WORKSHOPS IN COMPUTING
Series edited by C. J. van Rijsbergen

W0107541

Also in this series

Modelling Database Dynamics
Selected Papers from the Fourth International
Workshop on Foundations of Models and
Languages for Data and Objects, Volkse, Germany,
19–22 October 1992
Udo W. Lipeck and Bernhard Thalheim (Eds.)

14th Information Retrieval Colloquium
Proceedings of the BCS 14th Information
Retrieval Colloquium, University of Lancaster,
13–14 April 1992
Tony McEnery and Chris Paice (Eds.)

Functional Programming, Glasgow 1992
Proceedings of the 1992 Glasgow Workshop on
Functional Programming, Ayr, Scotland,
6–8 July 1992
John Launchbury and Patrick Sansom (Eds.)

Z User Workshop, London 1992
Proceedings of the Seventh Annual Z User
Meeting, London, 14–15 December 1992
J.P. Bowen and J.E. Nicholls (Eds.)

Interfaces to Database Systems (IDS92)
Proceedings of the First International Workshop
on Interfaces to Database Systems,
Glasgow, 1–3 July 1992
Richard Cooper (Ed.)

AI and Cognitive Science '92
University of Limerick, 10–11 September 1992
Kevin Ryan and Richard F.E. Sutcliffe (Eds.)

Theory and Formal Methods 1993
Proceedings of the First Imperial College
Department of Computing Workshop on Theory
and Formal Methods, Isle of Thorns Conference
Centre, Chelwood Gate, Sussex, UK,
29–31 March 1993
Geoffrey Burn, Simon Gay and Mark Ryan (Eds.)

**Algebraic Methodology and Software
Technology (AMAST'93)**
Proceedings of the Third International Conference
on Algebraic Methodology and Software
Technology, University of Twente, Enschede,
The Netherlands, 21–25 June 1993
M. Nivat, C. Rattray, T. Rus and G. Scollo (Eds.)

Logic Program Synthesis and Transformation
Proceedings of LOPSTR 93, International
Workshop on Logic Program Synthesis and
Transformation, Louvain-la-Neuve, Belgium,
7–9 July 1993
Yves Deville (Ed.)

Database Programming Languages (DBPL-4)
Proceedings of the Fourth International
Workshop on Database Programming Languages
– Object Models and Languages, Manhattan, New
York City, USA, 30 August–1 September 1993
Catriel Beeri, Atsushi Ohori and
Dennis E. Shasha (Eds.)

**Music Education: An Artificial Intelligence
Approach,** Proceedings of a Workshop held as
part of AI-ED 93, World Conference on Artificial
Intelligence in Education, Edinburgh, Scotland,
25 August 1993
Matt Smith, Alan Smaill and
Geraint A. Wiggins (Eds.)

Rules in Database Systems
Proceedings of the 1st International Workshop on
Rules in Database Systems, Edinburgh, Scotland,
30 August–1 September 1993
Norman W. Paton and
M. Howard Williams (Eds.)

Semantics of Specification Languages (SoSL)
Proceedings of the International Workshop on
Semantics of Specification Languages, Utrecht,
The Netherlands, 25–27 October 1993
D.J. Andrews, J.F. Groote and
C.A. Middelburg (Eds.)

Security for Object-Oriented Systems
Proceedings of the OOPSLA-93 Conference
Workshop on Security for Object-Oriented
Systems, Washington DC, USA,
26 September 1993
B. Thuraisingham, R. Sandhu and
T.C. Ting (Eds.)

Functional Programming, Glasgow 1993
Proceedings of the 1993 Glasgow Workshop on
Functional Programming, Ayr, Scotland,
5–7 July 1993
John T. O'Donnell and Kevin Hammond (Eds.)

Z User Workshop, Cambridge 1994
Proceedings of the Eighth Z User Meeting,
Cambridge, 29–30 June 1994
J.P. Bowen and J.A. Hall (Eds.)

6th Refinement Workshop
Proceedings of the 6th Refinement Workshop,
organised by BCS-FACS, London,
5–7 January 1994
David Till (Ed.)

continued on back page...

V.S. Alagar, S. Bergler and F.Q. Dong (Eds.)

Incompleteness and Uncertainty in Information Systems

Proceedings of the SOFTEKS Workshop
on Incompleteness and Uncertainty in
Information Systems, Concordia
University, Montreal, Canada,
8–9 October 1993

Published in collaboration with the
British Computer Society

Springer-Verlag
London Berlin Heidelberg New York
Paris Tokyo Hong Kong
Barcelona Budapest

V.S. Alagar, PhD

S. Bergler, PhD

F.Q. Dong, PhD

Department of Computer Science
Concordia University
1455 de Maisonneuve Blvd. West
Montreal, Quebec H3G 1M8
Canada

ISBN-13:978-3-540-19897-0   e-ISBN-13:978-1-4471-3242-4
DOI: 10.1007/978-1-4471-3242-4

British Library Cataloguing in Publication Data
A catalogue record for this book is available from the British Library

Apart from any fair dealing for the purposes of research or private study, or
criticism or review, as permitted under the Copyright, Designs and Patents Act
1988, this publication may only be reproduced, stored or transmitted, in any form,
or by any means, with the prior permission in writing of the publishers, or in the
case of reprographic reproduction in accordance with the terms of licences issued
by the Copyright Licensing Agency. Enquiries concerning reproduction outside
those terms should be sent to the publishers.

©British Computer Society 1994

The use of registered names, trademarks etc. in this publication does not imply,
even in the absence of a specific statement, that such names are exempt from the
relevant laws and regulations and therefore free for general use.

The publisher makes no representation, express or implied, with regard to the
accuracy of the information contained in this book and cannot accept any legal
responsibility or liability for any errors or omissions that may be made.

Typesetting: Camera ready by contributors

34/3830-543210 Printed on acid-free paper

Preface

The Software Engineering and Knowledgebase Systems (SOFTEKS) Research Group of the Department of Computer Science, Concordia University, Canada, organized a workshop on **Incompleteness and Uncertainty in Information Systems** from October 8–9, 1993 in Montreal. A major aim of the workshop was to bring together researchers who share a concern for issues of incompleteness and uncertainty. The workshop attracted people doing fundamental research and industry-oriented research in databases, software engineering and AI from North America, Europe and Asia. The workshop program featured six invited talks and twenty other presentations. The invited speakers were:

  Martin Feather (University of Southern California/Information Systems Institute)

  Laks V.S. Lakshmanan (Concordia University)

  Ewa Orłowska (Polish Academy of Sciences)

  Z. Pawlak (Warsaw Technical University and Academy of Sciences)

  F. Sadri (Concordia University)

  A. Skowron (Warsaw University)

The papers can be classified into four groups: rough sets and logic, concept analysis, databases and information retrieval, and software engineering. The workshop opened with a warm welcome speech from Dr. Dan Taddeo, Dean, Faculty of Engineering and Computer Science. The first day's presentations were in rough sets, databases and information retrieval. Papers given on the second day centered around software engineering and concept analysis. Sufficient time was given in between presentations to promote active interactions and numerous lively discussions. At the end of two days, the participants expressed their hope that this workshop would be continued. The wide range of topics and approaches, presented in a relaxed atmosphere that allowed sufficient room for discussion, was judged to be especially conducive to new collaborations and contacts. This volume contains full papers of the invited talks and most of the other presentations at the workshop. We hope that you find them interesting and useful in your own work.

The organization of the workshop was made possible due to generous voluntary help by the graduate students in the SOFTEKS research group.

Financial assistance from the Dean, Faculty of Engineering and Computer Science and Centre de Recherche Informatique de Montréal (CRIM) is gratefully acknowledged. Our thanks are due to Ms. Angie De Benedictis for providing excellent secretarial help for hosting the workshop and Mrs. Terry Czernienko for her superb professional assistance in the preparation of the papers for this volume.

April 1994   V.S. Alagar
                                                              S. Bergler
                                                              F.Q. Dong

Contents

Software Aberrations - Origins and Treatments

Martin S. Feather *

USC / ISI

4676 Admiralty Way

Marina del Rey, CA 90292

feather@isi.edu

Abstract

Within software, properties such as inconsistency and incompleteness are typically regarded as aberrations. Yet they are often the norm in both the course of the software development process, during which overly ideal requirements are compromised and approximated, and in the complexity of the resulting software itself, which must be tolerant of and responsive to aberrations arising from the environment within which the software is located. Some research that seeks to address these aberrations is summarized herein.

1 Origins of software aberrations

Developers of software must commonly deal with inconsistency, incompleteness, ambiguity and the like both in the course of the software development process itself, and in the environment within which the software will be fielded. I consider each of these in turn.

1.1 Aberrations in the software development process

Formal methods for software development employing formal specifications are being used to good effect in a number of real-world situations, e.g., see [17] for a discussion. Formal specifications are the keystone of these approaches, and to qualify as a 'good' specifications, are expected to be consistent, complete, unambiguous, etc.

The clarity of specifications comes from the ability to ignore efficiency concerns during their expression; specification languages provide constructs that permit the statement of *what* is to be achieved without necessitating the description of *how* it is to be accomplished. However, formal specifications of complex systems are themselves often large and complex. Thus the construction, comprehension and maintenance (modification) of formal specifications may itself be a difficult task. This difficulty is further exacerbated because specifications are supposed to codify the informal requirements desired of the software

---

*Support for the author has been provided by Defense Advanced Research Projects Agency contract No. BAPT 63-91-K-0006; views and conclusions in this document are those of the author and should not be interpreted as representing the official opinion or policy of DARPA, the U.S. Government, or any other person or agency connected with them.

they describe, yet statements of requirements are typically fragmentary, contra-dictory, incomplete, inconsistent and ambiguous. Furthermore, expression of requirements may employ widely varying levels of abstraction (e.g., concrete ex-amples, scenarios, general properties), styles (e.g., textual, graphical, formulae, domain-specific notations) and viewpoints (e.g., system-wide properties, single user viewpoints, snapshots of the entire state at one moment in time, historical traces of ongoing activity). Thus there is, in fact, often a large gap between requirements and specifications. Just as specifications (and the languages in which they are expressed) exhibit freedom from efficiency concerns, require-ments (and the languages in which they are expressed) exhibit freedom from specification concerns. The tools and techniques that deal with requirements must be not only tolerant of these aberrations, but must play an active role in supporting their resolution in order to emerge with a formal specification. In section 2, I describe the work our group has done in this regard, a key feature of which is its *incremental* nature, facilitating the gradual accommodation of multiple concerns.

Somewhat similar arguments have been made by Finkelstein et al., whose 'viewpoints' framework allows the separate statement of different aspects of software requirements, and facilitates the comparison and combination of those separate statements [14]. Also noteworthy is the Requirements Apprentice work [23] which provides tool support for, among other things, recognizing and dealing with informality, contradictions, incompleteness, and evolution.

1.2 Aberrations in the fielded software's environment

The previous section addressed the occurrence of aberrations in the software development process, the 'design time' phase. Aberrations may also occur at 'run time', when the software is placed in an environment that does not necessarily behave as perfectly as we would wish. Much of the complexity of systems comes from the need to build into them the ability to deal with 'exceptional' cases, which may occur only a small percentage of the time, but which may require a significantly larger percentage of the coding effort. It is useful to provide programming-level constructs which permit the separate expression of normal case behavior from expression of exceptional behavior. The exception mechanisms common to many programming languages are a small step in this direction. Our group has pursued a declarative style of expressing exceptions, and the reactions to them. This will be outlined in section 3.

1.3 Specification work at ISI

The Software Sciences division at ISI, headed by Bob Balzer, has worked with program specifications for a long period [2]. Much of this work has relevance to the issues raised above, and in the sections that follow I attempt to summarize it. The work has been done by many people — current and recent members of the group are: Dennis Allard, Bob Balzer, Kevin Benner, Don Cohen, Neil Goldman, Lewis Johnson, Jay Myers, K. Narayanaswamy, Dave Wile and Lorna Zorman. While the work has been done by the group, the inaccuracies and other failings of the descriptions that follow are due to me alone. I also must acknowledge many insights gained from discussions on these issues with Steve Fickas of the University of Oregon.

2 Dealing with design-time aberrations

Our approach to dealing with aberrations arising within the software development process is based upon the realization that development of a good specification is necessarily an *incremental* process.

In particular, development may proceed through stages in which the specification is known to be 'wrong' (inconsistent, incomplete, etc.), but which conveniently leads towards a specification with all the properties desired of such an object.

2.1 An *incremental* specification process

Our first foray into incremental specification was Goldman's observation that natural language descriptions of complex tasks often incorporate an evolutionary vein - the final description can be viewed as an elaboration of some simpler description, itself the elaboration of a yet simpler description, etc., back to some description deemed sufficiently simple to be comprehended from a non-evolutionary description [16]. He identified three 'dimensions' of changes between successive descriptions: *structural* - concerning the amount of detail the specification reveals about each individual state of the process, *temporal* - concerning the amount of change between successive states revealed by the specification, and *coverage* - concerning the range of possible behaviors permitted by a specification.

Balzer went on to provide a complete characterization of generic changes to the structure of a domain model, and considered propagating the effects of those changes through the operations that use the model and through the already-established data base of information [3].

These papers established the key ideas of our work on the incremental construction / explanation / modification of specification, namely that:

- the increments of the process often *change* the specified behavior in a manner that is not necessarily a pure refinement,

- there are different classes of such changes, and

- mechanical support is useful for conducting those changes over a large and detailed specification.

2.2 Benefits of incremental specification

The main benefits provided by this incremental approach are those of:

Specification Comprehension — to gain an understanding of a large and complex specification, we may begin from a simple starting point, and thereafter incrementally introduce only a palatable amount of additional information at each step, leading ultimately towards the fully detailed specification. Furthermore, because we are not limited to pure refinements (as would be the case in the methodology of stepwise refinement), the earlier stages of the specification need not be restricted to pure abstractions of the later stages. This permits the use of *'white lies'*, as Balzer has termed them, namely simplifying assumptions that we know to be untrue, and that we will later retract, but which permit the expression of a readily understood idealized specification.

Specification Construction — analogously to comprehension, it is far easier to construct a specification incrementally than to create the whole thing in one giant step (the pretence that we can do the latter has been called the 'big-bang' fallacy of specification construction). We set out to build mechanical support (beyond simply text editors or syntax-directed editors) for incremental construction. Our support took the form of a set of mechanized transformations.

The user, when wishing to make some change to the specification, would look to find a transformation that could accomplish this change, and (if successful) direct the system to apply the transformation to the selected portion of the specification. We came to call these 'evolution transformations', to emphasize that their very purpose is to evolve (change) the meaning of the specifications to which they are applied, in contrast to the more traditional meaning-preserving transformations that leave the meaning unchanged while changing some other aspect of the specification (typically efficiency or terminology). They share the benefits of traditional transformations in that they mechanically carry out the changes (which might be burdensome to perform manually, if the changes are complex and/or dispersed throughout the specification), and the record of application of transformations serves to encapsulate the development of (in our case) the specification itself. Note that even if the user is unable to find a transformation that accomplishes exactly the change desired, there may be a benefit to applying a transformation that accomplishes something close to the change desired, and thereafter modify the specification manually to achieve the precise result. This aspect greatly enhances the applicability of the transformations, without requiring that the set of them be complete in any sense.

Specification Modification and Reuse — one of the advantages of using specifications during software development is that they are more readily analyzable and maintainable (i.e., modifiable) than would be the corresponding efficient code. This permits the rapid exploration of alternatives during design. When analysis reveals that the specification needs to be modified, then evolution transformations ease this task. When a new task arises that is similar but not identical to some previous task, the specification of the previous task might be evolvable to form the specification of the new task, with less effort than it would take to construct that specification afresh.

2.3 Applications and elaborations of incremental specification

Our later work expanded upon the ideas of incremental specification:

2.3.1 Requirements and specifications

We built a system, ARIES, for the support of acquisition of requirements and development of specifications to meet those requirements [20]. Central to this system was the notion that the early stages of software design are a very exploratory process, involving repeated cycles of examination and adjustment of the emerging specification. To make formal specifications palatable to the user, ARIES provided several 'presentations' (e.g., of data flow, type hierarchy) through which the user could view various aspects of specifications. These presentations were used both for display to the user, and as a medium through which the user could *modify* specifications — the user's direct manipulation of these presentations were used to retrieve from the library of evolution transformations those that would achieve the change the user had indicated [19]. There was no need for all the requirements of some emerging system description to be complete, consistent, etc. Rather, it was the very purpose of the development activity to locate and respond to various failings of the requirements in the move towards a single, coherent specification. Note that this requires a shift of thinking: rather than assuming completeness, correctness, consistency, etc., to be the norm, these became the goals. For example, simulation (used to reveal consequences of the emerging descriptions) could not wait until the formal specification had been completely constructed, but rather had to work with the fragmentary early formulations [7].

2.3.2 Parallel elaboration (specification merging)

We extended the incremental development paradigm from a *linear* sequence of steps to a *tree* structure: starting from a single simple specification, different aspects of that specification were elaborated independently, leading to multiple specifications; these then were combined to achieve the all-inclusive specification [11]. This is very similar to the program merging of Reps et al [18] and the software prototype merging work of Berzins et al [8]. Several key assumptions underlly our particular style of merging:

- The parallel lines of incremental development are mostly independent. Thus incompatibilities arise relatively infrequently during combination; more commonly, combination of two lines of development gives rise to *additional* options from among which the user has to choose.

- Each of the specifications being merged has been derived from the single initial specification by a sequence of evolution transformations. As a result, some of the combination of the multiple specifications can be done by replaying the transformations in a linear order. Also, detection of clashes or further options that arise during combination can be determined by considering the transformation sequences that led to each of the specifications being combined [12].

2.4 Some related work

Fickas et al. have viewed specification development as a planning problem [1]; their *design operators* move within a search space of designs, transforming the specification as they do so. Interestingly, some of their work also uses a model of parallel elaboration (of requirements / specification) followed by combination, but in rather a different way: each elaboration is used to capture the ideal specification as seen by each different 'stakeholder' (e.g., intended user of the software system, administrator of the system, purchaser of the system). As a result, the ideal specifications that emerge from this process are very likely to be incompatible, and much of the combination process must deal with negotiation to reach an acceptable compromise among those divergent ideals [24].

The incremental approach to specification development is also being pursued by Souquières and Levy, who use their *development operators* (akin to our evolution transformations) to modify the emerging specification. Additionally, their development operators modify the *workplan*, an explicit record of the specification process, and modify the links between the emerging specification and that workplan [25]. This helps record the rationale of the specification process itself.

3 Dealing with run-time aberrations

Again, I trace the origins of our work on dealing with the 'run-time' aberrations of software to our group's focus on formal specification, and then follow how the ideas that arose from this work were adapted and extended as they were applied in a programming setting.

3.1 Constraints and specification

Balzer and Goldman identified the principles that underpin the specification of software systems [6], and it was on the basis of these principles that our specification language, Gist, was developed [5].

Among its features, Gist supports a 'generate and test' style of specification. A Gist specification may describe a set of straightforward possible behaviors, and use *constraints* to rule out the undesirable ones. For example, to specify the well-known eight-queens problem, in Gist we would simply state that each of the eight queens be placed somewhere on the squares of the chessboard, and separately state (as constraints) that no two queens could be on the same square, and that no two queens could attack one another by the chess' rules of queen movement. As another example, consider the use of elevators (lifts) to transport passengers between floors in a multi-story building; to specify this in Gist we would straightforwardly state the effects of passenger and elevator activity, and use constraints to rule out impossible (e.g., passengers entering/exiting an elevator whose doors were closed) and undesirable (e.g., passengers getting further from their destination floors) transportations. The key point here is that the denotation of the specification (e.g., placement of queens, movement of passengers and elevators) comprises those and only those behaviors that satisfy all the constraints. Thus constraints are a very powerful specification mechanism; they imply arbitrary lookahead (no painting oneself into a corner), and may require further subdivision if they span multiple components of a system (passengers and elevator controller) [10]. The use of program transformation to convert a Gist specification making significant use of constraints into an equivalent implementation is thus a potentially very difficult task.

3.2 Consistency (constraint) mechanisms in programming

Our group sought to make use of the ideas that arose from these specification-based investigations by incorporating some of Gist's ideas into a *programming* environment. In particular, a form of constraints became a programming-language concept, one that we term *'consistency rules'*. Unlike Gist constraints, these consistency rules[1] look ahead only to the next state of the computation, and thus do not prevent getting trapped in some dead-end which could have been avoided by having earlier made some different decision. Briefly, when the computation is about to transition to the next state, all the consistency rules are run on that prospective next state, and the transition is allowed to occur only if all those rules are satisfied. (In fact, they are allowed to examine both the prospective next state, and the state from which the transition is taking place. This allows them to be sensitive to transitions between states, e.g., an increase in some value). As described so far, these consistency rules are equivalent to the integrity constraints of databases.

Note the contrast with Prolog, in which backtracking is built in to allow the undoing of arbitrarily many computation steps. While arbitrary backtracking is satisfactory as an implementation mechanism for a large number of problems (as witnessed by the success of Prolog), there is nevertheless a wide class of other tasks for which backtracking is infeasible, typically those in which the activities of a program's environment, once committed to, cannot be undone. It is for tasks such as these that our programming-level consistency rules are designed.

3.3 Reacting to / recovering from inconsistencies

An important addendum to the behavior of our consistency rules concerns their behavior on detecting inconsistency.

By default, consistency rules simply give rise to a run-time break, in which the execution is interrupted. The user has the ability to study the transition and violated rules to see what the problem is, and choose to either give up on the transition entirely, or manually adjust the contents of the transition and try again. The mechanism ensures that, apart from this interrupted condition (in which the user's options are severely limited), the state of the computation can never be in violation of any of the consistency rules.

The programmer has the ability to associate with individual consistency rules so called *'repair rules'*, that are triggered into action when their corresponding consistency rules are violated by some attempted transition. A repair rule is allowed to examine the prospective state (that would violate its consistency rule) and the (valid) state from which the transition is occurring, and suggest *additional* changes to take place in the same transition. A trivial example of this is the notion of a single-valued place-holder; we might associate with the consistency rule that expresses its single-valuedness a repair rule that, in the case of a new (second) value being asserted, retracts the old value, thus restoring the single-valuedness. The additional changes suggested by all triggered repair rules are unioned with the changes already in the transition, to form a larger transition, which is then attempted in place of the original transition. Note the following consequences of this:

- The process is iterative — the new transition, formed by the union of the old transition and any additional changes suggested by the repair rules

---

[1] I will take care to say 'consistency rules' to refer to our programming language concept, and 'constraints' to refer to our specification language concept, with their similar, but not identical, semantics

— is attempted in place of the old transition. It is checked to see that it leads to a state that satisfies all the consistency rules; if any are violated, their repair rules are triggered, possibly leading to yet more changes to be added to the transition, repeating the process. This iterative process terminates either with a successful transition to a state that satisfies all of the consistency rules, or with a run-time break if either the number of cycles through this check consistency / run repair rules cycle has reached some pre-set limit, or because no additions to the transition are suggested by any repair rules.

- The only code that ever sees the world in an inconsistent state is that within the bodies of the triggered repair rules. The rest of the program, as before, sees only the states that result from transitions that satisfy all the consistency rules. This separation, of code that may assume all the consistency rules hold from code that is explicitly provided to (try to) recover from violations of consistency rules, is a crucial advantage that accrues from the use of these constructs.

- Repair rules can only suggest *additional* things to do in the same transition. In particular, they cannot suggest that something already part of the transition not be done. Thus if a transition is inconsistent because of two simultaneous contradictory actions, repair rules cannot recover from this (e.g., if a single-valued place-holder is simultaneously assigned two different values).

3.4 Applications

The consistency / repair rule mechanism described above proved useful within a wide range of programming activities that our group has pursued::

- a programming support environment, discussed in [15];

- the aforementioned ARIES system, that assists a user in requirements acquisition and specification development, and

- within automation of some administrative aspects of managing research projects within our institute.

3.5 Long transactions

In spite of the value we place on the use of consistency rules, they have some obvious limitations. In particular, the restricted lookahead to just the proposed next state, and the inability to backtrack over previous transitions, prove problematic when dealing with activities that would most naturally span multiple transitions. Such activities — 'long transactions' in database terminology — are at the heart of many real-world tasks. This is because it is typically infeasible to expect to come to an immediate decision as to how to resolve an inconsistency that has arisen. Perhaps multiple parties must negotiate to resolve the inconsistency, while the rest of the world is allowed to proceed. The challenge, therefore, is to allow inconsistency to occur without disrupting the rest of the program, and to work towards its resolution. We have employed three different strategies towards this end:

3.5.1 Tolerating inconsistency

Balzer suggested the approach in which selected consistency rules are changed from 'hard' requirements that can never be violated to 'soft' ones that can be violated, but, upon this occurring, cause all the data involved to automatically be marked as 'polluted' with respect to that consistency rule [4]. As a consequence:

- The existence of 'polluted' data is visible globally, hence any portion of the code that might be able to deal with such inconsistencies would be able to watch for the appearance of such data and react accordingly. This means that there is no need to hard-wire the origins of inconsistencies with the responses that fix them.

- Code that is written with the assumption that the consistency rule is not violated can be conditionalized to be on the watch for polluted data, and react accordingly (e.g., ignore it). Note, however, that the onus is on the programmer to locate all such code, and modify it accordingly.

We have continued this approach by implementing the notion of 'bounded obligations' on top of our consistency / repair rule mechanisms. Briefly, bounded obligations are the general form of requirements such as *'a library user must return a borrowed book on or before its due date'*. They have been suggested as a useful specification mechanism [21]. Their 'boundedness' comes from the need to achieve some condition at or before some other condition — the bound — arises (very often, a temporal condition, as in the due date example). 'Obligation' is very much the same as 'constraint' or 'consistency rule' — in the simplest form of some system, it expresses something that must be achieved. Of course, as argued earlier, in many systems the ideal behavior of the systems' environment cannot be assumed, and thus bounded obligations need to be weakened to allow their violation, which in turn triggers further action on the part of the system (e.g., impose a fine on a user who fails to return a book on time).

Our implementation translates a simple, declarative form of a bounded obligation into the equivalent data structures and operations necessary to ensure its adherence. Incremental development and exploration is achieved by modifying a 'strict' bounded obligation to become 'violatable' together with a way of recognizing when it has been violated — an application of Balzer's idea of weakening a constraint, and marking the data involved in its violations as 'polluted'. Again, a simple declaration to this effect is appropriately translated by our implementation. Finally, response to such violations can also be declared and automatically translated into running code, making use of the consistency / repair rules as the mechanism to achieve these effects [13].

One of the positive benefits of recognizing explicitly concepts such as bounded obligations is that it allows us to analyze proposed system designs in terms of these concepts. For example, it is reasonable to suggest and check that if an agent (person, computer program, hardware,...) is given an obligation, then that same agent should not also be given the ability to retract that obligation (e.g., the borrower of a library book should not be able to cancel the need to return that book! — note, however, that the librarian *might* both have both these abilities; having recognized this possibility, we might wish to consider whether or not to preclude it).

3.5.2 Pre-empting inconsistency

Narayanaswamy and Goldman proposed a different approach to accommodating long transactions that might violate consistency rules. They suggested that a transition that, as first formulated, would violate one or more consistency rules, be raised as a 'proposed' transition. Other code fragments that might be able to contribute to the transition to render it consistent with respect to all the consistency rules would then be invoked to inspect and possibly modify the transition, with the intention of getting it into a form which could be executed without violating any consistency rules [22]. They advocated this approach for cooperative software development, where teams of programmers would use this mechanism to coordinate their joint work. The ramifications of this approach are:

- The consistency rules are never actually violated, hence all code can be written with the assumption that it is run only in states valid with respect to all those rules.

- The exchange of information about proposed transactions must be coded separately from the consistency rule / repair rule mechanisms of the language.

3.5.3 Masking inconsistency

A third approach which on occasions was found useful was that of 'masking' inconsistencies so that they would not seem to arise.

For example, in the context of administering multiple researchers working on multiple projects, one key consistency rule stated that over each month the sum total of a researcher's work on individual projects would sum up to 100% of that researcher's time. Strict adherence to this rule constrains the flexibility of transferring researchers between projects. As a solution to this particular problem (which arose in our automation of aspects of our institute's project administration), a 'dummy' project was created to which any researcher could be deemed to be working. As a result:

- As with the case of pre-empting inconsistency, all consistency rules are ensured, hence all code (other than code within repair rules, of course) can assume them to hold.

- Although the inconsistency has been masked, the consequences of the masking may still be evident. For example, a query that asked for the number of projects that a researcher was working on would count the dummy project as it would any other project, unless explicitly modified.

- For those code fragments that might be able to react to the (masked) inconsistency, the existence of the condition can be readily recognized (in the example cited above, any researcher working for the dummy project would indicate this).

- It is not apparent how to mask *all* possible forms of consistency rules; thus this solution is not a general one, but rather of application in specific cases where a reasonable masking of the inconsistency can be programmed.

4 Inconsistency and incompleteness in a distributed setting

Finally, I mention some recent work of Balzer's that mixes the two themes described above, namely the treatment of aberrations in the software development process, and the use of run-time mechanisms that react to aberrations.

Balzer considered how to support multiple agents (people and/or programs) in a distributed setting working towards a globally complete and consistent state. Because of the distributed setting, no one person is likely has access to all the information, and for the tasks that he considered, a globally complete and consistent state is the end goal of the whole activity, so *incompleteness* and *inconsistency* predominates. He built a language mechanism that allows the simple statement of the following:

- Information transfer — what information to transfer among the agents. A simple object/attribute model of information is assumed, where typed objects have associated attribute values (which may be simple values such as numbers or strings, or other objects). Thus indicating what information to transfer is a matter of identifying which objects, and which of the attributes of those objects, should be transferred. Note that it is not necessary, and typically not desirable, to transfer all objects or all of the attribute values of an object.

- Workflow — when to transfer the information among the agents. For some tasks, when new information is made available by one agent, it is appropriate to have it immediately incorporated into the receiving agents' worlds; conversely, in other tasks, perhaps only the availability of such information is announced, and the importers are left to choose individually when to import the information. The language allows the expression of a range of possibilities.

- Correspondence — when one agent imports objects from another agent, the correspondence rules describe how to related the imported objects to the objects already present in the importing agent's world.

- Translation — during transfer of information between agents, the language mechanisms permit the renaming of the transferred information (so that different agents may ascribe different names to the same things), and even the re-representation of the transferred information (so that different agents may employ different data representations for the same, transferred, information).

- Completeness and consistency — these properties are easily defined on top of the simple data model. For example, a recurring form of completeness between two agents is that they both have a value for some attribute of the corresponding object. Similarly, consistency is that they have the *same* value for that attribute. The language facilitates the expression of rules such as these, which can be used to drive internal activities of the agents (e.g., display inconsistencies in some visual form), and/or drive the workflow activities between agents (e.g., when a complete and consistent state is achieved, then transfer the information to the next stage of processing).

Balzer has applied this to several radically different applications, two of which are the following:

Design of a message-processing system: Two developers are cooperating by developing different, but overlapping, parts of a message-processing system.

One developer is working on populating an overall language with concepts, while the other is working on using those concepts to state the processing rules for individual instances of those concepts. Completeness and consistency will have been attained when all the uses of concepts have corresponding definitions, and when all those uses agree with their definitions. The distributed system is organized to have a mediator between the two developers, which imports information from each of them, recognizes instances of incompleteness and inconsistency, and reflects back to them these problems when they are detected. The workflow is set up to notify the two users whenever the mediator has new information available for them, but allows them to choose when to import that information. Upon reaching a complete and consistent state, the mediator automatically forwards the information on to a compiler (a fourth agent) for production of the final system.

Battlefield sightings: Two 'observers' are cooperating to make sightings of some battlefield; they communicate directly to each other (i.e., in this system, there is no third-party mediator) about the sightings that they have made. Incompleteness arises when only one of them has made a sighting on some location; inconsistency arises when they both have made a sighting on some location, but they disagree about that sighting. The workflow is set up to have each agent automatically import the new sighting information from the other agent whenever it is made available.

Balzer's language allows the easy expression of the information transfer, workflow, etc., aspects each of these systems. Of particular relevance to this abstract is his treatment of incompleteness and inconsistency — as with the 'constraints' of our specification language, and the 'consistency rules' of our programming language, these conditions are stated declaratively. A difference, however, is the assumption that aberrations (incompleteness and inconsistency between agents) is the norm, rather than some temporary condition that must immediately be rectified.

5 Conclusions

I have tried to summarize the work that our group has done that has relevance to software 'aberrations'. Of necessity, this summary is very sketchy in nature, and readers interested in more details are encouraged to study the referenced material. In passing I have mentioned a few pieces of work done by people outside of our group, but I have not intended this to be anything close to a representative sampling of research in the area.

The two main themes that I have tried to suggest are:

- The need for *evolution* — software development is of necessity concerned with compromise and adaptation of idealized requirements, and thus the development process itself is a very iterative one, in which change (not simply pure refinement) predominates.

- The breadth of support programming-level that can be provided for dealing with run-time aberrations. The key to successful support is to permit the *declarative* statement of how to recognize and treat aberrations. Among its many benefits, it allows the programmer to state the recognition/treatment in one place, rather than be forced to distribute the equivalent code throughout the program. Such programs are thus more writable, readable and analyzable.

Lots of work remains to be done in these areas. One obvious avenue is the management of long transactions whose purpose is to resolve aberrations. For example, in the battlefield sightings application, there is currently no coordination imposed on the two observers when an inconsistency is detected; they could each change their sightings to what the other had reported, thus leading to a different, but no less inconsistent, state! The general issue concerns assurance that progress is being made towards restoration of consistency.

Another interesting area concerns the relationship between ideals, and the compromises that are necessary in a fielded system. How can we better make use of those ideals to direct the development process? For example, in [9] constraints are categorized into 'hard' and 'soft', and system design proceeds so as to prohibit 'hard' constraints from ever being violated, whereas can permit violations of 'soft' constraints, and links such violations with restoration activities that contribute to the re-establishment of the violated constraint. At run time, can the system take advantage of its knowledge of those ideals to operate more robustly? Many possibilities need to be explored.

References

[1] Anderson J, Fickas S. A proposed perspective shift: viewing specification design as a planning problem. In: Proc 5th Int'l Workshop on Software Specification and Design, Pittsburgh, PA, IEEE Computer Society Press, 1989, pp 177-184

[2] Balzer R. A 15 year perspective on automatic programming. IEEE Trans on Software Engineering 1985; SE-11(11):1257-1267

[3] Balzer R. Automated enhancement of knowledge representations. In: Joshi A (ed) Proc 9th Int'l Joint Conference on Artificial Intelligence, Los Angeles, CA, 1985, pp 203-207

[4] Balzer R. Tolerating inconsistency. In: Proc 13th Int'l Conference on Software Engineering, Austin, TX, IEEE Computer Society Press, 1991, pp 158-165

[5] Balzer R, Cohen D, Feather MS, Goldman NM, Swartout W, Wile DS. Operational specification as the basis for specification validation. In: Theory and practice of software technology, North-Holland, 1983, pp 21-49

[6] Balzer R, Goldman N. Principles of good software specification and their implications for specification languages. In: Specification of reliable software, IEEE Computer Society Press, 1979, pp 58-67

[7] Benner K. The ARIES simulation component (ASC). In: The Eighth KnowledgeBased Software Engineering Conference, Chicago, IL, 1993, pp 40–49

[8] Berzins V. Software merge: models and methods for combining changes to programs. Journal of Systems Integration 1991; 1(2):121–141

[9] Dardenne A, van Lamsweerde A, Fickas S. Goal-directed requirements acquisition, Science of Computer Programming 1993; 20(1-2):3–50

[10] Feather MS. Language support for the specification and development of composite systems. ACM Trans on Programming Languages and Systems 1987; 9(2):198–234

[11] Feather MS. Constructing specifications by combining parallel elaborations. IEEE Trans on Software Engineering 1989; 15(2):198–208

[12] Feather MS. Detecting interference when merging specification evolutions. In: Proc 5th Int'l Workshop on Software Specification and Design, Pittsburgh, PA, IEEE Computer Society Press, 1989, pp 169–176

[13] Feather MS. An implementation of bounded obligations. In: Proc 8th Knowledge-Based Software Engineering Conference, Chicago, IL, IEEE Computer Society Press, 1993, pp 114–122

[14] Finkelstein A, Kramer J, Nuseibeh B, Finkelstein L, Goedicke M. Viewpoints: a framework for integrating multiple perspectives in system development. Int'l Journal of Software Engineering and Knowledge Engineering 1992; to appear

[15] Goldman NM, Narayanaswamy K. Software evolution through iterative prototyping. In: Proc 14th Int'l Conference on Software Engineering, Melbourne, Australia, 1992

[16] Goldman NM. Three dimensions of design development. In: Proc 3rd National Conference on Artificial Intelligence, Washington, DC, 1983, pp 130–133

[17] Hall A. Seven myths of formal methods. IEEE Software 1990; 7(5):11–19

[18] Horwitz S, Prins J, Reps T. Integrating non-interfering versions of programs. ACM TOPLAS 1989; 11(3):345–387

[19] Johnson WL, Feather MS. Building an evolution transformation library. In: Proc 12th Int'l Conference on Software Engineering, Nice, FRA, IEEE Computer Society Press, 1990, pp 238–248

[20] Johnson WL, Feather MS, Harris DR. Representation and presentation of requirements knowledge. IEEE Trans on Software Engineering 1992; 18(10):853–869

[21] Kent SJH, Maibaum TSE, Quirk WJ. Formally specifying temporal constraints and error recovery. In: Proc IEEE Int'l Symposium on Requirements Engineering, San Diego, CA, IEEE Computer Society Press, 1993, pp 208–215

[22] Narayanaswamy K, Goldman N. "Lazy" consistency: a basis for cooperative software development. In: Proc of the Conference on Computer Supported Cooperative Work, Toronto, CAN, ACM Press, 1992, pp 257–264

[23] Reubenstein HB, Waters RC. The requirements apprentice: automated assistance for requirements acquisition. IEEE Trans on Software Engineering 1991; 17(3):226–240

[24] Robinson WN. Automated negotionated design integration: formal representations and algorithms for collaborative design. Technical Report CIS-TR-93-10, Department of Computer and Information Science, University of Oregon, April 1993

[25] Souquières J, Lévy N. Description of specification developments. In: Proc IEEE Int'l Symposium on Requirements Engineering, San Diego, CA, IEEE Computer Society Press, 1993, pp 216–223

Reasoning with Incomplete Information: Rough Set Based Information Logics

Ewa Orłowska

Institute of Theoretical and Applied Computer Science
Polish Academy of Sciences
Warsaw, Poland
orlowska@plearn.bitnet

1 Relative indiscernibility

The representation of uncertain information is a central task of AI systems and many different methods have been developed to address this issue. In this paper we discuss a rough set [27] perspective on uncertainty and we present a survey of logics that provide foundations for reasoning with incomplete information that is a source of that uncertainty. The rough set paradigm is based on the observation that characterization of individuals in observational terms is usually incomplete. Trying to describe continuous domains with discrete means we are faced with the problem of indiscernibility: We might not have enough discriminative resources to discern each individual in a domain under consideration from any others. In various fields of applications indiscernibility arises from different reasons. For instance, in information systems some objects might be indiscernible because they have the same description in terms of the attributes admitted in the system. In a more general setting, indiscernibility is determined by some parameters which reflect expressive and discriminative resources of a domain under consideration. Objects may be discernible with respect to one subset of parameters but indiscernible with respect to another. Whether or not objects are discernible from one another is thus a function of these parameters, or in other words, indiscernibility is relative to these parameters. In this paper several examples are discussed where relative indiscernibility plays a crucial role.

We consider domains which are characterized by specification of a nonempty set OB, a nonempty set PAR of parameters, and a family $\{IND(P)\}_{P \subseteq PAR}$ of binary relations in set OB. For a subset P of PAR relation $IND(P)$ is interpreted as indiscernibility relation relative to parameters from set P. Various intuitive interpretations can be associated with the elements of these sets. If a domain we are interested in is an information system, then we interpret elements of OB as objects in the system, and the elements of PAR as attributes. Intuition connected with decision theory would be that the elements of OB are decisions and the elements of PAR are consequences of the decisions. Under epistemic interpretation elements of OB are instances of concepts and elements of PAR are knowledge agents that learn or, generally speaking, acquire concepts. In the rough set theory the issue of indiscernibility-type incompleteness of information is addressed and uncertainty that is caused by incompleteness of information is the subject of investigations.

In this paper we concentrate on two logical systems with rough set semantics. The first system is aimed at representation of those notions and facts that are needed in rough set-based concept analysis that was originated in [15,23]. In the second system, proposed in [20,21], reasoning about uncertain knowledge of groups of agents is modelled. Both systems are strongly related to logic for reasoning with indiscernibility-type incomplete information proposed in [16]. In [18] some of the other types of incompleteness of information are discussed.

We assume that for any $P, Q \subseteq PAR$ following conditions are satisfied:

(IND1) $IND(P)$ is an equivalence relation,

(IND2) $IND(P \cup Q) = IND(P) \cap IND(Q)$,

(IND3) $IND(\oslash) = OB \times OB$.

The following proposition follows easily from these conditions.

Proposition 1

(a) $P \subseteq Q$ implies $IND(Q) \subseteq IND(P)$,

(b) The algebra $(\{IND(P)\}_{P \subseteq PAR}, \cap)$ is a lower semilattice, where $IND(PAR)$ is the zero element.

Let $R(o) = \{s \in OB : (o, s) \in R\}$ be an equivalence class of indiscernibility relation R. These classes satisfy the following conditions.

Proposition 2

(a) $R \subseteq S$ implies $R(o) \subseteq S(o)$

(b) $R \cap S(o) = R(o) \cap S(o)$.

Below several examples are given of relative indiscernibility relations.

Example 1 Let PAR be a family of subsets of a nonempty set OB, and for a set $P \subseteq PAR$ let $IND(P)$ be defined as follows:

$(o, o') \in IND(P)$ iff for all $p \in P$ we have $o \in p$ iff $o' \in p$.

Thus objects o and o' are indiscernible relative to set P if they are indiscernible with respect to every element p of P. The above scheme of relation corresponds closely to Leibnitz notion of identity. Assuming that elements of OB are individuals and elements of PAR are properties of these individuals, we consider two individuals o and o' to be equal up to properties from a set P whenever every property possessed by o is possessed by o' as well.

Example 2 Let OB be a family of subsets of a nonempty set PAR, and for any $P \subseteq PAR$ we define relation $IND(P)$ in OB as follows:

$(o, o') \in IND(P)$ iff for all $p \in P$ we have $p \in o$ iff $p \in o'$.

In this example the scheme of indiscernibility relations represents relativised equality of sets: As far as elements from subset P are concerned, sets o and o' are equal.

In the following example indiscernibility relations refer to objects that have the same type as parameters in the powerset hierarchy.

Example 3 Let OB and PAR be nonempty families of subsets of a certain nonempty set. We define two families of relative indiscernibility relations:

$(o, o') \in IND(P)$ iff for all $p \in P$ we have $o \subseteq p$ iff $o' \subseteq p$,

$(o, o') \in IND(P)$ iff for all $p \in P$ we have $p \subseteq o$ iff $p \subseteq o'$.

Example 4 We consider information system introduced in [13]. Let $OB = \{p, q, r, x\}$ be a set of objects such that $x \neq p, q, r$. Assume that p, q, r áre the attributes in this system as well. The values of these attributes are subsets of set OB. The assignment of values of attributes to the objects is given in the following table:

	p	q	r
p	$\{p\}$	$\{p, r, x\}$	$\{p, q, x\}$
q	$\{q, r, x\}$	$\{q\}$	$\{p, q, x\}$
r	$\{q, r, x\}$	$\{p, r, x\}$	$\{r\}$
x	$\{q, rx\}$	$\{p, r, x\}$	$\{p, q, x\}$

The system is self-referential, in a sense, because each attribute enables us to distinguish itself from the remaining objects, and any subset of attributes can discern just its elements from the remaining objects. The respective indiscernibility relations determine the following equivalence classes:

$$
\begin{array}{lllll}
IND(p): & \{p\} & \{q, r, x\} \\
IND(q): & \{q\} & \{p, r, x\} \\
IND(r): & \{r\} & \{p, q, x\} \\
IND(p,q): & \{p\} & \{q\} & \{r, x\} \\
IND(p,q,r): & \{p\} & \{q\} & \{r\} & \{x\}
\end{array}
$$

Example 5 Let $OB = \{1, 2, 3\}$ and let the set of attributes consists of all the subsets of set OB. Let values of the attributes be True (T) and False (F). The assignment of values of attributes to objects is given in the following table:

	$\oslash$	$\{1\}$	$\{2\}$	$\{1,2\}$	$\{3\}$	$\{1,3\}$	$\{2,3\}$	$\{1,2,3\}$
1	F	T	F	T	F	T	F	T
2	F	F	T	T	F	F	T	T
3	F	F	F	F	T	T	T	T

It is easy to see that the value of attribute a for object o equals $T(F)$ iff $o \in a$ ($o \notin a$). For each attribute a equivalence classes of a are set a itself and OB-a.

2 Representation of properties and property- forming operations

Equivalence classes of indiscernibility relations can be interpreted as properties of objects. We explain this idea by means of the following example.

Example 6 Let OB be the set of planets $OB = \{$Mercury (Me), Venus (V), Earth (E), Mars (Ma), Jupiter (J), Saturn (Sa), Uranus (U), Neptune (N), Pluto (P) $\}$. Let the set of attributes consists of three attributes: $D = $ 'distance from the Sun', $S = $ 'size', and $M = $ 'possession of a moon'. The values of attribute D are 'near' and 'far'; The values of attribute S are 'small', 'medium' and 'large'; The values of attribute M are 'yes' and 'no'. Assignment of values of the attributes to the objects is given in the following table:

	S	D	M
Me	small	near	no
V	small	near	no
E	small	near	yes
Ma	small	near	yes
J	large	far	yes
Sa	large	far	yes
U	med.	far	yes
N	med.	far	yes
P	small	far	yes

Equivalence classes of the indiscernibility relations determined by the attributes are as follows:

$IND(S): X1 = \{Me, V, E, Ma, P\}\quad X2 = \{J, Sa\}\quad X3 = \{U, N\}$

$IND(D): Y1 = \{Me, V, E, Ma\}\quad Y2 = \{J, Sa, U, N, P\}$

$IND(M): Z1 = \{Me, V\}\quad Z2 = \{E, Ma, J, Sa, U, N, P\}$

$IND(S,D): W1 = \{Me, V, E, Ma\}\quad W2 = \{J, Sa\}\quad W3 = \{U, N\}\quad W4 = \{P\}$

$IND(S,M): \{Me, V\}\quad \{E, Ma, P\}\quad \{J, Sa\}\quad \{U, N\}$

$IND(M,D): T1 = \{Me, V\}\quad T2 = \{E, Ma\}\quad T3 = \{J, Sa, U, N, P\}$

$IND(S,D,M): \{Me, V\}\quad \{E, Ma\}\quad \{J, Sa\}\quad \{U, N\}\quad \{P\}$

Observe that there is the following correspondence between equivalence classes and properties of planets:

$X1$: to be small $\qquad$ $X2$: to be large $\qquad$ $X3$: to be medium

$Y1$: to be near the Sun $\qquad$ $Y2$: to be far from the Sun

$Z1$: to possess no moon $\qquad$ $Z2$: to have at least one moon

$T2 = Y1 \cap Z2$: to be near the Sun and to have a moon

$W4 = X1 \cap Y2$: to be small and to be far from the Sun.

The example suggests that, at first, equivalence classes of indiscernibility relations can be identified with properties of objects, and second, that we can form new properties from some given properties by performing relational operations on the respective indiscernibility relations. In Example 6 the compound property $T2$ corresponds to conjunction of two properties. It is determined by indiscernibility relation $IND(M,D)$ which equals $IND(M) \cap IND(D)$. In a similar way, every property corresponding to an equivalence class of an indiscernibility $IND(P)$ for a certain finite set P of parameters is a conjunction of properties corresponding to equivalence classes of relations $IND(p)$ for $p \in P$.

New properties can also be constructed by forming the transitive closure of the union ($\cup^*$) of indiscernibility relations. Operation $\cup^*$ is characterized by the following conditions.

Proposition 3

(a) $R \cup^* S = \{(R \cup S)^i : i \geq 0\}$, where $(R \cup S)0 = $ Identity, $(R \cup S)i + 1 = (R \cup S); (R \cup S)^i$, and; is the composition of relations,

(b) $(R \cup^* S)(o) = \bigcup\{R(t) : t \in S(o)\} \cup \bigcup\{S(t) : t \in R(o)\}$.

whenever $R(x)$ included in $S(x)$ or $S(x)$ included in $R(x)$ for all x.

Since relation $R \cup^* S$ cannot be obtained from R and S by means of Boolean operations, the properties corresponding to its equivalence classes are not expressible as propositional combinations of properties corresponding to equivalence classes of R and S. Moreover, in general $IND(P) \cup^* IND(Q)$, is not of the form $IND(K)$ for some Boolean combination K of P and Q.

Example 7 Assume that we are given seven objects $o1, \cdots, o7$ consisting of circles and crosses, and attributes o = 'number of circles' and $+$ = 'number of crosses'. Values of these attributes are natural numbers. The assignment of values of the attributes to the objects is defined in the following table:

	o	$+$
$o1$	1	1
$o2$	1	2
$o3$	2	1
$o4$	2	2
$o5$	3	3
$o6$	3	4
$o7$	3	4

Equivalence classes of indiscernibility relations $IND(o)$ and $IND(+)$ are as follows:

$IND(o)$: $\{o1, o2\}$ $\{o3, o4\}$ $\{o5, o6, o71\}$
$IND(+)$: $\{o1, o3\}$ $\{o2, o4\}$ $\{o5\}$ $\{o6, o7\}$.

The transitive closure of the union of these relations provides the following equivalence classes:

$IND(o) \cup^* IND(+)$: $X1 = \{o1, o2, o3, o4\}$ $X2 = \{o5, o6, o7\}$.

Several applications of rough sets are concerned with definability of sets of objects in terms of some properties of these objects. However, incompleteness of information about individuals is the source of uncertainty of characterization of collections of individuals. Let R be an indiscernibility relation, we recall that the R-lower approximation and R-upper approximation of a set $X \subseteq OB$ is defined as follows:

$L(R)X$ = union of those equivalence classes of R that are included in X

$U(R)X$ = union of those equivalence classes of R that have an element in common with X.

If R is of the form $IND(P)$, then we write $L(P)$ and $U(P)$ instead of $L(IND(P))$ and $U(IND(P))$, respectively. Clearly, for any $X \subseteq OB$ we have $L(R)X \subseteq X \subseteq U(R)X$.

We say that set X is:
R-definable iff $L(R)X = X = U(R)X$
roughly R-definable iff $L(R)X \neq \oslash$ and $U(R)X \neq OB$
internally R-indefinable iff $L(R)X = \oslash$
externally R-indefinable iff $U(R)X = OB$
totally R-indefinable iff $L(R)X = \oslash$ and $U(R)X = OB$.

R-definability means that a given set X is the union of some of the equivalence classes of relation R, in other words X can be covered with equivalence classes of R. Since each equivalence class represents a property, we obtain the property that characterises the elements of set X by making disjunction of properties that correspond to the classes of the respective covering. For example in the domain from Example 6 set $\{Me, V, U, N, P\}$ is $\{D, S, M\}$-definable. After simple propositional transformation the corresponding property is 'no moon or far from the Sun and (medium or small)'.

In terms of approximations the relations of rough inclusion and rough equality are defined:

X is R-bottom included in Y iff $L(R)X \subseteq L(R)Y$
X is R-top included in Y iff $U(R)X \subseteq U(R)Y$
X is R-bottom equal to Y iff $L(R)X = L(R)Y$
X is R-top equal to Y iff $U(R)X = U(R)Y$.

The algebraic characterization of rough equalities can be found in [12,14,25].

Operation of intersection applied to indiscernibility relations enables us to define properties which are stronger than the properties which are determined by the components of intersection. According to 2(b) equivalence classes of intersection of indiscernibility relations are not bigger than equivalence classes of the components of intersection. Hence, properties obtained in this way provide a finer partition of the universe of objects and, as a consequence, approximations of any set X determined by $R \cap S$ are closer to X (with respect to inclusion) than approximations determined by R and S. Operation $\cup^*$ is used to obtain what is called strong definability [2]. We say that:

A set X of objects is strongly R-definable iff X is an equivalence class of R.

If a set is not strongly definable with respect to any indiscernibility relation in a given universe, then its strong definability could be achieved provided that characterization of objects is found by means of properties which are weaker than the properties determined by the original indiscernibility relations. In other words the new indiscernibility relation should determine bigger equivalence classes than the classes of the given partitions.

Example 8 Consider the set of objects and the set of attributes from Example 7 and set $X = \{o1, o2, o3, o4\}$. Neither $IND(o)$ nor $IND(+)$ (and clearly not $IND(o,+)$) provide its strong definability. However, set X strongly definable with respect to $IND(o) \cup^* IND(+)$.

We conclude that a logic for reasoning with indiscernibility-type incomplete information should satisfy the following conditions:

1. Formulas of the logic represent sets of objects,

2. Counterparts of set-theoretical operations and operations of lower and upper approximation are among propositional operations,

3. Approximation operations are determined by relative indiscernibility relations,

4. The family of indiscernibility relations is closed under intersection and transitive closure of union.

Conditions (1),(2) are not new, they are satisfied by several multimodal logics, where states in semantical structures are interpreted as objects, and operations of necessity and possibility are interpreted as operations of lower and upper approximation, respectively. To satisfy conditions (3) and (4) an essential extension of ordinary logics is needed.

The logics with propositional operations determined by relative relations are discussed in [17,22] and logics based on this idea were developed in [7, 9, 11, 16, 18, 19, 21, 24].

3 Logic of indiscernibility relations

The aim of the present section is to present logic $INDL$ of indiscernibility relations. The logic has been introduced in [23]. Some other versions of the logic are considered in [16,24]. In the logic the phenomenon of relativeness of indiscernibility relations can be dealt with. The logic is a multimodal logic with Kripke-style semantics, where indiscernibility relations play the role of accessibility relations. The essential difference between the standard modal logics and logic *INDL* is that in both syntax and semantics of *INDL* explicit reference is made to parameters which determine indiscernibility relations. In the language of *INDL* special expressions are introduced representing sets of parameters and their Boolean combinations. In the semantical structures of *INDL* relative indiscernibility relations are assumed.

The language of logic *INDL* is defined in two steps. First, the set of parameter expressions is introduced, and second, the set of formulas is constructed. Parameter expressions are built with symbols from the following disjoint sets:

CONPAR a set of constants representing sets of parameters,

$\{-, \cup, \cap\}$ the set of Boolean operations of complement, union, and intersection, respectively.

Set *EPAR* of parameter expressions is the smallest set satisfying the following conditions:

$CONPAR \subseteq EPAR$,

$P, Q \in EPAR$ imply $- P, P \cup Q, P \cap Q \in EPAR$.

Relational expressions of the language are constructed with parameter expressions by means of relational operations $\cap, \cup^*$ and with symbol *IND* of indiscernibility. Set *EREL* of relational expressions, interpreted as indiscernibility relations, is the smallest set satisfying the following conditions:

$P \in EPAR$ implies $IND(P) \in EREL$,

$R, S \in EREL$ imply $R \cap, R \cup^* S \in EREL$.

Formulas of the language are constructed with symbols from the following pairwise disjoint sets:

VARPROP a set of propositional variables interpreted as sets of objects,

$\{\neg, \vee, \neg, \rightarrow, \leftrightarrow\}$ the set of classical propositional operations of negation, disjunction, conjunction, implication, and equivalence, respectively,

$\{[], <>\}$ the set of modal propositional operations interpreted as operation of lower and upper approximation, respectively.

Set *FORI* of formulas of logic *INDL* is the smallest set satisfying the following conditions:

$VARPROP \subseteq FORI$,

$F, G \in FORI$ imply $\neg F, F \vee G, F \wedge G, F \rightarrow G, F \leftrightarrow G \in FORI$,

$F \in FORI, R \in EREL$ imply $[R]F, < R > F \in FORI$.

The semantics of the language is defined by means of the notion of model and satisfiability of formulas in a model. By a model we mean the system:

$M = (OB, PAR, \{IND(P)\} P \subseteq PAR, m)$,

where *OB* and *PAR* are nonempty sets whose elements are referred to as objects and parameters, respectively; For any $P \subseteq PAR$ relation $IND(P)$ is a binary relation in set *OB* satisfying conditions *(IND1),(IND2),(IND3)*; Function m : $CONPAR \cup VARPROP \rightarrow P(\text{PAR}) \cup P(OB)$ is a meaning function which provides interpretation of constants and variables of the language such that $m(P) \subseteq PAR$ for $P \in CONPAR$, and $m(p) \in OB$ for $p \in VARPROP$. We extend function m to arbitrary parameter expressions and relational expressions as follows:

$$m(-P) = -m(P), m(P \cup Q) = m(P) \cup m(Q), m(P \cap Q) = m(P) \cap m(Q),$$

$m(IND(P)) = IND(m(P))$,

$m(R \cap S) = m(R) \cap m(S), m(R \cup^* S) = m(R) \cup *m(S)$ for any indiscernibility relations R and S.

We say that a formula F is satisfied by an object o in model M (M, o sat F) iff the following conditions are satisfied:

M, o sat p iff $o \in m(p)$ for $p \in VARPROP$,

M, o sat $\neg F$ iff not M, o sat F,

M, o sat $F \vee G$ iff M, o sat F or M, o sat G,

M, o sat $F \wedge G$ iff M, o sat F and M, o sat G,

M, o sat $F \rightarrow G$ iff M, o sat $\neg F \vee G$,

M, o sat $F \leftrightarrow G$ iff M, o sat $(F \rightarrow G) \wedge (G \rightarrow F)$,

M, o sat $[R]F$ iff for all $s \in OB$ $(o,s) \in m(R)$ implies M, s sat F,

M, o sat $< R > F$ iff there is $s \in OB$ such that $(o, s) \in m(R)$ and M, o sat F.

We define extension of a formula F in model M ($ext_M F$):
$$ext_M F = \{o \in OB : M, o \text{ sat } F\} .$$

Proposition 4

(a) $ext_M p = m(p)$ for $p \in VARPROP$,

(b) $ext_M \neg F = -ext_M F$,

(c) $ext_M F \vee G = ext_M F \cup ext_M G$,

(d) $ext_M F \rightarrow G = ext_M \neg F \vee G$,

(e) $ext_M F \leftrightarrow G = ext_M (F \rightarrow G) \wedge (G \rightarrow F)$,

(f) $ext_M [R]F = L(m(R)) ext_M F$,

(g) $ext_M < R > F = U(m(R)) ext_M F$.

Proposition 4 says that classical propositional operations correspond to Boolean operations, and operations [] and <> correspond to operations of lower and upper approximation, respectively, determined by indiscernibility relation.

We say that a formula F is satisfied in a model M if there is on object o such that M, o sat F. A formula F is satisfiable iff there is a model M and an object o such that M, o sat F. A formula F is true in a model M ($| = MF$) iff M, o sat F for all $o \in OB$. Formula F is valid ($| = F$) iff F is true in all models.

The following two propositions say how basic properties of rough sets can be expressed in logic $INDL$.

Proposition 5

(a) $| = MF \rightarrow [R]F$ iff $ext_M F$ is $m(R)$-definable,

(b) $| = M \neg [R]F$ iff $ext_M F$ is internally $m(R)$-indefinable,

(c) $| = M < R > F$ iff $ext_M F$ is externally $m(R)$-indefinable,

(d) $\models M <R> F \wedge <R> \neg F$ iff $ext_M F$ is totally $m(R)$-indefinable.

Proposition 6

(a) $\models M [R]F \leftrightarrow [R]G$ iff $ext_M F$ bottom $m(R)$-equals $ext_M G$,

(b) $\models M <R> F \leftrightarrow <R> G$ iff $ext_M F$ top $m(R)$-equals $ext_M G$,

(c) $\models M [R]F \rightarrow [R]G$ iff $ext_M F$ is bottom $m(R)$-included in $ext_M G$,

(d) $\models M <R> F \rightarrow <R> G$ iff $ext_M F$ is top $m(R)$-included in $ext_M G$.

Proofs of these propositions are by verification. Below are listed examples of valid formulas.

Proposition 7 The following formulas are valid in *INDL*:

(a) $([R]F \vee [S]F) \rightarrow [R \cap S]F$

(b) $[R \cup^* S]F \rightarrow ([R]F \wedge [S]F)$

(c) $([IND(P)]F \vee [IND(Q)]F) \rightarrow [IND(P \cup Q)]F$

(d) $[IND(P \cap Q)]F \rightarrow ([IND(P)]F \wedge [IND(Q)]F)$.

Since indiscernibility relations are assumed to be equivalence relations, and so are their intersections and transitive closures of their unions, the operations $[R]$ and $<R>$ for any $R \in EREL$ are $S5$ modalities. Hence all formulas that are substitutions of theorems of logic $S5$ are valid in *INDL*.

The problem of complete axiomatization of the logic is open, however several results have been obtained for fragments of *INDL*, and several extensions of the logic have been introduced. In [3] completeness has been proved for the fragment of *INDL*, introduced in [2], without parameter expressions and with semantics restricted to models with what is called local agreement: for any indiscernibility relations R, S and for any object o either $R(o) \subseteq S(o)$ or $S(o) \subseteq R(o)$. Decidability of the validity problem for this fragment of *INDL* has been proved in [6]. Decidability of the validity problem for *INDL* has been proved in [10]. Generalization of *INDL* to non-transitive indiscernibility relations has been introduced in [18]. Logics of nondeterministic information with reflexive, symmetric relations (informational similarity of objects) and reflexive, transitive relations (informational inclusion of objects) and with some additional conditions reflecting relationship between these relations have been investigated in [11,28,33,34,35]. A generalization of *INDL* to arbitrary indiscernibility relations and modal operators corresponding to generalized approximation operations determined by arbitrary binary relations has been introduced in [17,22]. Application of relative indiscernibility relations to inductive reasoning is considered in [19].

Logics for reasoning about rough sets can also be found in [26,30,32,36,37,38].

4 Rough set semantics of knowledge operators

A formal logical analysis of reasoning about knowledge is a subject of investigations both in logic [5,8,40] and computer science [1,4] and several epistemic systems have been proposed to formalize the operator 'an agent knows'. In the present section we outline a formalism based on semantic treatment of knowledge within the framework of rough set theory [20,21]. Our approach is based on the following intuitions:

(1) Knowledge of an agent about a predicate F can be reflected by the ability of the agent to classify objects as instances or non-instances of F. For example, the sentence 'agent a knows green objects' is true whenever for any object o in a given domain agent a can decide whether o is green or not.

(2) Knowledge of an agent about a sentence F can be reflected by the ability of the agent to classify states of a given domain into those in which F is true and those in which F is false. For example, the sentence 'agent a knows that F is the case' is true whenever in any state agent a can decide whether F is true or not.

Assumptions (1) and (2) say that knowledge is understood as the ability to discern the thing which is claimed to be known from the other things. More generally, our intuition is that 'to know F' can be interpreted as 'to be able to decide the membership question for the extension of F, and according to the usual understanding of decidability, 'to decide the membership question' is to be understood as the ability to give yes-no answer to the question whether an element belongs to the set or not, for any element from a given universe. As a consequence, if we can answer the membership question for the extension of F, then we can also decide this question for the extension of the negation of F. The extension of a predicate (an open formula) is the set of those objects which satisfy the predicate, and the extension of a sentence (a closed formula) is the set of those states in which the sentence is true. In both cases a formula (open or closed) corresponds to a set which is a subset of the universe of a semantical structure for the language under consideration. The knowledge operators introduced in the present paper are defined semantically, they are functions which assign a subset of the universe to extension of the formula to which they are applied. This subset consists of those elements from the universe whose membership in the extension of the formula can be decided by an agent.

Our third assumption is concerned with relativity of knowledge. Usually, recognition of objects or states by an agent is not exact, it depends on his individual abilities. To reflect this fact we assume that:

(3) With each agent there is associated an indiscernibility relation, and the agent decides membership of objects or states up to this indiscernibility relation. As a consequence knowledge operators are relative to indiscernibility.

Let OB be a universe of objects and let AGT be a set of agents. For each $a \in AGT$ let $IND(a) \subseteq OB \times OB$ be an indiscernibility relation corresponding to agent a. For a set A of agents we define indiscernibility $IND(A)$ as follows:

$(s,t) \in IND(A)$ iff $(s,t) \in IND(a)$ for all $a \in A$,
$IND(\oslash) = OB \times OB$.

Hence, up to $IND(A)$ a state is discernible by A from some other state iff it is discernible by at least one agent from A. It is easy to see that relations $IND(A)$ satisfy conditions (IND1), (IND2), (IND3).

We recall that sets of A-positive, A-negative and A-borderline instances of a set $X \subseteq OB$ are defined as follows [15]:

$POS(A)X = L(A)X$
$NEG(A)X = OB - U(A)X$
$BOR(A)X = U(A)X - L(A)X$.

Intuitively, if $s \in POS(A)X$, then in view of agents from A element s is a member of X. If $s \in NEG(A)X$, then in view of agents from A element s is not a member of X. $BOR(A)X$ is the range of uncertainty. Element $s \in BOR(A)X$ whenever agents from A cannot decide whether s is a member of X or not.

Proposition 8

(a) $POS(A)X$, $NEG(A)X$, $BOR(A)X$ are pairwise disjoint

(b) $POS(A)X \cup NEG(A)X \cup BOR(A)X = OB$

(c) $POS(A)X$, $NEG(A)X$, $BOR(A)X$ are $IND(A)$-definable.

Proposition 9

(a) $A \subseteq B$ implies $POS(A)X \subseteq POS(B)X$, $NEG(A)X \subseteq NEG(B)X$, $BOR(B)X \subseteq BOR(A)X$

(b) $IND(A) \subseteq IND(B)$ implies $POS(B)X \subseteq POS(A)X$, $NEG(B)X \subseteq NEG(A)X$, $BOR(A)X \subseteq BOR(B)X$.

Proposition 10

(a) $POS(A)X \subseteq X$, $NEG(A)X \subseteq -X$

(b) $POS(A) \oslash = \oslash$, $NEG(A)OB = \oslash$

(c) $POS(\oslash)X = \oslash$ if $X \neq OB$, $POS(\oslash)OB = OB$

(d) $NEG(\oslash) X = \oslash$ if $X \neq \oslash$, $NEG(\oslash)\oslash = OB$

(e) $X \subseteq Y$ implies $POS(A)X \subseteq POS(A)Y$, $NEG(A)Y \subseteq NEG(A)X$.

Proposition 11

(a) $NEG(A)(X \cup Y) = NEG(A)X \cap NEG(A)Y$

(b) $NEG(A) X \cup NEG(A)Y \subseteq NEG(A)(X \cap Y)$

(c) $NEG(A)(-X) = POS(A)X$.

Proposition 12

(a) $BOR(A)(X \cup Y) \subseteq BOR(A)X \cup BOR(A)Y$

(b) $BOR(A)(X \cap Y) \subseteq BOR(A)X \cap BOR(A)Y$

(c) $BOR(A)(-X) = BOR(A)X$.

Proposition 13

(a) $POS(A)X \cup POS(B)X \subseteq POS(A \cup B)X$

(b) $POS(A \cap B)X \subseteq POS(A)X \cap POS(B)X$

(c) $NEG(A)X \cup NEG(B)X \subseteq NEG(A \cup B)X$

(d) $NEG(A \cap B)X \subseteq NEG(A)X \cap NEG(B)X$.

We define a family of knowledge operators $K(A)$ for $A \in AGT$:
$$K(A)X = POS(A)X \cup NEG(A)X.$$
Intuitively, $s \in K(A)X$ whenever s can be decided by agents from A to be an A-positive or A-negative instance of X.

Proposition 14

(a) $K(A)\oslash = K(A)OB = OB$

(b) $K(\oslash)X = \oslash$ if $\oslash \neq X \neq OB$

(c) $A \subseteq B$ implies $K(A)X \subseteq K(B)X$

(d) $IND(A) \subseteq IND(B)$ implies $K(B)X \subseteq K(A)X$

(e) If X is $IND(A)$-definable then $K(A)X = OB$.

We say that knowledge of agents A about X is:

complete	if $K(A)X = OB$
incomplete	if $BOR(A)X \neq \oslash$
rough	if $POS(A)X, NEG(A)X, BOR(A)X \neq \oslash$
pos-empty	if $POS(A)X = \oslash$
neg-empty	if $NEG(A)X = \oslash$
empty	if pos-empty and neg-empty

Example 9 Let $OB = \{s1, s2, s3, s4, s5, s6, s7\}$ and $A = \{a, b\}$. Assume that indiscernibility relations $IND(a)$ and $IND(b)$ provide the following equivalence classes:

$IND(a)$: $\{s1,s3\}$ $\{s2,s4,s5\}$ $\{s6,s7\}$
$IND(b)$: $\{s1, s2, s4\}\{s3, s6\}\{s5, s7\}$.

Clearly, $IND(\{a,b\})$ is the identity on OB. Assume that the extension of predicate 'green object' is $X = \{s1, s3, s4\}$. Then we have:

$POS(a)X = \{s1, s3\}$, $NEG(a)X = \{s6, s7\}$, $K(a)X = \{s1, s3, s6, s7\}$.

Hence, knowledge of agent a about concept 'green object' is not complete, up to indiscernibility $IND(a)$ the agent can only decide membership of $s1, s3, s6, s7$, for the remaining elements the agent does not know whether they are green or not. For the agent b we have:

$POS(b)X = \oslash$, $NEG(b)X = \{s5, s7\}$, $K(b)X = \{s5, s7\}$.

Knowledge of b about 'green object' is pos-empty, the agent can only decide that $s5$ and $s7$ are not green.

A joint knowledge of the group $\{a, b\}$ is complete, deciding together they can recognize for every object from OB whether it is green or not.

Observe that if knowledge of A about X is complete, then A can discern X from its complement. Every A has a complete knowledge about any $IND(A)$-definable set, in particular about $\oslash$ and OB. The fact that knowledge of any agent about the whole universe is complete should not be considered to be a paradox. A predicate whose extension equals OB provides a trivial, in a sense, information. In any particular example OB represents the set of 'all things perceivable by agents'. However, if OB consists of all formulas of the predicate calculus, and $X \subseteq OB$ is the set of all the valid formulas, then clearly not every agent has the complete knowledge about X, although he has the complete knowledge about OB, since in this example formulas are the only things he deals with. Observe that $X \subseteq Y$ does not necessarily imply $K(A)X \subseteq K(A)Y$, and $K(A)X$ is not necessarily included in X. These facts enable us to avoid the well known paradoxes of epistemic logic, where all the formulas known by anyone are valid, and every agent knows all the logical consequences of his knowledge.

The following theorems provide characterization of the types of knowledge defined in this section.

Proposition 15 The following conditions are equivalent:

(a) $K(A)X$ is complete

(b) X is $IND(A)$-definable

(c) $BOR(A)X = \oslash$

(d) $POS(A)X = -NEG(A)X$.

It follows that if agents A have complete knowledge about X, then they can tell X from its complement.

Proposition 16 The following conditions are equivalent:

(a) $K(A)X$ is rough

(b) X is roughly $IND(A)$-definable

(c) $\oslash \neq BOR(A)X \neq U$

(d) $\oslash \neq POS(A)X \subseteq -NEG(A)X$.

Proposition 17 The following conditions are equivalent:

(a) $K(A)X$ is pos-empty

(b) X is internally $IND(A)$-indefinable

(c) $K(A)X = NEG(A)X$

(d) $BOR(A)X = -NEG(A)X$.

Proposition 18 The following conditions are equivalent:

(a) $K(A)X$ is neg-empty

(b) X is externally $IND(A)$-indefinable

(c) $K(A)X = POS(A)X$

(d) $BOR(A)X = -POS(A)X$.

Proposition 19 The following conditions are equivalent:

(a) $K(A)X$ is empty

(b) X is totally $IND(A)$-indefinable

(c) $BOR(A)X = OB$.

Proposition 20

(a) $IND(A) = IND(B)$ iff $K(A)X = K(A)Y$ for all $X \subseteq OB$

(b) $IND(A) \subseteq IND(B)$ implies $K(B)X \subseteq POS(B)K(A)X$ and $POS(A)K(B)X$ $\subseteq K(A)X$

(c) $IND(A)$ is the identity on OB iff $K(A)X$ is complete for all X.

Proposition 21

(a) $K(A)\oslash$ is pos-empty, $K(A)OB$ is neg-empty

(b) $K(A)X = K(A)(-X)$

(c) $K(A)K(A)X = OB$

(d) $K(A)X \cup K(B)X \subseteq K(A \cup B)X$

(e) $K(A \cap B)X \subseteq K(A)X \cap K(B)X$.

Knowledge operators $K(A)$ are nonmonotonic.

Example 10 Consider $OB = \{s1, ..., s7\}$ and indiscernibility relation $IND(A)$ that provides the following equivalence classes: $\{s1, s2\}, \{s3, s4\}, \{s5, s6\}, \{s7\}$. Consider sets $X = \{s1, s2, s3\}$ and $Y = \{s1, s2, s3, s4, s5\}$. We have $K(A)X = \{s1, s2, s5, s6, s7\}$ and $K(A)Y = \{s1, s2, s3, s4, s7\}$.

Systems of the form:
$$E = (OB, AGT, \{IND(A)\}_{A \subseteq AGT}, \{K(A)\}_{A \subseteq AGT})$$
will be called epistemic systems. They serve as semantical structures for the epistemic logic defined in section 5.

Knowledge relative to indiscernibility $IND(A \cup B)$ can be considered to be a joint knowledge of the group consisting of all the agents from both A and B. By Proposition 1 we easily obtain the following lemma.

Proposition 22
$$K(A)X, K(B)X \subseteq K(A \cup B)X.$$

Hence a joint knowledge of a group of agents is not less than knowledge of any member of the group.

5 Logic with knowledge operators

We define a propositional language with a family of knowledge operators. Each operator is determined by a set of parameters interpreted as knowledge agents. Let $CONAGT$ be a set of constants which are to be interpreted as sets of agents. We define set $EAGT$ of agent expressions as follows:

$CONAGT \subseteq EAGT$

$A, B \in EAGT$ implies $-A, Q \cup B, A \cap B \in EAGT$.

Let $VARPROP$ be a set of propositional variables. Set FOR of formulas is the smallest set satisfying the following conditions:

$VARPROP \subseteq FOR$

$F, G \in FOR$ implies $\neg F, F \vee G, F \wedge G, F \rightarrow G, F \leftrightarrow G \in FOR$

$A \in EAGT, F \in FOR$ imply $K(A)F \in FOR$.

Hence the set FOR is closed with respect to classical propositional connectives and knowledge operators determined by agent expressions.

Let an epistemic system $E = (OB, AGT, \{IND(A)\}_{A \subseteq AGT}, \{K(A)\}_{A \subseteq AGT})$ be given. By a model we mean a system $M = (E, m)$, where m is a meaning function assigning sets of states to propositional variables, sets of agents to agent constants, and moreover m satisfies the following conditions:

$m(p) \subseteq OB$ for $p \in VARPROP$

$m(A) \subseteq AGT$ for $A \in CONAGT$

$m(A \cap B) = m(A) \cap m(B), m(A \cap B) = m(A) \cap m(B), m(-A) = -m(A)$.

In a similar way to that developed in Section 3 we define a family of extensions $ext_M F$ of formulas in a model for any $F \in FOR$. For formulas with knowledge operators we have:

$ext_M K(A)F = K(m(A))ext_M F$.

We say that a formula F is true in model M ($| =_M F$) iff $ext_M F = OB$, and a formula F is valid ($| = F$) iff it is true in all models.

Observe that formulas of the form $K(A)F \to F$ and $(F \to G) \wedge K(A)F \to K(A)G$ are not valid. This means that if F is known by an agent, then F is not necessarily true, and agents do not know all the consequences of their knowledge. Hence, the well known paradoxes of epistemic logics are eliminated in our system.

In the following we list some facts about knowledge of agents which can be expressed in the logic.

Proposition 23

(a) $| =_M K(A)F$ iff knowledge of $m(A)$ about $ext_M F$ is complete

(b) $| =_M \neg K(A)F$ iff knowledge of $m(A)$ about $ext_M F$ is empty

(c) not $| =_M K(A)F$ and not $| =_M \neg K(A)F$ iff knowledge of $m(A)$ about $ext_M F$ is rough

(d) $| =_M K(A)F \to K(B)F$ iff $K(m(A))ext_M F \subseteq K(m(B))ext_M F$.

Below are given examples of valid formulas.

Proposition 24 The following formulas are valid:

(a) $K(A)F \to K(A)K(A \cap B)F$

(b) $K(A \cup B)K(A)F \to K(A \cup B)F$

(c) $(K(A)F \vee K(B)F) \to K(A \cup B)F$

(d) $K(A \cap B)F \to K(A)F \wedge K(B)F$

(e) $K(A)F \leftrightarrow K(A)(\neg F)$

(f) $K(A)(K(A)F \to F)$.

Condition (c) says that knowledge of a group of agents exceeds knowledge of a part of the group.

Proposition 25

(a) $| = F \leftrightarrow G$ implies $| = K(A)F \leftrightarrow K(A)G$

(b) $|= F$ implies $|= K(A)F$.

Condition (b) says that agents A can discern extension of F from its complement iff they can discern extension of $\neg F$ from its complement. This fact is often considered to be a paradox of ideal knowers. However, with the interpretation of knowledge as the ability to decide the membership question it seems to be less paradoxical. It follows from the fact that the whole universe OB is $IND(A)$-definable for any A. In other words, whatever a perception ability of A is (whatever $IND(A)$ is), equivalence classes of all the elements from OB cover set OB.

For indiscernibility relations that are equivalence relations knowledge operators can be defined in the multimodal logic $S5$, namely $K(A)F$ is equivalent to $[IND(A)]F \vee [\ IND(A)](\ \neg F)$, where $[IND(A)]$ denotes the necessity operator determined by the accessibility relation $IND(A)$. Complete axiomatization of a fragment of this epistemic logic without explicit agent expressions has been presented in [39]. For nontransitive indiscernibility the respective formula with necessity operators from logic B is not equivalent to $K(A)F$, because in this case the operations of lower and upper approximation do not coincide with necessity and possibility, respectively.

According to the scheme suggested in the present section one can define knowledge operators determined by arbitrary binary relations, using the generalized notion of approximation of set and the respective modal operators introduced in [17,22]. The knowledge operators presented in this section are discussed in [29,31]

References

[1] Chandy KM, Misra J. How processes learn. Distributed Computing 1986; (1)40–52

[2] Farinas del Cerro L, Orlowska E. DAL-A logic for data analysis. Theoretical Computer Science 1985; (36)251–264

[3] Gargov G. Two completeness theorems in the logic for data analysis. ICS PAS Reports 581, 1986

[4] Halpern J (ed). Theoretical aspects of reasoning about knowledge. In: Proceedings of the 1986 Conference. Morgan Kaufmann, Los Altos, 1986

[5] Hintikka J. Knowledge and belief. Cornell University Press, 1962

[6] Kadota N, Nakamura A. A decidability result in a logic for data analysis. Tech Rep No C-22, Hiroshima University, 1988

[7] Konikowska B. A formal language for reasoning about indiscernibility. Bulletin of the PAS 35, Math 1987; 239–249

[8] Lenzen W. Recent work in epistemic logic. Acta Philosophica Fennica, 1978; (30)1–219

[9] Nakamura A. A logic for temporal data analysis. Tech Rep, Hiroshima University, 1988

32

[10] Nakamura A, Gao J-M. A decidability result in the logic of indiscernibility relations. Tech Rep, Hiroshima University, 1986

[11] Nakamura A, Gao J-M. A modal logic for similarity based data analysis. Tech Rep, Hiroshima University, 1988

[12] Nieminen J. Rough tolerance equality and tolerance black boxes. Fundamenta Informaticae, 1988; (11)289-296

[13] Novotny M. On sequents defined by means of information systems. Fundamenta Informaticae, 1981; (4)1041-1048

[14] Novotny M, Pawlak Z. On rough equalities. Bulletin of the PAS 33, Math, 1985; 99-104

[15] Orlowska E. Semantics of vague concepts. In: Dorn G, Weingartner P (eds) Foundations of logic and linguistics. Problems and solutions. (Selected contributions to the 7th International Congress of Logic, Methodology, and Philosophy of Science) Plenum Press, Salzburg, London, New York, 1983, pp 465-482

[16] Orlowska E. Logic of indiscernibility relations. Springer-Verlag, Berlin, Heidelberg, New York, 1984, pp 177-186 (Lecture notes in computer science no 208)

[17] Orlowska E. Kripke models with relative accessibility. ICS PAS Reports 569, Warsaw, 1985

[18] Orlowska E. Logic of nondeterministic information. Studia Logica XLIV, 1985; 93-102

[19] Orlowska E. Semantic analysis of inductive reasoning. Theoretical Computer Science 1986;43:81-89

[20] Orlowska E. Semantics of knowledge operators. Abstracts of the 8th Int'l Congress of Logic, Methodology, and Philosophy of Science, Moscow, 1987; (5)3:266-269. Also Bulletin of the PAS 35, Mathematics, 1987; pp 255-263

[21] Orlowska E. Logic for reasoning about knowledge. Bulletin of the Section of Logic, 1987; (16)1:26-38. Also Zeitschrift fur Mathematische Logik und Grundlagen der Mathematik, 1989; 35:559-572

[22] Orlowska E. Kripke models with relative accessibility and their application to inferences from incomplete information. Banach Center Publications, Polish Scientific Publishers Warsaw, 1987; 21:327-337

[23] Orlowska E. Logical aspects of learning concepts. International Journal of Approximate Reasoning 1988; (2)349-364

[24] Orlowska E. Representation of vague information. Information Systems, 1988; (13)167-174

[25] Pagliani P. A pure logic-algebraic analysis of rough top and rough bottom equalities. Manuscript, 1993

[26] Pawlak Z. Rough logic. Bulletin of the PAS 35, Ser Tech 1987; 253–258

[27] Pawlak Z. Rough sets. Kluwer, Amsterdam 1991

[28] Pliuskevicene A. A conservative extension of the logic of nondeterministic information. Proc of the Conference on Applications of Mathematical Logic. Tallin, 1986 (In Russian)

[29] Rasiowa H, Marek W. On reaching consensus by groups of intelligent agents. International Journal of Approximate Reasoning. 1989; 415–432

[30] Rasiowa H, Skowron A. Approximation logic. Proc of the Conference on Mathematical Methods of Specification and Synthesis of Software Systems. Berlin 1985, Akademi Verlag, Band 31, 1986; 123–139

[31] Rauszer C. Rough logic for multi-agent systems. Proc of the Conference Logic at Work. Amsterdam, 1992

[32] Szczerba L. Rough quantifiers. Bulletin of the PAS 35, Math 1987; 251–254

[33] Vakarelov D. Abstract characterization of some knowledge representation systems and the logic NIL of nondeterministic information. In: Jorrand Ph, Sgurev V (eds) Artificial Intelligence II, Methodology, Systems, Applications. North-Holland Amsterdam 1987; 255–260

[34] Vakarelov D. $S4$ and $S5$ together—$S4 + 5$. Abstracts of the 8th Int'l Congress of Logic, Methodology, and Philosophy of Science. Moscow, 1987; (5)3:271–274

[35] Vakarelov D. Modal logics for knowledge representation. Springer-Verlag, Berlin Heidelberg New York, 1989. pp 257–277 (Lecture notes in computer science no 363)

[36] Vakarelov D. Logical analysis of positive and negative similarity relations in property systems. Proc of the First World Conference on the Fundamentals of Artificial Intelligence, Paris, France, 1991, pp 491–500

[37] Vakarelov D. Rough polyadic modal logic. Journal of Applied Non-Classical Logics 1991; (1)9–34

[38] Vakarelov D. A modal logic for similarity relations in Pawlak knowledge representation systems. Fundamenta Informaticae 1991; (15)61–79

[39] Valiev MK. A modal logic interpreted as epistemic logic. Proc of the Conference Borzomi 88, 1988 (In Russian)

[40] Von Wright GH. An Essay in Modal Logic. North-Holland, Amsterdam, 1951

Knowledge and Uncertainty a Rough Set Approach

Zdzisław Pawlak

Institute of Computer Science

Warsaw Technical University

zpw@ii.pw.edu.pl

1   Introduction

The idea of a rough set has been proposed by the author as a new mathematical tool to deal with vagueness and uncertainty. It seems to be of fundamental importance to AI and cognitive sciences, in particular expert systems, decision support systems, machine learning, machine discovery, inductive reasoning pattern recognition, decision tables and others.

The rough set theory, besides its methodological significance, turn out to be very useful in practice and its importance to data analysis seems to be unquestionable. Main advantage of the rough set theory in applications is in discovering patterns in data, data reduction, discovering of data dependencies, data significance, decision algorithms generation from data, approximate classification of data, discovering similarities or differences in data, and others. Many real life applications of this concept have been implemented. More about the application of the rough set theory can be found in Slowinski [38].

In the lecture basic concepts of the rough set theory will be outlined and its philosophical background briefly presented. For more detailed exposition the reader is referred to Pawlak [26].

2   Knowledge and classification

Theory of knowledge for a long time has been subject of interest of philosophers and logicians [17,18,20,29]. Recently new momentum to this area of research have been given by AI researchers ([1,4,5,6,7,8,9,13,14,15,16,19,22,23,24,25,30, 31,32,33,39,40] and others). There is no till now, however, widely shared body of opinion, as to how understand, represent and manipulate knowledge.

Intuitively, the idea of knowledge seems to be best expressed by Russell, who says that "knowing" is a kind of relationship between an organism and the environment [35], which can be perceived as a body of information about some parts of reality that is needed to behave rationally in the real world.

It seems natural that this kind of understanding of knowledge must be based on the ability of an organism to classify various states of the real world and the organism states itself, and consequently that each organism must be equipped with a variety of classification skills, on concrete and abstract level.

For example, knowledge of any organism about its environment must be based on the ability to classify variety of situations (e.g. safe-unsafe, dark-bright, etc.). On more specific level classification of sensory signals, like color,

> "Apart from the known and the unknown, what else is there?"
>
> **Harold Pinter** in *The Homecoming*

temperature etc., seems to be of fundamental significance to acquire knowledge needed by any organism.

Therefore we will assume, that knowledge is based on the ability to classify objects, and by object we understand anything we can think of, for example entities, states, processes, abstract concepts, signals, events etc.

Classification requires that small differences between objects being classified must be postponed, i.e. object being in the same class are *indiscernible*. For example when classifying some objects according to color, in order to form a class of red objects, we have to postpone small differences between various shades of red, so that all objects in the same class are indiscernible. Therefore the indiscernibility is a fundamental concept in the presented approach.

3 Knowledge and information systems

As said before we assume that knowledge is manifested by the ability to classify. Therefore we will define formally knowledge as a family of partitions over a fixed, finite universe. For mathematical reasons instated of partitions we may also use the corresponding equivalence relations. Thus knowledge can be also defined as family of equivalence relations over the universe. Because we need a "language" to represent various partitions, we will employ to this end so called information systems, called also attribute-value tables.

An *information system* is a finite table rows of which are labelled by objects of the universe U, whereas columns - are labelled by attributes from a fixed set A and each entry of the table corresponding to object x and attribute a is an *attribute value*. The set of all values of an attribute a is called the domain of a and is denoted V_a . For example, if the attribute is COLOR then its domain may be *red, green, blue*, etc. An example of an information system is given in the table below.

U	COLOR	SHAPE	SIZE
1	*red*	*tri.*	*small*
2	*green*	*square*	*small*
3	*blue*	*round*	*large*
4	*red*	*square*	*small*
5	*green*	*round*	*large*

Table 1

The table contains data about five children toy blocks, described by three features (attributes) *COLOR*, *SHAPE* and *SIZE*. The domains of the corresponding attributes are {*red, blue, green*}, {*triangular, square*}, round and {*small, large*}.

It is easily seen that each subset of attributes determines partition of objects of the universe into blocks having the same features, i.e. being indiscernible by this features.

> "Knowing is a relation of the organism to something else or to a part of itself"
>
> **Bertrand Russel** in *An Inquiry into Meaning and Truth*

Formally an information system can be defined as a pair $S = (U, A)$, where U - is the universe and A - is the set of attributes. Each attribute a can be understood as a total function $a : U \rightarrow V_a$, which to every objects associates the attribute value.

With every subset of attributes $B \subseteq A$, we associate a binary relation $IND(B)$, called an *indiscernibility relation* and defined thus:

$$IND(B) = \{(x, y) \in U^2 : \text{ for every } a \in B, a(x) = a(y)\}.$$

Obviously *IND(B)* is an equivalence relation and

$$IND(B) = \bigcap_{a \in B} IND(a).$$

An equivalence class of the relation *IND(B)* containing the object x will be denoted $[x]_B$, and the partition generated by *IND(B)*, i.e. family of all equivalence classes of $IND(B)$, is denoted as $U/IND(B)$, or in short U/B.

Any subset of the universe will be called concept or category in $S = (U, A)$; in particular equivalence classes of any relation $IND(a)$ will be referred to as *primitive* concepts of a (in S), where as equivalence classes of any relation $IND(B)$ will be called basic concepts of B (in S), provided card $(B) > 1$.

An attribute value $a(x)$ can be viewed as a name (description, label)) of the it primitive category of a containing x (i.e.- the name of $[x]_a$), whereas the set $a(x)_{a \in B}$, can be considered as a name of the basic category $[x]_B$.

Remark. In fact we should distinguish between the name (intention), of a concept, e.g. *red*, and its meaning (extension), e.g. the set of all red objects, but for the sake of simplicity we will make not this distinction, whenever it will make no confusion.

For example if *U/COLOR* is a partition classifying objects according to color, than *red, green, blue*, etc., i.e. sets of red, green or blue objects, are primitive concepts of our knowledge; if elements of the universe are classified according to *COLOR (red, green, blue)*, and *SHAPE (triangle, square, round,)* then the corresponding basic categories would be *green and square* (green square) *red and triangular* (red triangle), etc. Thus basic categories are fundamental building blocks, or basic properties of the universe which can be expressed employing this knowledge. Hence an information system contains descriptions of all basic categories available in considered knowledge.

Knowledge in the presented approach can be viewed as a family of basic concepts or categories, which form elementary granules (atoms) of knowledge, i.e. having an information system $S = (U, A)$ knowledge determined by S can be defined as $K = U/A$. Many important problems can be formulated and solved in the proposed framework. For example we can easily define some useful notions. If $S = (U, B)$, $S' = (U, B')$ and $U/B = U/B'$ we will say that S is *equivalent* to S', symbolically $S \simeq S'$. If $IND(B') \subseteq IND(B)$, then and S will be called *finer* then S', or S' - *coarser* then S, symbolically $S' \leq S$.

"Reality, or the world we all know, is only
a description"

Carlos Castaneda in *Journey to Ixtlan:
The Lesson of Don Juan*

Often the question arises whether all primitive concepts in S are necessary
in order to define all basic concepts in S. This problem arises in many practical
applications—and will be referred to as *knowledge reduction*. Formally this can
be formulated in the discussed framework as follows. Suppose we are given
$S = (U, A)$ and $B \subseteq A$. The question is whether $U/B = U/A$?
To answer this question we need some auxiliary notions.

- Let $a \in B$. We will say that a is *superfluous* in B if $IND(B) = IND(B - \{a\})$, otherwise a is *indispensable* in B.

- The set of attributes B is *independent* if all its attributes are indispensable.

- The set B' is a *reduct* of B if

  - B is independent, and

  - $IND(B') = IND(B)$.

Thus a reduct of B is the minimal subset of B such that $U/B' = U/B$, i.e.
B' determines the same family of basic concepts as the set B. In other words
reduction of knowledge boils down to the elimination of superfluous attributes
in the information system.
    The set of all independent attributes in B is referred to as the *core* of B,
and is denoted $CORE(B)$. The following interesting property is valid:

$$CORE(B) = \cup RED(B), \tag{1}$$

where $RED(B)$ is the family of all reducts of B.

Remark. The problem of reduction of knowledge is related to the general idea
of independence discussed in mathematics as formulated by Marczewski [21]
see also an overview paper by Glazek [12].
    More about reduction of attributes can be found in [37].

4   Uncertainty, vagueness and rough sets

In this section we would like to discuss the central problem of our approach,
the problem of vagueness and uncertainty. There are many conceptions of
vagueness and uncertainty in logical and philosophical literature [2,3,10,34].
We present here so called "boundary-line" view, which is due to Frege, who
writes:
    *The concept must have a sharp boundary. To the concept without a sharp
boundary there would correspond an area that had not a sharp boundary-line
all around.* ([11]).

> "We must distinguish between truth, which is objective, and certainty, which is subjective"

Karl R. Popper (1992)

Thus Frege's idea of vagueness is based on the boundary-line cases. i.e. if a concept is precise every object can be classified as belonging to this concept or not, whereas for vague concepts this is not the case and some object cannot be classified to the concept or its complement, forming thus the boundary line cases. For example the concept of an *odd (even) number* is precise, because every number is either odd or even - whereas the concept of a *beautiful women* is vague, because for some women it cannot be decided whether they are beautiful or not, (there are boundary-line cases). Thus if a concept is vague we are uncertain whether some objects (the boundary-line cases) belong to the concept or not. Hence vagueness is a property of concepts (sets), whereas uncertainty is a property of objects (elements), i.e. if a concept is vague its extension is uncertain.

The ideas considered in the previous sections can be easily employed to express these considerations more precisely.

In the presented approach concept is a subset of the universe. Suppose we are given an information system $S = (U, A)$ and let $X \subseteq U$. The concept (set) X will be said to be precise, if it is an union of some basic concepts (sets) of S, otherwise the concept (set) is vague (rough). Thus precise concepts can be defined in terms of basic concepts in S, whereas this is not the case for vague concepts. (Let us note that some concepts can be precise in one information system but vague in another one).

Basic idea of our approach to vagueness consists in replacing vague concept by a pair of precise concepts, called its *lower* and *upper approximations*. The difference between the upper and the lower approximation is the boundary region. For example the lower approximation of the concept of a beautiful women contains all women which are beautiful with certainty, whereas the upper approximation of this concept contains all women which are possibly beautiful, and the boundary region of this concept is formed by all women which can not be classified with certainty as beautiful or not beautiful. The "size" of the boundary region can be used as a *measure* of vagueness of the vague concept. The greater the boundary region, the "more" vague is the concept; precise concepts do not have the boundary region at all.

Formally the above considerations can be presented as follows.

Let $S = (U, A)$ be an information system, $X \subseteq U$ and $B \subseteq A$. With each subset $X \subseteq U$ and the set of attributes B we associate two subsets:

$$\underline{B}X = \cup\{Y \in U/B : Y \subseteq X\}$$

$$\overline{B}X = \cup\{Y \in U/B : Y \cap X \neg \emptyset\}$$

called the $B - lower$ and the $B - upper$ approximation of X (in S) respectively.

Set $BN_B(X) = \overline{B}X - \underline{B}X$ will be called the $B - boundary$ of X. The set $\underline{B}X$ is the set of all elements of U which can be with *certainty* classified as elements of X, employing set of attributes B; the set $\overline{B}X$ is the set of elements of U which can be *possibly* classified as elements of X, employing the set of attributes B; the set $BN_B(X)$ is the set of elements which cannot be classified either to X or to $-X$ using B.

The boundary region is the undecidable area of the concept X, and none of the objects belonging to the boundary region can be classified with certainty to X or $-X$ by using the set of attributes B.

Obviously a concept X is vague (rough) with respect to B, if and only if $\overline{B}X \neq \underline{B}X$, otherwise the concept X is precise.

In order to express how "vague" is a concept we can use a numerical evaluation of vagueness by defining the accuracy measure

$$\alpha_B(X) = card\underline{B}/card\overline{B}$$

where $X \neq \emptyset$.

Obviously $0 \leq \alpha_B(X) \leq 1$, for every B and $X \subseteq U$; if $\alpha_B(X) = 1$ the boundary region of X is empty and the set X is precise with respect to B; if $\alpha_B(X) < 1$, the set X has some non-empty R-boundary region and consequently is vague with respect to B.

Besides characterization of vague concept by means of numerical values one can also define qualitative characterization of vagueness, showing that there are four basic classes of vagueness, as defined below.

a) If $\underline{B}X \neq \emptyset$ and $\overline{B}X \neq U$, then we say that X is *roughly B-definable*,

b) If $\underline{B}X = \emptyset$ and $\overline{B}X \neq U$, then we say that X is *internally B-undefinable*,

c) If $\underline{B}X \neq \emptyset$ and $\overline{B}X = U$, then we say that X is *externally B-undefinable*,

d) If $\underline{B}X = \emptyset$ and $\overline{B}X = U$, then we say that X is *totally B-undefinable*.

The intuitive meaning of this classification is the following:

If set X is roughly B-definable, this means that we are able to decide for some elements of U whether they belong to X or $-X$.

If X is internally B-undefinable, this means that we are able to decide whether some elements of U belong to $-X$, but we are unable to decide for any element of U, whether it belongs to X or not.

If X is externally B-undefinable, this means that we are able to decide for some elements of U whether they belong to X, but we are unable to decide, for any element of U whether it belongs to $-X$ or not.

If X is totally B-undefinable, we are unable to decide for any element of U whether it belongs to X or $-X$.

That means, that the set X is roughly definable if there are some objects in the universe which can be positively classified, to the set X employing the set of attribute B. This definition also implies that there are some other objects which can be classified without any ambiguity as being outside the set X.

External B-undefinability of a set refers to the situation when positive classification is possible for some objects, but it is impossible to determine that an object does not belong to X on the basis of its features expressed by the set of attributes B.

Having defined the vagueness we are now in a position to define uncertainty. As mentioned before uncertainty is related to elements of the universe and expresses how "strongly" an element belong to a concept. This idea can be expressed by the formula [27].

$$\mu_{X,B}(x) = card([x]_B \cap X)/cardX.$$

The intuitive meaning of the above formula is obvious. It is interesting to compare this formula with the membership function in the fuzzy set theory, but we will not discuss this problem here. More about it can be found in [27,28,36].

5   Conclusion

The rough set theory besides, its importance to data analysis, contributed also to understanding better vagueness and uncertainty.

References

[1] Aikins JS. Prototypic a knowledge for expert systems. Artificial Intelligence 1983; 20:163–210

[2] Black M. Vagueness. The Philosophy of Sciences 1937; 427–455

[3] Black M. Reasoning with loose concepts. Dialog 1963; 2:1–12

[4] Bobrow DG. A panel on knowledge representation. Proc Fifth Int'l Joint Conference on Artificial Intelligence, 1977, Carnegie-Melon University, Pittsburgh, PA

[5] Bobrow DG, Winograd T. An overview of KRL: a knowledge representation language. Journal of Cognitive Sciences 1977; 1:3–46

[6] Brachman RJ, Smith BC. Special issue of knowledge representation. SIGART Newsletter 1980; 70:1–138

[7] Brachman RJ, Levesque HJ. (eds) Readings in knowledge representation. Morgan Kaufmann Publishers Inc, 1986

[8] Buchanan B, Shortliffe E. Rule based expert systems. Addison-Wesley, Reading, Mass, 1984

[9] Davis R, Lenat D. Knowledge-based systems in artificial intelligence. McGraw-Hill, 1982

[10] Fine K. Vagueness, truth and logic. Synthese 1975; 30:265–300

[11] Frege G. Grundgesetze der arithmentik. 1903;2. Geach, Black (eds) In: Selections from the philosophical writings of Gotlob Frege, Blackweil, Oxford, 1970

[12] Glazek K. Some old and new problems in the independence theory. Colloquium Mathematicum 1979; 17:127–189

[13] Grzymala-Busse J. On the reduction of knowledge representation. Systems Proc of the 6th Int'l Workshop on Expert Systems and their Applications, Avignon, France, 1986; pp 463–478

[14] Grzymala-Busse J. Knowledge acquisition under uncertainty - a rough set approach. Journal of Intelligent and Robotics Systems 1988; 1:3–16

[15] Halpern J. (ed) Theoretical aspects of reasoning about knowledge. Proc of the 1986 Conference, Morgan Kaufman, Los Altos, CA 1986

[16] Hayes-Roth B, McDermott J. An inference matching for inducing abstraction. Communication of the ACM 1978; 21:401–410

[17] Hempel CG. Fundamental of concept formation in empirical sciences. University of Chicago Press, Chicago, 1952

[18] Hintika J. Knowledge and belief. Cornell University Press, Chicago, 1962

[19] Holland JH, Holyoak KJ, Nisbett RE, Thagard PR. Induction: processes of inference, learning, and discovery, MIT Press, 1986

[20] Hunt EB. Concept formation. John Wiley and Sons, New York, 1974

[21] Marczewski E. A general scheme of independence in mathematics, BAPS 1958; 731–736

[22] McDermott D. The last survey of representation of knowledge. Proc of the AISB/GI Conference on AI, Hamburg, 1978, pp 286–221

[23] Minski M. A framework for representation knowledge. In: Winston P (ed) The psychology of computer vision, McGraw-Hill, New York, 1975, pp 211–277

[24] Newell A. The knowledge level. Artificial Intelligence 1982; 18:87–127

[25] Orlowska E. Logic for reasoning about knowledge. Zeitshrift fur Math Logik und Grundlagen der Math 1989; 35:559–572

[26] Pawlak Z. Rough sets—theoretical aspects of reasoning about data. Kluwer Academic Publishers, 1991

[27] Pawlak Z, Skowron A. From the rough set theory to evidence theory. In: Fedrizzi M, Kacprzyk J, Yager RR (eds) Advances in the Dempster-Shafer theory of evidence, John Wiley and Sons, 1992 (to appear)

[28] Pawlak Z, Skowron A. Rough membership functions: a tool for reasoning with uncertainty. Algebraic Methods in Logic and Computer Science, Banach Center Publications, Institute of Mathematics, Polish Academy of Sciences, Warsaw, 1993; 28:135–150

[29] Popper K. The logic of scientific discovery. Hutchinson, London, 1959

[30] Rauszer C. Logic for information systems. Fundamenta Informaticae 1992 (to appear)

[31] Rauszer C. Knowledge representation for group of agents. In: Wolenski J (ed) Philosophical logic in Poland, Kluwer Academic Publishers, 1992 (to appear)

[32] Rauszer C. Rough logic for multi agent systems. Proc of the Conference Logic at Work, Amsterdam, 1992 (to appear)

[33] Rauszer C. Approximate methods for knowledge systems. Proc of the 7th Int'l Symposium on Methodologies for Intelligent Systems, Trondheim, 1993, pp 326–337

[34] Russell B. Vagueness. Australian Journal of Philosophy 1923; 1:84-92

[35] Russell B. An inquiry into meaning and truth. George Allen and Unwin, London, 1950

[36] Skowron A, Grzymala-Busse J. From the rough set theory to evidence theory. In: Fedrizzi M, Kacprzyk J, Yager RR (eds) Advances in the Dempster-Shafer theory of evidence, John Wiley and Sons, 1991 (to appear)

[37] Skowron A, Rauszer C. The discernibility matrices and functions in information systems, In: Slowinski R (ed) Intelligent decision support. Handbook of advances and applications of the rough set theory, Kluwer Academic Publishers, 1992, pp 311-362

[38] Slowinski R (ed) Intelligent decision support. In: Handbook of advances and applications of the rough set theory, Kluwer Academic Publishers, 1992

[39] Ziarko W. On reduction of knowledge representation. Proc 2nd Int'l Symp on Methodologies of Intelligent Systems, Charlotte, NC, 1987, pp 99–113

[40] Ziarko W. Acquisition of design knowledge from examples, Math Comput Modeling 1988; 10:551–554

A Formal Approach to Software Reusability

K. Periyasamy

Department of Computer Science

University of Manitoba

Winnipeg, Manitoba R3T 2N2, Canada

kasi@cs.umanitoba.ca

Abstract

Reuse of existing software, in part or as a whole, will save a significant portion of time and cost of software development and hence will increase the productivity of the software. One of the difficulties in this process is the identification and justification of existing software components for reuse. There exists a certain level of uncertainty in the justification process since the developer of the reusable components may not know much about the new environment in which the components will be reused. This paper is a contribution to the justification process for software reuse. It also takes into account the uncertainty of information concerning the new developing environment. In this paper, a formal approach is used. The formal specifications of requirements for both the reusable and the yet to be developed components are prepared using the same formal notation which are then used as the candidates for the justification process. The model-based formal specification technique Z is used for this purpose.

keywords: formal specifications, Z, software reusability

1   Introduction

Successful reuse of software components has been the dream of many software developers over a decade [3]. Reuse of existing software components will significantly improve productivity because of the reduction in the development cost and time. The overall cost of the reusability process lies in identifying, justifying and tailoring the reusable components; practical experience reveals that this cost is much lower than the actual development cost associated with the new product. Moreover, maintenance of reusable components is relatively easier compared to that of the newly developed ones.

Even though one could foresee a lot of benefits from software reuse, incorporating reusability into the software development process poses a number of additional problems. Among them, the justification and tailoring of reusable components seem to be the dominant factors. Maiden and Sutcliffe [4, 5] proposed a new method for software reuse through analogy. The examples presented in their papers illustrate how software from a different application domain can be reused. The approach relies on the functional behavior of the software to be reused and that of the software to be developed. However, the methodology for justifying the analogy has not been explained. Other researchers in this area concentrated on problems towards specific implementations and have not addressed the issues such as domain analysis and identification and justification of software at the design level.

The approach taken in this paper is somewhat similar to Maiden's approach based on analogy in the sense that it relies on comparing the functional behavior of the software being reused and that of the software to be developed. However, the methodology is different. In this paper, the formal specifications of the requirements for the two software are taken as candidates and then compared. This approach is more rigorous than analogy since it provides a mathematical basis for comparison. Moreover, the approach also takes into account the uncertainty regarding the environment of the newly developed software.

The current approach requires that the formal specifications of both the software to be reused and the software to be developed are prepared first. Since these two specifications are the candidates for further work, it is preferable to use the same specification notation to develop both the specifications. This is because, at present, the compatibility among various specification notations has not been well established and it is an area of research by itself.

The model-based specification technique Z is used in this paper. The choice of Z for this research are due to the following reasons: (1) Z has a well defined semantics which helps in reasoning. (2) Z allows modular specifications by which components can be specified independently and then integrated. (3) Refinement strategies for Z specifications have been well established and (4) Recent upgrades to Z include real-time and object-oriented extensions and hence the specifications can be applied to a wide range of application domains. A detailed description of the specification notation is beyond the scope of this paper; a list of Z notations used in this paper is given in Appendix A. Interested readers are recommended to refer to [8, 11] for a detailed treatment on Z.

2   The justification process

Justification requires a strong mathematical basis in order to provide reasoning. It is well known in Software Engineering that formal methods applied to the software development process enable the designer to reason about the behavior of the software. Moreover, the analysis on whether to reuse an existing software component X in place of the yet to be developed software component Y should be carried out much earlier in the software development process, typically during *requirements analysis and specifications* [5]. It is because (1) the specifications of the requirements describe the behavior of the software; (2) the designer can justify that the behavior of X satisfies, either partially or completely, the expected behavior of Y and (3) the designer has more freedom to alter the design and/or implementation of X to suit that of Y. It is therefore decided to use the formal specifications of the requirements of the software as the candidate for comparing and justifying reusability of the components.

There exists certain level of uncertainty of information in the justification process. Consider the reuse of X in place of Y. The developer of X may not know the environment in which Y is intended to be developed and/or the environment in which Y is going to be used. One possible solution for this problem is to develop generic components as suggested in [3, 7, 9] that may be used in several contexts. However, experience shows that the diverse application of such generic components is very limited. Moreover, such generic components are available only at the implementation level such as library of modules in the procedural paradigm and library of classes in the object-oriented paradigm. Obviously, justification is difficult at the implementation level. On the other hand, formal specifications of requirements are independent of the design and implementation level and also are mathematically based. If the formal specifications of requirements for X are available, then the designer of Y can simply match them with those of Y in order to justify reusability. It is thus the responsibility of the designer of Y to make use of the formal

specifications for X as such or to tailor them towards the new environment. In this way, the designer of X is neither constrained to know about Y or its environment, nor design a generic component. Thus the formal approach provides a partial solution to the uncertainty problem for software reuse.

The major problem with this approach is that if the requirements specifications for X have already been developed in the same notation as is intended for Y, then one could directly compare them. Otherwise, there may require a reverse engineering approach to specify X in the same notation used for Y.

3   The approach

For simplicity, let us analyze reusability at the components level. Consider a component X to be reused and a component Y yet to be developed. The specification of X contains the structure $Sturct_X$ and the behavior $Behave_X$ of X. In a similar way, the specification of Y contains the structure $Struct_Y$ and the behavior $Behave_Y$ of Y.

In order to reuse X in place of Y, two conditions are to be satisfied:

Structural Compatibility This requires *renaming* of individual components of $Struct_X$ to a set of corresponding components in $Struct_Y$ and then establishing *type compatibility* between the two structures. In addition, the type invariant of X must imply the type invariant of Y.

Behavioral Satisfaction This requires that the behavior of Y must imply the behavior of X. Notice that unlike type invariants, the implication for behavior satisfaction is reversed. This indicates that $Behave_X$ must be weaker and hence can be used in several contexts. Moreover, the component Y may require additional information and hence may have additional constraints imposed.

3.1   Structural compatibility

By structure in this paper, it is meant a declaration of an entity in Z. A declaration in Z may be simple such as <variable> : < type> or, it may be a composite structure defined by a schema such as

$$
\begin{array}{|l}
\hline
\_S\_\rule{0pt}{0pt}\\
\hline
x : \mathbf{Z}\\
y : \mathbf{N}\\
\hline
x \le y\\
\hline
\end{array}
$$

Based on these concepts, the following are defined:

Definition 1 *A structure is simple if it is represented by $<name : type>$.*

Definition 2 *A structure is composite if it is represented as*
$< s_1 : t_1; s_2 : t_2; \ldots; s_n ; t_n > $ *and* $n > 0$.
A composite structure may have a type invariant represented by a conjunction of predicates.

Definition 3 *The cardinality of a structure is defined as the number of elements in it.*

It is easy to observe that *cardinality* of a structure must always be greater than zero; *cardinality* $= 1$ implies that the structure is simple and *cardinality* > 1 implies that the structure is composite.

Since schemas (the composite structures as defined in this paper) can also be used as types in Z, the type compatibility is defined first before establishing structural compatibility. Type compatibility is defined as follows:

Definition 4 *A type T_1 is compatible to another type T_2 if and only if every instance of T_1 also respects the behavior defined by T_2; stated otherwise, an instance of a type T_1 can be assigned to an instance of type T_2.*

Lemma 1 *Every type is compatible to itself.*

Proof: The proof for this lemma is obvious from the definition of type compatibility.

Lemma 2 *A subtype is compatible to its parent type.*

Proof: A subtype is created by enforcing additional constraints on the behavior of its parent type. For example, the numeric enumeration type $\{1 .. 100\}$ is a subtype of N whose instances are restricted to the values between 1 and 100. Thus, an instance of the enumerated type can be assigned to an instance of type N.

Notice that for user defined primitive types in Z, such as *String*, it is difficult to assert type compatibility since the behavior of its instances is not defined. Hence the task of ensuring type compatibility using the user defined primitive types in Z is left to the designer.

Using these definitions, the compatibility between two structures S_1 and S_2 is now defined as follows:

Definition 5 *S_1 is structurally compatible with S_2 if and only if*
(a) both S_1 and S_2 are simple and type(S_1) and type(S_2) are compatible; or,
(b) both S_1 and S_2 are composite structures such that
   (i) cardinality of S_1 = cardinality of S_2;
   (ii) for each element $< s_{1i} : t_{1i} >$ in S_1, there exists an element
     $< s_{2i} : t_{2i} >$ in S_2 such that such that t_{2i} is type compatible to t_{1i}, $1 \leq i \leq n$ and
     (iii) type_invariant $(S_1) \Rightarrow$ type_invariant (S_2), with
      each s_{2i} renamed to s_{1i}, $1 \leq i \leq n$.

The result of establishing structural compatibility is to create a renaming table which contains names from each of these structures. The same table will be used for matching the type invariants and for ensuring behavioral satisfaction.

It is to be noted that for two given composite structures, there might be several combinations which satisfy structural compatibilities. It is the designer's responsibility in such situations to choose the right renaming table. The behavioral satisfaction process might indicate the wrong selection in which case the designer can choose the alternate table.

3.2   Behavioral satisfaction

The behavior of an entity in Z is specified by a series of operations performed on that entity. Typically, the set of operations in Z which use or affect the structure of a software component is considered to be its behavior. Therefore, behavioral satisfaction is a process of establishing a relationship between the operations of the two software components - X, the component to be reused and Y, the component yet to be developed.

For behavioral satisfaction, the behavior of Y must imply the behavior of X. This is because, as stated earlier, the weaker the conditions defining the behavior the more contexts the component X can be used. An operation in Z is specified by a set of predicates expressed in conjunctive normal form. Hence it is easier to show the implication. This process makes use of the same renaming table created earlier. While ensuring behavioral satisfaction, more entries may be added to the renaming table due to the parameters of the operations, as defined later in this paper. It is required to ensure the structural compatibility between these parameters as well.

These concepts are formalized in the following definitions.

Definition 6 *Behavior of a software component is expressed by a set of operations. Behavioral satisfaction is the process of establishing*

$$Op_{21} \Rightarrow Op_{11} \wedge Op_{22} \Rightarrow Op_{12} \wedge \ldots \wedge Op_{2n} \Rightarrow Op_{1n}, \forall i : 1 .. n, \text{ where}$$
Op_{1i} refers to an operation performed on X and Op_{2i} is an operation performed on Y.

The implications between operations as defined in the behavioral satisfaction process is not a simple task. Each operation in Z is specified is specified by a set of predicates expressed in conjunctive normal form such as

$$Op_1 = A_1 \wedge A_2 \wedge \ldots \wedge A_n$$
$$Op_2 = B_1 \wedge B_2 \wedge \ldots \wedge B_m$$

To ensure that $Op_2 \Rightarrow Op_1$, it is to be shown that

$$B_1 \wedge B_2 \wedge \ldots \wedge B_m \Rightarrow A_1 \wedge A_2 \wedge \ldots \wedge A_n$$

Since Op_2 and Op_1 may belong to two different application domains, the set of variables involved in each one of these operations might be different. The renaming table contains the mapping from the set of variables in Op_1 (and operations belonging to the same application as that of Op_1) to those in Op_2 (and operations belonging to the application domain in which Op_2 is specified). Therefore, if S_2 is the set of variables involved in Op_2 (including parameters) and S_1 represents the set of variables involved in Op_1 (including parameters), then the implication in the behavioral satisfaction process is to be written as

$$Op_2 \Rightarrow Op_1[S_2 \leftarrow S_1]$$

where $Op_1[S_2 \leftarrow S_1]$ indicates that the variables of Op_1 are renamed with that of Op_2.

The behavioral satisfaction process also requires the identification of *free* and *bound* variables in each predicate in the operations. Only the *free* variables are used in renaming. For example, consider the quantified expression $\forall x : \mathbb{N} \mid x > 0 \bullet x \neq y$; the free variables in this expression are $\mathbb{N}$ and y; the variable x is bound and has its scope limited to the expression itself. The symbols $0, +, >$ and $\neq$ are treated as constant symbols in Z. Due to space limitations, only the set of rules for identifying the free variables in Z is given in the Appendix B and the readers are recommended to refer to [12] for further details.

The behavioral satisfaction process might require user intervention. For example, the predicate $x \in S$ (where S is a set) might be required to imply the predicate $(\exists i : 1 .. \#T \bullet T(i) = x)$ and it is true if and only if the sequence T has the same *type* of elements and *cardinality* as that of S and has no duplicates; in other words, T is structurally compatible to S. Since there is no rule in predicate logic to assert such implication directly, it is the designer's responsibility to ensure the implication.

3.3 Example

In this section, the concepts of reusability defined in the previous section are illustrated through an example. Here, the possibility of reusing a flight reservation system for a course registration system is considered. Due to space limitations, the exact matching of the specifications is not illustrated. The current example illustrated the partial matching and tailoring of the reusable components. In addition, the informal descriptions augmented with the specifications are kept minimal due to space scarcity.

3.3.1 Flight Reservation System

```
┌─ Flight1 ──────────────────────────────────────────────────
│  number : N₁
│  departure, arrival : N₁
│  seats : seq N
├─────────────────────────────────────────────────────────────
│  arrival > departure
│  (∀ i, j : 1 .. #seats •
│        i ≠ j ∧ seats(i) > 0 ∧ seats(j) > 0 ⇒ seats(i) ≠ seats(j))
└─────────────────────────────────────────────────────────────
```

A flight's information contains a unique flight number, its departure and arrival time and the passengers. Each passenger is given a unique identification number and a unique seat number. In the above specification, $seat(i)$ represents the ith seat and the corresponding passenger number who reserved that seat. It is assumed that the seats with passenger number zero are empty. The invariant ensures that no passenger can occupy more than one seat at any time. It is to be noted that *arrival* in the above structure denotes the arrival of the flight at its destination and *departure* denotes its departure at the origin.

```
┌─ Passenger1 ─────────────────────────────────────────────
│ token : N₁
│ reserved : Flight1 ⇸ N₁
├──────────────────────────────────────────────────────────
│ (∀ f₁, f₂ : dom reserved •
│     (f₁.departure ≠ f₂.departure ∧
│      f₁.departure < f₂.departure ⇒ f₁.arrival < f₂.departure)) ∧
│ (∀ f : dom reserved •
│     ∃₁ i : 1 .. #(f.seats) •
│         (f.seats(i) = token ∧ reserved(f) = i))
└──────────────────────────────────────────────────────────
```

The passenger's structure indicates the unique identification number for the passenger, the flights reserved by the passenger and the seat numbers in each of these flights. Since a passenger cannot fly in more than one flight simultaneously, it is ensured in the type invariant that the arrival time of a flight f_1 reserved by the passenger must be earlier than the departure time of the flight f_2 reserved by the same passenger, if the departure time of f_1 is earlier than that of f_2. Notice that the specification does not indicate how the passenger can come back to the origin before f_2 departs. This information is out of scope for the current specification. The consistency of seat numbers between the passenger and the flight structures is also ensured by the invariant.

An auxiliary function called *elems* is defined to get the set of elements from a sequence (by eliminating the duplicates); it is used in subsequent specifications.

```
╔═ [X] ═════════════════════════════════════════════════════
║ elems : seq X ⟶ P X
╟────────────────────────────────────────────────────────────
║ ∀ s : seq X • elems s = {t : X | ∃ i : 1 .. #s • s(i) = t}
╚════════════════════════════════════════════════════════════
```

```
┌─ Reservation1 ────────────────────────────────────────────
│ flights : P Flight1
│ passengers : P Passenger1
├───────────────────────────────────────────────────────────
│ (∀ f₁, f₂ : flights • f₁.number = f₂.number ⇒ f₁ = f₂)
│ (∀ p₁, p₂ : passengers • p₁.token = p₂.token ⇒ p₁ = p₂)
│ (∀ f : flights •
│     elems f.seats = {p : passengers | f ∈ dom p.reserved ∧
│             p.reserved(f) ∈ 1 .. #(f.seats) • p.token}) ∧
│ (∀ p : passengers • dom p.reserved ⊆ flights)
└───────────────────────────────────────────────────────────
```

The state space of the reservation system is defined next. It contains a set of flights and a set of passengers. The consistency between the information in these two sets is stated as the state space invariant.

The behavior reservation system is illustrated by defining an operation on the state space. The operation to reserve a seat for a passenger is given next. The variable *seatno?* in the specification of the operation represents the seat number requested by the user. The validity of this seat number (within its range) is also ensured in the specification.

```
┌─ ReserveSeat1 ─────────────────────────────────────────────
│ ΔReservation1
│ f? : Flight1
│ p? : Passenger1
│ seatno? : N₁
├────────────────────────────────────────────────────────────
│ f? ∈ flights
│ p? ∈ passengers
│ f? ∉ dom p?.reserved
│ p?.token ∉ elems f?.seats
│ 1 ≤ seatno? ≤ #(f?.seats)
│ flights' = flights \ {f?}∪
│       {(μ f : Flight1 | f.number = f?.number ∧ f.departure =
│               f?.departure ∧ f.arrival = f?.arrival ∧
│               (∀ i : 1 .. seatno? − 1 • f.seats(i) = f?.seats(i)) ∧
│               f.seats(seatno?) = p?.token ∧
│               (∀ j : seatno? + 1 .. #(f?.seats) • f.seats(j) = f?.seats(j))
│       • f)}
│ passengers' = passengers \ {p?}∪
│       {(μ p : Passenger1 | p.token = p?.token ∧
│               p.reserved = p?.reserved ⊕ {f? ↦ seatno?} • p)}
└────────────────────────────────────────────────────────────
```

3.3.2 Course Registration System

Next, the specification for the course registration system is given. Each course contains a unique course number, starting time, ending time and a set of students attending the course.

```
┌─ Course ───────────────────────────────────────────────────
│ courseno : N₁
│ start, end : N₁
│ registered : P N
├────────────────────────────────────────────────────────────
│ start < end
└────────────────────────────────────────────────────────────
```

Every student has a unique i.d. number. The set of courses taken by each student is also modeled as part of the student information. Once again, irrelevant details such as name, address and phone number are ignored. The invariant asserts that the student cannot attend two different courses simultaneously.

```
┌─ Student ──────────────────────────────────────────────────
│ id : N
│ taken : P Course
├────────────────────────────────────────────────────────────
│ ∀ t₁, t₂ : taken •
│       (t₁.start ≠ t₂.start ∧
│       t₁.start < t₂.start ⇒ t₁.end < t₂.start)
└────────────────────────────────────────────────────────────
```

The course registration system contains a set of courses and a set of students. Invariant asserts that all courses taken by the students are offered and all courses contain students who are all registered in the system. Uniqueness of course numbers and student i.d. numbers are also expressed as part of the invariant.

System

$courses$: $\mathbb{P}\ Course$
$students$: $\mathbb{P}\ Student$

$(\forall\ c_1, c_2 : courses \bullet c_1.courseno = c_2.courseno \Rightarrow c_1 = c_2)$
$(\forall\ s_1, s_2 : students \bullet s_1.id = s_2.id \Rightarrow s_1 = s_2)$
$(\forall\ c : courses \bullet c.registered = \{s : students \mid c \in s.taken \bullet s.id\})$
$(\forall\ s : students \bullet s.taken \subseteq courses)$

As in the flight reservation system, there is an operation to register a particular student for a particular course. After validating the student and the course information, the database is updated.

Reserve

$\Delta System$
$c?$: $Course$
$s?$: $Student$

$c? \in courses$
$s? \in students$
$s?.id \notin c?.registered$
$c? \notin s?.taken$
$courses' = courses \setminus \{c?\} \cup$
$\qquad \{(\mu\ c : Course \mid c.courseno = c?.courseno \wedge c.start = c?.start \wedge$
$\qquad\qquad c.end = c?.end \wedge c.registered = c?.registered \cup \{s?.id\} \bullet c)\}$
$students' = students \setminus \{s?\} \cup$
$\qquad \{(\mu\ s : Student \mid s.id = s?.id \wedge s.taken = s?.taken \cup \{c?\} \bullet s)\}$

3.3.3 Justification Process

In this section, it is justified that the flight reservation system can be reused in place of the course registration system. The structural compatibility is ensured by matching the appropriate declarations as indicated in the renaming table /refrevised.

Notice that the mapping between *registered* and *seats* is valid only if the sequence *seats* contains no duplicates. A close look at the type invariant for *Flight*1 ensures this validity. The structure *Passenger*1 has an additional constraint to ensure the consistency of information stored in the seat numbers and the passenger id, for which there is no equivalent constraint in the structure *Student*. Since *Passenger*1 is the reusable component, this additional constraint will not bother the reusability of *Passenger*1 in place of *Student*. It is also to be noted that structural compatibility is ensured between a function (*reserved* in *Passenger*1) and a set (*taken* in *Student*); this is valid since the domain of the function is the same set as required by the new component.

The process of establishing behavioral satisfaction is attempted next. With the use of the renaming table, it is clear that the first four predicates of the

courseno	←	number
start	←	departure
end	←	arrival
registered	←	seats
Course	←	Flight1
id	←	token
taken	←	reserved
Student	←	Passenger1
System	←	Reservation1
courses	←	flights
students	←	passengers

Table 1: Renaming Table for Flight-Course Example

specification *ReserveSeat*1 for the flight reservation system imply the first four predicates of *Reserve* for the course registration system. The predicate

$$1 \leq seatno? \leq \#(f?.seats)$$

is due to the newly added variable *seatno?* in *ReserveSeat*1 for which there is no equivalent in *Reserve*. This requires user intervention in tailoring *ReserveSeat*1 in order to match with *Reserve*. Since the variable is introduced to explicitly address the seat number which is not required in the new component, *ReserveSeat*1 is modified into *ReserveSeat*2 as follows:

$$
\begin{array}{l}
\rule{2cm}{0.4pt}\ ReserveSeat2 \rule{6cm}{0.4pt} \\
\Delta\, Reservation1 \\
f? : Flight1 \\
p? : Passenger1 \\
\rule{14cm}{0.4pt} \\
f? \in flights \\
p? \in passengers \\
f? \notin \mathrm{dom}\, p?.reserved \\
p?.token \notin \mathrm{elems}\, f?.seats \\
(\exists\, seatno : 1 .. \#(f?.seats) \bullet \\
\quad flights' = flights \setminus \{f?\} \cup \\
\quad\quad \{(\mu f : Flight1 \mid f.number = f?.number \wedge f.departure = \\
\quad\quad\quad f?.departure \wedge f.arrival = f?.arrival \wedge \\
\quad\quad\quad (\forall i : 1 .. seatno - 1 \bullet f.seats(i) = f?.seats(i)) \wedge \\
\quad\quad\quad f.seats(seatno) = p?.token \wedge \\
\quad\quad\quad (\forall j : seatno + 1 .. \#(f?.seats) \bullet f.seats(j) = f?.seats(j)) \\
\quad\quad \bullet f)\} \wedge \\
\quad passengers' = passengers \setminus \{p?\} \cup \\
\quad\quad \{(\mu p : Passenger1 \mid p.token = p?.token \wedge \\
\quad\quad\quad p.reserved = p?.reserved \oplus \{f? \mapsto seatno\} \bullet p)\})
\end{array}
$$

The predicate

$$c.registered = c?.registered \cup \{s?.id\} \qquad\qquad\qquad \dots P_1$$

in the schema *Reserve* in course registration system indicates that the set *registered* is updated with one more entry $s?.id$. Whereas the corresponding predicate in *ReserveSeat2*

$$(\forall i : 1 .. seatno? - 1 \bullet f.seats(i) = f?.seats(i)) \land$$
$$f.seats(s?) = p?.token \land$$
$$(\forall j : seatno? + 1 .. \#(f?.seats) \bullet f.seats(j) = f?.seats(j)) \qquad \ldots P_2$$

indicates that the information on seats is updated but it also specifies the location. In the modified version, the seat number is no longer passed as input and any seat satisfying this condition will ensure the completion of the operation. Therefore, $P_1 \Rightarrow P_2$ and hence behavioral satisfaction is ensured.

4   Conclusion

One of the major problems in software reusability is the justification that an already developed software component X can be reused in place of an yet to be developed component Y. This requires a mathematical basis for reasoning. In this paper, formal specifications of requirements has been chosen as the representative for the justification process. A methodology has been proposed to use the formal specification of requirements for both the reusable component as well as the yet to be developed component and justify reusability. Since compatibility between different formal notations is not well established until now, it has been decided to use the same formal notation for both the software components. The formal specification notation Z is used in this paper.

The justification process outlined in this paper is only the beginning of the author's research on reusability. There are a lot of problems yet to be addressed; some of them are given below:

Type Compatibility While it is easy to establish type compatibility among primitive types such as N (natural numbers) and Z (integers), it is difficult to match user defined types such as *String* in the specification. Such user defined types commonly occur in Z specifications. Therefore, the process of establishing type compatibility requires user interaction.

Partial Reusability The process of deciding partial reusability may not be cost-effective. It requires a great deal of support from the specification technique.

Design and Implementation The justification process outlined in this paper is based on the formal specification of requirements and consequently matches only the functional behavior of the components involved. More work is needed to evaluate the suitability of the design and implementation of the reusable components with respect to the new environment.

References

[1] Basili VR, Rombach HD. Support for comprehensive reuse. Software Engineering Journal 1991; 6(9):303–316

[2] Batory D, O'Malley S. The design and implementation of hierarchical software systems with reusable components. ACM Trans on Software Engineering and Methodology 1992; 1(4):355–398

[3] Griss ML. Software reuse at Hewlett Packard. Technical Report HPL-91-38, Software and Systems Laboratory, Hewlett Packard, CA, March 1991

[4] Maiden NA. Analogy as a paradigm for specification reuse. Software Engineering Journal 1991; 6(1):3–15

[5] Maiden NA, Sutcliffe AC. Exploiting reusable specifications through analogy. Communications of the ACM 1992; 35(4):55–64

[6] Morrison R, Dearle A, Connor RCH, Brown AL. An AdHoc approach to the implementation of polymorphism. ACM Trans on Programming Languages and Systems 1991; 13(3):342–371

[7] Meyer B. Lessons from the design of the Eiffel libraries. Communications of the ACM 1990; 33(9):69–88

[8] B. Potter, J. Sinclair and D. Till, **An Introduction to Formal Specification and Z**, Prentice Hall International Series in Computer Science, 1991.

[9] Prieto-Diaz R. Software reuse. Communications of the ACM 1991; 34(5):89–97

[10] Ratcliffe MB, Gautier RJ. System development through the reuse of existing components. Software Engineering Journal 1991; 6(11):406–412

[11] Spivey JM. The Z notation: a reference manual. Second Edition, Prentice Hall International Series in Computer Science, 1992

[12] Woodcock JCP. Formal development using Z - a tool-based course, Tulane University, LA, April 1993

Appendix

A Z Notation

We here provide the notations used in Z specifications in this paper and their meanings. As stated in the previous sections, for a complete syntax of the Z specification language, the reader is referred to [11].

$\rightarrowtail$	*partial function*	**P**	*power set*
$f\,x$	*function f applied to x*	$\emptyset$	*empty set*
$\wedge$	*logical AND*	$\#$	*cardinality of a set*
$\vee$	*logical OR*	$\subseteq$	*subset*
$\neg$	*logical NOT*	$\cup$	*set union*
$\forall$	*forall*	$\cap$	*set intersection*
$\exists$	*there exists*	$\in$	*set membership*
$\exists_1$	*there exists exactly one*	$\Rightarrow$	*implies*
		$\Leftrightarrow$	*if and only if*

Δ *Schema_name* indicates that the composite data type is changed due to the operation.

B   Rules for Free Variables Substitution

In the following rules, the notations ϕ_p denotes a functions which maps a predicate to the set of free variables in it. In a similar way, the notations ϕ_e and ϕ_d refer to the functions which map an expression and a declaration respectively to its respective free variables. In addition, p and q denote predicates, s, t and u denote expressions, d, d_1 and d_2 denote declarations, R denotes a relational expression, x denotes a variable and c denotes a constant symbol defined in the Z language (e.g.; $+$, 4).

$\phi_p(\neg p) = \phi_p p$

$\phi_p(p \wedge q) = (\phi_p p) \cup (\phi_p q)$

$\phi_p(p \vee q) = (\phi_p p) \cup (\phi_p q)$

$\phi_p(p \Rightarrow q) = (\phi_p p) \cup (\phi_p q)$

$\phi_p(p \Leftrightarrow q) = (\phi_p p) \cup (\phi_p q)$

$\phi_p(t = u) = (\phi_e t) \cup (\phi_e u)$

$\phi_p(t \in u) = (\phi_e t) \cup (\phi_e u)$

$\phi_p(sRu) = (\phi_e s) \cup (\phi_e R) \cup (\phi_e u)$

$\phi_p(\forall d \mid p \bullet q) = \phi_d(d \mid p) \cup (\phi_p q \setminus \alpha d)$

$\phi_p(\exists d \mid p \bullet q) = \phi_d(d \mid p) \cup (\phi_p q \setminus \alpha d)$

$\phi_e(\mathbf{P}\, t) = \phi_e t$

$\phi_e(t_1 \times t_2) = (\phi_e t_1) \cup (\phi_e t_2)$

$\phi_e\{t_1, t_2\} = (\phi_e t_1) \cup (\phi_e t_2)$

$\phi_e\{d \mid p \bullet t\} = \phi_d(d \mid p) \cup (\phi_e t \setminus \alpha d)$

$\phi_e(st) = (\phi_e s) \cup (\phi_e t)$

$\phi_e x = \{x\}$

$\phi_e c = \emptyset$

$\phi_d(d \mid p) = \phi_d d \cup (\phi_p p \setminus \alpha d)$

$\phi_d(d_1; d_2) = (\phi_d d_1) \cup (\phi_d d_2 \setminus \alpha d_1)$

$\phi_d(x : s) = \phi_e s$

In the above rules, the function α maps a declaration to the set of variables it declares and it can be inductively defined as follows:

$\alpha(d \mid p) = \alpha d$

$\alpha(d_1; d_2) = (\alpha d_1) \cup (\alpha d_2)$

Modeling Uncertainty in
Object-Oriented Databases

Fereidoon Sadri *
Department of Computer Science
Concordia University
Montreal, Canada
sadri@cs.concordia.ca

Abstract

The Information Source Tracking (IST) Method has been recently proposed for the modeling and management of uncertain and inaccurate information in relational and deductive database systems. In this paper we will discuss the application of IST to object-oriented databases (OODBs). We will compare and contrast forms of uncertainty in OODBs with those studied in classical (relational) databases, and discuss how IST techniques can be applied to model and manage such uncertainties. We also represent an architecture for the implementation of IST-based uncertain OODBs.

1 Introduction

The Information Source Tracking (IST) Method has been recently proposed for the modeling of uncertainty and inaccuracy in relational and deductive database systems [13, 23, 24, 25]. In this paper we will discuss the application of IST to object-oriented databases (OODBs).

Previous approaches to the modeling and management of uncertainty and inaccuracy in databases can be categorized into two broad categories, *numerical* and *non-numerical*. Numerical techniques use a numerical measure for uncertainty, and manipulate these measures to obtain numerical measures for the uncertainty of derived data, such as answers to a query. Mycin's certainty factors [28], fuzzy sets and possibility theory, e.g. [30, 31, 32], techniques bases on Dempster-Shafer theory of evidence [14, 15], and probabilistic measures, e.g. [2, 3], are examples of the numerical approaches.

Non-numerical techniques are often based on partitioning the data into "definite" and "indefinite" components, and extend the classical relational algebra operations to manipulate these components. These techniques date back to the early days of relational databases research, and has been triggered by an attempt to incorporate "null" values in databases. Codd's "maybe" operations [4] is an early representative of non-numerical approaches. Other examples include [5] and [16, 17].

---
*Supported by grants from the Natural Sciences and Engineering Research Council of Canada (NSERC), and Fonds pour la Formation de Chercheurs et l'Aide a la Recherche (FCAR) of Quebec.

Information Source Tracking (IST) is a *hybrid* technique. The main idea behind IST is that information is supplied, or confirmed, by information sources. The database stores each "piece" of information, e.g. a tuple in a relational database, together with (the identity of) the confirming source(s). Query processing manipulates data as usual, but also manipulates the information about sources of data. For each answer to a query, the information sources contributing to the answer, as well as the nature of the contribution, are identified. Up to this moment, the IST technique is non-numerical. As an optional second phase in query processing, a certainty figure can be calculated for each answer to a query, as a function of the reliabilities of the contributing information sources. These reliabilities can be supplied by the users, or the database system might estimate them based on the past performance of information sources [8, 9]. The numeric paradigm (e.g. probabilistic, possibilistic, or evidential) is orthogonal to the first phase of query processing in IST. Thus far we have concentrated on the probabilistic approach for this phase. A brief description of the IST method is Section 4. Details can be found in [13, 23, 24, 25, 26].

This paper is concerned with the modeling and management of uncertain and inaccurate data in object-oriented databases (OODBs). In particular, we are interested in the application of the IST method to OODBs. A brief description of the object-oriented database model is presented in Section 2, and the types of uncertainties in OODBs are discussed in Section 3. We argue that, in addition to the usual data uncertainties and inaccuracies that have been studied in database systems, the concept of "class uncertainty" needs to be addressed in object-oriented databases. Section 4 is a brief overview of the IST method, and in Section 5 we discuss the application of IST techniques to OODBs. Implementation issues of IST-based uncertain OODBs are also discussed. Conclusions and future research directions are presented in Section 6.

2   Object-oriented database model

In this section we will briefly describe the object-oriented database model. The database community has very much converged on a "standard" object-oriented database model [1, 12], summarized below.

A database is a collection *objects*. An object is an instance of a *class* that describes the structure and the behavior of the object. Alternatively, we can say that similar objects are classified into a class. A class declaration consists of a set of *attributes* (or *variables*), and a set of *methods* (also called *operations*, or *actions*). Attributes and methods describe the *structure* and the *behavior* of the objects (instances) of a class.

Classes are organized into a *class hierarchy* according to the generalization/specialization relationship among them. A subclass *inherits* the declarations of its superclasses. That is, a class inherits the attributes and the methods of its ancestors in the class hierarchy. A class can also have attributes and methods of its own, i.e. attributes and methods that are not declared in any ancestor in the hierarchy. It is also possible to redefine (override) inherited attributes and methods in a (sub)class.

When an object is created, it is declared to be an instance of a class. In other words, each object has a type which is the class of which it is an instance. We can think of an object (instance) of a class C as a mapping from the set of attributes of C to values. These values can be atomic (e.g. integer, character string, etc...) or they can be objects. Each object has a unique object identifier that is used to refer to it.

3 Types of uncertainty in OODBs

In this section we will discuss types of uncertainties in object-oriented database systems, and contrast them with those of the relational model. We will concentrate on uncertainty in data, that is, objects (instances) and their attribute values. It is possible, in general, to have uncertainty in *metadata*, such as class structures and hierarchy. In this paper, though, we will not address metadata uncertainty.

Probably the simplest form of uncertainty in an object-oriented database system is uncertainty regarding values of the attributes. This is comparable to the relational model, when the attribute values can be uncertain. A number of techniques has been proposed to handle uncertainty at the attribute level in the relational model, such as [2, 14, 15, 18]. Most of these techniques assume single-valued attributes, for example, restricted by a functional dependency or a key dependency, and propose techniques to represent the uncertainty in the form of one out of a set of possible values. In object-oriented databases, in general, we can have single-valued attributes as well as multiple-valued (or set-valued) attributes. The uncertainty for a single-valued attribute is again in the form of one out of a set of possible values. This "functionality constraint", e.g. single-valued attribute, is often difficult to model precisely in uncertain databases. The system should be intelligent enough to recognize that multiple values for a single valued attribute at a given instant represents an inconsistency. Most current systems designed to handle uncertainty produce an incorrect response to queries of the form "list objects having values of v_1 and at the same time v_2 for a single-valued attribute. The uncertainty for multiple-valued attributes is more subtle, and can be in the form of one set out of a collection of possible sets of values.

We should also mention that the techniques developed for the modeling of uncertainty at the tuple level in the relational model can also be used for the representation of uncertainty at the attribute level. At the extreme, we need to fully normalize and decompose relations into binary relations to achieve this goal. Some of these methods will be discussed below.

The next form of uncertainty in the object-oriented databases is the uncertainty at the object level. In particular, when answering a query, the membership of the objects in the answer will have varying certainty degrees. This also applies to intermediate results and views, so, an uncertain object-oriented database should also have facilities for modeling uncertainty at the object level. This form of uncertainty is roughly similar to the uncertainty at the tuple level in the relational model. The proposals for incorporating this type of uncertainty in the relational model often use an extended relational model and extended relational algebra operations for query processing [16, 17, 23, 24]. Related works in deductive databases, quantitative logic programming, and probabilistic logic also explore similar notions of uncertainty [10, 11, 13, 19, 20, 22, 29]

The next form of uncertainty, which we will call *class* or *type* uncertainty has not been addressed in the context of relational databases. There are situations where we are not certain about the type (class) of an object. Consider, for example, a database of UFO (Unidentified Flying Objects) sightings. For a particular sighting, there may be differences in the eye witnesses accounts. We might have different types for UFOs (types 1, 2, and 3), and the sighting might be of different types depending on the witness. Note that we even have a structural uncertainty in this type of uncertainty. The structure of the object depends on its type, and we are not certain about the type. This situation, roughly speaking, corresponds to the relational case where we have a tuple, but are not certain about the relation where the tuple belongs. Further, the set of attributes relevant to the tuple also depends on the relation where it should be placed.

We would like to point out the similarity between class uncertainty and the concept of "multityping" [7]. Multityping was studied in the context of temporal object-oriented databases, where the type (class) of object may change over time (*dynamic* multityping). We also contemplated *static* multityping, i.e. the case when an object demonstrates behavior relevant to multiple classes concurrently, as an alternative to multiple inheritance.

There is, though, a subtle difference between "class uncertainty" and "static multityping". We expect, in most cases of class uncertainty, the object to actually have a unique type in reality, rather than exhibiting multiple behavior. This might be an integrity rule resulting from the nature of application being modeled. Whereas in static multityping it is understood that the object is in fact demonstrating multiple behavior concurrently. The type uniqueness requirement in the uncertain paradigm will necessitate special techniques such as those proposed in [26].

Modeling class uncertainty might affect the performance of the uncertain object-oriented database systems considerably. When a method is invoked on an object, it is imperative to access the code that implements the method rapidly to be efficient. Often the object identifier "encodes" the class of the object, e.g. a pointer to the class object is included in the identifiers of the corresponding objects. Class uncertainty renders these techniques unapplicable to a large extent.

Finally we would like to mention that it is also possible to have meta-data level uncertainty. In the object-oriented paradigm. Classes, their structures and behaviors, and class hierarchy might be subject to uncertainty. This is similar to the relational case where the relation schemes and integrity constraints could be uncertain. We will not pursue this type of meta-data level uncertainty in this paper.

4 Review of IST

In this section we give a brief review of the Information Source Tracking (IST) method [13, 23, 24, 25]. In the IST approach we assume that information is supplied, or confirmed, by information sources, and the reliability of the contributing source determines the certainty of information. For each "piece" of data in the database, e.g. for each tuple or attribute in the relational model, or each fact or rule in deductive databases, we also record the contributing information source(s). Query processing algorithms handle data as well as sources information. An answer to a query also identifies sources contributing to the answer and their nature of contribution. The calculation of certainties are left as the (optional) last step of query processing. IST provides a clean and effective framework to deal with the issue of dependent and independent data, an issue which creates substantial difficulties with other techniques.

One way of recording information source(s) contributing to data is to associate with each piece of data a set of vectors representing the role of information sources. Each vector has the form $(a_1 \cdots a_k)$, where k is the number of information sources, and $a_i \in \{0, -1, +1, \top\}$. Intuitively, the elements $\{0, -1, +1, \top\}$ denote, respectively, no contribution, negative contribution, positive contribution, and over specification (or inconsistency). When IST is applied to the relational model, the relational algebra operations projection, selection, join, Cartesian product, union, intersection, and set difference are extended to manipulate these source vectors as well as the data. In the application of IST to deductive databases, counterparts to logical connectives conjunction, disjunction, and negation has been devised to manipulate the source vectors accordingly. In what follows we will give a summary of the second approach. Details can be found in [13].

An *information source vector* (*source vector*, for short) is a vector $v = (a_1 \cdots a_k)$, $a_i \in \{0, -1, +1, \top\}$, $i = 1, \ldots, k$, where k is the number of information sources. We require that a source vector should have at least one non-zero element. We also permit special source vectors T and F, intended for *true* and *false*, to data that is known to be correct and incorrect, respectively. The intended meaning of source vectors is explained below.

The source constants, $\{0, -1, +1, \top\}$, are used to specify the role of an information source in a piece of data. In a source vector $v = (a_1 \cdots a_k)$, corresponding to the data d, the value of a_i specifies the role of the information source S_i as follows:

$$a_i = \begin{cases} 0 & S_i \text{ neither confirms nor denies } d \\ -1 & S_i \text{ denies } d \\ +1 & S_i \text{ confirms } d \\ \top & S_i \text{ is inconsistent with respect to } d \end{cases}$$

A source vector $v = (a_1 \cdots a_k)$ specifies the conjunction of the roles of each information source S_i as given by a_i. A set of source vectors $x = \{v_1, \ldots, v_m\}$ specifies the disjunction of the specification of the vectors $v_1, \ldots, v_m$. More precisely, the role of information sources is captured by the *expression* corresponding to a set of source vectors defined as follows:

We associate a Boolean variable s_i with each information source S_i, $i = 1, \ldots, k$. Let $v = (a_1 \cdots a_k)$ be a source vector, then the set of information sources $S^+ = \{S_i \mid a_i = +1 \text{ or } a_i = \top\}$ are contributing positively to v, while the set of information sources $S^- = \{S_i \mid a_i = -1 \text{ or } a_i = \top\}$ are contributing negatively. Note that the case of inconsistent information source, $a_i = \top$, is treated as the source s_i is contributing positively as well as negatively to the corresponding information. The expression $e(v)$ corresponding to the source vector $v = (a_1 \cdots a_k)$, is defined as:

$$e(v) = \bigwedge_{S_i \in S^+} s_i \bigwedge_{S_j \in S^-} \neg s_j$$

Note that $e(v) = false$ if $a_i = \top$ for at least one i, $1 \leq i \leq k$.

The expression $e(x)$ corresponding to a set x of source vectors is

$$e(x) = \bigvee_{v \in x} e(v)$$

The expressions corresponding to the special source vectors T and F are *true* and *false*, respectively.

4.1 Source vector operations

The query processing in IST-based uncertain databases uses the information source vector operations *s-conjunction*, *s-disjunction*, and *s-negation* described below.

First, we observe that the information source constants $\{0, -1, +1, T\}$ form a lattice structure, with the top and bottom elements T and 0 respectively. The partial order among the elements are as follows: $0 \prec 1 \prec T$ and $0 \prec -1 \prec T$. The bottom element, 0, can be considered as designating *under specified*, and the top element, T, designates *over specified* (or *inconsistent*).

Given two source vectors $v = (a_1 \cdots a_k)$ and $w = (b_1 \cdots b_k)$, their *s-conjunction* $u = v \overset{s}{\wedge} w$ is the source vector $u = (c_1 \cdots c_k)$, where $c_i = lub(a_i, b_i)$ The *lub* is the least upper bound with respect to the lattice of information source constants.

The cases where one or both operands are the special source vectors T or F are handled in the obvious way, namely:

$F \overset{s}{\wedge} v = v \overset{s}{\wedge} F = F$, for all source vectors v, and

$T \overset{s}{\wedge} v = v \overset{s}{\wedge} T = v$, for all source vectors v.

The s-conjunction of two sets of source vectors x and y is performed as follows

$$x \overset{s}{\wedge} y = \{v \overset{s}{\wedge} w \mid v \in x \text{ and } w \in y\}$$

The *s-disjunction* of two sets of source vectors x and y, written $x \overset{s}{\vee} y$, is their union

$$x \overset{s}{\vee} y = x \cup y$$

The *s-negation* of a source vector $v = (a_1 \cdots a_k)$, written $\overset{s}{\neg} v$, is defined as follows: let u_i denote the source vector $(b_1 \cdots b_k)$ where $b_i = +1$ and $b_j = 0$, for $j \neq i$, and similarly let w_i denote the source vector $(b_1 \cdots b_k)$ where $b_i = -1$ and $b_j = 0$, for $j \neq i$, then

$$\overset{s}{\neg} v = \{u_i \mid a_i = -1 \text{ or } a_i = T\} \cup \{w_i \mid a_i = +1 \text{ or } a_i = T\}$$

The s-negation of the special source vectors T and F are F and T, respectively.

The s-negation of a set $x = \{v_1, \ldots, v_m\}$ of source vectors is calculated as follows:

$$\overset{s}{\neg} x = (\overset{s}{\neg} v_1) \overset{s}{\wedge} (\overset{s}{\neg} v_2) \overset{s}{\wedge} \ldots \overset{s}{\wedge} (\overset{s}{\neg} v_m)$$

The following results are from [23]. In the following x, y, and z are sets of source vectors, and $e(x)$, $e(y)$, and $e(z)$ are their corresponding expressions, respectively.

Theorem 1 *Let $z = x \overset{s}{\wedge} y$. Then $e(z) = e(x) \wedge e(y)$.*

Theorem 2 *Let $z = x \overset{s}{\vee} y$. Then $e(z) = e(x) \vee e(y)$.*

Theorem 3 *Let $z = \overset{s}{\neg} x$. Then $e(z) = \neg e(x)$.*

5 Uncertain OODBs

In this section we explore the application of Information Source Tracking (IST) techniques to uncertain object-oriented databases. We will consider attribute, object, and class uncertainties at this point. First we discuss the modeling, and next the query processing in an uncertain OODB.

Attribute uncertainty can be handled by associating source vectors with each value of an attribute of a given object. We need to distinguish between single-valued and multiple-valued attributes. For single-valued attributes a "reliability adjustment" approach [26] is needed when contradictory information is supplied by information sources. In general, there is a possibility of conflicting information from different sources whenever integrity constraints, such as single-valued attributes, are present. In a regular database conflicting information, i.e. information violating integrity constraints, is simply disallowed. In an uncertain database, however, we must be able to cope with conflicting information. In [26] we discuss integrity constraints of the single-valuedness form, such as functional dependencies in the relational model, and propose techniques to cope with them in IST-based uncertain databases. The same approach can be applied to uncertain object-oriented databases.

To handle the object uncertainty we can associate source vectors with each object as well. In most cases all objects in the database will have the *true* source vector T to start with. Then, in the course of query processing or view materialization, attribute and type uncertainties, as well as object uncertainties, will affect the object vectors. For example, consider the query "list the boards in which the IC chip DNA220016 has been used". The uncertainty regarding the attribute "IC chips" of the objects "boards" will be reflected in the object vectors of the answer to the query. Query processing in uncertain OODBs is discussed in more detail below.

Class uncertainty is a novel concept which has not been addressed before. It is the association between an object and its type (class) which is uncertain, and we can use source vectors as well for their modeling. In most cases, there is a single-type integrity constraint for each object. This should be handled in a similar manner as discussed in the case of single-valued attributes.

5.1 Query processing in uncertain OODBs

The "pure" object-oriented paradigm designates methods as the sole means for retrieving and/or updating attribute values. Yet the database community regards the ability to process *ad hoc* queries as a basic requirement of a database system. As a result we have witnessed general purpose query processing facilities, such as various *object SQLs*, functional languages, and logic programming based facilities being proposed and developed for OODBs. The IST method is compatible with all of these approaches. What needs to be added to the query facility is the ability to manipulate source information. If numerical measures of source reliabilities are provided, then the last (optional) step of the query processing would be the calculation of the reliability of the answer as a function of the source reliabilities.

The main idea is to use the source vector operations s-conjunction, s-disjunction, and s-negation to manipulate source information concurrently with data manipulation. The techniques discussed in [13] for query processing in uncertain deductive databases can be readily extended to an OODB with a logic-programming based query facility.

An object SQL facility with simple (non-nested) queries is also easy to handle. We have demonstrated the feasibility of this approach for the relational model by a prototype implementation [6]. The case for OODBs needs some extensions. The structure of the *where* clause determines the source vector operations. A complex predicate, i.e. a predicate on a contiguous sequence of attributes along a branch of the composition hierarchy, can be handled easily. The "traversal" of the composition hierarchy amounts to the s-conjunction of the source vectors corresponding to the attributes along the path. More research is needed for efficient processing of nested SQL queries.

We should add that the situation becomes more complicated with aggregate queries, i.e. queries incorporating *max, min, count, sum*, and *average* operators. In [27] we discuss some of the issues regarding aggregate queries.

A method facility using a general purpose programming language is more complicated to extend to incorporate uncertainty. Methods used for insertions, deletions, and modifications of data should be enhanced to record the contributing source, and to detect inconsistencies and initiate the reliability adjustment process [26].

Methods that implement query processing facility should also be enhanced to maintain and manipulate source information (e.g. in the form of source vectors). If an SQL or logical query sublanguage is used then the approaches mentioned above can be used. Otherwise the source manipulation routines should be coded into the methods. Some automation can be achieved through techniques similar to those used in code generation in compilers and interpreters.

Example 1 Let's consider a simple OODB of (digital) systems, boards, and IC chips. There are three classes, System, Board, and Chip. The class System has an attribute, Boards, that is of type Board. This attribute is multiple-valued, and lists the boards used in a System. The class Board has an attribute, Ics, that is of type Chip. This attribute is also multiple-valued, listing all Ics used on the board.

The database contains information about two systems, S_1 and S_2, three boards B_1, B_2, B_3, and five chips $C_1, \ldots, C_5$. The information is provided by four information sources $s_1, \ldots, s_4$, and is depicted below. For example, according to the information source s_1, the system S_1 contains boards B_1 and B_2, while according to the source s_2 the system S_1 contains boards B_1 and B_3.

System S_1

Boards:				
B_1	1	0	0	0
B_2	1	0	0	0
B_1	0	1	0	0
B_3	0	1	0	0

System S_2

Boards:				
B_1	1	0	0	0
B_1	0	1	0	0
B_3	0	1	0	0
B_3	0	0	0	1

Board B_1

Chips:				
C_1	1	0	0	0
C_2	1	0	0	0
C_3	0	0	0	1

Board B_2

Chips:				
C_2	0	1	0	0
C_3	0	0	1	0
C_5	0	0	0	1

Board B_3

Chips:				
C_4	1	0	0	0
C_4	0	0	1	0
C_3	0	0	1	0

Now let us consider the query "list systems that use the IC chip C_4". This query can be specified in object SQL as follows:

```
select systems
where System.Boards.ICs = ''C_4''
```

Note that the "path" expression `System.Boards.ICs` in the `where` clause specifies a traversal of the composition hierarchy.

The answer to the query contains the objects S_1 and S_2. The corresponding (object) source vectors can be obtained as:

$$\{(0\ 1\ 0\ 0)\} \overset{s}{\wedge} \{(1\ 0\ 0\ 0),(0\ 0\ 1\ 0)\} = \{(1\ 1\ 0\ 0),(0\ 1\ 1\ 0)\}$$

and

$$\{(0\ 1\ 0\ 0),(0\ 0\ 0\ 1)\} \overset{s}{\wedge} \{(1\ 0\ 0\ 0),(0\ 0\ 1\ 0)\} = \{(1\ 1\ 0\ 0),(0\ 1\ 1\ 0),(1\ 0\ 0\ 1),(0\ 0\ 1\ 1)\}$$

If we had numerical measures of sources' reliabilities, we could calculate certainties of the above answers using one of the two algorithms from [23]. For example, let the reliabilities of the sources $s_1, \ldots, s_4$ be 95%, 90%, 85%, and 80%, respectively. Then the systems S_1 and S_2 are answers to the above query with certainties 89.325% and 97.265%, respectively.

5.2 Implementation

In this section we will explore how an uncertain object-oriented database system can be implemented. It is our thesis that the user interface of an uncertain OODB should not be any different from a conventional OODB, except that the system can (optionally) provide additional information to the users regarding the certainty of the answers to queries. Hence the only differences visible to the users of an uncertain database are:

- Users should identify contributing information source(s) when inserting (e.g. creating objects), deleting, or modifying data.

- In addition to producing answers to users' queries, the system identifies contributing information source(s) involved in the inclusion of each object in the answer to a query.

- The system can calculate the certainty of each object in the answer to a query. The certainty is a function of the reliabilities of contributing information sources, which should be supplied by users.

In an uncertain OODB attribute uncertainty and object uncertainty are simple to implement. We can associate source vectors with each attribute value of an object, as depicted in Example 1, for attribute uncertainty. Similarly, we can associate source vectors with each object to model object uncertainty. These source vectors are generated by the system using the information provided by the users at the time of object creation, and are hidden from the users. They are manipulated by the query processing subsystem to identify contributing sources, and optionally compute certainties of answers to queries.

Implementing class uncertainty is more complicated. We propose the use of *generic* object identifiers for uncertain objects. A generic identifier determines a special object, which we will call an *association* object, which provides the mapping to the realizations of the uncertain object. A *realization* of an uncertain object is simply an ordinary object as an instance of a single class, with its own unique identifier. As mentioned above, attribute values of uncertain objects are <value, source-vector> pairs. The value could be atomic, or it could be a generic identifier. The users are only aware of generic object identifiers, and utilize them to access and manipulate the objects.

A reference to a class-uncertain object, hence, will consist of a reference to its association object through its generic identifier, followed by references to the realizations of the object. The same behavior also takes place when traversing a composition hierarchy, since generic object identifiers are stored as attribute values used in the traversal. Association objects, in general, are very small, and should be cached in memory after the first reference. This will eliminate extra disk traffic (or client-server traffic) and will achieve a performance that is comparable with a regular OODB system.

6 Conclusions

We investigated uncertainty and inaccuracy in object-oriented databases, and highlighted its similarities and differences with relational databases. It was argued that in addition to attribute and object uncertainties, the concept of "class uncertainty" needs to be addressed in uncertain OODBs. We also explored the application of the Information Source Tracking (IST) method to the modeling and handling of uncertainty in OODBs. Techniques developed for IST, such as source vector operations, reliability adjustment process to preserve integrity rules, and the results regarding aggregate operations can be used in the context of object-oriented databases. We also presented an architecture for efficient implementation of uncertain OODBs.

Many questions remain open regarding the modeling and manipulation of uncertain data in databases and in particular in OODBs. We are currently investigating the extension of query processing to full SQL and OSQL (Object SQL) queries. For OODBs utilizing a general purpose language for the coding of methods, routines to handle source vectors that are used to model uncertainty should be coded into the methods. Investigation into the automation of this process is another direction for future investigations.

References

[1] Atkinson M, Bancilhon F, Dewitt D, Dittrich K, Maier D, Zdonik S. The object-oriented database systems manifesto. Proc First Int'l Conf on Deductive and Object-Oriented Databases, 1989, pp 40–57

[2] Barbara B, Garcia-Molina H, Porter D. The management of probabilistic data. IEEE Trans on Knowledge and Data Engineering 1992; 4(5):487–502

[3] Cavallo R, Pitarelli M. The theory of probabilistic databases. Proc of the 1987 Int'l Conference on Very Large Databases, 1987, pp 71–81

[4] Codd EF. Extending the database relational model to capture more meaning. ACM Trans on Database Systems 1979; 4(4):397–434

[5] DeMichiel LG. Resolving database incompatibility: an approach to performing operations over mismatched domains. IEEE Transactions on Knowledge and Data Engineering 1989; 1(4):485-493

[6] Doyon B. Reliability of answers to an SQL query. Department of Computer Science, Concordia University, 1990

[7] Goyal P, Qu YZ, Sadri F. The temporal object model. In: Srinivasan B, Zeleznikow J (eds) Research and Practical Issues in Databases. 1992, pp 36-50 (Proc of the 3rd Australian Database Conference)

[8] Jamil H, Sadri F. Trusting an information agent. Proc of the International Workshop on Rough Sets and Knowledge Discovery, Banff, Canada, 1993, pp 348-359

[9] Jamil H, Sadri F. Recognizing credible experts in inaccurate databases. Manuscript, December 1993

[10] Kifer M, Li A. On the semantics of rule-based expert systems with uncertainty. In: Gyssens M, Paredaens J, Van Gucht D (eds) Springer-Verlag, 1988, pp 102-117 Proc of the 2nd International Conference on Database Theory (Lecture notes in computer science no 326)

[11] Kifer M, Subrahmanian VS. Theory of generalized annotated logic programming and its application. Journal of Logic Programming 1992; 12(4):335–367

[12] Kim W. Introduction to object-oriented databases. The MIT Press, 1990

[13] Lakshmanan VS, Sadri F. Modeling uncertainty in deductive databases. Manuscript, May 1993

[14] Lee SK. Imprecise and uncertain information in databases: an evidential approach. Proc of the 1992 IEEE Int'l Conference on Data Engineering 1992; 614–621

[15] Lee SK. An extended relational database model for uncertain and imprecise information. Proc of the 1992 Int'l Conference on Very Large Databases, 1992, pp 211–220

[16] Liu KC, Sunderraman R. Indefinite and maybe Information in Relational Databases. ACM Trans on Database Systems 1990; 15(1):1–39

[17] Liu K-C, Sunderraman R. A generalized relational model for indefinite and maybe information. IEEE Transactions on Knowledge and Data Engineering 1991; 3(1):65–77

[18] Morrissey JM. Imprecise information and uncertainty in information systems. ACM Trans on Information Systems 1990; 8(2):159–180

[19] Ng R, Subrahmanian VS. Probabilistic logic programming. Information and Computation, 1990

[20] Ng R, Subrahmanian VS. A semantical framework for supporting subjective and conditional probabilities in deductive databases, Technical Report No. CS-TR-2563, Department of Computer Science, University of Maryland, November 1990.

[21] Ng R, Subrahmanian VS. Stable semantics for probabilistic deductive databases. Technical Report no CS-TR-2573, Department of Computer Science, University of Maryland, December 1990

[22] Nilsson NJ. Probabilistic logic. Artificial Intelligence 1986; 28:71–87

[23] Sadri F. Reliability of answers to queries in relational databases. IEEE Trans on Knowledge and Data Engineering 1991; 3(2):245–251

[24] Sadri F. Modeling uncertainty in databases. Proc of the 1991 IEEE Int'l Conference on Data Engineering 1991; 122–131

[25] Sadri F. Information source tracking: efficiency issues. Manuscript, submitted for publication

[26] Sadri F. Integrity constraints in the information source tracking method. IEEE Transactions on Knowledge and Data Engineering to appear

[27] Sadri F. Aggregate operations in the information source tracking method. In: Alagar VS, Lakshmanan VS, Sadri F (eds) Formal Methods in Databases and Software Engineering. Springer-Verlag, 1993, pp 24–39 (Proc of the 1992 Montreal Workshop on Formal Methods in Databases and Software Engineering)

[28] Shortliffe EH, Buchanan BG. A model of inexact reasoning in medicine. Mathematical Biosciences 1975; 23:351–379

[29] Van Emden MH. Quantitative deduction and its fixpoint theory. Journal of Logic Programming 1986; 4(1):37–53

[30] Zadeh LA. Fuzzy sets as a basis for a theory of possibility. Fuzzy Sets Syst 1978; 1(1):3–28

[31] Zadeh LA. Knowledge representation in fuzzy logic. IEEE Trans on Knowledge and Data Engineering 1989; 1(1):89–100

[32] Zemankova M. Implementing imprecision in information systems. Information Sciences 1985; 37:107–141

Management of Uncertainty in AI: A Rough Set Approach

Andrzej Skowron

Institute of Mathematics

Warsaw University

skowron@mimuw.edu.pl

Abstract

We present some consequences of the assumption that objects are classified on the basis of a partial information about them encoded in information systems. The presented results are based on the rough set approach [14] and boolean reasoning [1].

1   Introduction

We present some consequences of the assumption stating that objects are classified on the basis of a partial information about them encoded in information systems.

The access to the information about objects allow us to define the rough membership functions [12] computable from information systems. Among consequences of properties [12] of the rough membership functions the most important seems to be the statement that logical systems for reasoning with uncertainty are intentional. We apply properties of rough sets and, in particular properties of rough membership functions, for proving correctness of inference rules with embedded certainty coefficients.

We also show that the belief functions [17] are computable from the information encoded in information systems. One of the consequence of our approach is that the Dempster-Shafer rule of evidence combination is valid for independent products [25] of information systems.

We present a method for synthesis of decision rules with coefficients related to belief functions [27, 28].

The paper is organized as follows. In Section 2 we recall some basic notions of rough set theory [14, 13, 12]. In particular we define the membership functions (rm-functions) and we present their basic properties. We also describe some methods for decision rules synthesis from consistent decision tables [28]. In Section 3 we present properties of membership functions related to set theoretical operations of union and intersection. One can prove that for some boundary regions it is not possible to compute the values of the rm-functions for union $X \cup Y$ and intersection $X \cap Y$ knowing the values of rm-functions for X and Y only (if information encoded in information systems is not accessible and some special relations between sets X and Y do not hold). These results show that the assumptions about properties of the fuzzy membership functions (see, e.g. [4] p.11) related to the union and intersection should be modified if one would like to take into account that objects are classified on the basis of a partial information about them. We also give the necessary and sufficient conditions for the following equalities to be true:

$\mu_{X \cup Y}^{\mathbb{A}}(x) = \max(\mu_X^{\mathbb{A}}(x), \mu_Y^{\mathbb{A}}(x))$ and

$\mu_{X \cap Y}^{\mathbb{A}}(x) = \min(\mu_X^{\mathbb{A}}(x), \mu_Y^{\mathbb{A}}(x))$ for any $x \in U$.

These conditions are expressed by means of the boundary regions of a partition of U defined by sets X and Y or by means of some relationships which should hold for the sets X and Y. In particular one can show [12] that the above equalities are true for arbitrary information system $\mathbb{A}$ iff $X \subseteq Y$ or $Y \subseteq X$. In Section 4 we apply properties of rough membership functions (and their extensions) to show some relationships between certainty coefficients attached to formulas in some rules of inference like modus ponens or inference rule based on similization transmutations [10]. In Section 5 we discuss some basic relationships between rough set theory and evidence theory [21, 22, 23, 25]. In particular an interpretation of belief and plausibility functions in terms of lower and upper approximation is given. We also show [23], [25] that the Dempster-Shafer rule of evidence combination is valid if the information source corresponding to the combination of two independent sources of information is represented by the independent product of information systems related to these independent sources. We apply the methods developed for consistent decision tables to inconsistent decision tables for synthesis of decision rules with certainty coefficients. At the end we suggest some other applications of rough set theory for management of uncertainty in particular those related to data filtering and compression.

2 Rough sets preliminaries

Information systems [11, 14] are used for representing knowledge. Rough sets have been introduced [14] as a tool to deal with inexact, uncertain or vague knowledge in artificial intelligence applications. In this section we recall some basic notions related to information systems and rough sets.

An *information system* is a pair $\mathbb{A} = (U, A)$, where U is a non-empty, finite set called the *universe* and A – a non-empty, finite set of *attributes*, i.e. $a : U \to V_a$ for $a \in A$, where V_a is called the *value set* of a.

Elements of U are called *objects* and interpreted as, e.g. cases, states, processes, patients, observations. Attributes are interpreted as features, variables, characteristic conditions etc.

Every information system $\mathbb{A} = (U, A)$ and non-empty set $B \subseteq A$ determine a *B-information function*

$$Inf_B : U \to \mathbb{P}(B \times \bigcup_{a \in B} V_a)$$

defined by $Inf_B(x) = \{(a, a(x)) : a \in B\}$. The set $\{Inf_B(x) : x \in U\}$ is called the *B-information set* and it is denoted by $INF(B)$. The A-information set is also denoted by $INF(\mathbb{A})$. Elements of $INF(\mathbb{A})$ are called *information vectors*.

We consider a special case of information systems called decision tables. A *decision table* is any information system of the form $\mathbb{A} = (U, A \cup \{d\})$, where $d \notin A$ is a distinguished attribute called *decision*. The elements of A are called *conditions*.

One can interpret a decision attribute as a kind of classification of the universe of objects given by an expert, decision-maker, operator, physician, etc. Decision tables are called training sets of examples in machine learning [8].

The cardinality of the image $d(U) = \{k : d(s) = k\}$ for some $s \in U$ is denoted by $r(d)$. We assume that the set V_d of values of the decision d is equal to $\{1, \ldots, r(d)\}$. The decision d determines the partition $\{X_1, \ldots, X_{r(d)}\}$ of the universe U, where $X_k = \{x \in U : d(x) = k\}$ for $1 \leq k \leq r(d)$. The set X_k is called the k-th decision class of $\mathbb{A}$.

Let $\mathbb{A} = (U, A)$ be an information system. With every subset of attributes $B \subseteq A$, an equivalence relation, denoted by $IND_{\mathbb{A}}(B)$ (or $IND(B)$) called the *B-indiscernibility relation*, is associated and defined by

$$IND(B) = \{(s, s') \in U^2 : \text{ for every } a \in B, a(s) = a(s')\}$$

Objects s, s' satisfying relation $IND(B)$ are indiscernible by attributes from B.

Let $\mathbb{A}$ be an information system with n objects. By $M(\mathbb{A})$ [26] we denote an $n \times n$ matrix (c_{ij}), called the *discernibility matrix of* $\mathbb{A}$ such that

$$c_{ij} = \{a \in A : a(x_i) \neq a(x_j)\} \text{ for } i, j = 1, \ldots, n.$$

A *discernibility function* $f_{\mathbb{A}}$ for an information system $\mathbb{A}$ is a boolean function of m boolean variables $\overline{a}_1, \ldots, \overline{a}_m$ corresponding to the attributes $a_1, \ldots, a_m$, respectively, and defined by

$$f_{\mathbb{A}}(\overline{a}_1, \ldots, \overline{a}_m) = \bigwedge \{\bigvee \overline{c}_{ij} : 1 \leq j < i \leq n, c_{ij} \neq \emptyset\}$$

where $\overline{c}_{ij} = \{\overline{a} : a \in c_{ij}\}$.

It can be shown [26] that the set of all *prime implicants* of $f_{\mathbb{A}}$ determines the set of all *reducts of* $\mathbb{A}$.

If $\mathbb{A} = (U, A)$ is an information system, $B \subseteq A$ is a set of attributes and $X \subseteq U$ is a set of objects then the sets

$$\{s \in U : [s]_B \subseteq X\} \text{ and } \{s \in U : [s]_B \cap X \neq \emptyset\}$$

are called *B-lower* and *B-upper approximation* of X in $\mathbb{A}$, and they are denoted by $\underline{B}X$ and $\overline{B}X$, respectively.

The set $BN_B(X) = \overline{B}X - \underline{B}X$ will be called the *B-boundary* of X. When $B = A$ we write also $BN_{\mathbb{A}}(X)$ instead of $BN_A(X)$.

Sets which are unions of some classes of the indiscernibility relation $IND(B)$ are called definable by B. The set X is B-definable iff $\overline{B}X = \underline{B}X$. Some subsets (categories) of objects in an information system cannot be expressed exactly by employing available attributes but they can be defined roughly. The set $\underline{B}X$ is the set of all elements of U which can be with certainty classified as elements of X, having the knowledge represented by attributes from B; $BN_B(X)$ is the set of elements which one can classify neither to X nor to $-X$ having knowledge B.

If $X_1, \ldots, X_{r(d)}$ are decision classes of $\mathbb{A}$ then the set

$$\underline{B}X_1 \cup \ldots \cup \underline{B}X_{r(d)}$$

is called *the B-positive region of* $\mathbb{A}$ and is denoted by $POS_B(d)$.

If $\mathbb{A} = (U, A \cup \{d\})$ is a decision table then we define a function $\partial_A : U \rightarrow \mathbb{P}(\{1, \ldots, r(d)\})$, called *the generalized decision in* $\mathbb{A}$, by

$$\partial_A(x) = \{i : \exists x' \in U(x' IND(A)x \text{ and } d(x') = i)\}.$$

A decision table $\mathbb{A}$ is called *consistent (deterministic)* if $|\partial_A(x)| = 1$ for any $x \in U$, otherwise $\mathbb{A}$ is *inconsistent (non-deterministic)*. It is easy to see that a decision table $\mathbb{A}$ is consistent iff $POS_A(d) = U$. Moreover, if $\partial_B = \partial_{B'}$ then $POS_B(d) = POS_{B'}(d)$ for any non-empty sets $B, B' \subseteq A$.

A subset B of the set A of attributes of decision table $\mathbb{A} = (U, A \cup \{d\})$ is *a relative reduct* of $\mathbb{A}$ iff B is a minimal set with the following property: $\partial_B = \partial_A$, where ∂_B is the generallized decision of $(U, B \cup \{d\})$. The set of all relative reducts in $\mathbb{A}$ is denoted by $RED(\mathbb{A}, d)$.

If $B \in RED(\mathbb{A}, d)$ then the set $\{(\{a = a(x) : a \in B\}, d = d(x)) : x \in U\}$ is called the *trace of* B *in* $\mathbb{A}$ and is denoted by $Trace_\mathbb{A}(B)$.

The rough membership functions (rm-functions) have been introduced in [20] as a tool for reasoning with uncertainty. The definition of these functions is based on the observation that objects are classified by means of available partial information about them.

Let $\mathbb{A} = (U, A)$ be an information system and let $\emptyset \neq X \subseteq U$. The *rough* $\mathbb{A}$-*membership function of the set* X (or, *rm-function*, in short) denoted by $\mu_X^\mathbb{A}$, is defined by:

$$\mu_X^\mathbb{A}(x) = \frac{|[x]_A \cap X|}{|[x]_A|}, \quad \text{for } x \in U$$

One can observe a similarity of the expression on the right hand side of the above definition with the expression used to define the conditional probability.

Proposition 2.1.[20] *Let* $\mathbb{A} = (U, A)$ *be an information system and let* $X, Y \subseteq U$. *The rm-functions have the following properties:*

(i) $\mu_X^\mathbb{A}(x) = 1$ *iff* $x \in \underline{A}X$;

(ii) $\mu_X^\mathbb{A}(x) = 0$ *iff* $x \in U - \overline{A}X$;

(iii) $0 < \mu_X^\mathbb{A}(x) < 1$ *iff* $x \in BN_\mathbb{A}(X)$;

(iv) If $IND(A) = \{(x, x) : x \in U\}$ *then* $\mu_X^\mathbb{A}$ *is the characteristic function of* X;

(v) If x $IND(A)$ y *then* $\mu_X^\mathbb{A}(x) = \mu_X^\mathbb{A}(y)$;

(vi) $\mu_{U-X}^\mathbb{A}(x) = 1 - \mu_X^\mathbb{A}(x)$ *for any* $x \in X$;

(vii) $\mu_{X \cup Y}^\mathbb{A}(x) \geq \max(\mu_X^\mathbb{A}(x), \mu_Y^\mathbb{A}(x))$ *for any* $x \in U$;

(viii) $\mu_{X \cap Y}^\mathbb{A}(x) \leq \min(\mu_X^\mathbb{A}(x), \mu_Y^\mathbb{A}(x))$ *for any* $x \in U$;

(ix) If $\mathbb{X}$ *is a family of pairwise disjoint subsets of* U *then*

$$\mu_{\cup \mathbb{X}}^\mathbb{A}(x) = \sum_{X \in \mathbb{X}} \mu_X^\mathbb{A}(x) \text{ for any } x \in U$$

□

Now we recall the definition of decision rules. Let $\mathbb{A} = (U, A \cup \{d\})$ be a decision table and let

$$V = \bigcup_{a \in A} V_a \cup V_d \,.$$

The atomic formulas over $B \subseteq A \cup \{d\}$ and V are expressions of the form $a = v$, called descriptors over B and V, where $a \in B$ and $v \in V_a$. The set $\mathbb{F}(B, V)$ of formulas over B and V is the least set containing all atomic formulas over B and V and closed with respect to the classical propositional connectives $\vee$ (disjunction) and $\wedge$ (conjunction).

Let $\tau \in \mathbb{F}(B, V)$. Then by $\tau_{\mathbb{A}}$ we denote the set of all objects of $\mathbb{A}$ with property τ, defined inductively as follows:

1. if τ is of the form $a = v$ then $\tau_{\mathbb{A}} = \{x \in U : a(x) = v\}$;

2. $(\tau \wedge \tau')_{\mathbb{A}} = \tau_{\mathbb{A}} \cap \tau'_{\mathbb{A}}$; $(\tau \vee \tau')_{\mathbb{A}} = \tau_{\mathbb{A}} \cup \tau'_{\mathbb{A}}$.

Let us note that the complement of any definable set is definable by union and intersection.

The set $\mathbb{F}(A, V)$ is called the set of *conditional formulas of* $\mathbb{A}$ and is denoted by $\mathbb{C}(A, V)$.

A decision *rule of* $\mathbb{A}$ is any expression of the form

$$\tau \Rightarrow d = v \text{ where } \tau \in \mathbb{C}(A, V) \text{ and } v \in V_d \,.$$

The decision rule $\tau \Rightarrow d = v$ for $\mathbb{A}$ is *true* in $\mathbb{A}$ iff $\tau_{\mathbb{A}} \subseteq (d = v)_{\mathbb{A}}$; if $\tau_{\mathbb{A}} = (d = v)_{\mathbb{A}}$ then we say that the rule is $\mathbb{A}$-*exact*.

We present now two methods for synthesis of different forms of decision rules from consistent decision tables. The methods are based on some properties of the discernibility matrices [26] and their modifications.

The first method consists of two steps. In the first step we show how to modify the discernibility matrix notion to compute the set $RED(\mathbb{A}, d)$ of all relative reducts of $\mathbb{A}$. In the second step we show how any relative reduct $B \in RED(\mathbb{A}, d)$ allows directly to obtain the description of each decision class in the form of the decision rule. On the left hand side of all decision rules only attributes from B occur. The description of the decision classes is minimal in the following sense: it is not possible to obtain a description of all decision classes by applying any proper subset of B.

Let $\mathbb{A} = (U, A \cup \{d\})$ be a consistent decision table and let $M(\mathbb{A}) = (c_{ij})$ be its discernibility matrix. We construct a new matrix $M'(\mathbb{A}) = (c'_{ij})$ assuming $c'_{ij} = \emptyset$ if $d(x_i) = d(x_j)$ and $c'_{ij} = c_{ij} - \{d\}$, otherwise. The matrix $M'(\mathbb{A})$ is called *the relative discernibility matrix of* $\mathbb{A}$. Now one can construct the *relative discernibility function* $f_{M'(\mathbb{A})}$ of $M'(\mathbb{A})$ in the same way as the discernibility function was constructed from the discernibility matrix. One can show that the following proposition is true:

Proposition 2.2.[28] *For any $B \subseteq A$ the following conditions are equivalent:*
(i) $B \in RED(\mathbb{A}, d)$;
(ii) $\wedge B$ s a prime implicant of $f_{M'(\mathbb{A})}$.

□

In condition (ii) the elements of B are treated as boolean variables corresponding to attributes. Proposition 2.2 allows to compute the set of all relative reducts by computing the set of all prime implicants of $f_{M'(\mathbb{A})}$.

Now, for any $B \in RED(\mathbb{A}, d)$ we construct the set $Trace_{\mathbb{A}}(B)$.

To obtain the decision rule corresponding to the i-th decision it is enough to take all pairs from $Trace_{\mathbb{A}}(B)$ with the second element equal to $d = i$ and create the disjunction α_i of all conjunctions of descriptor sets occurring on the first position in those pairs. The constructed decision rule has the form

$$\alpha_i \Rightarrow d = i$$

Proposition 2.3.[28] *Let $\mathbb{A} = (U, A \cup \{d\})$ be a consistent decision table and let $B \in RED(\mathbb{A}, d)$. The decision rules*

$$\alpha_i \Rightarrow d = i \text{ where } i = 1, ..., r(d)$$

are exact in $\mathbb{A}$ and the descriptions of decision classes defined by them are minimal, i.e. for any $B' \subset B$ do not exist formulas β_i for $i = 1, \ldots, r(d)$ from $\mathbb{C}(B', V)$ such that the decision rules $\beta_i \Rightarrow d = i$ are exact in $\mathbb{A}$ for $i = 1, ..., r(d)$. □

The second method allows to construct a description of the decision classes by exact in $\mathbb{A}$ decision rules

$$\alpha_i \Rightarrow d = i$$

where $\alpha_i \in \mathbb{C}(A, V)$ is a disjunction $\bigvee \wedge \gamma_i$ of conjunctions $\wedge \gamma_i$ of minimal sets γ_i of descriptors for $i = 1, \ldots, r(d)$. The set γ_i defines in $\mathbb{A}$ a non-empty set of objects, i.e. $(\wedge \gamma_i)_{\mathbb{A}} \neq \emptyset$ and is minimal in the following sense: the decision rule

$$\wedge \gamma'_i \Rightarrow d = i$$

is no longer valid in $\mathbb{A}$ for any $\gamma'_i \subset \gamma_i$ satisfying $(\wedge \gamma'_i)_{\mathbb{A}} \neq \emptyset$. The decision rule with the above property is called *minimal with respect to the descriptors in $\mathbb{A}$*.

The method allows to generate decision rules with one more property, namely if

$$\bigvee \wedge \gamma_i \Rightarrow d = i$$

is any of the constructed decision rules for $\mathbb{A}$ and δ is a set of descriptors such that

$$\wedge \delta \Rightarrow d = i$$

is valid in $\mathbb{A}$ and $(\wedge \delta)_{\mathbb{A}} \neq \emptyset$ then $\gamma_i \subseteq \delta$ for some i. The decision rules with the above property are called *complete with respect to the descriptors in $\mathbb{A}$*.

Now we present a method allowing to compute for a given consistent decision table $\mathbb{A}$ the description of all decision classes of $\mathbb{A}$ in the form of exact in $\mathbb{A}$ decision rules which are complete and minimal with respect to descriptors in $\mathbb{A}$.

Let $\mathbb{A} = (U, A \cup \{d\})$ be a consistent decision table and $M'(\mathbb{A}) = (c'_{ij})$ be its relative discernibility matrix. We construct a new matrix

$$M(\mathbb{A}, k) = (c^k_{ij}) \text{ for any } x_k \in U$$

assuming $c^k_{ij} = c'_{ij}$ if $d(x_i) \neq d(x_j) \& (i = k \vee j = k)$ and $c^k_{ij} = \emptyset$, otherwise. The matrix $M(\mathbb{A}, k)$ is called *the k-relative* discernibility matrix of $\mathbb{A}$. Now one can construct the *k-relative discernibility function* $f_{M(\mathbb{A},k)}$ of $M(\mathbb{A},k)$ in the same way as the discernibility function was constructed from the discernibility matrix.

Let $Atr(\tau)$ denote the set of all attributes occurring in the prime implicant τ of $f_{M(\mathbb{A},k)}$ and let us denote by

$$Trace(\mathbb{A},k)$$

the following set of descriptor conjunctions:

$$\{\bigwedge\{a = a(x_k) : a \in Atr(\tau)\} : \tau \text{ is a prime implicant of } f_{M(\mathbb{A},k)}\}.$$

Now let α_p for any $p \in \{1, \ldots, r(d)\}$ be a disjunction of all formulas from the set $\bigcup\{Trace(\mathbb{A},k) : d(x_k) = d(x_p)\}$.

One can show that the following proposition is true:

Proposition 2.4.[28] *Let* $\mathbb{A} = (U, A \cup \{d\})$ *be a consistent decision table. The decision rules:*

$$\alpha_p \Rightarrow d = p \text{ where } p \in \{1, \ldots, r(d)\}$$

are complete and minimal with respect to descriptors in $\mathbb{A}$. $\quad\square$

The above method has been applied for solving a real-time state identification problem [30]. One can observe some similarities of generated rules to those discussed in [8] for AQ algorithms.

3 Rough membership functions for union and intersection

First we present formulas for computing the rm-function values $\mu^{\mathbb{A}}_{X \cup Y}(x)$ and $\mu^{\mathbb{A}}_{X \cap Y}(x)$ from the values $\mu^{\mathbb{A}}_{X}(x)$ and $\mu^{\mathbb{A}}_{Y}(x)$ (when it is possible, i.e. when classified objects are not in a particular boundary region) if information encoded in the information system $\mathbb{A}$ is accessible. In the construction of those formulas we apply a partition of boundary regions related to X and Y. One can interpret these results as follows: the computation of rm-function values $\mu^{\mathbb{A}}_{X \cup Y}(x)$ and $\mu^{\mathbb{A}}_{X \cap Y}(x)$ (if one exclude a particular boundary region !) is *extensional* for a given information system.

Let $\mathbb{A} = (U, A)$ be an information system and let $\mathbb{X}, \mathbb{Z}$ be families of subsets of U such that $\mathbb{Z} \subseteq \mathbb{X}$ and $|\mathbb{Z}| > 1$, where $|\mathbb{Z}|$ denotes the cardinality of $\mathbb{Z}$. The set

$$\bigcap_{X \in \mathbb{Z}} BN_{\mathbb{A}}(X) \cap \bigcap_{X \in \mathbb{X} - \mathbb{Z}} (U - BN_{\mathbb{A}}(X))$$

is said to be the $\mathbb{Z}$-boundary region defined by $\mathbb{X}$ and $\mathbb{A}$ and is denoted by $Bd_{\mathbb{A}}(\mathbb{Z}, \mathbb{X})$.

Lemma 3.1[20] *Let* $\mathbb{A} = (U, A)$ *be an information system,* $X, Y \subseteq U$ *and* $\mathbb{X} = \{X \cap Y, X \cap -Y, -X \cap Y, -X \cap -Y\}$. *If* $x \in U - Bd_{\mathbb{A}}(\mathbb{X}, \mathbb{X})$ *then*

$$\mu^{\mathbb{A}}_{X \cap Y}(x) =$$

if $x \in Bd_{\mathbb{A}}(\{X \cap -Y, -X \cap Y\}, \mathbb{X}) \cup Bd_{\mathbb{A}}(\{X \cap -Y, -X \cap Y, -X \cap -Y\}, \mathbb{X})$

then 0
else if $x \in Bd_{\mathbb{A}}(\{X \cap Y, X \cap -Y, -X \cap Y\}, \mathbb{X})$ then $\mu_X^{\mathbb{A}}(x) + \mu_Y^{\mathbb{A}}(x) - 1$
    else $\min(\mu_X^{\mathbb{A}}(x), \mu_Y^{\mathbb{A}}(x))$

$\square$

Lemma 3.2.[20] *Let* $\mathbb{A} = (U, A)$ *be an information system,* $X, Y \subseteq U$ *and* $\mathbb{X} = \{X \cap Y, X \cap -Y, -X \cap Y, -X \cap -Y\}$. *If* $x \in U - Bd_{\mathbb{A}}(\mathbb{X}, \mathbb{X})$ *then*

$$\mu_{X \cup Y}^{\mathbb{A}}(x) =$$

if $x \in Bd_{\mathbb{A}}(\{X \cap -Y, -X \cap Y\}, \mathbb{X}) \cup Bd_{\mathbb{A}}(\{X \cap -Y, -X \cap Y, -X \cap -Y\}, \mathbb{X})$
  then $\mu_X^{\mathbb{A}}(x) + \mu_Y^{\mathbb{A}}(x)$
  else if $x \in Bd_{\mathbb{A}}(\{X \cap Y, X \cap -Y, -X \cap Y\}, \mathbb{X})$ then 1
    else $max(\mu_X^{\mathbb{A}}(x), \mu_Y^{\mathbb{A}}(x))$

$\square$

One can prove that the assumptions from Lemma 3.1 and Lemma 3.2 related to the boundary region $Bd_{\mathbb{A}}(\mathbb{X}, \mathbb{X})$ cannot be removed because otherwise it will not be possible to compute the values of $\mu_{X \cup Y}^{\mathbb{A}}(x)$ and $\mu_{X \cap Y}^{\mathbb{A}}(x)$ knowing the values $\mu_X^{\mathbb{A}}(x)$ and $\mu_Y^{\mathbb{A}}(x)$ only.

From Lemma 3.1 and Lemma 3.2 we have the following:

Theorem 3.3.[20] *Let* $\mathcal{A}$ *be the class of all information systems with the universe including non-empty sets* X *and* Y. *The following conditions are equivalent:*

(i) $\mu_{X \cap Y}^{\mathbb{A}}(x) = \min(\mu_X^{\mathbb{A}}(x), \mu_Y^{\mathbb{A}}(x))$ *for any* $x \in U$ *and* $\mathbb{A} = (U, A) \in \mathcal{A}$

(ii) $Bd_{\mathbb{A}}(\mathbb{Y}, \mathbb{X}) = \emptyset$ *for any* $\mathbb{X} \supseteq \mathbb{Y} \supseteq \{X \cap -Y, -X \cap Y\}$ *and* $\mathbb{A} = (U, A) \in \mathcal{A}$, *where* $\mathbb{X} = \{X \cap Y, -X \cap Y, X \cap -Y, -X \cap -Y\}$.

$\square$

Theorem 3.4[20] *Let* $\mathcal{A}$ *be the class of all information systems with the set of objects including non-empty sets* X *and* Y. *The following conditions are equivalent:*

(i) $\mu_{X \cup Y}^{\mathbb{A}}(x) = \max(\mu_X^{\mathbb{A}}(x), \mu_Y^{\mathbb{A}}(x))$ *for any* $x \in U$ *and* $\mathbb{A} = (U, A) \in \mathcal{A}$

(ii) $Bd_{\mathbb{A}}(\mathbb{Y}, \mathbb{X}) = \emptyset$ *for any* $\mathbb{X} \supseteq \mathbb{Y} \supseteq \{X \cap -Y, -X \cap Y\}$ *and* $\mathbb{A} = (U, A) \in \mathcal{A}$, *where* $\mathbb{X} = \{X \cap Y, -X \cap Y, X \cap -Y, -X \cap -Y\}$.

$\square$

A characterization of the conditions related to the boundary regions occurring in Theorem 3.3 and Theorem 3.4 is given in Lemma 3.5.

Lemma 3.5.[20] *Let* $\mathcal{A}$ *be the class of all information systems with the set of objects including non-empty sets* X *and* Y. *The following conditions are equivalent for arbitrary* $\mathbb{A} = (U, A) \in \mathcal{A}$:

(i) $Bd_A(\mathbb{Y}, \mathbb{X}) = \emptyset$ for any $\mathbb{X} \supseteq \mathbb{Y} \supseteq \{X \cap -Y, -X \cap Y\}$, where $\mathbb{X} = \{X \cap Y, -X \cap Y, X \cap -Y, -X \cap -Y\}$;

(ii) $\alpha \vee \beta \vee \gamma \vee \delta \vee \epsilon$ holds where

$\alpha := (X \subseteq Y \, or \, Y \subseteq X)$;

$\beta := (X - Y \neq \emptyset \, and \, Y - X \neq \emptyset \, and \, X \cup Y = U \, and \, X \cap Y = \emptyset \, and \, Bd_A(\{X \cap -Y, -X \cap Y\}, \mathbb{X}) = \emptyset)$;

$\gamma := (X - Y \neq \emptyset \, and \, Y - X \neq \emptyset \, and \, X \cup Y = U \, and \, X \cap Y \neq \emptyset \, and \, Bd_A(\{X \cap -Y, -X \cap Y\}, \mathbb{X}) = \emptyset \, and \, Bd_A(\{X \cap -Y, -X \cap Y, X \cap Y\}, \mathbb{X}) = \emptyset)$;

$\delta := (X - Y \neq \emptyset \, and \, Y - X \neq \emptyset \, and \, X \cup Y \neq U \, and \, X \cap Y = \emptyset \, and \, Bd_A(\{X \cap -Y, -X \cap Y\}, \mathbb{X}) = \emptyset \, and \, Bd_A(\{X \cap -Y, -X \cap Y, -X \cap -Y\}, \mathbb{X}) = \emptyset)$;

$\epsilon := (X - Y \neq \emptyset \, and \, Y - X \neq \emptyset \, and \, X \cup Y \neq U \, and \, X \cap Y \neq \emptyset \, and \, Bd_A(\{X \cap -Y, -X \cap Y\}, \mathbb{X}) = \emptyset \, and \, Bd_A(\{X \cap -Y, -X \cap Y, -X \cap -Y\}, \mathbb{X}) = \emptyset \, and \, Bd_A(\{X \cap -Y, -X \cap Y, X \cap Y\}, \mathbb{X}) = \emptyset \, and \, Bd_A(\{X \cap -Y, -X \cap Y, X \cap Y, -X \cap -Y\}, \mathbb{X}) = \emptyset)$.

Let us remark that only when the condition α holds, i.e. when $X \subseteq Y$ or $Y \subseteq X$, the corresponding condition is independent from the properties of boundary regions.

The presented below Theorems 3.6 and Theorem 3.7 show that our approach is intensional with respect to the set of all information systems (with a universe including sets X and Y), namely it is not possible, in general, to compute the rm-function values $\mu_{X \cup Y}^A(x)$ and $\mu_{X \cap Y}^A(x)$ from the values $\mu_X^A(x)$ and $\mu_Y^A(x)$ when information about A is not accessible.

Theorem 3.6.[20] There is no function

$$F : [0,1] \times [0,1] \rightarrow [0,1]$$

such that for any information system $A = (U, A)$ and any finite sets X and Y $(X, Y \subseteq U)$ the following equality holds:

$$\mu_{X \cup Y}^A(x) = F(\mu_X^A(x), \mu_Y^A(x)) \text{ for any } x \in U.$$

$\square$

Theorem 3.7.[20] There is no function

$$F : [0,1] \times [0,1] \rightarrow [0,1]$$

such that for any information system $A = (U, A)$ and any finite sets X and Y $(X, Y \subseteq U)$ the following equality holds:

$$\mu_{X \cap Y}^A(x) = F(\mu_X^A(x), \mu_Y^A(x)) \text{ for any } x \in U.$$

$\square$

In [20] we presented an algorithm for computing the rm-function values $\mu_X^A(x)$ for $x \in X$, where X is any set generated by the set theoretical operations $\cup, \cap, -$ from a given family of finite sets. The algorithm for computing values of rm-functions is based on the properties of the atomic components of the sets. The rm-functions are computable and their values can be derived without the help of an expert.

4 Properties of inference rules with certainty coefficients

First we show how to estimate the certainty of the modus ponens rule conclusion on the basis of certainty coefficients of the premises of that rule. We assume that certainty factors are expressed by means of the membership functions.

We assume that $\mathbb{A}$ is an information system and $\alpha, \beta, \gamma \in \mathbb{F}(A, V)$. By $\mu(\alpha, \cdot)$ we denote the rough membership function $\mu_X^{\mathbb{A}}$ where $X = \alpha_{\mathbb{A}}$.

Proposition 4.1. *Let $\mathbb{A}$ be an information system and let $\alpha, \beta, \gamma \in \mathbb{F}(A, V)$. Then the following equality holds:*

$$\mu(\beta, x) = \mu(\alpha, x) + \mu(\alpha \rightarrow \beta, x) - 1 + \mu(\neg \alpha \wedge \beta, x)$$

$\square$

From Proposition 4.1 we have the following inequalities:

$$\mu(\alpha \rightarrow \beta, x) + \mu(\alpha, x) - 1 \leq \mu(\beta, x) \leq \mu(\alpha \rightarrow \beta, x)$$

allowing us estimate the value of the membership function for the conclusion of the modus ponens rule on the basis of the values of the membership functions for premises of that rule. One can see that in some sense it is not possible to improve the above inequality. Indeed, we obtain the equality instead of the inequality on the right hand side when $(\neg \alpha)_{\mathbb{A}} \subseteq \beta_{\mathbb{A}}$ and we have the equality instead of the inequality on the left hand side when $(\beta)_{\mathbb{A}} \subseteq \alpha_{\mathbb{A}}$. Let us observe that the error of the truth degree estimation for β on x is non greater than $1 - \mu(\alpha, x)$.

One can also calculate that the following fact holds:

Proposition 4.2. *Let $\mathbb{A}$ be an information system and let $\alpha, \beta, \gamma \in \mathbb{F}(A, V)$. If $\mu(\alpha, x) \in [a.A]$ and $\mu(\alpha \rightarrow \beta, x) \in [b, B]$ then $\mu(\beta, x) \in [c, C]$, where $c = max(a + b - 1, 0)$ and $C = B$.* $\square$

Let us now consider another rule of inference introduced in [10] and related to the so called similization transmutation. We show that the rule presented in [10] is only asymptotically true. To show this we introduce a definition of the similarity relation in a given context. Let $\mathbb{A} = (U, A)$ be an information system and let $a, b, c \in A$ and $\epsilon > 0$. Assume also that $V_a = \{v_a^1, \ldots, v_a^k\}$, $V_b = \{v_b^1, \ldots, v_b^k\}$, $V_c = \{v_c^1, \ldots, v_c^k\}$. The attributes a, b are ϵ-similar in the context c in $\mathbb{A}$, symbolically $aSIM_\epsilon(\mathbb{A})b$ in $CTX(c)$, iff for any i $(1 \leq i \leq k)$ and $v \in V_c$ the following inequality holds:

$$|\{x \in U : a(x) = v_a^i \& c(x) = v\} \div \{x \in U : b(x) = v_b^i \& c(x) = v\}| \leq \epsilon|U|$$

If α and β are formulas over A and V then we write

$$\alpha \rightarrow_{A,k} \beta$$

where $k \in [0, 1]$ iff the following inequality holds:

$$|\alpha_{\mathbb{A}} \cap \beta_{\mathbb{A}}| \geq k|\alpha_{\mathbb{A}}|$$

Some properties of this kind of partial dependencies are given in [25].

The following theorem establishing the asymptotical truth of the inference rule based on the similization transmutation holds:

Theorem 4.3. *Let* $\mathbb{A} = (U, A)$ *be an information system and let* $a, b, c, d \in A$ *with* $V_a = \{v_a^1, \ldots, v_a^k\}$, $V_b = \{v_b^1, \ldots, v_b^k\}$, $V_c = \{v_c^1, \ldots, v_c^k\}$, $V_d = \{v_d^1, \ldots, v_d^k\}$. *For arbitrary* $k' \in (0, 1)$ *there exist* $\epsilon > 0$ *and* $k \in [0, 1]$ *such that the following implication holds:*

if $(aSIM_\epsilon(\mathbb{A})b$ in $CTX(c))$&
$(a = v_a^i \to_{\mathbb{A}} d = v_d^i)$&
$(c = v_c^i \to_{\mathbb{A},k} d = v_d^i)$ then $(b = v_b^i \to_{\mathbb{A},k'} d = v_d^i)$

□

One can also apply the rough set approach for analysis of properties of inference rules with certainty coefficients expressed by belief functions.

5 Decision rules for inconsistent decision tables

The classification problems are central for the rough set approach [14] as well as for the evidence theoretic approach [17].

In evidence theory [17] the information about sets creating a given partition is embedded directly in some numerical functions called the basic probability assignment, belief function and plausibility function whereas in the case of the rough set approach the information about classified sets and objects is included in a decision table. The evidence theory approach is based on the idea of placing a number from the interval $[0, 1]$, given, e.g. by an expert, to indicate a degree of belief for a given proposition on the basis of a given evidence.

It is possible to compute the basic functions of evidence theory from a given decision table [25]. First we recall some basic notions of evidence theory [17].

A frame *of discernment* Θ is a finite non-empty set.

The basic probability assignment (bpa) on Θ is any function $m : \mathbb{P}(\Theta) \to \mathbb{R}_+$, where $\mathbb{R}_+$ is the set of non-negative reals, satisfying the following two conditions:

$$m(\emptyset) = 0 \text{ and } \sum_{\Delta \subseteq \Theta} m(\Delta) = 1$$

For a given bpa m two functions are defined.

A function $Bel : \mathbb{P}(\Theta) \to \mathbb{R}_+$ is called *the belief function over* Θ (generated by m) iff for any $\theta \subseteq \Theta$

$$Bel(\theta) = \sum_{\Delta \subseteq \theta} m(\Delta)$$

A function $Pl : \mathbb{P}(\Theta) \to \mathbb{R}_+$ is called *the plausibility function over* Θ (generated by m) iff for any $\theta \subseteq \Theta$

$$Pl(\theta) = \sum_{\Delta \cap \theta \neq \emptyset} m(\Delta)$$

A function $Q : \mathbb{P}(\Theta) \to \mathbb{R}_+$ is called *the commonality function* iff for any $\theta \subseteq \Theta$

$$Q(\theta) = \sum_{\theta \subseteq \Delta} m(\Delta)$$

The plausibility function Pl is definable by the belief function, namely: $Pl(\theta) = 1 - Bel(\Theta - \theta)$ for $\theta \subseteq \Theta$.

Now we will describe how decision tables determine these functions.

A decision d in the decision table $\mathbb{A} = (U, A \cup \{d\})$ defines set $\Theta_\mathbb{A} = \{1, \ldots, r(d)\}$ called the *frame of discernment defined by d in $\mathbb{A}$*. We say that the frame of discernment Θ is compatible with $\mathbb{A}$ if $r(d) = |\Theta|$. In the sequel to simplify notation we assume $\Theta = V_d = \Theta_\mathbb{A} = \{1, \ldots, k\}$, where $k = r(d)$ for considered decision tables and frames of discernment.

The classification of objects can be based on the following observation [25]:

Proposition 5.1. *Let $\mathbb{A} = (U, A \cup \{d\})$ be a decision table. The family of all non-empty sets from*

$$\{\underline{A}X_1, \ldots, \underline{A}X_{r(d)}\} \cup \{Bd_\mathbb{A}(\theta) : \theta \subseteq \Theta_\mathbb{A} \text{ and } |\theta| > 1\}$$

(where $Bd_\mathbb{A}(\theta) = \bigcap_{i \in \theta} BN_A(X_i) \cap \bigcap_{i \notin \theta} -BN_A(X_i)$) is a partition of the universe U. Moreover the following equality holds:

$$\bigcup_{i \in \theta} \underline{A}X_i \cup \bigcup_{\Delta \subseteq \theta, |\Delta| > 1} Bd_\mathbb{A}(\Delta) = \underline{A}\bigcup_{i \in \theta} X_i \text{ for } \theta \subseteq \Theta_\mathbb{A} \text{ with } |\theta| > 1.$$

$\square$

By $APP\_CLASS_\mathbb{A}(d)$ we denote the family:

$$\{\underline{A}X_1, \ldots, \underline{A}X_{r(d)}\} \cup \{Bd_\mathbb{A}(\theta) : \theta \subseteq \Theta_\mathbb{A} \text{ and } |\theta| > 1\}$$

There is a natural correspondence between subsets of $\Theta_\mathbb{A}$ and elements of $APP\_CLASS_\mathbb{A}(d)$, which can be expressed by the following function:

$$F_\mathbb{A}(\theta) = \begin{cases} \underline{A}X_i & \text{if } \theta = \{i\} \text{ for some } i \ (1 \leq i \leq r(d)) \\ \emptyset & \text{if } \theta = \emptyset \\ Bd_\mathbb{A}(\theta) & \text{if } |\theta| > 1 \end{cases}$$

It is easy to observe that the generalized decision ∂_A has the following property: $\partial_A(x)$ is the unique subset θ of Θ such that $x \in F_\mathbb{A}(\theta)$ for any $x \in U$. The function $\partial_\mathbb{A}$ can be treated as a new decision attribute (defined by conditions in $\mathbb{A}$) approximating the decision d.

The function $m_\mathbb{A} : \mathbb{P}(\Theta) \to \mathbb{R}_+$, called the *standard basic probability assignment of $\mathbb{A}$* is defined by

$$m_\mathbb{A}(\theta) = \frac{|F_\mathbb{A}(\theta)|}{|U|} \text{ , for any } \theta \subseteq \Theta.$$

Proposition 5.2. [25] *The function $m_\mathbb{A}$ defined above is a basic probability assignment (in the sense of evidence theory).* $\square$

The *belief function $Bel_\mathbb{A}$ of $\mathbb{A}$* is defined by

$$Bel_\mathbb{A}(\theta) = \sum_{\Delta \subseteq \theta} m_\mathbb{A}(\Delta)$$

where $\theta \subseteq \Theta$ and m_A is the standard probability assignment of A.

The interpretation of the above definition is given by the following theorem [25]:

Theorem 5.3. *Let* $A = (U, A \cup \{d\})$ *be a decision table. For arbitrary* $\theta \subseteq \Theta$ *the following equality holds:*

$$Bel_A(\theta) = \frac{|\underline{A}\bigcup_{i \in \theta} X_i|}{|U|}$$

The belief function Bel_A *is Bayesian iff all decision classes of* A *are definable by the set* A *of conditions. In particular, the belief function* $Bel_{A'}$ *where* $A' = (U, A \cup \{\partial_A\})$, *is Bayesian.*

□

Corollary 5.4. *Let* $A = (U, A \cup \{d\})$ *be a decision table. For arbitrary* $\theta \subseteq \Theta$ *the following equality holds:*

$$Pl_A(\theta) = \frac{|\overline{A}\bigcup_{i \in \theta} X_i|}{|U|}$$

□

The commonality function of A *is defined by*

$$Q_A(\theta) = \sum_{\Delta \subseteq \theta} m_A(\Delta)$$

where $\theta \subseteq \Theta$.

The Dempster-Shafer rule of combination allows to compute a new belief function from the combined evidence of several belief functions over the same frame of discernment if they are based on entirely distinct (independent) sources of evidence. The general formulation is due to Dempster [3].

The presented below [25] results show that for the belief functions based on standard basic probability assignment it is possible to formulate precisely the meaning of "independent sources of information" and on that basis to prove the compatibility of our approach with the Dempster-Shafer combination rule.

Let Θ be a frame of discernment compatible with the decision tables

$$A_1 = (U_1, A_1 \cup \{d_1\}) \quad \text{and} \quad A_2 = (U_2, A_2 \cup \{d_2\}).$$

The decision table $A = (U, A \cup \{d\})$ is called a Θ-independent product of decision tables A_1 and A_2 iff the following conditions hold:

1. $U = U_1 \times U_2 - U_1 \otimes U_2$,
   where $U_1 \otimes U_2 = \{(s_1, s_2) : U_1 \times U_2 : \partial_{A_1}(s) \cap \partial_{A_2}(s) = \emptyset\}$;

2. $d(s_1, s_2) = \partial_{A_1}(s) \cap \partial_{A_2}(s)$ for any $(s_1, s_2) \in U$;

3. $A = A_1 \dot\cup A_2$ (i.e. A is the disjoint union of A_1 and A_2 defined by $A_1 \times \{1\} \cup A_2 \times \{2\}$).

4. $(a, i)(s_1, s_2) = a(s_i)$ for $(a, i) \in A$, $i = 1, 2$ and $(s_1, s_2) \in U$

The independent product of decision tables A_1, A_2 is denoted by $A_1 \odot A_2$. The decision in $A_1 \odot A_2$ has values in $\mathbb{P}(\Theta)$. We take $\Theta_o = \mathbb{P}(\Theta)$ as the frame of discernment for $A_1 \odot A_2$ and we consider the standard basic probability assignment

$$m_{A_1 \odot A_2} : \mathbb{P}(\Theta_o) \longrightarrow \mathbb{R}_+ .$$

We have the following property:

$$m_{A_1 \odot A_2}(\Delta) = 0 \text{ if } (|\Delta| > 1 \text{ and } \Delta \subseteq \Theta_o) \text{ or } \Delta = \{\emptyset\} ;$$

so the belief function corresponding to $m_{A_1 \odot A_2}$ is Bayesian.

Hence the classification determined by the decision d in $A_1 \odot A_2$ is definable by conditions of $A_1 \odot A_2$.

The theorem formulated below gives the rule for computing the values

$$m_{A_1 \odot A_2}(\Delta) \text{ for } |\Delta| = 1 \text{ and } \Delta \subseteq \Theta_o, \Delta \neq \{\emptyset\} .$$

Theorem 5.5. [25] *Let $A_1 \odot A_2$ be a Θ-independent product of decision tables A_1 and A_2. Then for every $\emptyset \neq \theta \subseteq \Theta$ we have the following equality, called Dempster's combination rule:*

$$m_{A_1 \odot A_2}(\{\theta\}) = \frac{\displaystyle\sum_{\theta_1 \cap \theta_2 = \theta} m_{A_1}(\theta_1) m_{A_2}(\theta_2)}{1 - \displaystyle\sum_{\theta_1 \cap \theta_2 = \emptyset} m_{A_1}(\theta_1) m_{A_2}(\theta_2)}$$

□

Let us consider again a frame of discernment Θ compatible with decision tables

$$A_1 = (U_1, A_1 \cup \{d_1\}) \text{ and } A_2 = (U_2, A_2 \cup \{d_2\})$$

and Θ-independent product $A_1 \odot A_2 = (U, A \cup \{d\})$ of decision tables A_1 and A_2. Any decision table $A = (U, A \cup \{d^*\})$ satisfying the following conditions:

1. $\bigcup_{s \in U} d(s) = \bigcup_{s \in U} \{d^*(s)\}$ and

2. $\{d^*(s) : s \in x\} = \theta$ for any equivalence class x of the indiscernibility relation $IND_A(A)$ included in $\partial_{A_1 \odot A_2}^{-1}(\{\theta\})$ where $\theta \subseteq \Theta$;

is called the realization of $A_1 \odot A_2$ and is denoted by $d^*[A_1 \odot A_2]$.

We have the following property :

Corollary 5.6. [25] *Let $d^*[A_1 \odot A_2]$ be a realization of $A_1 \odot A_2$. Then for any $\theta \subseteq \Theta$ the following equality holds:*

$$m_{A_1 \odot A_2}(\{\theta\}) = m_{d^*[A_1 \odot A_2]}(\theta)$$

□

Corollary 5.7. [25] *Let $A_1 \odot A_2$ be a Θ-independent product of decision tables A_1 and A_2 and let $d^*[A_1 \odot A_2]$ be an arbitrary realization of $A_1 \odot A_2$. Then for* *every $\emptyset \neq \theta \subseteq \Theta$ we have the following equality, called Dempster's combination rule:*

$$m_{d^*[\mathbb{A}_1 \odot \mathbb{A}_2]}(\theta) = \frac{\displaystyle\sum_{\theta_1 \cap \theta_2 = \theta} m_{\mathbb{A}_1}(\theta_1) m_{\mathbb{A}_2}(\theta_2)}{1 - \displaystyle\sum_{\theta_1 \cap \theta_2 = \emptyset} m_{\mathbb{A}_1}(\theta_1) m_{\mathbb{A}_2}(\theta_2)}$$

□

Let us now consider inconsistent decision tables. One can transform an arbitrary inconsistent decision table $\mathbb{A} = (U, A \cup \{d\})$ into a consistent decision table $\mathbb{A}_\partial = (U, A \cup \{\partial_A\})$ where $\partial_A : U \to \mathbb{P}(\Theta)$ is the generalized decision of $\mathbb{A}$ defined in Section 2 and $\Theta = \{1, \ldots, r(d)\}$. It is easy to see that $\mathbb{A}_\partial$ is a consistent decision table. Hence one can apply to $\mathbb{A}_\partial$ the methods presented in Section 2 to obtain for any $\theta \subseteq \Theta$ with $(\partial_A = \theta)_{\mathbb{A}_\partial} \neq \emptyset$ the decision rules of the form:

$$\alpha_\theta \Rightarrow \partial_A = \theta$$

We have the following proposition relating these rules to the standard basic probability assignment of $\mathbb{A}$:

Proposition 5.8. *If $\alpha_\theta \Rightarrow \partial_A = \theta$ is a decision rule obtained by applying to $\mathbb{A}_\partial$ any method presented in Section 2 and $(\partial_A = \theta)_{\mathbb{A}_\partial} \neq \emptyset$ then*

(i) $\{x \in U : \partial_A(x) = \theta\} = (\alpha_\theta)_{\mathbb{A}} = (\partial_A = \theta)_{\mathbb{A}_\partial}$

(ii) $m_{\mathbb{A}}(\theta) = \dfrac{|\{x \in U : \partial_A(x) = \theta\}|}{|U|}$

□

In a similar way one can get rules related to the lower approximation of the union of decision classes X_i where $i \in \theta$. The cardinality of this set is related to the value $Bel_{\mathbb{A}}(\theta)$. It is enough to construct a decision table

$$\mathbb{B}_\theta = (U, A \cup \{b_\theta\})$$

where $b_\theta(x) = 1$ if $\partial_A(x) \subseteq \theta$ and $b_\theta(x) = 0$, otherwise.
It is easy to observe that $\mathbb{B}_\theta$ is a consistent decision table.

Proposition 5.9 *If $\beta_\theta \Rightarrow b_\theta = 1$ is a decision rule obtained by applying to $\mathbb{B}_\theta$ any method presented in Section 2 and $(b_\theta = 1)_{\mathbb{B}_\theta} \neq \emptyset$ then*

(i) $\{x \in U : \partial_A(x) \subseteq \theta\} = (\beta_\theta)_{\mathbb{A}} = (b_\theta = 1)_{\mathbb{B}_\theta}$

(ii) $Bel_{\mathbb{A}}(\theta) = \dfrac{|\{x \in U : \partial_A(x) \subseteq \theta\}|}{|U|}$

□

In a similar way one can get a rule related to the upper approximation of the union of decision classes X_i where $i \in \theta$. The cardinality of this set is related to the value $Pl_{\mathbb{A}}(\theta)$. It is enough to construct a decision table

$$\mathbb{P}_\theta = (U, A \cup \{p_\theta\})$$

where $p_\theta(x) = 1$ if $\partial_A(x) \cap \theta \neq \emptyset$ and $p_\theta(x) = 0$, otherwise.
It is easy to observe that $\mathbb{P}_\theta$ is a consistent decision table.

Proposition 5.10 *If $\gamma_\theta \Rightarrow p_\theta = 1$ is a decision rule obtained by applying to $\mathbb{P}_\theta$ any method presented in Section 2 and $(p_\theta = 1)_{\mathbb{P}_\theta} \neq \emptyset$ then*

$(i) \quad \{x \in U : \partial_A(x) \cap \theta \neq \emptyset\} = (\gamma_\theta)_A = (p_\theta = 1)_P,$

$(ii) \quad Pl_A(\theta) = \dfrac{|\{x \in U : \partial_A(x) \cap \theta \neq \emptyset\}|}{|U|}$

$\square$

One can apply the same method for the generation of decision rules related to the commonality function.

Our method of decision rules synthesis is based on application of boolean reasoning [1] to boolean functions built from discernibility matrices and their modifications. One can observe that this method can be applied for synthesis of any decision rule corresponding to a given decision table $A = (U, A \cup \{d\})$ if this rule describes a decision class definable by conditions of A (see, e.g [35]).

Conclusions

There are some other important problems strongly related to management of uncertainty which we shall investigate in our next paper. Among them the most interesting seem to be the applications of rough sets to data filtering and compression [29], [15]. We also would like to study the relationships of rough sets with random sets and chaos theory.

References

[1] Brown EM. Boolean Reasoning. Kluwer,Dordrecht, 1990

[2] Bhatnager RK, Kanal LN. Handling uncertain information: a review of numeric and non-numeric methods. In: Kanal LN, Lemmer JF (eds) Uncertainty in Artificial Intelligence. North-Holland, Amsterdam, 1986

[3] Dempster AD. Upper and lower probabilities induced by multivalued mapping. Annals of Mathematical Statistics 1967; 38:325–339

[4] Dubois D, Prade H. Fuzzy sets and systems: theory and applications. Academic Press, 1980

[5] Dubois D, Prade H. Combination and propagation of uncertainty with belief functions - a reexamination. Proc of the 9th IJCAI'85 Conference, Los Angeles, CA, 1985, pp 111–113

[6] Fagin R, Halpern JY. Reasoning about knowledge and probability. In: Proc of the 2nd Conf on Theoretical Aspects of Reasoning about Knowledge, Morgan-Kaufmann, San Mateo, 1988, pp 277–293

[7] Grzymala-Busse JW. Managing uncertainty in expert systems. Morgan Kaufmann, San Mateo, 1991

[8] Kodratoff Y, Michalski R. Machine learning: an artificial intelligence approach. Morgan Kaufmann, San Mateo, 1990

[9] Kruse R, Schwecke E, Heinsohn J. Uncertainty and vagueness in knowledge based systems: numerical methods. Springer-Verlag, Berlin, Heidelberg, 1991

[10] Michalski R. Inferential theory of learning: developing foundations for multistrategy learning. Reports Machine Learning and Inference Laboratory ML192-3, George Mason University, 1993, pp 1–42

[11] Pawlak A. Rough sets. Basic notions. Report no 431, Institute of Computer Science, Polish Academy of Sciences, 1981. Also in Int'l Journal of Computer and Information Sciences 1982; 11:344–356

[12] Pawlak Z, Skowron A. Rough membership functions. In: Fedrizzi M, Kacprzyk J, Yager RR (eds) Advances in the Dempster-Shafer Theory of Evidence, John Wiley and Sons, New York (to appear)

[13] Pawlak Z, Skowron A. A rough set approach for decision rules generation. ICS Research Report 23/93, Warsaw University of Technology. Proc of the IJCAI'93 Workshop The Management of Uncertainty in AI, France, 1993

[14] Pawlak Z. Rough sets: theoretical aspects of reasoning about data. Kluwer, Dordrecht, 1991

[15] Polkowski L, Skowron A. Analytical morphology (in preparation)

[16] Shachter RD, Levitt TS, Kanal LN, Lemmer JF. Uncertainty in artificial intelligence. Machine Intelligence and Pattern Recognition, 9, North Holland, Amsterdam, 1990

[17] Shafer G. Mathematical theory of evidence. Princeton University Press, 1976

[18] Shafer G. Constructive probability. Synthese 1981; 48:1–60

[19] Shafer G. Probability judgment in artificial intelligence. In: Kanal LN, Lemmer JF (eds) Uncertainty in Artificial Intelligence. North Holland, Amsterdam, 1986, pp 127–135

[20] Shafer G, Pearl J. Readings in uncertain reasoning. Morgan Kaufmann, San Mateo, 1990

[21] Skowron A. The evidence theory and decision tables. Bulletin of the European Association for Theoretical Computer Science 1989; 39:199–204

[22] Skowron A. The rough sets theory and evidence theory. Fundamenta Informaticae 1990; 13:245–262

[23] Skowron A. The rough set theory as a basis for the evidence theory. ICS Research Report 2/91, Warsaw University of Technology, 1991, pp 1–53

[24] Skowron A, Grzymala-Busse JW. From the rough set theory to the evidence theory. ICS Report 8/91, Warsaw University of Technology, 1991, pp 1–49

[25] Skowron A, Grzymala-Busse JW. From rough set theory to evidence theory. In: Fedrizzi M, Kacprzyk J, Yager RR (eds) Advances in the Dempster-Shafer theory of evidence. John Wiley and Sons, New York, to appear

[26] Skowron A, Rauszer C. The discernibility matrices and functions in information systems. In: Slowiński R (ed) Decision support by experience-applications of the rough sets theory. Kluwer, Dordrecht, 1992, pp 331-362

[27] Skowron A. Boolean reasoning for decision rules generation. In: Komorowski J, Ras Z (eds) Proc of the 7th Int'l Symposium (ISMIS'93), Trondheim, Norway. Springer-Verlag, 1993, pp 295-305 (Lecture notes in artificial intelligence no 689)

[28] Skowron A. A synthesis of decision rules: applications of discernibility matrices. Proc of the Conf. Intelligent Information Systems, Augustow, June 7-11, 1993

[29] Skowron A. Extracting laws from decision tables-A rough set approach. (invited lecture) Proc of the Int'l Workshop on Rough Sets and Knowledge Discovery (RSDK'93), Banff, Canada, 1993, pp 101-105

[30] Skowron A, Suraj Z. A rough set approach to the real-time state identification. EATCS Bulletin of the European Association for Theoretical Computer Science, 1993; 50:264-275

[31] Smets P. Belief functions. In: Smets P, Mamdami EH, Dubois D, Prade H (eds) Non-standard logics for automated reasoning. Academic Press, London, 1988, pp 253-286

[32] Yager RR. On the Dempster-Shafer framework and new combination rules. Info Sci 1987; 41:93-137

[33] Zadeh LA. Fuzzy sets. Information and Control 1965; 8:338-353

[34] Zadeh LA. A simple view of the Dempster-Shafer theory of evidence and its implication for the rule of combination. AI Magazine, 1986; 7:85-90, 1986

[35] Ziarko W. Analysis of uncertain information in the framework of variable precision rough set model. In: Int'l workshop rough sets: State of the art and perspectives. Poznan-Kiekrz, Poland. Extended Abstracts. 1992, pp 74-77

Rough Sets and Data Dependencies

Debby Keen[*]   Arcot Rajasekar[†]

Department of Computer Science

University of Kentucky

{keen,sekar}@ms.uky.edu

1   Introduction

Many methods have been used to express the relationships between different pieces of data. In the beginning, all relationships were assumed to be rigid and precise. Objects were either in a set or they were not. All data followed a rule or was incorrect. Traditional database systems are well-suited for storing knowledge explicitly and for deducing definite information from the stored knowledge through explicitly defined rules.

This is efficient use of the definite data that exists, but it does not capture the irregularities of the real world. Realistic data may not follow any rules precisely, data may be missing, data may be vague or ambiguous or just incorrect. We can apply some techniques from artificial intelligence to handle these problem areas. Similarity-based and statistical-based measures can provide information that is unavailable using only static rules. Classification techniques that were developed for machine learning may be applied to databases.

Pawlak and Marek [10, 15] first described rough sets in the early 80's. Rough sets have been considered for use in machine learning[11], logic [8] and non-monotonic reasoning [18], as a mathematical theory for information systems [14, 9, 13], expert systems [12], and data analysis [12].

Data dependencies used in conjunction with databases subdivide the data into subsets, sometimes into partitions. These partitions can be viewed as rough sets in a sense. The mathematical expression of rough sets can be useful as a theory to express interactions between partitions of tuples in a database. In this paper we explore this interconnection between rough sets and dependencies in relational databases.

2   Data dependencies

Here we define and review some of the dependencies that can be used in databases. The simplest dependencies are those that assume the relationship holds for all data under consideration, that there are no exceptions to the rule. In the database area, this kind of relationship is expressed by functional dependencies. They are very restrictive.

[*]Research partly supported by a fellowship from the Pew Foundation and a grant from Pikeville College

[†]Research partly supported by NSF Grant CCR-9110721

Partitioning dependencies loosen the requirements slightly. They allow one X-value to determine more than one Y-value. They separate the data into "congruent" groups. But partitioning dependencies force the groups to be disjoint.

Inductive dependencies are the least restrictive of these dependencies. They allow the data to be loosely grouped, by allowing the groups to overlap in some ways.

One question that dependencies try to answer is what data is relevant to the user's query. Functional dependencies assume that only one tuple has the information required, or else the data is not in the database. Partitioning dependencies allow other tuples that have a matching value to be considered relevant, the tuples that are in the same partition as the tuple in question. Inductive dependencies go beyond that and allow tuples from other subsets to be considered relevant, as long as they have some connection to the subset in question.

The reader is referred to [17] for details on the database terminology used in the paper. We use the usual meanings of databases, relations, schemas, and attributes.

2.1 Functional dependencies

Functional dependencies are used for many purposes. They are used to design database schemas, ensuring that the data is stored with a minimal number of redundancies. They are used to validate new data being input to the system; if the new data violates the dependency, it is rejected or corrected. Functional dependencies can also be used to infer information when data is missing, to replace null values [1, 2, 4, 6, 17, 3].

A simple definition of a functional dependency from X to Y, written as $X \to Y$, is that each X value is associated with exactly one Y value. If two tuples have matching X-values their Y-values should also be the same.

Functional dependencies have been extended in terms of numeric dependencies where an X-value is restricted to associating with a fixed number of Y-values [5].

2.2 Partitioning dependencies

Consider a relationship that is not a function, yet still very structured. The X-values do not functionally determine Y-values; one X-value will be associated with several Y-values (not a fixed number of values), but no two X-values are associated with the same Y-value. That is, the relationship forms disjoint partitions of the Y-values. The X-values can be said to group the Y-values together into groups that are "congruent" according to X. A formal definition of a partitioning dependency is as follows:

Definition 1 *Let r be a relation under schema $R(A_1, A_2, \ldots, A_n)$. Let X and Y be subsets of $R(A_1, A_2, \ldots, A_n)$.*
Define $Q = \{q_i \mid \exists t \in R \text{ such that } t[X] = q_i\}$ (Q is the set of all X values that occur in R) and $p_i = \{t[Y] \mid t \in R, t[x] = q_i, q_i \in Q\}$.
$X \nrightarrow Y$ is a partitioning dependency on relation $\mathbf{R}$ if $\forall_{i,j} i \neq j \to p_i \cap p_j = \emptyset$.
X is the "partitioning" attribute, and Y is the "partitioned" attribute.

Note: the term *partitioning dependency* has been used in other contexts, e.g., with regard to nesting relations. We trust there will be no confusion in our use of the term as we define it here.

Example 1 *This table supports a partitioning dependency, $X \twoheadrightarrow Y$.*

X	a	a	a	b	b	b
Y	1	2	4	3	7	8
Z	35	99	79	42	99	32

The partitions induced by X on Y are $\{1, 2, 4\}$ and $\{3, 7, 8\}$. Note that X does not partition Z.

Partitioning dependencies are closely related to functional dependencies. Essentially they are the 'reverse' or converse of a functional dependency.

Theorem 1 *Let A and B be attributes or sets of attributes in relation R. Then $A \twoheadrightarrow B$ iff $B \to A$.*

Discussion: Since the values of A partition the values of B, each value for B is placed in a subset corresponding to one value of A. These subsets are disjoint, by the definition of a partitioning dependency. So each value of B uniquely identifies one value of A. This is the definition of a functional dependency $B \to A$.

Because of the functional dependency, each B-value has exactly one A-value associated with it. There may be several B-values associated with the same A-value, but no B-value will be associated with more than one A-value.

This means that one A-value will have one or more B-values associated with it, a subset of B-values which is a partition because one B-value will never appear in more than one of the subsets. And since each B-value has exactly one A-value, every B-value will appear in *some* subset.

This set of subsets is a partitioning of the B-values by A. or $A \twoheadrightarrow B$.

The proof is in two parts. First part: If $A \twoheadrightarrow B$ then $B \to A$.

Let $Q = \{a| \exists t \in R, t[A] = a\}$ and let partitions generated by the partitioning dependency be $p_i = \{t[B]| \; t[A] \in q_i (q_i \in Q)\}$. The p_i's are disjoint, by the definition of a partitioning dependency. Therefore any value of B is placed in exactly one p_i. Each p_i is associated with one element from Q, q_i, and each element of Q is a value of A, so each p_i is associated with one value of A. Thus, for any B-value, $b_j \in p_i$ associates b_j with q_i, so there is a functional relationship between B and A, or $B \to A$.

Second part: If $B \to A$ then $A \twoheadrightarrow B$.

Let $Q = \{b| \exists t \in R, t[B] = b\}$ and let the partitions generated by the functional dependency be $p_i = \{t[A]| \; t[b] \in q_i (q_i \in Q)\}$. Each p_i is of size one, since each B is associated with exactly one A. It is possible that several p_i's will be equal, will have the same value in them, because different B-values may be associated with the same A-value. If the p_i's that are equal are grouped together, or equivalently, if the b-values that are associated with the same A-value, are grouped together, the groups form partitions because each B-value is associated with exactly one A-value. $M_j = \{b_i| \; p_i = \{a_j\}\}$. M_j's are partitions of B-values and each is associated with an A-value. Thus each A-value is associated with a partition of B-values, or $A \twoheadrightarrow B$.

□

2.3 Inductive dependencies

In concept, inductive dependencies are similar to functional dependencies, but inductive dependencies define approximate relationships, whereas the functional dependencies provide rigid connections[7]. They are "orthogonal" to each other. That is, functional dependencies can be seen as providing data dependency information in a horizontal direction (along the rows of relations) whereas inductive dependencies can be seen as having an additional component in the vertical direction (along the columns of a relation). Intuitively, if a tuple in a relation has an undefined value in a column, then an approximate value can be computed from a *subset of values* present in that column in the relation, from a subset of tuples that are *similar* to the one in question.

Inductive dependencies use inductive knowledge to answer queries. Consider that in the database we have 10 people with *Terry* as their first names of which 8 are female and 2 are male. If we use the database as our repertoire of experience in first names, we can provide an approximate answer that a Terry whose sex is unknown is a female rather than a male. The reasoning behind our approach is similar to the *closed world assumption* [16], but we assume that the world is *inductively closed* as opposed to only *deductively closed*.

Query processing in a (relational) database context has been mainly confined to deducing information that is available in the database. That is, the answers given to queries are supported by available data in the database and are computed using the classical operations of select, project and join. When the query cannot be answered using the above operations the database system returns an empty answer.

But when it is not possible to deduce an answer to a query from a tuple, it would be worthwhile to provide an approximate answer using information which is *similar* to the one from which the query would be answered. Inductive dependencies provides an approximate answer to a query using available related information from the database. This can be illustrated as follows. Consider that someone is checking to see if a particular stock was up or down at today's opening of the market. Assume that the stock information database does not contain the desired information. But there is information regarding other stocks that are "similar" that indicates they are all "down". This data can be used to provide an approximate answer for our original query. It is our contention that the inquirer would be happier with the approximate answer, "the stock you asked about is probably down", rather than with a null answer for the query. We made use of an inductive dependency which can be loosely stated as follows: "The direction of change of a particular stock inductively depends upon the direction of change of the other stocks in the same category." We made use of this inductive dependency to answer the query which otherwise has no derivable answer from the database.

A practical need for inductive dependencies can be justified as follows: even though for some sets of data it is not possible to provide a strict dependency, it may be possible to provide a looser dependency among the data. Such types of information are very often used in statistics and probability theory to provide approximate answers to queries for which there are no precise answers. Inductive dependencies make these notions user-definable and precise. Consider the following relationships for which one cannot write any rigid dependency criterion:

- The salaries of assistant managers with similar experience are similar.

- Similar houses in the same locality cost the same amount.

- A materials research database may have null values for materials that have not been investigated yet. These values may be approximated by comparing the properties to those of known similar materials.

- A family generally shares the same surname, but this is not a true functional dependency, due to remarriages, etc. If a census database included the members of a family but some last names were missing, they could be inferred by using the head of household's last name.

The above 'rules of thumb' are not inflexible dependencies which can be enforced in a database nor are they rules which can be used to provide precise answers from a database. But they are rules which can provide approximate answers which are often sufficient for human uses. Inductive dependencies are unusual in that they are flexible enough to be used in many different areas, from null values to heterogeneous databases, just about anywhere a "heuristic" rule is needed.

Definition 2 *[7]*
Inductive Dependency

Let $\mathbf{R}(A_1, A_2, \ldots, A_n)$ be a relation scheme, and let X be a (possibly null) subset of $\{A_1, A_2, \ldots, A_n\}$ and Y be an element in $\{A_1, A_2, \ldots, A_n\}$ such that Y is not in X. We say $X \hookrightarrow Y$, read "X inductively determines Y" or "Y inductively depends upon X", if whatever relation r is the current value for $\mathbf{R}$, and if r has a set of tuples, r', which agree in the components for all attributes in the set X, then any null (or undefined) value for Y in any tuple in r' can be approximately determined (using an approximation function) from the non-null values of attribute Y in r'. The set of tuples in r' which have non-null values for attribute Y is called an inductive determinant. □

Inductive dependencies are used as follows. Assume that given a value for attributes X one wants to find an approximate value for attribute Y in a relation state r of scheme R. We first make the following assumptions. One, X is a key and two, the Y value is undefined for that X value. The assumption of X being a key is made so that X is non-null and uniquely determines a tuple. (Actually, the assumption that the tuple be uniquely determined can be relaxed, but we retain the assumption to simplify our procedure.) Let t be the tuple given by the value for attribute X. Let $Z \hookrightarrow Y$ be an inductive dependency in R. Let z be the value for attribute Z in tuple t. Again we assume that z is non-null, otherwise we will not be able to apply the inductive criterion. Next, we select all tuples in r which have $Z = z$. This set of tuples, say r', forms the inductive determinant. The Y attribute is next projected and given as input to an approximation function. The value returned by the function provides an approximate answer for the query.

Besides using inductive dependencies for replying to queries, they can be used to do an integrity check when the database is being updated with new data. If the new data does not 'fit' with the existing data, an empty determinant will result. This can give a warning that the entered data is not within "normal" bounds.

Say somebody is entering a salary as $100,000 for a sales-clerk and the induced value for sales-clerks in that store is around $20,000. Then a warning can be given to show that the new value is well beyond the range of norms. Or if a user leaves a field empty, the value calculated by the inductive dependency on similar tuples can be suggested as a possible value. The user may elect to allow the data to be processed as entered anyway, of course.

An important advantage of inductive dependencies is their flexibility. Integrity constraints in relational databases used to check for errors in data entry are normally "static". If the nature of the input data changes, the constraints have to be updated manually and possibly the entire database will have to be rechecked with the new constraint. Inductive dependencies can provide dynamic error checking. A value can be checked against the induced values provided by an inductive dependency. If a value falls out of "normal" bounds, the user could still allow the data to be entered. This data will then be taken into account automatically when the next data is checked. Inductive dependencies are more in tune with the changing context of a fluctuating database.

3 Rough and crisp sets

First we discuss the terminology of rough sets. The definitions are taken from Pawlak [15].

Definition 3 *Let U be a certain set called the* **universe** *and let R be an equivalence relation on U. The pair $A = (U, R)$ is called an approximation space. R is an indiscernibility relation: if $x, y \in U$ and $(x, y) \in R$ then x and y are indistinguishable in $A[15]$.*

Equivalence classes of the relation R will be called elementary sets in A. The empty set is also elementary in every A. Every finite union of elementary sets in A is a composed set. If X is a subset of U, the best upper approximation of X in A, written $\overline{Apr_A(X)}$, is the least composed set in A containing X. The best lower approximation of X in A, written $\underline{Apr_A(X)}$, is the greatest composed set contained in X. [15]

So each elementary set is a set of objects which are indistinguishable as far as A is concerned.

For the next four definitions, let $A = (U, R)$ be an approximation space and let $X, Y \subset U$. [15]

Definition 4 *The sets X, Y are "roughly-bottom equal" in A, in symbols $X \overline{\approx}_A Y$, iff $\underline{Apr_A}(X) = \underline{Apr_A}(Y)$.*

Definition 5 *The sets X, Y are "roughly-top equal" in A, in symbols $X \underline{\sim}_A Y$, iff $\overline{Apr_A}(X) = \overline{Apr_A}(Y)$.*

Definition 6 *The sets X, Y are "roughly equal" in A, in symbols $X \approx_A Y$, iff $X \overline{\approx}_A Y$ and $X \underline{\sim}_A Y$.*

Definition 7 *Equivalence classes of the relation $\approx_A$ $(\overline{\approx}_A, \underline{\sim}_A)$ will be called rough (lower, upper) sets.*

Crisp sets are sets in which the membership function is complete and precise. An element is either in the set or not. These are the sets usually dealt with in set theory. If the upper and lower approximations of a rough set coincide, the set is a *crisp set*. This is also described as a *measurable* set in a later section.

Rough sets have elements about which there is some uncertainty as to whether they are in the rough set or not. Rough sets can be used to express uncertainty in different ways. The lower approximation is the set of objects that are definitely in X; the upper approximation contains objects that *may* be in X. These sets assume that a set may contain several items which are indistinguishable as far as the attributes given. This is usually assumed **not** to be the case with database relations since each relation has no duplicate tuples. It is possible, however, to consider a more restricted view of "indistinguishable", using only some of the attributes given about the objects.

4 Rough sets and dependencies

In this section we define concepts in data dependencies in the terms and terminology of rough sets. First we define the basis for our application of rough set concepts to database systems. Assume that there is a data dependency from X to Y, that is, given a value of X, there are some values of Y connected with that value of X. Let all values of Y connected with one value of X be taken to be "indiscernible" according to X.

Definition 8 I-equivalence
Let t_i and t_j be two tuples from R and let X be an attribute from R's relational schema. t_i and t_j are i-equivalent according to X if their values for the X attribute are equal, written $t_i \doteq_X t_j$. I-equivalence ($\doteq_X$) partitions a relation R into disjoint sets. The definition of $\doteq_{\overline{X}}$ can be given in a similar fashion where $\overline{X}$ is a set of attributes.

Definition 9 *An elementary set is a set of tuples that are all i-equivalent ($\doteq_X$) to each other, where X is a subset of R's attributes. A composed set is any finite union of elementary sets. Note that the elementary sets are disjoint according to the values of the X attribute.*

Definition 10 Cover(S)
Let S be a subset of values in U. The cover(S) is the smallest set of elementary sets that will include all the values given in S. It may be larger than S if the elementary sets include other values also; it may be equal to S, if S is an elementary set or a composed set itself. Cover(S) can also be defined in terms of $\doteq$.

$Cover(S)$ is $\underline{Apr}_X(S)$ unioned with the minimum number of other elementary sets that are needed to include *all* elements of S. The second part of this union may be empty, if S is a composed set, or it may add some of the elementary sets that are *i-equivalent* to elements of S. If an element of S is already in the $Cover(S)$, there is no need to add any elements not in S that are i-equivalent to it.

From Pawlak, the lower approximation of a set, S, is the set of all elementary sets that fit completely inside S. It is the same in database terms. If an X-value occurs in a tuple which has a Y-value in S but the X-value also occurs in a tuple which has a Y-value outside of S, then its elementary set is *not* included in $\overline{Aprx}(S)$.

The upper approximation of a set, S, is the smallest set of elementary sets that can "cover" all of the values in S. In database terms, the upper approximation of S is the smallest set of elementary sets such that $S \cap e_i$ ($e_i \in \overline{Aprx}(S)$) $\neq \emptyset$ and $S \cap (\bigcup_i e_i) = S$. **Cover(S)** $= \overline{Aprx}(S)$.

To express the lower approximation with database concepts, imagine that a set, S, of values is given from a relation R. Let X be an attribute from R. If all tuples with a particular X-value appear in S, then S can be said to contain an "elementary set" as described above. If some tuples having a particular X-value appear in S, and some with the same X-value appear outside of S, then the elementary set is *not* contained in S. This group of sets is called the $Kernel_X(S)$. This set will be no larger than S, and it may be much smaller, even empty.

Definition 11 *If an attribute X exists in relation R, let $Kernel_X(S) = S -$ {values which represent tuples which are $\doteq_X$ with a tuple who is outside of S}*

To find the $Kernel_X$ of S, begin with $Kernel_X(S) = S$.
$\forall valuesv_j \in S$,   if $\exists t_1 \in R$ such that $t_1 \in S$ and also $\exists t_2 \in R$ such that $t_2 \notin S$ and $t_2 \doteq_X t_1$ then remove v_j from $Kernel_X(S)$

This Kernel function performs the same operations as the lower approximation of a set. To belong to either the lower approximation or the kernel, all items which are considered indistinguishable inside set S must not also appear outside of set S. $Kernel_X(S) = \underline{Aprx}(S)$

4.1   Functional dependencies and crisp sets

Theorem 2 *If a functional dependency is given on R, any subset of R would be a crisp set, based on the partitioning induced by the dependency.*

Given a functional dependency, $X \rightarrow Y$, let the subsets of Y-values generated by it be p_i, each associated with an x_i from some tuple in R. $p_i = \{t[Y] \mid t \in R, t[X] = x_i\}$ By the definition of a functional dependency, each x_i has exactly one y_i associated with it, so each p_i should be of size exactly one. Some p_i's may be the same set, since different X-values are allowed to be associated with the same Y-value.

Let S be an arbitrary set of Y-values. $\underline{Aprx}(S)$ is the union of the elementary sets that are contained in S, by definition. By the above discussion, each Y-value in S is, by itself, an elementary set. Thus, the union of the elementary sets in S is the union of the *values* in S, or S itself. So $\underline{Aprx}(S) = S$.

$\overline{Aprx}(S)$ is the smallest union of elementary sets that contains S, by definition. $= \{p_j | y_j \in S and y_j \in p_j\}$ This union would contain all elementary sets whose Y-values appear in S, and no elementary sets whose Y-values did not appear in S, since each elementary set corresponds to one Y-value. Thus the union would have exactly all Y-values that appear in S, or S itself. $\overline{Aprx}(S) = S$.

Therefore S is crisp. Since S is an arbitrary set of Y-values, any subset of R would be a crisp set using a functional dependency.

$\square$

4.2 Partitioning dependencies and crisp sets

Partitioning dependencies generate partition subsets (elementary sets) that are disjoint from each other, since each X-value may have more than one Y-value but each Y-value is associated with *exactly* one X-value.

It is possible for lower approximations and upper approximations to be different in these circumstances, however. If a set, S, of Y-values is given which includes, say, just part of an elementary set, the upper approximation will be the entire elementary set. So the upper approximation is not equal to S, but is larger than S. Therefore the elementary sets formed by partitioning dependencies are not crisp.

Theorem 3 *Let the relation R have the attributes $A = \{A_1, A_2, \ldots, A_n\}$. And let X be a subset of A and $Y = A - X$. Then the partition induced by $\doteq_X$ is the same as the partition induced by the partitioning dependency $X \nrightarrow Y$.*

This proof is by contradiction and is included below.

Assume that it is true that $\mathcal{P}_{\doteq_X}$ (the partitioning generated by $\doteq_X$) is *not* the same as the partition generated by $X \nrightarrow Y$. That means that there is some element in R that falls into different subsets in the two partitionings. Call this tuple t. t must belong to *some* subset in the partitioning dependency partitioning, if it belongs to R. (Call this subset s_i.) This means that it has an X-value that caused it to be placed in that subset, say $t[x]$. The other tuples in the subset, s_i, have the same value of X as t does.

But since the other tuples in s_i do have the same value of X as t, t would be $i - equivalent\, according\, to\, X$ or $\doteq_X$ to all of them. Thus the $\doteq_X$ operator would place t in s_i, the same subset as the partitioning dependency would. This is a contradiction of the initial assumption.

□

We develop the relationship between partitioning dependencies and rough sets in a later section.

5 Multiple dependencies and rough sets

In databases one can have multiple dependencies in the same relation.

Example 2

X_1	X_2	Y	Z
p	1	a	7
q	1	a	8
q	2	b	9
r	2	c	10
r	3	c	11
s	3	d	12

Let $X \rightsquigarrow Y$ mean that the values of Y are grouped by X-values. In other words, there is some data dependency between X and Y.

Assume that there are two dependencies supported by the table above, $X_1 \rightsquigarrow Y$ and $X_2 \rightsquigarrow Y$. Hence there are two different definitions of elementary sets of Y, one based on X_1 and one on X_2. So given a set $S \subseteq Y - values$, we can find approximations according to X_1 and X_2. Elementary sets of Y according

to $X_1 = \{a\}, \{a, b\}, \{c\}, \{d\}$.
Elementary sets of Y *according to* $X_2 = \{a\}, \{b, c\}, \{c, d\}$.

Let $A = \{a\}$. $Apr_{X_1}(A) = \{a\}$, $Apr_{X_2}(A) = \{a\}$, $\overline{Apr_{X_1}}(A) = \{a\}$, $\overline{Apr_{X_2}}(A) = \{a\}$.

Let $B = \{a, b\}$. $Apr_{X_1}(B) = \{a, b\}$, $Apr_{X_2}(B) = \{a\}$, $\overline{Apr_{X_1}}(B) = \{a, b\}$, $\overline{Apr_{X_2}}(B) = \{a, b, c\}$.

Let $C = \{b, c\}$. $Apr_{X_1}(C) = \{c\}$, $Apr_{X_2}(C) = \{b, c\}$, $\overline{Apr_{X_1}}(C) = \{a, b, c\}$, $\overline{Apr_{X_2}}(C) = \{b, c\}$.

With multiple dependencies, one can extend the concept of approximation further. Suppose that we need to find a consensus on the values of Y which are i-equivalent to a set S of Y-values. Separately one can define $Apr_{X_1}(S), \overline{Apr_{X_1}}(S), Apr_{X_2}(S), \overline{Apr_{X_2}}(S)$. Then there are three ways of combine X_1 and X_2 to form approximations. The first method is mentioned in Pawlak[15], in an example using many experts.

The second method is to use X_1, X_2 together as a partitioning attribute and compute the approximation. Then we have the following theorems.

Theorem 4 $Apr_{X_1}(S) \subseteq Apr_{X_1 X_2}(S)$.

Theorem 5 $\overline{Apr_{X_1}}(S) \subseteq \overline{Apr_{X_1 X_2}}(S)$.

The third method is to use the knowledge given by X_1, X_2 in a recursive fashion to identify further indistinguishability. Consider, for example, that the elements (tuples) in one subset are "indistinguishable" from each other - that the values of the "partitioned" attribute in this subset are the same as far as the inductive dependency is concerned. In some sense they are "equivalent" to each other; if a tuple were requested with that value of the "partitioning" attribute, any one of the tuples in the subset would suffice. Now consider that one of the "partitioned" attribute's values may also appear in *another* subset, that it appears in the "overlapping" portion of both subsets, in their intersection. In this case, the notion of equivalence leads to viewing tuples given in both sets to be equivalent in a very broad sense. Consider that an agent A knows that $\{1,3,5,7\}$ are equivalent and an agent B knows that $\{7,9,11,13\}$ are equivalent. Then when they combine their knowledge, one can conclude that $\{1,3,5,7,9,11,13\}$ are equivalent in a broad sense, even though the reason of equivalence for individual agents may differ.

We want to define such an I-equivalence according to both X_1 and X_2. We denote it by $X_1 \odot X_2$.

Example 3

X_1	a1	a1	a1	a2	a2	a2
X_2	b1	b1	b2	b2	b3	b4
Y	y1	y2	y3	y4	y5	y6

According to X_1 *the elementary sets are* $\{y1, y2, y3\}$ *and* $\{y4, y5, y6\}$. *According to* X_2 *the elementary sets are* $\{y1, y2\}, \{y3, y4\}, \{y5\}$, *and* $\{y6\}$.

By using just the X_1-*values,* $\{y1, y2, y3\}$ *are indistinguishable, and* $\{y4, y5, y6\}$ *are indistinguishable. Combining the two dependencies, all the elements in the union of the two sets* $\{y1, y2, y3, y4, y5, y6\}$ *are indistinguishable. This holds because the tuples are individually i-equivalent to each other; strictly the union would be formed because* $y1 \doteq_{X_1} y3$ *and* $y3 \doteq_{X_2} y4$, *therefore* $y1 \doteq_{X_1 \odot X_2} y4$, *and so on.*

The partitioning obtained through $\doteq_{X_1 \odot X_2}$ over Y is denoted by $I - closure_{X_1, X_2, Y}(P)$. Note that the partition given by $\doteq_{X_1 \odot X_2}$ is different from that given by $t_1 \doteq_{X_1, X_2} t_2$, which partitions such that $t_1[X_1] = t_2[X_1]$ and $t_1[X_2] = t_2[X_2]$. One can define partitioning by Y with $\doteq_{X_1 \odot X_2}$ using $\doteq_{X_1}$ and $\doteq_{X_2}$.

Definition 12 *Let P be a partition of R's Y-values. If there are two dependencies on R, $X_1 \rightsquigarrow Y$ and $X_2 \rightsquigarrow Y$, then the $I-closure_{X_1, X_2, Y}(P) = \{p | \forall a_1, a_2 \in p, it\ is\ true\ that\ a_1, a_2 \in P\ and\ either\ a_1 \doteq_{X_1} a_2\ or\ a_1 \doteq_{X_2} a_2\}$.*

Procedure 1 Procedure for finding a "partition"'s i-closure
Input consists of X_1 and X_2, the two attributes that partition the relation R into subsets which may or may not be disjoint; and P, the subset whose I-closure is to be calculated.

Output is a subset of the same relation R which includes all elements of R that are I-equivalent to the elements in P, through either X_1 or X_2. This subset will be disjoint from the rest of R.

Start Q (the output partition) out as P. Let P_1 be the partitioning induced by X_1 and similarly for P_2.
Repeat the following until there is no change to Q
　　$\forall p_{1i} \in P_1 and p_{2j} \in P_2$,
　　　　if any element of Q is I-equivalent with p_{1i} add p_{1i} to Q
　　　　if any element of Q is I-equivalent with p_{2j} add p_{2j} to Q

Q finishes as the I-closure of P, possibly equal to P if P is disjoint from all other subsets of P_1 and P_2, or possibly equal to R if there are "indistinguishabilities" from P to all other subsets of P_1 and P_2.

The 'repeat the following' above is required, since something added to Q when checking a p_{2j} may make other i-equivalences possible with one of the p_{1i}'s which had already been checked.

It is possible that an *i-closure* partition could include the entire relation (it would be the only partition, obviously). It is also possible that this process will not combine *any* subsets if no subsets overlap; in this case, they already formed a partitioning.

Fixed Point Operator
Consider a lattice which is formed by partitions of sets of tuples in R. This lattice is complete. We can define an operator T on the elements of the lattice as follows:

$T_{X,Y}(P) = \{s_1 \cup s_2$ if $s_1, s_2 \in P$ and s_1 and s_2 have at least one common Y-value with respect to $X\}$

T operates on partitions to produce partitions. T has two parameters because the partition P is partitioned according to the X attribute and the subsets will be combined if they have any common Y-values.

One can apply the operator iteratively for X_1 and X_2 as follows:
$T_{X_1, X_2, Y}(P) = T_{X_1, Y}(T_{X_2, Y}(P))$. The least fixed point for $T_{X_1, X_2, Y}$ exists.

The result of T operating on P is used to replace the individual subsets in P. Repeating this operation on P causes the partitioning to reduce in rank, as individual partitions grow in size. Each iteration will reduce the rank by one until there are no more subsets with common Y-values, so the rank is monotonically decreasing towards 1. It is assumed that P started with a finite number of partitions in it. Since T is monotonic and the lattice of partitions is complete and continuous, $T_{X_1,X_2,Y}$ has a least fixed point. The relationship between the *I-closure* and T can be seen from the following.

Theorem 6 $I - \text{closure}_{X_1,X_2,Y}(P) = T_{X_1,X_2,Y}(P) \uparrow \omega$.

6 Partitioning and inductive dependencies and rough sets

In this section we consider partitioning dependencies, inductive dependencies and their relationship to rough sets.

6.1 Partitioning dependencies and rough sets

A partitioning dependency would produce a partitioning of R in which the subdivisions would be elementary sets.

The lower approximation of a set S when the partition is induced by a partitioning dependency would be the largest composed set contained in S. In database terms, if S has *all* the Y-values associated with a particular X-value then the tuples that they represent would be in the lower approximation. The upper approximation of a set S when the partition is induced by a partitioning dependency would be the smallest composed set that contains S. If S has *any* of the Y-values associated with a particular X-value, then all the tuples associated with that X-value are in the upper approximation.

Partitioning dependencies produce partitions of the relation that behave very much like the "pure" elementary sets of Pawlak. The partitions are disjoint and all elements of each subset are "indistinguishable" in one sense.

Inductive dependencies produce looser divisions of the relation, subdivisions which may have overlap. This is where Kernel and Cover may be clearer than elementary sets, since the elementary sets with respect to X will not be true partitions.

6.2 Properties of dependency-related rough sets

These are a few of the properties of rough sets [15]. The properties are stated first in Pawlek's notation, then in our notation.

Let R be the relation of tuples, and let S be a subset of tuples in R.

- The *boundary* of S for X is $\overline{Apr_X(S)} - \underline{Apr_X(S)}$.
  $boundary_X(S) = Cover(S) - Kernel_{X,Y}(S)$

  which would be the set of tuples that would not have the same X-value as the ones in the lower approximation, but would have a Y-value matching one of their Y-values (that's how the tuple would get into the Cover).

- The internal edge, $\underline{Edge_X}(S)$, would be $S - \underline{Apr_X(S)}$.
  $\underline{Edge_X}(S) = S - Kernel_{X,Y}(S)$

- The external edge $\overline{Edge_X}(S)$ would be $\overline{Aprx(S)} - S$.

  $\overline{Edge_X}(S) = Cover(S) - S$

  This would be very close to the description of the boundary, but would also include some tuples which did have the same value of X as the tuples in S, but did not match them in some other way.

- $Aprx(R) = R$ (where R is the whole relation)

  $Kernel_{X,Y}(R) = R$

  since the least composed set that represents the values of X in the tuples in R would require all the elementary sets, which is R.

- $\overline{Aprx(R)} = R$

  $Cover(R) = R$

- $Aprx(S) \subseteq S \subseteq \overline{Aprx(S)}$

  $Kernel_{X,Y}(S) \subseteq S \subseteq Cover(S)$

- $Aprx(\emptyset) = \emptyset$

  $Kernel_{X,Y}(\emptyset) = \emptyset$

  $\overline{Aprx(\emptyset)} = \emptyset$

  $Cover(\emptyset) = \emptyset$

6.3 Accuracy of approximation

Considering the size of the partitions formed in the rough sets and the comparative sizes of partitions of different attributes can provide some additional insight into the data.

If the size of $Aprx(S)$ is equal to the size $\overline{Aprx(S)}$, then S is said to be *measurable*. Also S is either an elementary set or a union of such[15]. S is also *crisp*.

The accuracy of approximation of S for X (this only involves one attribute) is the ratio of the size of the lower approximation of S for X to the size of the upper approximation of S for X or, the ratio of all tuples that *are* indistinguishable from the tuples in S to the tuples that *may be* indistinguishable from the tuples in S.

$$\frac{|Aprx(S)|}{|\overline{Aprx(S)}|}$$

If the accuracy is 1, then S is *measurable*. The accuracy of S for X is 0 iff the size of the $Aprx(S)$ is 0, meaning there are *no* tuples in the lower approximation. The tuples in S do not match their X-values with anything in R. The i-closure is always a true partition of the values and would give an accuracy of 1. When the accuracy is between 0 and 1, it indicates there is *some* information known about the values of X, but not complete information[15].

The accuracy of approximation of Y by X (given a partitioning dependency $X \xrightarrow{P} Y$) would be 1, since every value of Y appears in only one partition of X.

Mrozek [12] defines exactly the same ratio to be the accuracy of the approximation of S according to X. He also describes a different ratio, the accuracy of approximation of Y's partitioning by X's partitioning. This ratio is the size of the Y partitions that are completely included in X's partitions, divided by the size of the universe U. For inductive dependencies, this measurement is different from the dynamic confidence factor (a measurement of the size of a partition) [7]; it's more a measure of how well the "partitioning" matches up. It would be dynamic, it would change as more data was added. It could be called a measure of how much one attribute depends on another. If the accuracy is 1, then there is a perfect match between the determining attribute's values and the values of the determined attribute. If the accuracy is 0, there is no match between partitions at all; no partition of X contains a whole partition of Y. When the accuracy of approximation is between 0 and 1, it indicates there is some relationship between X and Y, that there is some information in X's values that can be used to (loosely) determine Y's values.

Example 4

X	1	1	1	2	2	2	3	3	3
Y	2	2	3	3	4	4	5	5	7
Z	3	4	5	6	7	8	9	10	11

The accuracy of approximation of X for Y would be (2 + 2 + 2 + 1) /9. The Y partitions are { (1,2,3), (1,2,4)}, {(1,3,5),(2,3,6)}, {(2,4,7), (2,4,8)}, {(3,5,9), (3,5,10)} and {(3,7,11)}. The X partitions are {(1,2,3), (1,2,4), (1,3,5)}, {(2,3,6), (2,4,7), (2,4,8)}, and {(3,5,9), (3,5,10), (3,7,11)}. Only the 3's that overlap between the 1-partition and the 2-partition would not be included in any one partition and would not contribute to the accuracy of approximation.

7 Conclusion

Rough sets are a powerful way of expressing uncertainty in set membership. Partitioning and inductive dependencies are extensions of functional dependencies that add flexibility and abilities to the relational database concept.

We have shown that rough sets can furnish a sound theoretical basis for data dependencies, especially those that express approximate relationships. In particular the grouping of a relation by $\doteq$ can be used as an equivalence class for approximate reasoning with rough sets. This can be useful in giving mathematical background to practical applications, such as the handling of null values in databases and for considering multiple dependencies.

References

[1] Biskup J. A formal approach to null values in database relations. In: Minker J, Nicholas JM (eds) Advances in database theory: vol 1. Plenum, New York, 1981, pp 299–341

[2] Codd EF. Extending the database relational model to capture more meaning. ACM Trans on Database Systems 1979; 4(4):394–434

[3] Date CJ. An introduction to database systems. Addison-Wesley, Reading, Mass, 1986

[4] Grant J. Null values in a relational database. Information Processing Letters 1977; 6(5)

[5] Grant J, Minker J. Inferences for numerical dependencies. Theoretical Computer Science 1985; 41:271-287

[6] Imielinski T, Lipski W. Incomplete information in relational databases. J ACM 1984; 31(4):761-791

[7] Keen D, Rajasekar A. Inductive dependencies and approximate databases. In: First Int'l Conference on Information and Knowledge Management. International Society for Computers and their Applications, 1992

[8] Krynicki M. A note on rough concepts logic. Fundamenta Informaticae 1990; XIII:227-235

[9] Marek W, Pawlak Z. Information storage and retrieval systems: mathematical foundations. Theoretical Computer Science 1976; 1:331-354

[10] Marek W, Pawlak Z. Rough sets and information systems. Technical Report 441, Polish Academy of Science, 1981

[11] Marek W, Pawlak Z. Rough sets and information systems. Fundamenta Informaticae 1984; VII.1:105-115

[12] Mrozek A. Rough Sets and dependency analysis among attributes in computer implementations of expert's inference models. Int'l Journal of Man-Machine Studies 1989; 30:457-473

[13] Novotny M, Pawlak Z. Algebraic theory of independence in information systems. Fundamenta Informaticae 1991; XIV:454-476, 1991

[14] Pawlak Z. Information systems theoretical foundations. Information Systems 1981; 6(3):205-218

[15] Pawlak Z. Rough sets. Int'l Journal of Computer and Information Sciences 1982; 11(5):341-356

[16] Reiter R. On closed world data bases. In: Gallaire H, Minker J (eds) Logic and Data Bases, Plenum Press, New York, 1978; 55-76

[17] Ullman JD. Principles of database and knowledge-base systems. Computer Science Press, Rockville, MD, 1988

[18] Vakarelov D. A modal logic for similarity relations in Pawlak knowledge representation systems. Fundamenta Informaticae 1991; XV:61-79

Situation Theory and Dempster-Shafer's Theory of Evidence for Information Retrieval

M. Lalmas   C.J. van Rijsbergen

Department of Computing Science

University of Glasgow

Scotland, G12 8QQ

{mounia,keith}@dcs.glasgow.ac.uk

Abstract

We propose a model of information retrieval systems that is based on a Theory of Information and a Theory of Uncertainty, respectively Situation Theory and Dempster-Shafer's Theory of Evidence. These were selected because they allow us to tackle two of the main problems that confront any attempt to model an information retrieval system: the representation of information and its flow; and the uncertainty engendered by the complexity and ambiguity arising when dealing with information.

1 Introduction

An *Information Retrieval* (IR) system is a tool [17] that stores information and enables retrieval of this information for a variety of uses. We consider only written information[1] (in a natural language) stored as a set of *documents*. A user requiring information communicates with an IR system by submitting a *query* which expresses her information need. The IR system task is to identify the documents that satisfy the query. These documents are *retrieved* and *displayed* to the user, very often in *order* of their supposed *degree of relevance* to the query. There are many models for IR systems; the best known are the Boolean, the Vector Space and the Probabilistic models. These models seem to have reached their maximum potential because they use simple representations of the semantics and pragmatics of natural language. It has been suggested that a model be developed using a *logic-based* approach [18]. This arises out of two observations: i) a logic provides all the necessary formalism to model the different functions of an IR system and, ii) a logic handles natural language more thoroughly.

Let d and q be the sentences in a logic that formalise, respectively, the information content of the document and the information need phrased within the query. In classical logic, the validity of $d \rightarrow q$ would mean that the document is somewhat *relevant*[2] to the query. We define a logic-based framework in which implication provides an appropriate modelling of relevance. The evaluation of the implication should reflect the possibilities that, two documents are relevant

---

[1] The work carried out here can be applied to any type of media.

[2] Here we are not talking of the user relevance judgement, but the system relevance assessment.

to the same query to a different degree; and that the document is partially relevant to the query.

The use of *classical logic* is not appropriate because of the semantics associated with the material implication. Indeed, in classical logic, $d \rightarrow q$ is equivalent to $\neg d \vee q$, which leads to two difficulties with regard to IR: i) how should we interpret the negation of a formula ($\neg d$)? and, ii) if we admit negation as in classical logic, should we (incorrectly) assert relevance when the implication $d \rightarrow q$ is valid as a result of the validity of $\neg d$? This problem is extensively discussed in [9].

The exclusive use of a *binary logic* is not sufficient. Indeed, basing the relevance assessment on the validity or non-validity of $d \rightarrow q$ entails that either too many or too few documents are retrieved. We are interested in evaluating the extent to which $d \rightarrow q$ can be said to be valid. So the evaluation of $d \rightarrow q$ involves uncertainty[3], thus the goal is the computation of $u(d \rightarrow q)$. This expresses the extent to which a document satisfies the query upon which the determination of the relevance degree is based. Therefore, a theory of uncertainty is required. This approach was recommended in [18] under the name of the Logical Uncertainty Principle. We give a slightly modified principle that is more IR-oriented, called the *Relevance Principle*:

"The extent to which d is relevant to q, that is, the evaluation of d → q relative to a given data set, is based on the minimal extent to which it is necessary to add information to d for it to become d' such that d' → q is valid".

A non truth-based logic is more appropriate because a model of an IR system is more concerned with *information content* rather than truth-values. Indeed, what does it mean to say that a formula is *true* in a document? What is an *interpretation* with respect to a document? We believe that the way forward is to base our model on a *theory of information*, which can also have the advantage of representing *partial* information. Partiality is an important feature of an IR system because it is often not known whether a document is about a given item of information, but this can be found out eventually when additional information becomes available.

Finally, in IR it is very often the case that not all of the information content of a document is equally *significant*, so it would be advantageous to express the significance of the information in the document. This could be done by using a framework that assigns weights. We use a theory of uncertainty for this purpose.

We put forward a logic-based model that follows the Relevance Principle and preferably satisfies the four following criteria: the logic[4] should be non-classical, deals with uncertainty, weights information items according to their significance and embodies a formalism of the data set. To our knowledge, there are no logics that fulfil these requirements. However, after a large review of existing literature, we have selected two theories: Situation Theory [1,2,5,6] and Dempster-Shafer's Theory of Evidence [14]. The former is a 'logic of informa-

---

[3]Two approaches are possible. The evaluation of the implication might lead to a value in [0,1]; that is, the uncertainty is intrinsic to the logic. Alternatively, a measure u could capture the uncertainty of the implication. We opt for the second approach.

[4]By the logic, we mean any formalism that allows a representation of information, that is, a 'logic of information' or a 'theory of information'.

tion' which provides a modelling of information and its behaviour, whereas the latter provides a model of the uncertainty and the weighting mechanisms. We borrow terminology from Scott Domains [15] and Data Semantics [11] which make the formulation of the model simpler.

We develop the model in two phases. In the first phase we ignore the significance of the information. We use Situation Theory. The uncertainty is modelled by a general framework like that adopted in expert systems [7]. In the second phase, we extend the model to deal with significance using Dempster-Shafer's Theory of Evidence. We divide this paper into several parts. First we introduce Situation Theory and show its potential in modelling an IR system. Thus, we model the data set and develop the model for unweighted information. Then we introduce Dempster-Shafer's Theory of Evidence, which extends the previous model to incorporate weighted information.

2   Situation theory

Situation Theory is a theory of information which, by following a mathematical approach, models more naturally the way humans handle information and its flow. It can be compared to Quantum Mechanics, where, an ideal representation of an electron is adopted, even if it is not well understood what an electron *is*. Hence, it becomes possible to model the behaviour and interaction of electrons. Situation Theory adopts the same approach. It proposes first to represent the notion of *information* without really indicating what information *is*; from this, a model of the *flow of information* [5] is derived. An IR system is constantly 'confronted with information and its flows. For example, there is the flow that conveys the information we are reading from what we are actually reading in terms of words, letters, etc. Here, we only consider flows that cater for the semantics and the pragmatics of natural language.

Consider a situation about an office where a person Mounia is working. A person entering this office, let's say Keith, is able to extract information that resides in the situation. Keith acts as a *cognitive agent*. The extracted information depends strongly on his *focus of attention* and *perception capability*. In Situation Theory, an item of information is considered as an entity and is represented by an *infon*. For example, the information concerning the fact that Mounia is working is modelled by the infon $\ll$ *Working, Mounia, Office; 1* $\gg$. If the information was that Mounia is not working, the corresponding infon would be $\ll$ *Working, Mounia, Office; 0* $\gg$, which is called the *dual* infon of the above. Nothing is said so far about the truth or falsity of the two infons above; they are representations of information items. What makes them true is any situation which includes or pertains to them. If we call s the situation Keith is confronted with, we write $s \models \ll$ *Working, Mounia, Office; 1* $\gg$ to say that s *supports* the corresponding infon.

The purpose of Situation Theory is to represent the fact that a situation *supports* some information and that it *carries* additional information, where carrying information signifies that an information item often contains information about other information items, so the information that is supported by a situation contains information about other situations. Carrying information corresponds to a flow of information, which is formally defined below. We can already sense that situations and infons show similarities with documents and their information content. Supported information corresponds to the *explicit* information content of the document, whereas carried information corresponds to its *implicit* information content.

The two following infons: $\ll$ *Working, Mounia, Office, 11am; 1* $\gg$ and $\ll$ *Working, Mounia, Home, 9pm; 1* $\gg$ have in common the information that Mounia is working. What differs is the place and the time of the action. This similarity is represented in the theory by *types of situations*, or simply *types*. Here the corresponding type would be, $\varphi = [\dot{s} | \dot{s} \models \ll Working, Mounia, \dot{p}, \dot{t}; 1 \gg]$, which classifies all the situations where a person referred to as Mounia is working at a given time and place. Here $\dot{s}$, $\dot{p}$ and $\dot{t}$ are parameters, standing respectively for a situation, a place and a time. Any situation that supports the information that Mounia is working at a given time and place is said to be *of type* φ: we write $s \models \varphi$ as well (in [2], this is written as $s : \varphi$).

Two types may be connected together to form a *constraint*. For example the two types $\varphi = [\dot{s} | \dot{s} \models \ll present, smoke, \dot{p}, \dot{t}; 1 \gg]$ and $\psi = [\dot{s} | \dot{s} \models \ll present, fire, \dot{p}, \dot{t}; 1 \gg]$ are not independent. The information they represent is *informationally* related because most humans know that if they see smoke in a place, then there was (or is) a fire nearby. There is a flow that indicates that a situation which supports φ additionally carries the information that some other situations support ψ. The constraint, written $\varphi \rightarrow \psi$, is introduced to model this flow, which happens between two situations, let say s_1 and s_2. The constraint $\varphi \rightarrow \psi$ applied to these situations, means that the fact that $s_1 \models \varphi$ implies that $s_2 \models \psi$, where s_2 can be either the same as s_1 or different. This latter case arises because a situation can carry information about other situations as well as itself. A typical IR example is that we can use constraints to model synonymous terms. More elaborately, the rules in expert systems could be modelled by constraints.

3 Uncertainty in situation theory

A flow does not always materialise because of the unpredictable nature of situations; thus indicating that flows are often uncertain. In Situation Theory, an uncertain flow is modelled by a *conditional* constraint, that is, $\varphi \rightarrow \psi | B$, which highlights the fact that the constraint $\varphi \rightarrow \psi$ holds if some background conditions captured within B are met. This is the way uncertainty is captured in Situation Theory. Such a representation is not sufficient for our purposes because in IR we need to quantify the uncertainty. So we replace the background condition by a degree of certainty indicating the extent to which the constraint holds. Let T be the set of types. The function $cert : (T \rightarrow T) \rightarrow [0, 1]$ evaluates the certainty of the constraints. The value 0 means that the constraint does not exist whereas the value 1 means that the constraint is absolute (always holds).

A flow is either certain or uncertain. Both types link either the same situation or two different situations. In the former case, additional information about the situation is obtainable. In the latter case information about other situations is obtainable. We consider two types of flow. If the flow is certain, then the additional information is about the same situation. If the flow is uncertain, then another situation is built that contains the additional information. We are working on the problem of identifying the constraints and computing their certainty. This issue goes beyond the scope of this paper. In what follows, we assume that constraints are given together with their certainty values.

We have introduced Situation Theory, which we have extended in order to have a numerical representation of uncertainty. Next, we describe the first component of our model, that is the data set as mentioned in the Relevance Principle.

4   The data set

The data set contains the semantics and pragmatics of natural language, upon which the addition process is based. In IR, a data set is in most cases a *thesaurus* (terminology we shall use from now on), that is, a set of relationships between information items. Classical examples of these relationships include synonymy or broadness. Thus we treat the thesaurus as a set of constraints.

Let p be the representation of an explicit information item contained in a document. Let the constraint $p \to p'$ be a relationship stored in the thesaurus. If $cert(p \to p') = 1$ then p' is part of the information content of the document. Otherwise the document is extended to a *fictive* document which has p' in its information content. The certainty associated with this document is $cert(p \to p')$. So addition to a situation means extension of that situation. If the thesaurus contains the two constraints $p \to p'$ and $p \to p''$ then adding information is an ambiguous operation. The values $cert(p \to p')$ and $cert(p \to p'')$ help to give an indication of the appropriateness of the addition. An overall value is computed which depends on the type and the amount of added information, and the relationship itself[5]. This value is the degree of relevance.

Constraints are the perfect tool to represent thesaural, or any semantic or pragmatic relationships. A document, if viewed as a situation, supports information and often carries implicit information that depends on the available constraints. To summarise, we have a set of situation S, a set of types T and thesaurus denoted Th that is, a set of constraints together with the function $cert : (T \to T) \to [0, 1]$. We describe next the model of an IR system where the significance of the information is not taken into account.

5   Unweighted information

A document is an object that purveys information, so a document is modelled as a situation d. A query is an information need, so a query is modelled as a type φ. The cognitive agent, that is, the IR system determines to what extent d supports φ. If $d \models \varphi$ then φ is part of the information content of the document. Otherwise, constraints from Th are used to find a flow that leads to a situation that supports φ. If such a flow exists, its certainty is computed. This value reflects the fact that the larger the flow, the less relevant the document is. Our model is presented in two stages. Firstly, we deal with single type queries and secondly with complex queries (that are constituted of several types).

---

[5]The relationships between information items vary in strength. For example, the synonymy relationship links more strongly two terms than does the narrowness relationship. Also, among synonym, two terms can be more 'synonymous' than two others (specially, when polysemy occurs).

The translation of the information content into types enters the area of natural language processing (NLP). There is an extensive literature on NLP, the one that is most relevant to our context is called Situation Semantics [1,8]. We assume that the NLP phase has already been performed and that we are in the presence of types.

5.1 Unweighted model: single type query

We define the function $\mathcal{R} : S \times T \rightarrow [0,1]$, where $\mathcal{R}(d,\varphi)$ is the degree of relevance of the document with respect to the query. The computation of $\mathcal{R}(d,\varphi)$ results in two cases. First, $d \models \varphi$ then the document is relevant, thus $\mathcal{R}(d,\varphi) = 1$. Secondly, $d \not\models \varphi$, however $d \models \psi$ and $\psi \rightarrow \varphi \in Th$, then $\mathcal{R}(d,\varphi) = cert(\psi \rightarrow \varphi)$ implying that the degree of relevance corresponds to the certainty of the constraint. Two cases arise. If $cert(\psi \rightarrow \varphi) = 1$, then $d \models \varphi$ and $\mathcal{R}(d,\varphi) = 1$. Otherwise, d is extended into a situation d', which is a situation supporting all information supported by d as well as φ. Several constraints might be required to arrive at φ, either in sequence or in parallel. We borrow terminology from Landman [11], which leads to simpler definitions within Situation Theory ontology. We take the definitions of extension, chain, branch from the same source, and we adapt them to our ontology.

A situation s' is an *extension* of the situation s, denoted $s \rhd s'$, iff every type that s supports is supported by s'. We write $E(s)$ the set of extensions of a situation s. Extensions exist because of constraints. A situation $s \models \psi$ is extended to a situation $s' \models \varphi$ due to the fact that $\psi \rightarrow \varphi \in Th$, where $cert(\psi \rightarrow \varphi) < 1$. The certainty of the extension is $cert(\psi \rightarrow \varphi)$, which can also be interpreted as the certainty of s' being the appropriate extension of s. We take our motivation for extension from [11] but we enhance Landmans approach by specifying how to obtain these extensions.

C is a *chain* in $E(s)$ if C is a subset of $E(s)$ and for all $s', s'' \in C$, either $s' \rhd s''$ or $s'' \rhd s'$. A *branch* b is a chain in $E(s)$ starting from s (called the *root*), that is, for all $s' \in b$, $s \rhd s'$. We note $B(s)$ the set of all branches with root s. A leaf s' of a branch is the end point situation of that branch. Branches are used to model the sequence of extensions.

From a situation, there are often alternative extensions. This is modelled by what we call the *split-up* of a situation. If a situation $s \models \psi$ and $\{\psi \rightarrow \psi_i, i = 1, n\} \subset Th$, then s can be extended into n different situations s_i. The certainty of the extension of s into s_i is of value of $cert(\psi \rightarrow \psi_i)$.

We next define the certainty of obtaining a situation from a sequence of extensions. Consider $b = \{s_1, \cdots, s_n\}$ where $s_1 \rhd \cdots \rhd s_n$, and let the extension of s_i into s_{i+1} arise from $\psi_i \rightarrow \psi_{i+1} \in Th$ where $cert(\psi_i \rightarrow \psi_{i+1}) < 1$. The certainty of the branch b, denoted $\partial(b)$ corresponds to the certainty of obtaining the situation s_n from s_1, which is given by[6]:

$$\partial(b) = \prod_{i=0, n-1} cert(\psi_i \rightarrow \psi_{i+1})$$

This formula reflects the fact that the more information is added (the more extensions are required) the less relevant the document is. The process of

---

[6]In cavéat, this formula put in the context of Probability Theory assumes independence of data. Better formulae should be looked at. However, product and sum make computation simpler.

extending a situation ceases in two cases: when the requested information is found, that is, the branch leads to a situation leaf s_f such that $s_f \models \varphi$ (we also say that s_f is *relevant* with respect to φ); or, when the branch cannot be extended anymore, that is, there is no constraint that can arise from its situation leaf. We say that the branch $b \in B(s)$ is a *minimal branch* with respect to φ if its leaf is the only situation in that branch that supports φ. We write $B(s, \varphi)$ the set of minimal branches with root s with respect to φ.

Given the situation d and the type φ, the set $B(d, \varphi)$ must be investigated to assess the relevance. This can be viewed schematically as follows.

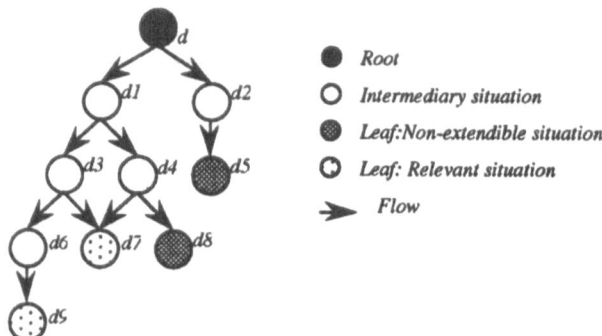

The situation d is the original document. d_7 and d_9 are the relevant leaves and $B(d, \varphi)$ contains $\{d, d_1, d_3, d_6, d_9\}$, $\{d, d_1, d_3, d_7\}$ and $\{d, d_1, d_4, d_7\}$. The overall certainty of obtaining φ from d gives the values of the degree of relevance is given by:

$$\mathcal{R}(d, \varphi) = \sum_{b \in B(d,\varphi)} \partial(b)$$

where the following property is imposed:

$$\forall \psi \in T, \sum_{\substack{\psi \to \psi_i \in Th \\ i=1,n}} cert \, (\psi \to \psi_i) = 1$$

which ensures that the value of $\mathcal{R}(d, \varphi)$ remains in the interval $[0,1]$. The formula above means that the set $\{\psi_1, \cdots, \psi_n\}$ has the same *semantic informativeness* that the type ψ itself. The function *cert* can easily be made to satisfy this property via normalisation[7]. We have chosen this formulation because this model is extended to cater for weighted information. There we want that the summation of the certainty of all extensions of a situation to equal the certainty associated with that situation (the reason is explained in the section dealing with the weighted model). Let us illustrate our point with an example.

From the definition of split-up, if $\{\psi_0 \to \psi_i | cert(\psi_0 \to \psi_i) < 1, i = 1, n\} \subset Th$ then $d_0 \models \psi_0$ is extended into n situations.

---

[7]However, this property is not necessary if other formulae of relevance are used (for example, maximum instead of sum).

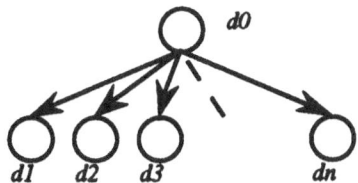

From the above property, we obtain:

$$\sum_{i=1,n} \partial(\{d_0, d_i\}) = \sum_{i=1,n} cert(\psi_0 \rightarrow \psi_i) = 1$$

If b is the branch that extends d to d_0, the certainty of the branch being $\partial(b)$, then:

$$\sum_{i=1,n} \partial(b \cup \{d_i\}) = \sum_{i=1,n} \partial(b)^* cert(\psi_0 \rightarrow \psi_i) = \partial(b)^* \sum_{i=1,n} cert(\psi_0 \rightarrow \psi_i) = \partial(b)$$

where $b \cup \{d_i\}$ is the branch b with one more extension d_i. Furthermore, the expression of $\mathcal{R}(d, \varphi)$ entails that the summation of the certainty of all the branches with root d comes to one, since the certainty originated from d is one (the empty branch).

To finish, if for some $d' \models \varphi$, then any extension of d' leads to a situation that supports φ. The certainty involved, when added, is equal to the certainty already qualifying d'. Therefore, there is no point to extend a relevant situation.

5.2 Unweighted model: complex query

We extend the model to incorporate complex queries, that is, queries that request several items of information. These are modelled by a set of types Φ. We extend the definition of the support relation to deal with set of types. In this case, a situation s supports Φ, written $s \models \Phi$, if $s \models \varphi$ for all $\varphi \in \Phi$. The function $\mathcal{R}(d, \Phi)$ becomes defined on $\mathcal{R} : S \times 2^T \rightarrow [0, 1]$, where d is the situation modelling the document.

The extensions of a situation do not always generate situations that support all the types in Φ. So we differentiate between branches whose leaves support the complete query to the ones that only partially support it. These are called respectively relevant and partially relevant branches, which are denoted by the sets $B_t(d, \Phi)$ and $B_p(d, \Phi)$.

The expression of the relevance degree of the document with respect to the query becomes:

$$\mathcal{R}(d, \Phi) = \sum_{b \in B_t(d, \Phi)} \partial(b) + \sum_{b \in B_p(d, \Phi)} \partial(b)$$

Let $Ex(d, \Phi)$ and $Sp(d, \Phi)$ be respectively the two sums of the equation above. $Ex(d, \Phi)$ measures the *exhaustivity* of the document. If $Ex(d, \Phi) = 0$ then the document is not exhaustive because no extension supports the total query. If $Ex(d, \Phi) > 0$ then the document is exhaustive because there is at least one extension that yields to a situation that supports Φ. $Sp(d,\Phi)$ gives an indication about the *specificity* of the document. If all the extensions lead to partially relevant branches then $Sp(d,\Phi) = 1$. This reflects the fact that the document is specific to the query since all extensions lead to relevant information[8]. The interpretation of $Ex(d,\Phi)$ and $Sp(d,\Phi)$ are so far speculative and experiments are necessary to find out empirically if $Ex(d,\Phi)$ and $Sp(d,\Phi)$ reflect the exhaustivity and specificity of the document.

We have presented a model of an IR system for unweighted information. Next, we extend the model to deal with weighted information.

6 Weighted information

In this section we present the model where information is weighted according to its significance. The information in a document can be structured in different ways: syntactically as in paragraphs, sentences or words; semantically through synonyms; or pragmatically as in discourse. We concentrate on the use of semantic structures which we believe to be the most difficult and most important to handle correctly within IR.

In the unweighted model, a document was modelled by one situation d. Let us suppose that a document is constituted of structures. Then, the document is modelled by a set of situations, one for each structure. The union of the situations is that situation d, thus the situations modelling the different structures are sub-situations of d. An item of information can be common to two situations, for example, whenever the item has several meanings. A weight is assigned to each situation, which represents the significance of the information it supports.

6.1 Theory of evidence

We use Dempster-Shafer's theory, as the framework to build our model for weighted situations. Given a *frame of discernment* Θ, a density function m : $2^{\Theta} \rightarrow [0,1]$ called *basic probability assignment* (BPA) is defined on Θ such that:

$$m(\oslash) = 0 \text{ and } \sum_{A \subseteq \Theta} m(A) = 1$$

$m(A)$ represents the degree of belief that is committed exactly to A. Every element A such that $m(A) > 0$ is called a *focal element*. A *belief function* $Bel : 2^{\Theta} \rightarrow [0,1]$ is defined in terms of a BPA m as follows:

$$Bel(A) = \sum_{B \subseteq A} m(B)$$

where $Bel(A)$ is the total belief committed to A. A frame of discernment Ω can be obtained from Θ by splitting some or all elements of Θ. This is defined by the *refinement* function $\omega : 2^{\Theta} \rightarrow 2^{\Omega}$ where:

(i) $\omega(\{p\}) \neq \oslash$ for all $p \in \Theta$

---

[8]The terms exhaustivity and specificity are motivated by their traditional use in IR.

(ii) $\omega(\{p\}) \cap \omega(\{p'\}) = \oslash$ if $p \neq p'$

(iii) $\bigcup_{p \in \Theta} \omega(\{p\}) = \Omega$

In the unweighted model, situations were extended. In the weighted model, the document is modelled by several situations, which are eventually extended. Since we would like to keep the same sort of framework between extensions, we deal with several frames of discernment. A refinement is the functional tool that leads one frame to the other. For simplicity we write $\omega(\{p\}) = \omega(p)$. Then for any subset A:

$$\omega(A) = \bigcup_{p \in A} \omega(p)$$

where $\omega(A)$ consists of all the possibilities in Ω that are obtained by splitting all the elements in A. Going from Θ to Ω is called refinement. The belief functions Bel_Θ (with BPA m_Θ) and Bel_Ω (with BPA m_Ω) defined respectively on Θ and Ω are consistent iff $Bel_\Theta(A) = Bel_\Omega(\omega(A))$. We admit that [14] $m_\Theta(A) \geq m_\Omega(\omega(A))$ which means that refining decreases beliefs.

Next we show how we use this theory to build our framework. We are still working on S the set of situations, T the set of types and Th the set of constraints. The general idea is that a document is a frame of discernment, a focal element is a situation. The focal elements are simultaneously extended, leading to another frame of discernment. This corresponds to the refinement defined above[9]. Belief functions indicate the information content in the different frames of discernment, their values for a given query are combined to form the degree of relevance.

7 Description of the weighted model

We define the frame of discernment as a subset $T_D \subseteq T$, which is the set of types that correspond to the document information contents. A focal element is a basic situation, that is, a situation s which is not an extension of any other situation (except for the empty situation, written e^{10}). We distinguish basic situations because a BPA value is assigned to them, which represents the belief committed exactly to each of them. Beliefs of non-basic situations are computed from the BPA of basic situations. The document is constituted of semantic structures, which we model by basic situations.

We call the set of basic situations related to a frame of discernment a $domain^{11}$, denoted D. So in the weighted model, a document is modelled

---

[9] In fact, a situation is extended means that additional information becomes available. This is very much compatible with the notion of refinement of information in Dempster-Shafer's framework.

[10] The situation that supports no information, or too much information.

[11] Domain is a terminology borrowed from Scott domains [15]. Work has been done to show the connection between an extension of Situation Theory and Scott Domains [3]. This issue though interesting goes beyond the scope of this paper, however, this observation convinced us of the well foundness of our representation.

by a domain. The situations in D are the situations that support types in T_D. A BPA is a function $m : D \rightarrow [0, 1]$ defined by:

$$m(e) = 0 \text{ and } \sum_{s \in D} m(s) = 1$$

The weight $m(s)$ represents the significance of the situation with respect to the overall information content of the document. We are working on building basic situations, and on the computation of m, but one method can be found in [16]. The approach that we are thinking of is based on Rough Set Theory [13].

To evaluate the quantity of information supported by the different situations of the domain we use a belief function $Bel : 2^D \times 2^T \rightarrow [0, 1]$ which is defined in terms of a BPA m by:

$$Bel(A, \Gamma) = \sum_{\substack{s \models \varphi \\ s \in D \, \varphi \in \Gamma}} m(s)$$

$Bel(A, \Gamma)$ represents the belief that the information Γ is supported by situations in $A \subseteq D$. The set A is introduced because we are only concerned with some of the basic situations in the domain (the reason is explained when we formulate the relevance degree from belief functions). We say that a situation is *relevant* with respect to a set of types Γ, if that situation supports *at least one* type in Γ (we do not distinguish any longer between relevant and partially relevant situations). A document is modelled as a set of situations D, as a result, its relevance, with respect to the query modelled by Γ, is defined in terms of the relevant situations in D with respect to Γ. From now on, we are dealing with two notions of relevance, with respect to a document and with respect to a situation.

In the weighted model, a belief function defined on a domain enables us to determine the relevance of a document with respect to the explicit information. As implicit information arises from constraints, the situations in the domain can be extended. These extensions constitute a refinement between domains, that is a function $\omega : 2^D \rightarrow 2^{D'}$, between the two domains D and D', such that:

$$\bigcup_{s \in D} \omega(s) = D'$$

Unlike Dempster-Shafer's definition, we explicitly build the refinement from the constraints in Th. For this purpose, we define the set $E_d(s)$ of direct extensions from s that is any extension which arises from the awareness of a single constraint. So we have:

$$\text{for all situations } s \in D, \quad \omega(s) = \begin{cases} E_d(s) & \text{if} & E_d(s) \neq \varnothing \\ \{s\} & \text{if} & E_d(s) = \varnothing \end{cases}.$$

Our construction ensures that $w(s) \neq \varnothing$. Indeed, if $E_d(s) = \varnothing$, that is, s cannot be extended, then the refinement of s is s itself.

There are differences between Dempster-Shafer's refinement function and ours. First, the refinement of two situations can lead to a same situation, which reflects the fact that two items of information can be refined to a common item.

As a result, the property $m_D(s) \geq m_{D'}(\omega(s))$ does not always hold. Secondly, in our model situations are refined and not the elements of the frame. However, a situation is extended or refined (from now on we use alternatively the two terms), based on the types it supports and the constraints related to these types. Moreover, types are analogous to the elements of the frame of discernment. In our case, one type per situation is used for refinement, whereas in the original definition, all elements of the frame are simultaneously refined. Nevertheless, a refinement is based on the types supported by situations and the constraints, so the two definitions are compatible.

The representation of implicit certain and uncertain information in the unweighted model is easily mapped onto a domain D. Let $s \in D$ such that $s \models \varphi$ and $\varphi \rightarrow \psi \in Th$. If $cert(\varphi \rightarrow \psi) = 1$ then $s \models \psi$. Thus, implicit certain information is inherent to D^{12}. Otherwise, s is extended into s' such that $s' \models \psi$, the certainty of the extension is $cert(\varphi \rightarrow \psi)$. Since, a situation that is the extension of another situation cannot be basic, we get that $s' \notin D$, hence the extension of a situation in D leads to another domain[13]. This mechanism has the advantage that it caters for the fact that an item of information can be both explicit and implicit in a document.

Let ω_i be the refinement function between the two domains D_i and D_{i+1}, with respective BPA m_i and m_{i+1}. Both properties below are required:

$$\sum_{s \in D_i} m_i(s) = 1 \quad \text{and} \quad \sum_{s \in D_{i+1}} m_{i+1}(s) = 1$$

The BPA m_i is already known, so what is left is to determine the BPA m_{i+1}. Let $s \in D_i$ and $b = \{s, s'\}$ a branch in $E_d(s)$ that arises from the constraint $\varphi \rightarrow \psi$. We define:

$$m_{i+1}(s') = \partial(b)^* m_i(s) = cert(\varphi \rightarrow \psi)^* m_i(s)$$

Several branches starting from situations in D_i could lead to s'. We generalise:

$$\sum_{s \in \omega_i^{-1}(s')} \partial(\{s, s'\})^* m_i(s) = m_{i+1}(s')$$

where $\omega_i^{-1}(s')$ is the set of situations in D_i that are extended into s'. It is easy to verify that m_{i+1} is a BPA[14]. There is a distinction to be made between the interpretation of m_0 and $m_i (i > 0)$. The BPA $m_i(s')$ represents the certainty that s' is obtaining from the original domain after i refinements. The quantity $m_0(s)$ is the importance of the situation s in the original domain. The quantities $m_i(s')$ (for $i > 0$) are computed from m_0 and the certainty degrees of constraints while m_0 is established when processing the document.

---

[12] An element of a Scott Domain is an intentional object that is described by some properties. These entail other properties, which also describe that object. The analogy with situation is patent, a situation is an element, types are the properties of the elements, and constraints gives other properties of that element

[13] Two Scott Domains can be linked by an *approximate function* [15], the properties of which are compatible with the ones of the Dempster-Shafer's refinement function.

[14] This is compatible with the way many model the propagation of uncertainty; the $m_i(s)$ correspond to uncertain facts, $\partial(b)$ to uncertain rules, both upon which $m_{i+1}(s')$ is based. The choice of the product and sum is debatable, other combinations might be more appropriate.

Let d be the situation modelling the document as in the unweighted model, from where the initial domain D_0 is built. Given a query modelled by a set of types Φ, its belief is computed in each domain by summing the BPA of the relevant situations with respect to Φ. We give an example to illustrate our formulation of $\mathcal{R}(d, \Phi)$.

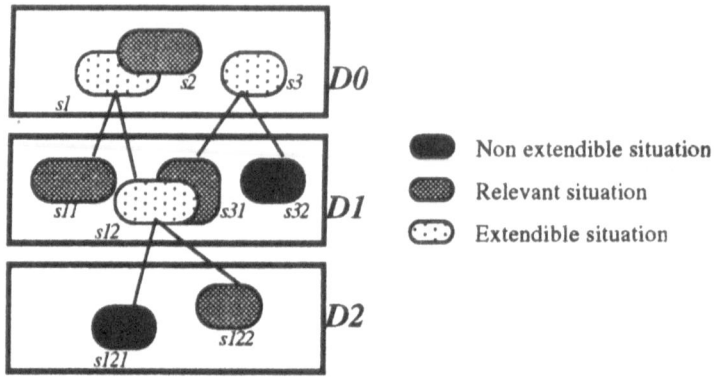

In this figure, we have for example, $\omega_0(s_1) = \{s_{11}, s_{12}\}$. The non-relevant and extendible situations are refined, leading to the next domain. We define the two sets:

$$R(A, \Phi) = \{s \in A | \exists \varphi \in \Phi, s \models \varphi\}$$

$$NE(A, \Phi) = \{s \in A | E_d(s) = \oslash\}$$

of respectively relevant situations and non-extendible situations in A. The belief values are added together to form the degree of relevance $\mathcal{R}(d, \Phi)$ as follows:

$$\mathcal{R}(d, \Phi) = \sum_{i=1,n} Bel(\Gamma_i, \Phi)$$

where:

$$\Gamma_i = \omega_{i-1}(\Gamma_{i-1} - R(\Gamma_{i-1}, \Phi) - NE(\Gamma_{i-1}, \Phi)) \text{ for } i > 0$$

Γ_i is the set $\omega_i(\Gamma_{i-1})$ where all relevant and non-extendible situations have been discarded from Γ_{i-1}. In a domain, the evaluation of Bel includes relevant situations that are not the extensions of already relevant situations in the previous domains. Moreover, non-extendible situations are not included in the refinement since they will never lead to the sought information. This explains why we express beliefs from a subset of situations. For example, we get:

	Γ_i	$R(\Gamma_i, \Phi)$	$NE(\Gamma_i, \Phi)$
$i = 0$	$\{s_1, s_2, s_3\}$	$\{s_2\}$	$\oslash$
$i = 1$	$\omega_0(\{s_1, s_3\}) = \{s_{11}, s_{12}, s_{31}, s_{32}\}$	$\{s_{11}, s_{31}\}$	$\{s_{32}\}$
$i = 2$	$\omega_1(\{s_{12}\}) = \{s_{121}, s_{122}\}$	$\{s_{122}\}$	$\{s_{121}\}$

In the example, $\Gamma_3 = \oslash$, so we get $\mathcal{R}(d, \Phi) = m_0(s_2) + m_1(s_{11}) + m_1(s_{31}) + m_2(s_{122})$.

As for the unweighted model, we could have separated among relevant and partially relevant situations, which would have allowed to measure the exhaustivity and the specificity of the document. Though we have not done this, it would be easy to do the split.

8 Conclusion

We have suggested a model for IR systems based on Situation Theory and Dempster-Shafer's Theory of Evidence. The model offers a representation of information and its flow (semantics and pragmatics), allows partiality and provides a mechanism that caters for the significance of information. We use Situation Theory to model information and its flow. We use Dempster-Shafer's theory of Evidence to structure information according to its significance. Our contribution is to show that a theory of information together with a theory of certainty are both necessary and sufficient to build a model for IR systems.

We found that Situation Theory is an appropriate formalism for modelling the qualitative aspect of an IR system (that is, information, flow, information containment) whereas Dempster-Shafer's Theory of Evidence provides the quantitative aspect of the model (weighted information, measure of amount of information). We also found that Situation Theory and Dempster-Shafer's Theory of Evidence are compatible, therefore, both can be mapped onto each other to provide the model. And nonetheless, from the fact that we have borrowed the terminology from Scott Domains and Data Semantics (both can be used as theory of information), we can see that all the theories we have used are compatible, leading us to think that our approach is well founded.

9 Future work

The model is now being implemented, this will fairly soon which will allow us to draw conclusions about the validity of our model. We will also be able to provide answers to the questions: Is our model consistent and appropriate? Do we deal correctly with the combination and propagation of uncertainty? Do we cover every case regarding the extension with respect to information containment? What about if an extension leads to contradictory information?

We have assumed several mathematical hypotheses in our model. We will study those to find out whether they can be weakened. We will proceed further with our theoretical work, refining the accuracy of the model. Furthermore, we will assess the efficacy of our model and compare it to similar models implemented using different approaches.

References

[1] Barwise J, Perry J. Situations and Attitudes, Bradford Books, MIT Press, 1983

[2] Barwise J. The situation in logic. CSLI lecture notes no 17, 1989

[3] Barwise, J. Information links in domain theory. Proc Conference on Mathematical Foundations of Program Semantics, Springer-Verlag, 1991 (Lecture notes in computer science) to appear

[4] Chiaramella Y, Chevallet JP. About retrieval models and logic. The Computer Journal (special issue) 1992; 35(3):233–242

[5] Devlin KJ. Logic and information. Cambridge University Press, 1991

[6] Dretske F. Knowledge and flow of information. Bradford Books, MIT Press, 1981

[7] Dubois D, Prade H. Combinations d'information incertaines. Equipe Intelligence Artificielle et Robotique, Communication, Decision, Raisonement, 1987 (Rapport LSI no 263)

[8] Fenstad JE, Halvorsen PK, Langholm T, van Benthem J. Situations, language and logic. Reidel, 1987

[9] Harper WL, Stalnaker R, Pearce G. (eds) Ifs. Reidel, 1981

[10] Lalmas M, van Rijsbergen CJ. A Logical model of information retrieval based on situation theory. Proc of the BCS 14th Information Retrieval Colloquium, 1992, pp 1–13

[11] Landman F. Towards a theory of information. The status of Partial Objects in Semantics, Foris, 1986

[12] Nie J. Towards a probabilistic modal logic for semantic-based information retrieval. In: Belkin N, Ingwersen P, Pejtersen AM (eds) ACM/SIGIR92, conference proceeding, 1992, pp 140–141

[13] Pawlak Z. Rough sets. Int'l Journal of Information and Computing Science 1982; (5):119–123

[14] Shafer's G. A mathematical theory of evidence. Princeton University Press, 1976

[15] Scott DS. Domains for denotational semantics. (Lecture notes in computing science no 140), 1982

[16] Teixera de Silva W, Milidiu RL. Belief function model for information retrieval. Journal of the American Society for Information Science 1993, 4(1):10–18

[17] van Rijsbergen CJ. Information retrieval. 2nd Edition. Butterworths, London, 1979

[18] van Rijsbergen CJ. A non-classical logic for information retrieval. The Computer Journal 1986; 29:481–485

Completeness in Statechart Models for Reactive Systems

Vangalur S. Alagar   Fangqing Dong   Ramesh Achuthan

Department of Computer Science
Concordia University
Montreal, Canada
{alagar,fqdong,ramesh}@cs.concordia.ca

Abstract

A necessary condition for ensuring robustness and safety in reactive systems is to ensure that system specification is complete with respect to the initial requirements. In this paper, we introduce the notion of totality for requirements and formalise the notion of completeness of system specification with respect to requirements. The paper illustrates a method for checking completeness using disjunctive logic programs.

1   Introduction

In this paper, we present a formal notion of *completeness* in statechart-based modeling of reactive systems. The notion of completeness is useful for establishing whether or not a reactive system model represented in statechart adequately captures the requirements of the system.

Reactive systems [9] are systems that continually interact with their environment. Process control systems, telephony applications and human-computer interface systems are typical reactive systems. The typical requirement of such systems are that they satisfy stringent timing constraints and avoid unsafe execution paths. An important inherent feature of reactive systems is concurrency, since the environment always works concurrently with the system itself.

Statecharts were proposed by Harel [4] to provide a simple solution to the specification of reactive systems. Statecharts are state transition-based formalisms extended to allow the representation of concurrency and hierarchy of states. An important feature of statecharts is the broadcast mechanism, which provides an effective way to express system response to environmental stimulus. The modular and hierarchical nature of statecharts lead to a succinct description of state transitions and provide visual appeal while reducing the state explosion problem. Parallel composition of concurrent components in reactive systems can be efficiently represented using orthogonal composition in statecharts. Recently statecharts have been used to model process-control systems [8] and avionics systems [6].

Statecharts have formal semantics making them executable; that is, the behavior of the system modeled by a statechart can be obtained by simulating it. In order to remain useful and trustworthy the simulated behavior must confirm with the expected behavior implied by the requirements. Hence, ensuring the completeness of specifications is an important issue since the lack of completeness in specifications can have a major impact on testing, formal verification and software reuse. In the context of system modeling and software specifications the notion of completeness itself has not been satisfactorily formalized. The two recent works [7, 5] present the notion of internal completeness of requirements and provide an approach for ascertaining whether or not a given set of requirements is internally complete. They provide certain criteria for triggers and output events in real time blackbox requirements specification to be internally complete. The main issues concerning this approach are: 1) the notion of completeness studied is limited to input/output specifications, 2) they lack the formalism needed to ascertain whether or not a given model adequately represents the requirements.

Our goal in this paper is to provide a theoretical foundation for the notion of completeness for reactive system modeling and to provide a formal basis for ascertaining whether or not a given statechart model is complete (i.e., adequately represents) with respect to the requirements. Since the concept of completeness is defined with respect to the information available in the requirements, it is necessary that the requirements be *total*.

The following section describes the specification media we use for requirements and the system design. In section 3, Allen's temporal logic [2] is reviewed. Section 4 formally defines the requirements specification and the notion of totality. Section 5 discusses logical characterization of statechart models and software requirements using disjunctive logic programs. Section 6 formally introduces the concept of completeness with respect to requirements and then discusses the computational complexity for determining the completeness.

2 Specifications of reactive systems

In the development of reactive systems, we assume a two language view [10] where the requirements are specified using one representation and the architectural system designs are specified using another representation. We use a declarative medium like SCR-model [1] for requirements specification. This medium is semi-formal and is convenient for representing requirements from a users point of view. We use statecharts for representing the system specification of a reactive system. The following two subsections describe the specification media through an example.

2.1 Requirements specification using SCR-model

Instead of directly using logic to specify system requirements, we make use of the Software Cost Reduction (SCR) model to specify requirements specifications, since this model has been successfully used to specify the requirements specifications of many practical systems, and demonstrated to be an adequate methodology to characterize event-driven systems like reactive systems. In this model, the behavioral requirements of a reactive system can be specified as a set of finite mode-machines, where

- each *mode* represents a class of system states which share a set of common observable attributes, and different modes have distinct attributes;

- *mode transitions* signify system state changes;

- *transition conditions* specify the enabling conditions of a mode transition; and

- *events* with associated conditions define the times when mode transitions occur.

The behaviors of a system component can be described using a mode-machine, and the behaviors of whole system can be defined by the union of mode-machines of all system components.

To specify a reactive system, we view such a system as a black-box, and the behaviors of the system can be characterized in terms of observable inputs (triggers) and outputs of the system [5]. The following diagram shows an example alarmclock system which has two subsystems: bell window and system clock[1]. The alarmclock allows the alarm to be *set* or *canceled*. Once *ringing*,

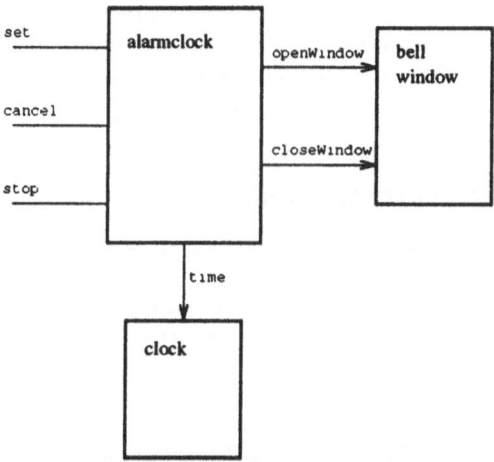

Figure 1: Alarm Clock Configuration Diagram

the alarm can be *stopped*. Stopping the alarm causes the bell window to be *closed*. The alarmclock periodically *polls* the clock for the actual time (1 sec). The alarmclock can *open* and *close* the bell window. When the alarm time is reached the alarmclock causes the bell window to *open*. If the alarm is not *stopped* the bell window is *closed* after a *fixed duration* (60 seconds).

The following table shows the SCR-model of the requirements specification of the alarmclock system. Observable behavior of the system is the status of the alarm system: opening/closing of the alarmwindow, or quiet/ringing of the system. Inputs to the system are operations of set, stop, or cancel. Time is also an observable event, since the opening or closing of the bell window depend on the alarm time and the interval of ringing. Note that the system is quiet only when the alarmwindow is iconized, and it is ringing only if the alarmwindow opens. So, this system can be characterized by two modes: quiet (when the

---

[1]This example is due to [3] with some adaptation.

bell window is closed) and ringing (when the bell window opens).

Current Mode	$set(C_1)$	$cancel(C_1)$	stop	$time(t)$	New Mode
quiet	$@T(C_1)$	$@T(\neg C_1)$	–	–	quiet
	–	–	–	$@T\ When(C_2)$	ringing
ringing	–	–	$@T$	$@T\ When(C_3)$	quiet

where $C_1 = alarmtime(t^*)$, $C_2 = alarmtime(t)$, and $C_3 = in\ ringing\ 60s$.

An expression of the form $@T$ represents an event occurring at the time interval. An expression of the form $@T(Cond)$ represents an event occurring at the time interval and $Cond$ is a postcondition of this event. An expression of the form $@T\ When(Cond)$ represents an event occurring at the time interval while condition $Cond$ is true.

2.2 System specifications using statecharts

Statecharts are structured visual formalisms that extend the conventional finite state machines by AND/OR decompositions of states together with inter-level transitions and a broadcast mechanism for communication between concurrent components. Hence there is both hierarchy (for depthwise descriptions) and orthogonality for breadthwise compositions). The hierarchy of statecharts facilitates the modeling of reactive system in a top-down way. The orthogonal composition in statecharts are very powerful to represent interaction among concurrent components. The semantics of interaction between concurrent components is slightly different from that in Harel's statechart. In this paper, the semantics of concurrent components ensures any transition shared (i.e., synchronous) between components to be taken only simultaneously. Fig. 2 shows the system specification of the already discussed alarmclock using statecharts. This statechart consists of three parallel components: alarmclock (middle component) and system clock (left-hand component) and bell system (right-hand component). In the description of the alarmclock system, the state *alarmon* contains a substatechart which represents the details of the system behavior when the alarm is on. According to the semantics, the shared transition open-Window in the orthogonal components alarmclock and bell system should happen synchronously. Similarly, the shared transition closeWindow should also synchronize.

A system specification represented in statecharts can be formalized in Allen's temporal logic [2] by transforming the statecharts into a set of Allen's temporal logical formulas. We prefer Allen's temporal logic due to the following reasons: 1) it has plenty of temporal predicates to represent various temporal relations; 2) syntactically it is much easier to distinguish between transitions and properties associated with transitions; and 3) both SCR and statecharts can be translated into Allen's logic.

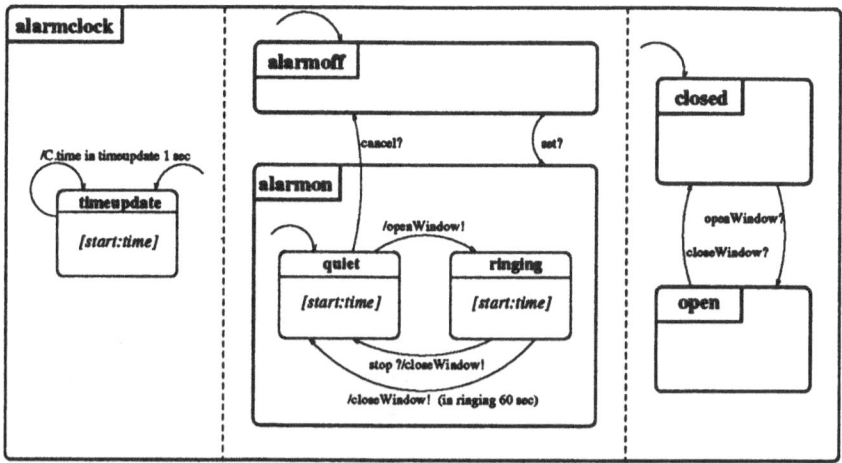

Figure 2: Alarm Clock Statechart

3 Temporal logic and time structures

We use Allen's temporal logic as an intermediate form in the process of developing disjunctive logic programs from i) requirement specification represented in SCR; ii) system specifications represented in statecharts. In this paper, we refer to Allen's temporal logic simply as temporal logic. Temporal logic of Allen is a (syntactically) second-order logic, which makes use of two higher-order predicates $holds, occur$. The predicate $holds(A, t)$ asserts that A holds over a time interval t, and in any subinterval of t. The predicate $occur(A, t)$ states that event A occurs over the smallest time interval t. The temporal logic also has several temporal predicates $before, meets, overlays, starts, finishes, during$ and $equal$. Intuitively, temporal predicates assert the temporal relationship of two time intervals t_1 and t_2. The predicate $before(t_1, t_2)$ states t_1 is a time interval temporally before the time interval t_2. Similarly the predicate $meet(t_1, t_2)$ means that the time interval t_2 starts immediately after the time interval t_1. The intuitive meaning of other predicates can be obtained directly from the predicate symbols themselves. For more details on these predicates readers are referred to [2].

We define the notion of a *time structure* to bring out the relationship between statecharts and Allen's temporal logic. The motivation for establishing the relationship is to develop a formal methodology for Allen's logic characterization of a system specification represented in statecharts.

A time structure **T** is a (finite or infinite) tree where each arc represents a time/subtime interval of arbitrary but finite length. A time interval is either a basic time interval (*e.g.* t_0 and t_{01}) in time structure, or a composed time interval (*e.g.* $t_0 t_1$, and $t_1 t_{10} t_{101}$), which is a sequence of subtime intervals in time structure. In other words, a time interval is a path and the various arcs in the path form subintervals. A path in the structure corresponds to some property which may *hold* in the interval. The nodes in the structure correspond to the *occurrence* of events which are assumed to be instantaneous. The occurrence

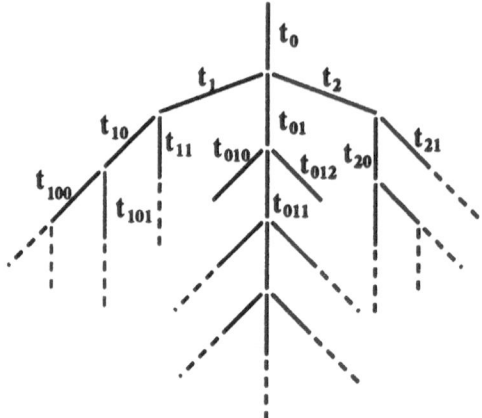

Figure 3: Time Structure

of an event may mark the end of a subinterval if a property which was holding true is not affected by the occurrence or it may mark the end of an interval if a property changes its truth value due to the occurrence of the event. It is to be noted that, the tree nature of the structure does not imply any branching-time behavior. Instead it could represent properties which could be true in overlapping time intervals.

The computation in a statechart can also be represented by such a time structure. An arc in the structure corresponds to a state in the statechart where some property may hold true. A path having two or more arcs may represent a superstate in which some property which holds in the interval represented by the path is true. Subintervals in a structure may correspond to substates in a statechart. Two or more arcs leaving a node may correspond to state changes in orthogonal components of the statecharts. Nonterminating computation in statecharts which does not have any periodic behavior will have to be represented by infinite tree structure. However, terminating computations and nonterminating computations which have periodic behavior can be represented by infinite tree structure.

3.1 Expressing requirements in temporal logic

Here we show how the requirements of the alarmclock example discussed before can be formalized in temporal logic. From the structure of the SCR-based requirements specification it is clear that such specifications can be easily represented in first-order logic using temporal predicates. A mode transition in the SCR requirements can be expressed in the form:

$$holds(Current\_Mode, t) \land occur(Event, t) \land meets^*(t, t') \rightarrow holds(New\_Mode, t').$$

Intuitively, this expression says that at any time interval t, if system state is in *Current Mode* and event *Event* occurs, then at the following time interval t' system state changes to *New Mode*. The rules 1-5 are the temporal formulas transformed from the SCR-model above. The rules 6-9 essentially assert that the truth value of attributes *quiet*, *alarmtime(t)*, $\neg$ *alarmtime(t)*, or *ringing* would not be changed simply due to the progress of time. In other words, the truth value of the attributes should be inherited from previous mode. We call these rules *persistence rules*. Note that these rules have to be included in the requirements specification, since otherwise the so called *frame problems* would arise in the reasoning using temporal knowledge.

Let $meets^*(t, t') \equiv_{def} meets(t, t') \wedge \neg \exists t'' within(t'', t')$.

1. $holds(quiet, t) \wedge occur(set(alarmtime(t^*)), t) \wedge meets^*(t, t')$
$$\rightarrow holds(alarmtime(t^*), t').$$

2. $holds(quiet, t) \wedge occur(cancel(alarmtime(t^*)), t) \wedge meets^*(t, t')$
$$\rightarrow \neg holds(alarmtime(t^*), t').$$

3. $holds(ringing, t) \wedge occur(stop, t) \wedge meets^*(t, t') \rightarrow holds(quiet, t')$.

4. $holds(alarmtime, t) \wedge meets^*(t, t') \rightarrow holds(ringing, t')$.

5. $holds(ringing, t) \wedge holds(ringing\_in\_60s, t) \wedge meets^*(t, t')$
$$\rightarrow holds(quiet, t').$$

6. $holds(quiet, t) \wedge meets^*(t, t') \wedge \neg holds(alarmtime(t'), t') \rightarrow holds(quiet, t')$.

7. $holds(quiet, t) \wedge holds(alarmtime(t^*), t) \wedge \neg occur(cancel(alarmtime(t^*)), t') \wedge$
$$meets^*(t, t') \rightarrow holds(alarmtime(t^*), t').$$

8. $holds(quiet, t) \wedge \neg holds(alarmtime(t^*), t) \wedge \neg occur(set(alarmtime(t^*)), t') \wedge$
$$meets^*(t, t') \rightarrow \neg holds(alarmtime(t^*), t').$$

9. $holds(ringing, t) \wedge meets^*(t, t') \wedge \neg holds(stop, t') \wedge$
$$holds(ringing\_less\_60s, t) \rightarrow holds(ringing, t').$$

$holds(ringing\_in\_60s, t) \equiv_{def} meets^*(t, t_1) \wedge \neg holds(ringing, t_1) \wedge$
$$holds(ringing, t) \wedge length(t) = 60s$$

$holds(ringing\_less\_60s, t) \equiv_{def} meets^*(t, t_1) \wedge \neg holds(ringing, t_1) \wedge$
$$holds(ringing, t) \wedge length(t) < 60s$$

Finally, we need axioms to classify the relationship among modes and among inputs to the system. For this purpose we add the following axioms. These are also necessary for an unambiguous interpretation of the requirements.

A_1 $holds(quiet, t) \oplus holds(ringing, t)$.
A_2 $holds(open, t) \leftrightarrow holds(ringing, t)$.
A_3 $holds(closed, t) \leftrightarrow holds(quiet, t)$.
A_4 $occur(set, t) \oplus occur(cancel, t) \oplus occur(stop, t) \vee occur(tick, t)$.

The axiom A_1 asserts that the modes *quiet* and *ringing* are exclusive. The axiom A_2 states that *window-opening* is an attribute associated with the mode *ringing*, while the axiom A_3 says *window-closed* is an attribute associated with the mode *quiet*. The fourth axiom A_4 expresses that all the inputs *set*, *stop* and *cancel* are exclusive, while they are inclusive with time passing. *tick* is special constant which expresses a primitive time interval.

4 Totality in requirements

In this section, we formally define the notion of totality of a requirement specification. Intuitively the requirements specification of a reactive system is considered to be total, if the truth of the output attributes can be uniquely determined. In other words, with respect to every input to the system, all the aspects of the system behaviors such as state transitions, true/false of state attributes, can be determined uniquely. Before defining totality we give a formal definition of requirements specifications for reactive systems. Based on this definition we formalize the notion of totality.

4.1 Requirements specification without time

The *requirements specification* R of a system S is a first-order theory (I, S, A), where

1. I is the input specification. Among the predicate symbols occurring in S, we identify a subset $\{p_1, \cdots, p_m\}$ of them, called input predicate symbols. Each input predicate p (of arity n) is specified by a set $I_p = \{p(\bar{d}_1), \cdots, p(\bar{d}_l)\}$, where $\bar{d}_j$ is a tuple $(c_{j1}, \cdots, c_{jn})$ of constants. The input specification is the Cartesian product $I_{p_1} \times \cdots \times I_{p_m}$. An input to the system S is any element of the input specification, *i.e.*, $E \in I_{p_1} \times \cdots \times I_{p_m}$, sometimes, denoted by the set $E = \{p_1(\bar{d}_1), \cdots, p_m(\bar{d}_m)\}$.

2. S is the requirements of the system S, which is a set of first-order logic formulas over a finite domain $\{c_1, \cdots, c_k\}$.

3. A is a set of axioms consisting of *Domain Closure Axiom*: $\forall X [X = c_1 \vee \cdots \vee X = c_k]$; and *Unique Name Axioms*: $c_i \neq c_j$, for each pair of distinguished constants c_i and c_j.

Intuitively, the domain closure axiom asserts that variables can be replaced only by constants in the domain, and the unique name axioms state that all constants in the domain are distinguishable.

4.2 Requirements specification with time

The specification $R = (I, S, A)$ of a system S is a first-order theory, where

1. I is the input specification of the system S *w.r.t.* input predicate symbols $p_1, \cdots, p_m$. The input specification for an input predicate symbol p at time t is a set of predicates

$$I_p(t) = \{ \; occur(p(\bar{d}_1), t), \; \cdots, \; occur(p(\bar{d}_l), t), \; occur(tick, t) \; \}.$$

where each $p()$ is a system related event and $\bar{d}_j$ is a tuple $(c_{j1}, \cdots, c_{jn})$ of constants. The predicate $occur(tick, t)$ corresponds to the passage of time when no system related event happens. The input specification I for the system S consists of the Cartesian products *w.r.t.* each time t. An input to the system S at time t is any element $E(t)$ of $I_{p_1}(t) \times \cdots \times I_{p_m}(t)$, sometimes, denoted by the set $E(t) = \{occur(p_1(\bar{d}_1), t), \cdots, occur(p_m(\bar{d}_m), t)\}$. If there is no input to the system at time t, then $E(t)$ consists of all negations of inputs, *i.e.*,

$$E(t) = \{\neg occur(p_j(\bar{d}_j), t) \mid p_j(\bar{d}_j) \in I_{p_j}(t), \; \forall j\}.$$

An input to the system S over a time structure $\mathbf{T}$ is a collection of inputs to the system S over time t: $E = \bigcup_t E(t)$.

2. S is a set of first-order logic formulas in Allen's temporal logic over a finite domain $\{c_1, \cdots, c_k\}$.

3. A is a set of axioms consisting of *Domain Closure Axiom* and *Unique Name Axioms*.

4.3 Totality of requirement specification

Let $R = (I, S, A)$ be the specification of a system S. Then the requirement R of S is *total*, if for each input E to S, $S^+ = S \cup E \cup A$ satisfies the following *totality condition(s)*.

1. $T(S^+)$ is closed under first-order consequence.

2. $T(S^+ \cup \{B \mid S^+ \models B\} \cup \{\neg B \mid S^+ \not\models B\}) = T(S^+)$, where B is any variable-free predicate.

3. $T(S^+)$ is consistent.

For the alarmclock system S, the system specification S consists of all temporal logical formulas transformed from SCR-model of the requirements specification. The input specification I consists of only one predicate, say *in*, and

$$I_{in}(t) = \{occur(in(set), t), occur(in(stop), t), occur(in(cancel), t), occur(tick, t)\}.$$

5 Representation using disjunctive logic programs

A *disjunctive logic program* is a finite set of disjunctive clauses of the following form:

$$A_1 \vee \cdots \vee A_k \leftarrow B_1, \cdots, B_n, not\ C_1, \cdots, not\ C_m.$$

Intuitively, a disjunctive clause says that if all B_is are true, and all C_js are false, then either A_1, or $\cdots$, or A_k is true. Among the disjunctive logic programs, we are particularly interested in disjunctive stratified logic programs and locally stratified logic programs. A disjunctive logic program is *stratified*, if all the predicate symbols occurring in the program can be decomposed into disjoint sets so that negative results can be concluded by applying CWA (Closed World Assumption) to predicates based on the hierarchy of predicate symbols. A disjunctive logic program is *locally stratified*, if all the ground atoms (propositions) occurring in the program can be decomposed into disjoint sets so that negative results can be concluded by applying CWA. If every clause in a disjunctive stratified logic program is definite (*i.e.*, $k = 1$), then the program is called *a stratified logic program*.

Stratified logic programs preserve many attractive properties. First of all, every stratified logic program must have a unique canonical (Herbrand) model, called *perfect model* of that program. The perfect model of a stratified program is also a minimal (Herbrand) model, but minimal models may not be perfect. The semantics of a stratified program can be uniquely determined by its perfect model: every ground atom in the perfect model is interpreted as *true*; otherwise, *false*. A disjunctive stratified logic program must have perfect models, but may not be unique due to the existence of disjunctive conclusions. On the other hand, a disjunctive stratified logic program can be reduced into a set of stratified logic programs for each disjunctive inputs. The perfect models of those reduced stratified logic programs coincide with the perfect models of the disjunctive logic programs. In other words, if non-determinism in a disjunctive stratified program is ruled out, the disjunctive stratified program can then be reduced to a stratified logic program. More details on stratified logic programs and disjunctive (locally) stratified logic programs can be found in [11].

5.1 Expressing requirement specification in disjunctive logic programs

The total requirement specification of a reactive system represented in temporal logic can be transformed into disjunctive logic program in a straightforward manner. This fact can be easily understood, since a proposition B cannot be derived in the logic program if and only if its negation can be derived in the total temporal logic requirements. In other words, a total requirement in temporal logic can be rewritten into a disjunctive logic program by dropping all negative conclusions of temporal formulas. Negative results in a disjunctive logic program can be concluded based on closed world assumptions (CWA). In fact, the requirements expressed in disjunctive logic programs will be more concise than the requirements expressed in temporal logic. The notion of totality in the general context of first order theory as defined in section 3, can be re-formalized to suit the disjunctive logic programs by the following theorem.

Theorem: Let $R = (I, S)$ be the specification of a system S expressed in the form of a disjunctive stratified logic program. Then the requirement R of S is *total*, if for each input E to S, $P = S \cup E$ has a unique perfect model M.

Note that the uniqueness of the perfect model implicitly says that the non-determinism in a disjunctive logic program of the system requirements is due to non-determinism of inputs to the system. Whenever the inputs to the system are known, the system behavior would be completely determined. Note also that P must satisfy the domain closure axiom and unique name axioms, since the perfect model semantics of stratified programs are based on the Herbrand interpretation of logic programs.

5.2 Representing statecharts in disjunctive stratified logic programs

A system specification represented in statecharts can be formalized in Allen's temporal logic by transforming the statecharts into a set of Allen's temporal logical formulas.

Statecharts expressed in Allen's logic can be transformed to a disjunctive logic program if the pre- and post-conditions associated with each transition can be expressed in the form of disjunctive clauses. Expressing statecharts in a disjunctive logic program can help us reduce the expressive complexity and the computational complexity for determining the completeness of statechart-based modeling of a reactive system (to be discussed in section 6). The possibility of expressing statecharts in disjunctive stratified logic program is due to the fact that each individual statechart can be transformed into a finite/ infinite tree structure by associating a time (point or interval) with each occurrence of all states. Based on this tree structure of transition graph, we can arrange all of states and transitions occurring in the tree structure into a hierarchy.

A statechart can be transformed into a disjunctive logic program, using the following four group of rules: *transition rules, initial rules, hierarchical rules*, and *persistent rules*. Transition rules are obtained from transitions and describe the change of state effected by the occurrence of the transition. Initial rules show the triggering conditions of initial transitions for system components and all substatecharts. Hierarchical rules describe the relationships between statecharts and their components. Persistent rules, as initially discussed in the Section 4, are used to assert that truth values of attributes at each state would not be changed due to the progress of time.

The disjunctive logic program corresponding to the system specification of the example alarmclock represented in statechart is shown in Fig.4. Due to lack of space, we show only the final temporal logical formulas but not the intermediate forms in the process of deriving logic programs from the statechart of Fig. 2.

6 Completeness

Informally, the modeling of a reactive system is said to be complete with respect to the requirements of that system if the behaviors formalized in the modeling of that system coincide with the behaviors expressed by the requirements. Since both the requirements and the system specification (model) can be represented in the form of disjunctive logic programs, the completeness of the model with respect to the requirements in terms of logic programs can be understood intuitively as the semantic equivalence of the logic programs expressing the requirements and the model.

On the other hand, during the development process of the system specification represented in statecharts, a possible state in the requirements may be refined into several disjoint substates, or many intermediate states might be introduced. To capture the relationship between the states in the requirement specification and in the system specification, we make use of a *state refinement table*: each proposition B (constant c) available in the requirement is associated with a set of propositions $\{B_1, \cdots, B_k\}$ (a set of constants $\{c_1, \cdots, c_k\}$), where each B_j (c_j) expresses a refined state associated with B (c). This kind of information can also be formalized in a disjunctive formula of the following form:

$$holds(B, t) \leftrightarrow holds(B_1, t) \vee \cdots \vee holds(B_k, t),$$

This can be represented in the form of disjunctive logical rules:

$$holds(B_1, t) \vee \cdots \vee holds(B_k, t) \leftarrow holds(B, t).$$
$$holds(B, t) \leftarrow holds(B_1, t).$$
$$\cdots$$
$$holds(B, t) \leftarrow holds(B_k, t).$$

Transition Rules

$hold(quiet, t) \land occur(openWin, t) \land meets^*(t, t') \rightarrow hold(ringing, t')$.

$hold(ringing, t) \land occur(stop, t) \land meets^*(t, t') \rightarrow occur(closeWin, t')$.

$hold(ringing, t) \land meets^*(t, t') \land length(t + t') = 60s$
$\rightarrow occur(closeWin!, t')$.

$occur(closeWin!, t) \land meets^*(t, t') \rightarrow hold(quiet, t')$.

$hold(quiet, t) \land occur(cancel, t) \land meets^*(t, t') \rightarrow hold(alarmoff, t')$.

$hold(timeupdate, t) \land occur(C.time, t') \land finish(t', t) \land length(t) = 60s \land$
$meets^*(t', t'') \rightarrow occur(C.time, t'')$.

$hold(alarmoff, t) \land occur(set, t) \land meets^*(t, t'') \rightarrow occur(initAlarmon, t')$.

$occur(openWin!, t) \rightarrow occur(openWin?, t)$.

$occur(closeWin?, t) \rightarrow occur(closeWin!, t)$.

$occur(closeWin!, t) \rightarrow occur(closeWin?, t)$.

$occur(closeWin?, t) \rightarrow occur(closeWin!, t)$.

Initial Rules

$occur(initAlarmclock, t) \rightarrow occur(initAlarmclock.A, t)$.

$occur(initAlarmclock, t) \rightarrow occur(initAlarmclock.B, t)$.

$occur(initAlarmclock, t) \rightarrow occur(initAlarmclock.C, t)$.

$occur(initAlarmclock.A, t) \land meets^*(t, t') \rightarrow hold(timeupdate, t')$.

$occur(initAlarmclock.B, t) \land meets^*(t, t') \rightarrow hold(alarmoff, t')$.

$occur(initAlarmclock.C, t) \land meets^*(t, t') \rightarrow hold(closed, t')$.

$occur(initAlarmon, t) \land meets^*(t, t') \rightarrow hold(quiet, t')$.

Hierarchical Rules

$hold(alarmclock, t) \rightarrow hold(alarmclock.A, t)$.

$hold(alarmclock, t) \rightarrow hold(alarmclock.B, t)$.

$hold(alarmclock.A, t) \rightarrow hold(timeupdate, t)$.

$hold(timeupdate, t) \rightarrow hold(alarmclock.A, t)$.

$\vdots$

Persistent Rules

$holds(alarmoff, t) \land \neg occur(set, t) \land meets^*(t, t') \rightarrow holds(alarmoff, t')$.

$holds(quiet, t) \land \neg occur(openWin!, t) \land meets^*(t, t') \rightarrow holds(quiet, t')$.

$holds(ringing, t) \land \neg occur(stop, t) \land \neg occur(closeWin!, t)$
$\land meets^*(t, t') \rightarrow holds(ringing, t')$.

$holds(timeupdate, t) \land \neg occur(C.time?, t) \land meets^*(t, t') \rightarrow holds(timeupdate, t')$.

$holds(closed, t) \land \neg occur(openWin?, t) \land meets^*(t, t') \rightarrow holds(closed, t')$.

$holds(open, t) \land \neg occur(closeWin?, t) \land meets^*(t, t') \rightarrow holds(open, t')$.

Figure 4: Disjunctive logic program for the alarmclock example

Information corresponding to constant refinement can be captured in a similar way.

Let P_r be the disjunctive logical program for requirement, and P_m be the disjunctive logical program for modeling. Let $\mathcal{P}$ be all logical symbols occurring in P_r. Then we say the modeling P_m is *complete w.r.t.* the requirement P_r if both the following conditions are satisfied:

- for each perfect model [11] $\mathcal{M}_r$ of P_r, there exists a perfect model $\mathcal{N}_m$ of P_m such that the extension of $\mathcal{N}_m$ w.r.t. $\mathcal{P}$ coincides with $\mathcal{M}_r$; and

- for each perfect model $\mathcal{N}_m$ of P_m, there exists a perfect model $\mathcal{M}_r$ of P_r such that the extension of $\mathcal{N}_m$ w.r.t. $\mathcal{P}$ coincides with $\mathcal{M}_r$.

In the alarmclock example, the state-refinement can be captured using the following *state refinement table*:

Req.States	SystemStates
quiet	alarmoff quiet
ringing	ringing
open	open
closed	closed

Note that the mode *quiet* in the system requirement is refined into two distinct states *alarmoff* and *quiet* which is a substate of *alarmon*.

To determine whether the statechart-based model of the alarmclock system is complete, we first transform the first-order theory (represented in temporal logic) obtained from SCR-model into a disjunctive logic program. Then we can compute all the perfect models of the disjunctive logic program obtained from requirements and all the perfect models of the disjunctive logic program obtained from the system model. After computing the perfect models, we can decide the completeness by checking the completeness criteria.

7 Discussion

One important issue is the computational complexity and decidability for determining the completeness of a specification model with respect to total requirements. For models without time or for models involving finite time structures, this turns out to be decidable, although it is an NP-hard problem. One brutal way to decide the completeness is to Herbrand instantiate the disjunctive logic programs obtained from requirements and system model, and then to compute a perfect model using truth tables. Due to the finiteness of the Herbrand bases of the associated programs, clearly, the number of perfect models for those programs are finite, as well. Therefore, the completeness of a specification model with respect to total requirements is decidable. However, for models involving infinite time structures, the problem of determining completeness is undecidable.

The importance for ensuring completeness makes this work valuable. The importance for completeness stems from the necessity for robustness and safety in reactive system. A model that is complete with respect to the total requirement specification will necessarily satisfy robustness and all safety properties implied by the system requirements. Robustness is satisfied, since a complete model of a system can appropriately handle all circumstances a system may have, and yields an output with respect to any external and internal stimuli. Safety properties are the logical consequences of the totality of a correct requirement specification. So, robustness and safety properties are the implications of the completeness of the modeling with respect to the total requirement specification.

References

[1] Atlee J, Gannon J. State-based model checking of event-driven system requirements. Software Engineering Notes December 1991

[2] Allen JF. Towards a general theory of action and time. Artificial Intelligence 1984; (23)

[3] Coleman D, Hayes F, Bear S. Introducing objectcharts or how to use statecharts on object-oriented design. IEEE Trans Soft Engg January 1992

[4] Harel D. Statecharts: a visual formalism for complex systems. Science of Computer Programming 1987; (8)

[5] Jaffe MS, Leveson NG, Heimdhal MPE, Melhart BE. Software requirements analysis for real-time process-control systems. IEEE Trans Soft Engg 1991; (3)

[6] Leveson NG, Heimdhal M, Hildreth H, Reese J, Ortega R. Experiences using statecharts for a system requirement specification. In: Proc Sixth Int'l Workshop on Software Specification and Design, 1991

[7] Melhart BE, Leveson NG, Jaffe MS. Analysis capabilities for requirements specified in statecharts. In: Proc Fifth Int'l Workshop on Software Specification and Design, 1989.

[8] Ostroff JS. A verifier for real-time properties. Journal of Real-Time Systems 1992; (4)

[9] Pnueli A. Application of temporal logic to specification and verification of reactive systems: a survey of current trends. In: de Roever WP, de Bakker JW, Rozenberg G (eds) Current trends in concurrency. Springer-Verlag, 1986 (Lecture notes in computer science no 224)

[10] Pnueli A. Specification and development of reactive systems. In: Information processing. Elsevier Science Publishers, 1986

[11] Przymusinski TC. On the declarative semantics of deductive databases and logic programming. In: Minker J (ed) Foundations of deductive databases and logic programming. Morgan-Kaufmann, 1988

Knowledge Recovery and Development

W.M. Jaworski   R. Shinghal

Department of Computer Science

Concordia University

Montreal, Canada

{jaworski,shinghal}@cs.concordia.ca

1   Introduction

There is a generic uncertainty in information systems, and this uncertainty is amplified by lack of direct connectivity between components and structures, resulting mostly from the limitations of the multitude of notations and formats being used.

In this paper, we present a meta-notation named InfoSyntax [2] that enables us to recover and normalize knowledge from existing information systems. The different representations or disjointed views used in information systems force developers and users to create taxing mental connections between parts of an information system. Often, existing notations are redundant: they require multiple copies of the same object. Our proposed syntax identifies each object in one place, but then allows it to be referenced repeatedly in many contexts.

Existing notations are based on sequences of expressions, which are them-selves represented by a sequence of symbols. It is extremely difficult to define multidimensional objects in such sequential notations. Therefore, we need a notation with a capability to deal with this multidimensionality. In the In-foSyntax notation, we introduce sets and the relationships among them. By treating each set as representing a dimension, we are able to model multidi-mensional information systems. The vocabulary of the schemata covers whole concepts of information systems, that is, the modelling of objects, functionality, and dynamics.

Schemata and concepts can be developed while we are creating an informa-tion system or inspecting it for incompleteness and uncertainty. Only a limited number of generic schemata need to be introduced. We use our representation to define the structures and concepts as they were intended to be, that is, in a uniform, normalized format.

The schemata are developed stepwise by producing sets, structures, and their relationships. They provide templates for process, data flow, and data model definition; for instance, execution tracing for verification and perfor-mance evaluation is possible.

2   A toy expert system example

To illustrate our approach, we adapt the tongue-in-cheek expert system UN-PERS [4], which seeks to infer the position of a university person by observing him/her on campus. The nine **prodrules** (short for production rules) are the following:

1. If *he is a student,he is emaciated*, and *he wears a helmet*, then *he is a undergraduate student.*

2. If *he is a student*, and *he is emaciated*, then *he is a graduate student.*

3. If *he is an academic*, and *he eats junk food*, then *he is a student.*

4. If *he is an administrator*, and *he talks to himself*,then *he is a secretary.*

5. If *he is an academic, he talks to himself*, and *he takes long lunches*,then *he is a professor.*

6. If *he is an administrator, he writes memos*, and *he takes long lunches*, then *he is a dean.*

7. If *he wears a suit*, and *he shuffles papers*, then *he is an administrator.*

8. If *he looks confused*, then *he is an academic.*

9. If *he looks sleepy*, then *he is an academic.*

As can be discovered by studying the above, UNPERS has five **final hypotheses**: the person is *an undergraduate student, a graduate student, a secretary, a professor, a dean.* UNPERS has three **intermediate hypotheses**: the person is *a student, an academic, an administrator.* The intermediate hypotheses are inferred as transitional results in the processing of the prodrules. They appear as antecedents, too, in prodrules, and then for notational clarity they are known as **intermediate evidence**. The **initial evidence** to infer a person's role is drawn from the following: the person is *emaciated, wears a helmet, eats junk food, talks to himself, takes long lunches, writes memos, wears a suit, shuffles papers, looks confused*, and *looks sleepy.*

For our further discussion of this example, let us assume that if we can infer more than one hypothesis from a set of prodrules, then we retain only the hypothesis that requires the most specific evidence. This imposes a priority ordering on the prodrules. Now, given the initial evidence that a person observed is *emaciated, wears a helmet, eats junk food*, and *looks confused*, we reason sequentially through prodrules 8, 3 and 1 to infer that the person is *an undergraduate student.* The procedure used exemplifies **forechaining** (short for forward chaining), since we start from initial evidence and reason 'forward' to conclude a final hypothesis.

Alternatively, we can reason by **backchaining** (short for backward chaining). For example, we first conjecture the final hypothesis that the person is *an undergraduate student.* We then confirm our conjecture by reasoning 'backward' through the prodrules to establish the initial evidence to be that *he is emaciated, wears a helmet, eats junk food*, and *looks confused.*

We can use the notation of AND/OR graphs to show the reasoning required for undergraduate student using an inference net (Figure 1). We next present in Figures 2 to 9 the InfoMap representations of the above discussion.

Figure 2a shows a subschema for the text of UNPERS prodrules. Its last row says that the nine prodrules should be in sequence. In Figure 2b, the above subschema is loaded with the text of the nine prodrules. Its first column defines the sequence of the prodrules.

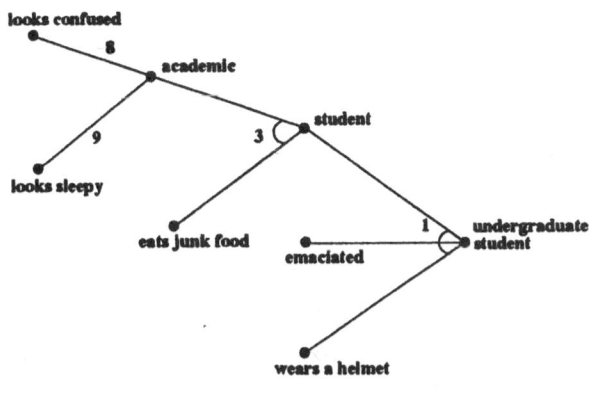

Figure 1: An inference net in UNPERS.

The subschema of Figure 3a permits classification of evidence and hypotheses in the prodrules. Figure 3b displays this classification for the evidence and hypotheses of UNPERS; for example, the third column identifies the five final hypotheses.

The subschema of Figure 4a allows the representation of prodrules declaratively. Individual columns of Figure 4b show the individual prodrules parsed into evidence and hypothesis. An evidence is denoted by 't', a hypothesis by 'T'.

Figure 5a delineates the processing order for forechaining, assuming that the initial evidence is given by the first column. The processing order is presented as the last row in the {VIEW} of Figure 5b. Then Figure 5c shows the prodrules sorted columnwise in processing order. Figure 6, parts a, b and c are for backchaining; they correspond to the parts a, b and c of Figure 5. Similarly, parts a, b and c of Figure 7 for the inference net of Figure 1 correspond to parts a, b and c of Figure 5.

Till now, we have presented our material incrementally in Figures 2 to 7. These figures are extractions from a knowledge base built by us incrementally in a non-deterministic fashion. The InfoSchema of this knowledge base is given in a graphical and a tabular form in Figure 8. Each set is represented by a large rectangle (not to be confused with the small rectangles or squares) in Figure 8a. The rectangle contains the set name and its cardinality. Each set plays roles, which are shown by small squares containing letters designating the specific role. This is similar to the roles attached to entities in data modeling [1]. The relationships between the sets is shown by edges. The cardinality of the relationship is shown by a number next to the edge. In short, the relationship cardinality specifies the number of relevant columns in the Infomap built using the InfoSchema. The small rectangles in the righthand side of Figure 8a contain the set roles and the possible member roles for that set role. An InfoSchema, developed incrementally, for the structures of the information systems is shown in Figure 9. Finally, Figure 10 is developed to illustrate the approach described by Zahnister [5].

3   Conclusion

We agree with Parnas [3] that information systems should be created and presented in small chunks. The InfoMaps are supporting the cross-functional team, and allow N-dimensional system modeling as well as concurrent development, which are the three paradigms required by Zahnister [5]. Infomaps with proper display equipment offer media equivalent to those suggested by Zahnister, that is, storyboard, whiteboard, flipcharts, and a CASE tool. Zahnister also suggests a repository for views and a CASE tool to ensure consistency of inter-relationships among the views. InfoMaps offer an environment for creating an integrated representation of an information system incrementally and displaying the required standard or views defined by queries. In addition to a series of displays, as suggested by Parnas [3], there is also a need for an SQL-equivalent for querying a repository of knowledge about information systems. We are in the process of developing such a system.

References

[1] Booch G. Object oriented design with applications. Benjamin/Cummings, 1992

[2] Jaworski WM, Cummings T. Program normalization and optimization: using InfoMaps as inspection and program testing tool. Canadian Conference on Electrical and Computer Engineering, Quebec City, Canada, 1991

[3] Parnas DL, Madey J, Iglewski M. Formal documentation of well-structured programs. CRL Report 259, Communications Research Laboratory, McMaster University, Hamilton, Canada, 1992

[4] Shinghal R. Formal concepts in artificial intelligence. Chapman & Hall, London, UK. co-published in the US with Van Nostrand, New York, 1992, pp 324–339

[5] Zahnister RA. Design by walking around. Communications of the ACM 1993; 36(10):115-123

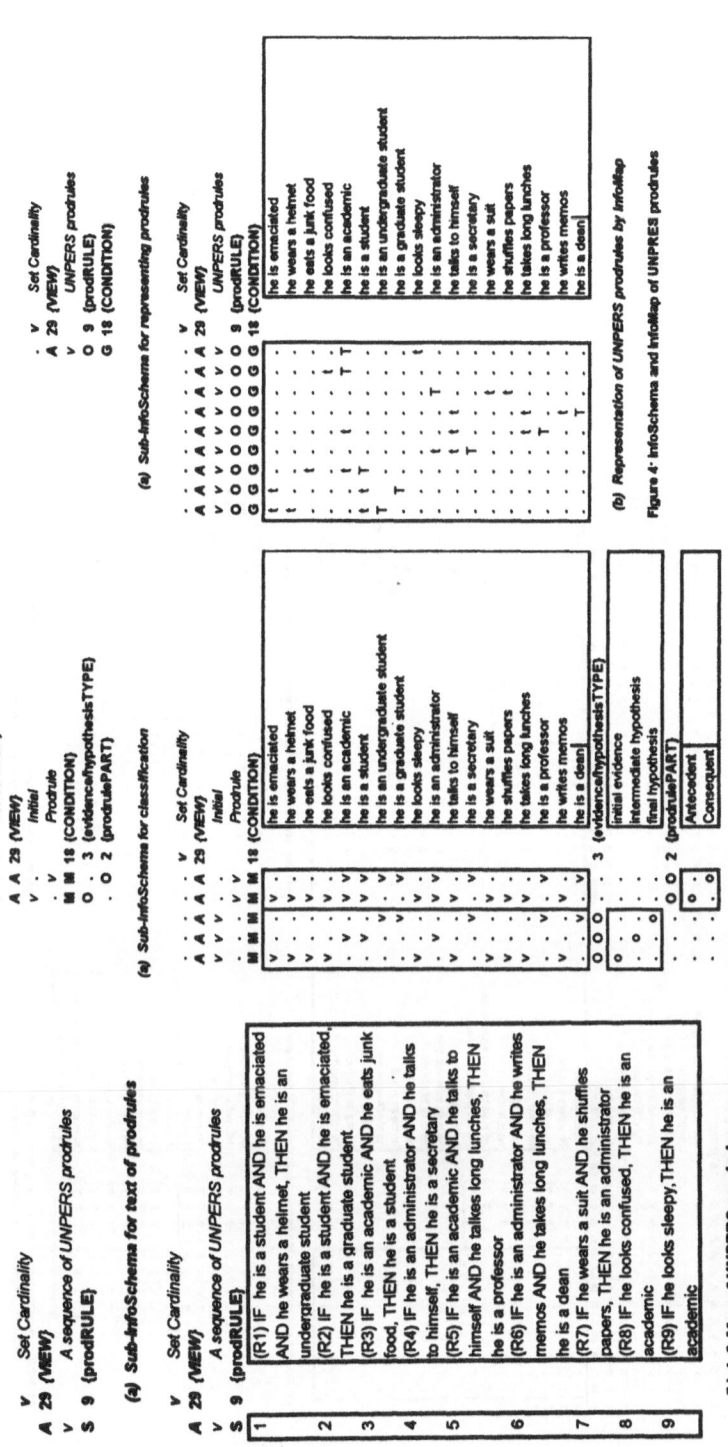

(a) Sub-InfoSchema for text of prodrules

(b) InfoMap of UNPERS prodrules

Figure 2: An example of InfoSchema and InfoMap

(a) Sub-InfoSchema for classification

(b) InfoMap with classification of UNPERS

Figure 3: An example of InfoSchema and InfoMap

(a) Sub-InfoSchema for representing prodrules

(b) Representation of UNPERS prodrules by InfoMap

Figure 4: InfoSchema and InfoMap of UNPRES prodrules

(R1) IF he is a student AND he is emaciated AND he wears a helmet, THEN he is an undergraduate student

(R2) IF he is a student AND he is emaciated, THEN he is a graduate student

(R3) IF he is an academic AND he eats junk food, THEN he is a student

(R4) IF he is an administrator AND he talks to himself, THEN he is a secretary

(R5) IF he is an academic AND he talks to himself AND he takes long lunches, THEN he is a professor

(R6) IF he is an administrator AND he writes memos AND he takes long lunches, THEN he is a dean

(R7) IF he wears a suit AND he shuffles papers, THEN he is an administrator

(R8) IF he looks confused, THEN he is an academic

(R9) IF he looks sleepy, THEN he is an academic

136

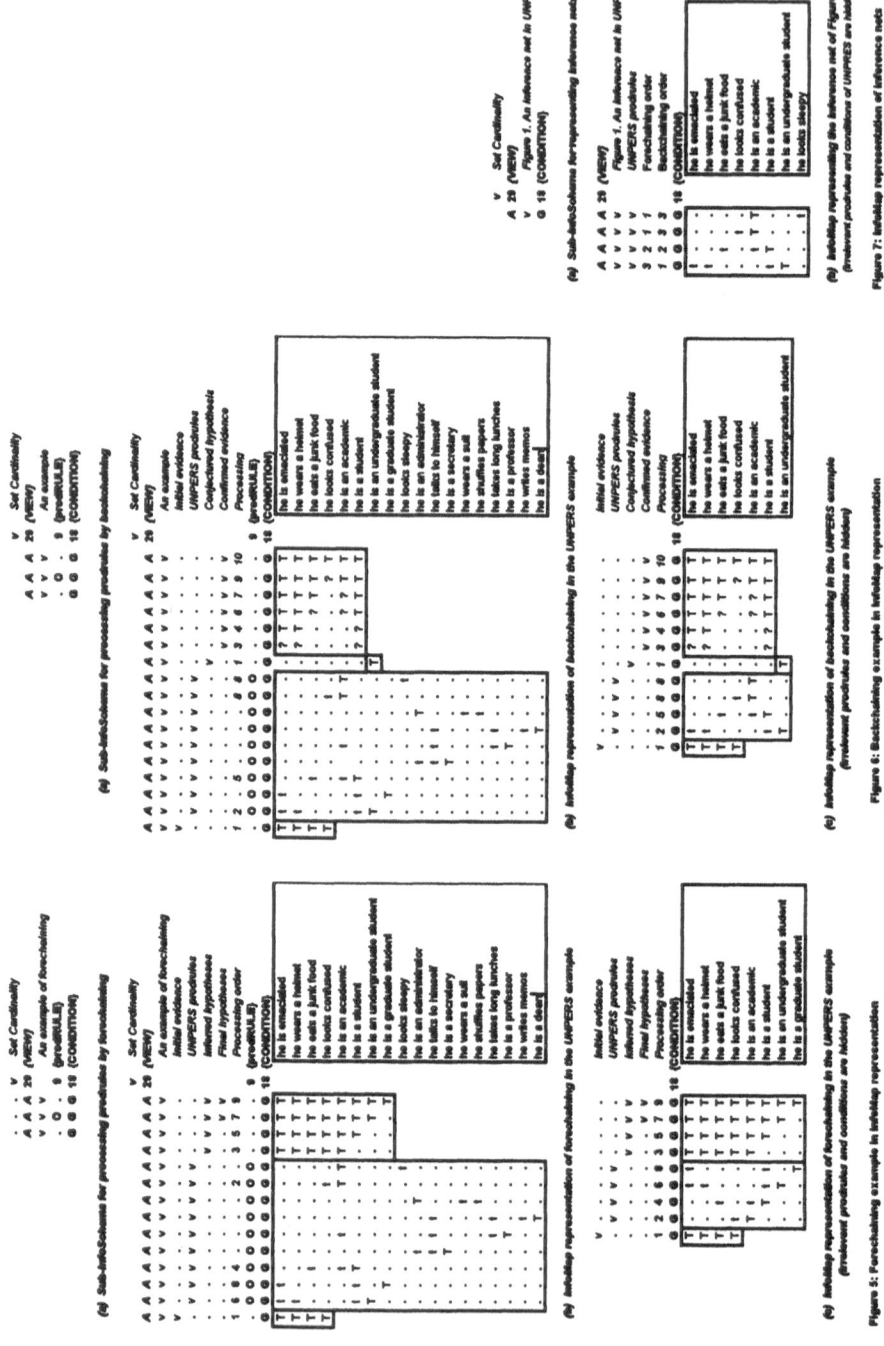

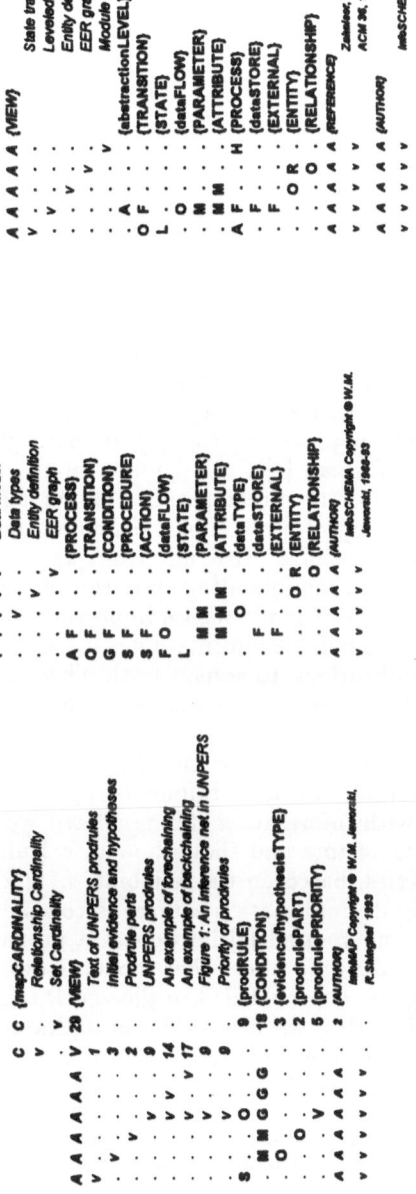

Figure 8 a: Tabular InfoSchema for UNPERS

Figure 8 b: Graphical InfoSchema for UNPERS

Figure 9: A Composite InfoSchema

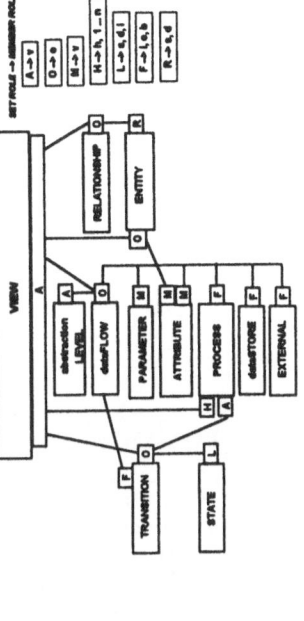

Figure 10 a: A tabular InfoSchema for the Structured Systems

Figure 10 b: Graphical InfoSchema for the Structured Systems

137

A Relational Data Model for Manipulating Probabilistic Knowledge*

Laks V.S. Lakshmanan   Heather L. Johnstone

Department of Computer Science

Concordia University

Montreal, Canada

{laks,heather}@cs.concordia.ca

1 Introduction

Reasoning with uncertain knowledge is an activity that arises in many areas
of computer science, including knowledge-base systems and expert systems. It
is well known that existing expert systems handle reasoning with uncertainty
mostly with ad hoc techniques with little theoretical justification [12, 18]. Many
systems of reasoning with uncertainty have been developed in recent times, including fuzzy set based approaches (*e.g.*, see Zadeh [20], Raju and Majumdar
[15]), quantitative approaches to reason with knowledge (*e.g.*, van Emden [19]
and Steger *et al* [18]) and probabilistic approaches (*e.g.*, [7], Halpern [9]), and
the classical works (for example see Carnap [3]). A highlight in the area of
reasoning with probabilistic knowledge is the recent proposal by Ng and Subrahmanian [13] of a comprehensive theory of probabilistic logic programming.
While these works provide tools for reasoning with uncertain knowledge, a
closely related area of reasoning with and manipulating an uncertain database
has received scant attention. This area is of fundamental importance as there
are many database applications where available information is uncertain (*e.g.*,
stock market predictions, medical applications, to name a few). There is thus a
definite need for a formal model of databases for representation, manipulation,
and reasoning involving uncertain information.

In this paper, we choose probability theory for modeling uncertainty in
databases, owing to its solid foundation and its well-founded theory for manipulating probabilities associated with information. Some related works are
the following. Sadri [16] uses source vectors and shows how to calculate the
reliability metrics of answers to queries, based on the reliability of the stored
information. The reliability of separate information sources is considered independent in this model. Gelenbe and Hebrail [8] introduces a probabilistic
relational model and studies query processing under that model. However, no
algebra comparable to relational algebra is provided. Cavallo and Pittarelli [5]
propose a theory in which it is required that the probability of tuples in a relation sum to 1. Thus, the tuples are considered as alternates so that effectively,
a probabilistic relation can only model a classical relation in which one tuple

---

*This research was supported in part by a grant from the Natural Sciences and Engineering
Research Council of Canada and in part by a grant from the Fonds Pour Formation De
Chercheurs Et L'Aide À La Recherche of Quebec.

exists. Barbara *et al* [2] propose a data model and study an algebra. They treat the attribute (rather than the tuple) as the entity on which probabilities are assigned. Their probabilistic relations are polarized into deterministic(key) and non-deterministic attributes and the probability is interpreted as the conditional probability that an attribute takes on a certain value given its key value. The conditional probability distributions assigned to keys throughout the database are considered independent.

Bayesian Decision Methods (see [1], [4], [6], [10], [17]) have been studied in the context of AI and expert systems. This approach requires that a **complete** probabilistic model be specified i.e. **all** the probabilities required to determine the probability of a certain event must be provided. In practice, this is usually not possible (nor, perhaps, desirable). Thus, some works (e.g. [14]) assume independence between events, in order to circumvent this.

Our probabilistic relational data model is motivated by a need to *(i)* develop a formal basis for assimilating and manipulating uncertain information available about a problem domain based on probability theory, and *(ii)* extend the popular relational database technology to support the activity of *(i)*. The following features contrast our models from previously proposed ones:

1. The model is not simply an extension of the relational model where tuples/attributes come with probabilities already attached. Rather, we introduce a language using which one can specify how the probabilities of tuples should be assigned.

2. In this sense, our framework offers a methodology for collecting "raw" uncertain information into a probabilistic database based on **available** (uncertain and possibly incomplete) knowledge.

3. We do not assume events to be universally independent or mutually exclusive. Nor do we work with complete ignorance of their interdependence. Our language allows a user to express the extent of interdependence among events in the form of constraints.

4. Since the framework allows for an incomplete probabilistic model, it can **estimate** the probabilities of tuples with the information that **is** specified.

Figure 1 shows an architectural view of the system. The knowledge-base (KB) stores rules in the form of probabilistic statements expressed in a precise language. In some sense, this corresponds to the "raw" information available on the problem domain. There is a precise sense in which the KB corresponds to a set of probabilistic relations (p-relations). This correspondence is established via the mathematical program corresponding to the logic rules in the KB (see section 4 for an example). These p-relations are virtual, analogous to the views in standard RDBMS and enable the users to formulate their queries conveniently. Queries can be expressed using a probabilistic relational algebra (pRA) and are processed by generating exactly those constraints which are needed to process them. These constraints are fed to a mathematical programming package (the constraint solver) to derive the probability of each answer tuple. Interfacing this with an RDBMS enables us to take advantage of the (classical) query processing capabilities of existing database technology.

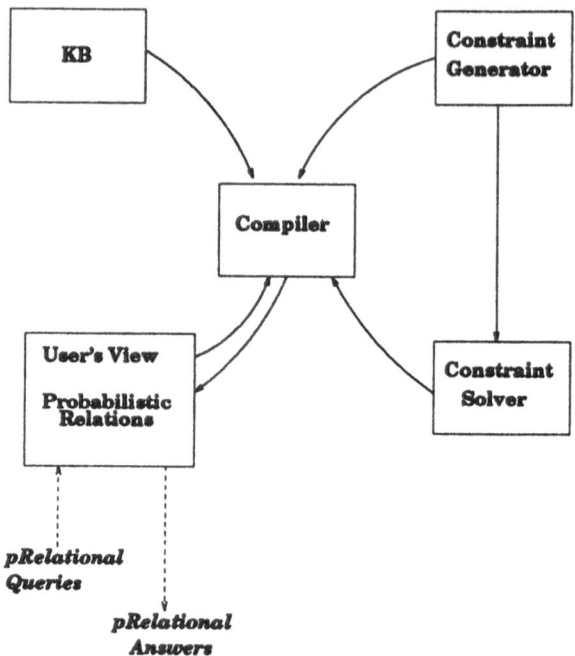

Figure 1: Architecture of Knowledge Base

2 The language

Let $\mathcal{L}$ be a first-order language containing infinitely many variable symbols and infinitely many constant and predicate symbols but no function symbols. The comparison predicates, $<$, $>$, $=$, etc., are built in to the language. Atomic formulas are defined in the usual manner and literals are atoms or negation of atoms. A general formula is a conjunction of literals, $L_1 \wedge \ldots \wedge L_n$.

Let α and β be real numbers in the interval [0,1] and let F_i be a (general) formula. A *probabilistic statement* is a statement of one of the following forms:

1. $\alpha \leq prob(F_1|F_2) \leq \beta$, where F_1, F_2 contain no variables.

2. $(\forall \mathbf{X})(\alpha \leq prob(F_1|F_2) \leq \beta)$ where $\mathbf{X}$ is the tuple of variables occurring in F_1 and F_2.

3. $\alpha \leq prob(F_1|F_2) < op_1 > \ldots < op_k > prob(F_{n-1}|F_n) \leq \beta$, where $< op_i >$ is either $+$ or $-$, and F_i contains no variables.

4. $(\forall \mathbf{X})(\alpha \leq (prob(F_1|F_2) < op_1 > \ldots < op_k > prob(F_{n-1}|F_n)) \leq \beta)$, where $\mathbf{X}$ is the tuple of variables occurring in $F_1, \ldots, F_n$.

We now turn to an example which will be used to illustrate the syntax of the language and serve as a running example throughout the paper.

Example. Car Insurance. An insurance company would like to keep probabilistic information on each of its insureds. Examples of such information include: what is the probability that a given insured will file an accident claim in the next year, what is the probability that a given insured will be a victim of theft in the next year, etc.

The company has access to some statistical data from a previous year or years derived from a sample (or samples) of insured drivers. Suppose among other things, these statistics indicate that of insured drivers the proportion who filed an accident claim in a year is 0.2. Assume that the predicate $Claim(X, Y)$ has the intended meaning that insured X has made a claim of type Y (accident, theft etc). The probabilistic information above can be formalized by the following statement of our language:

(1) $(\forall X)(0.2 \leq (prob(Claim(X, accident) \leq 0.2)$

3 The probabilistic data model

In this section we present our probabilistic data model which makes use of the language $\mathcal{L}$.

A central notion in our probabilistic data model is that of a *probabilistic knowledge base* (KB). The KB consists of *(i)* a set of rules (statements of the language $\mathcal{L}$), termed the *probabilistic rulebase, (ii)* a set of facts which we call the probabilistic factbase, *(iii)* a set of relation schemes, *(iv)* a set of scopes (a finite subset of a domain) and a *(v) relevancy base*.

In order to illustrate the components of the KB we will expand the insurance example from the previous section. Appendix A shows what the rulebase for our insurance example might contain.

Note that in addition to the predicate *Claim*, we introduce two new predicates to express some more information : $Residence(X, Y)$ where X lives in Y area of the city, $Owns(X, Y)$ where X owns a car of type Y and $Payment(X, Y)$ asserts that the cost of a claim of type X to the company falls within the range of Y.

Rules 1 through 8 are the kind of rules which would have come about from a statistical sample. For example, rule 5 states that the probability of an insured owning a Honda given that insured had made a theft claim is 0.33. Rules 9 through 12, on the other hand, may not have come directly from a statistical sample, but are rather "common sense" or "expert rules" i.e. rules one would expect to hold on a sample. For example, rule 9 states that there can only be one (total) payment amount for any given type of a claim. Rule 11 indicates that whatever effect both living downtown and owning a Honda have on the probability of having one's car stolen, it is not less than the probability of the same given that one lives downtown (i.e owning a Honda does not decrease the effect of living downtown on the probability of theft).

The relevancy base is similar to the rulebase but is used specifically to store information about independent events. Normally, this information is also "common sense" or "expert" opinion. The language $\mathcal{L}$ is also used in the relevancy base. For example, we might want to say that one person's claim is independent of another person's claim:

$(\forall XYZW)(0 \leq prob(Claim(X, Y)|Claim(Z, W) \wedge X \neq Z) - prob(Claim(X, Y)) \leq 0)$

The predicates in the rulebase are partitioned into two types : *definite predicates* and *probabilistic predicates*. For the insurance example, the definite predicates are *Residence* and *Owns*. The probabilistic predicates are *Claim*,

INS_NAME	TYPE	P
fred	accident	[0.2, 0.2]
wilma	accident	[0.2, 0.2]
fred	theft	[0, 1]
wilma	theft	[0.33, 0.52]

TYPE	AMT	P
accident	$1000 - $2000	[0.8, 0.8]
accident	$2001 - $3000	[0.2, 0.2]
theft	$1000 - $2000	[0, 1]
theft	$2001 - $3000	[0, 1]

INS_NAME	AREA	P
fred	suburb	[1, 1]
wilma	downtown	[1, 1]

INS_NAME	CAR_TYPE	P
fred	honda	[1, 1]
wilma	honda	[1, 1]

Figure 2: Probabilistic Relations for Insurance Example

and *Payment*. The reason for this partitioning will be apparent as we turn our attention now to the factbase.

The factbase contains ground atoms of definite predicates. Assume that we have some information about the insureds of the insurance company. For simplicity we focus our attention on two particular insureds, Fred and Wilma. Fred lives in the suburbs and owns a Honda and Wilma lives downtown and owns a Honda.

We represent this in the factbase as:

$FB=\{$ *Residence(fred, suburb), Residence(wilma,downtown), Owns(fred,honda), Owns(wilma,honda)* $\}$

Facts pertinent to the definite predicates that are left out of the factbase are implicitly false.

Recall that among the components of the KB are a set of relation schemes and a set of scopes. The relation schemes correspond to the predicates found in the language $\mathcal{L}$ with attributes introduced. Let the relation schemes for the insurance example be claim(INS_NAME,TYPE), payment(TYPE,AMT), residence(INS_NAME,AREA), owns(INS_NAME,CAR_TYPE).

We will let the scopes be: $scope$(INS_NAME) = $\{fred, wilma\}$, $scope$(TYPE) = $\{accident, theft\}$, $scope$(AMT) = $\{\$1000 - \$2000, \$2001 - \$3000\}$, $scope$(AREA) = $\{downtown, suburb\}$, $scope$(CAR_TYPE) = $\{honda\}$.

The RB and FB along with the relation schemes and scopes, generate what are termed *probabilistic relations*.

Let r be a classical real-world relation whose contents are unknown to us. This uncertainty is captured by a probabilistic relation in the following way: if r is over attributes $A_1, \ldots, A_n$, then for each $t \in dom(A_1) \times \ldots \times dom(A_n)$, $r_p(t) = [\alpha, \beta]$, where the probability that t is an element of r falls in the range $[\alpha, \beta]$. We call t a *pure tuple*.

We can display a probabilistic relation in tabular form and for convenience treat the codomain as an attribute which we give the special name P. Any tuple which maps to $[0, 0]$, i.e. is false, is left out of the table. We illustrate in Figure 2 the probabilistic relations generated by the RB and FB of the insurance example.

In Figure 2 the probability that the tuple $< wilma, accident >$ is an element of the relation $Claim$ (for example) falls between α and β.

Note that all the entries for $Owns_p$ and $Residence_p$ were taken directly from the factbase. These are actually classical relations but probabilistic relations are really a generalization of classical relations and can thus represent them.

The entries for the *Claim$_p$* and *Payment$_p$* relations were derived from the information in both the FB and RB. In the next section, the way in which these probabilistic relations are generated is discussed.

4 Generation of probabilistic relations

In this section, we describe how the probabilistic relations are generated.

Recall that the rulebase may contain statements with variables. Each statement with variables can be expanded into a set of statements containing only constants and we call this the *expanded rulebase*. Generating the expanded rulebase from the RB involves replacing the variables with constants from the appropriate scope.

The relevancy base can likewise be expanded and is called the *expanded relevancy base*. Each rule of the expanded relevancy base expresses the independence of two events. We further attach the following implicit semantics to the relevancy base: whenever the relevancy base indicates that an event e_i is independent of an event e_j and an event e_k, then e_i is also independent of the joint occurrence of e_j and e_k. This notion if formalized by an *independence convention* defined next.

Definition. Independence Convention.

1. If the relevancy base states that event e_i is independent of event e_j and e_i is independent of e_k then e_i is independent of the joint occurrence of e_j and e_k.

2. If event e_a is independent of event e_b and event e_a is independent of event e_c, then e_a is also independent of any joint occurrence of e_b and e_c.

□

We next introduce the notion of an *event*. Recall that the RB, KB and relevancy base generate probabilistic relations. For each pure tuple, t, of probabilistic relation, r_p, $r(t)$ is the event that $t \in r$ where r is the (unknown) classical relation whose uncertainty is represented by $r_p(t)$. We concern ourselves only with finding the probability range of events for the probabilistic relations corresponding to probabilistic predicates.[1] The events for a probabilistic relation are all those pure tuples which can be formed from the respective database scopes, i.e. the Cartesian Product of those scopes. An example of an event from the insurance example is *Claim(wilma, accident)*.

It is now possible to illustrate how the probabilistic relations are generated from the expanded RB, FB and expanded relevancy base. Finding the probability range for each pure tuple (or event) in a probabilistic relation amounts to generating that probabilistic relation. Consider an event e. We will model the effect of the expanded rulebase and expanded relevancy base, along with the events of a KB on the probability of e, as a mathematical program. An objective function for the event which is specified using the pertinent information in the factbase, can be minimized and maximized against the constraints of the

---

[1] Recall that the pure tuples of the probabilistic relations of definite predicates map to $[1,1]$

mathematical program. This minimum and maximum will give the probability range for the event.

There are four steps to deriving the probability of the event that a pure tuple is in a relation. These are : (1) Find the Affecting set for the event, (2) Find the set of rules for the event, (3) Set up the constraints for the event, (4) Generate and minimize and maximize the objective function for an event.

We will discuss each of these steps briefly.

Affecting Set. Assume that the event of interest is e. It is necessary to find the set of events which (recursively) affect e (i.e. the events upon which event e is conditional). These events can be extracted from the expanded relevancy base. This set, along with e, is called the *affecting set*, E, for e.

Rules for an Event. Once the set E is compiled, the set of rules which contain these events in their head or body can be extracted from the expanded rulebase and relevancy base.

Constraints for an Event. Consider for a moment two arbitrary events e_1 and e_2. There are four possible combinations of the occurrence of these events: $e_1 \wedge e_2$, $e_1 \wedge \neg e_2$, $\neg e_1 \wedge e_2$, $\neg e_1 \wedge \neg e_2$. The possible occurrences can be formalized in the form of *possible worlds*. We can associate a probability with each possible world. Note that the possible worlds are mutually exclusive and exhaustive. Thus, the probability of event e_2, for example, can be expressed as $prob(e_1 \wedge e_2) + prob(\neg e_1 \wedge e_2)$.

In the same way as above, possible worlds can be associated with the events in set E. The relevant rules can thus be transformed from the language $\mathcal{L}$ into mathematical constraints using the possible worlds as variables. Recall the form of the rules (statements) from definition 1 of section 2. Let W be the set of possible worlds generated by the events in E. A rule is transformed in the following way. For each atom in the rule of the form $prob(e_1 | e_2 \wedge \cdots \wedge e_n)$ (where e_i is an event in E), replace the atom with the expression $(w_1 + \cdots + w_n)/(w_i + \cdots + w_j)$ where $\{w_i, \ldots, w_j\}$ is the set of probabilities of worlds in which $e_2 \wedge \ldots \wedge e_n$ is true and $\{w_1, \ldots, w_n\} \subset \{w_i, \ldots, w_j\}$ are the probabilities of worlds in which e_1 is true. [2]

Once all the rules for an event are transformed, some additional rules can be added. A rule can be added that specifies that the sum of the probabilities of the non-zero worlds is 1. [3] Also, a rule can be added for each non-zero world, constraining its probability to be between 0 and 1.

Note that the set of constraints for an event in general constitutes a non-linear mathematical program.

Objective Function. The truth values of the pertinent facts in the factbase are used to specify an objective function which is used against the program to calculate the bounds on an event. Some of the events in the affecting set E for an event e are composed of definite predicates. The factbase can be perused to determine the truth value of these definite predicates. If $e_1, \ldots, e_n$ are the events in E corresponding to definite predicates that are true and $e_i, \ldots, e_j$ are the events in E corresponding to definite predicates that are false, then the objective function for event e if formed from the expression $prob(e | e_1 \wedge \ldots \wedge e_n \wedge \neg e_i \wedge \ldots \wedge \neg e_j)$. This expression is transformed into an

---

[2] In practice, there are some heuristics which can be applied to decrease the number of worlds

[3] As the worlds are mutually-exclusive and exhaustive

objective function in exactly the same way as the rules were transformed into constraints.

The objective function is then minimized and maximized against the mathematical program to yield the bounds on the probability of the event e.

5 A probabilistic relational algebra

A probabilistic relational algebra which operates over probabilistic relations is defined in this section. The algebra is analogous to that of classical relational databases with the operations projection, selection, Cartesian Product, union and subtraction defined on relations.

Assume that r_p is a probabilistic relation over $A_1, \ldots, A_n$. Recall the intuitive semantics of r_p is that it represents the uncertainty of a classical relation, r, over the same attributes. When defining operators over a relation such as r_p, the result relation represents the uncertainty of the classical result relation of the operation. The result of a probabilistic relation is itself a probabilistic relation.

We use the same symbols, $\prod$, σ, $\times$, $\cup$. and $-$ for the probabilistic operators as for the classical operators. Whether the operator is acting as the classical version is the probabilistic version will be obvious from the type of relation(s) it is working over (i.e. classical or probabilistic).

5.1 Projection

Consider the probabilistic relation r_p which models the uncertainty of r. For each tuple t in the projection of the events of r_p [4] on a set of attributes, $\mathbf{A}$, there exists a set of tuples $t_1, \ldots, t_n$ whose restriction on $\mathbf{A}$ is t. Thus, the probability that t is in $\prod_{\mathbf{A}}(r)$ is the probability that at least one of $t_1, \ldots, t_n$ is in r i.e. $prob(r(t_1) \vee \cdots \vee r(t_n))$.

Example 4.1. $\prod_{TYPE}(Claim_p)$. Suppose that for each claim type, we wanted to find the probability that someone would make that type of claim in the next year. This would be expressed as $\prod_{TYPE}(Claim_p)$. The set of events of $claim_p$ is:

> $\{e_1: Claim(fred, accident)$,$e_2: Claim(wilma, accident)$,$e_3: Claim(fred, theft)$,
> $e_4: Claim(wilma, theft)\}$.

Thus, $\prod_{TYPE}(sup(Claim_p)) = \{< accident >, < theft >\}$. The events e_1 and e_2 both contribute to $< accident >$ thus finding $prob(\prod_{TYPE}(sup(Claim_p))$ $(< theft >)$ amounts to calculating $prob(e_3 \vee e_4)$. The affecting sets for both e_3 and e_4 are found and their union is taken. The union of the affecting sets is $\{e_3, e_4, e_9, e_{10}, e_{11}, e_{12}, e_{13}, e_{14}\}$. Algorithm 3 is used to generate the set of rules from the affecting set. The constraints are set up and the resulting mathematical program is solved for the objective function $prob(e_3 \vee e_4 | e_9 \wedge e_{10} \wedge \neg e_{11} \wedge e_{12} \wedge e_{13} \wedge \neg e_{14})$ $prob(\prod_{TYPE}(< accident >))$ is calculated in the same way and the result is the probabilistic relation below:

---

[4] Recall that the set of events of r_p is the classical relation formed by the Cartesian Product of the scopes of r_p

TYPE	P
accident	$[0.36, 0.36]$
theft	$[0.33, 1]$

□

5.2   Selection

The selection operator, $\sigma_C(r_p)$ simply selects tuples in the events of r_p which satisfy the condition C and maps those tuples to the same interval values that they are mapped to in r_p. The condition C is as in classical relational algebra. Specifically, C is of the form $A_i \theta A_j$ or $A_i \theta v$ where A_i, A_j are attributes, v is a value in the domain of A_i and θ is one of $=, \neq, >, <, \leq, \geq$. Any finite boolean combination of the above is also allowable.

Example 4.2. $\sigma_{NAME='wilma'}(Claim_p)$
We want to select those tuples in $Claim_p$ which pertain to Wilma. The result of this operation is shown below:

NAME	TYPE	P
wilma	accident	$[0.2, 0.2]$
wilma	theft	$[0.33, 0.52]$

□

5.3   Cartesian product

In classical relational algebra, a tuple $t = t_1 \circ t_2$ is in the Cartesian Product of relations r and s when t_1 is in r and t_2 is in s. Thus, for the probabilistic Cartesian Product, it is necessary to find the probability that t_1 is in r **and** t_2 is in s.

Calculating $prob(r(t_i) \wedge r(t_j))$ is analogous to that of projection, except that the probability of $r(t_i) \wedge s(t_j)$ given the relevant facts of the factbase, is used as the objective function to the mathematical program generated by the events $r(t_i)$ and $s(t_j)$.

5.4   Union

In classical relational algebra, a tuple, t, is in the union of two relations if it is an element of either relation. The probabilistic union thus finds the probability that a tuple occurs in either relation.

Again, $prob(r(t) \vee s(t))$ given the relevant facts of the factbase becomes the objective function to the mathematical program generated by the events $r(t)$ and $s(t)$.

5.5   Subtraction

In classical relational algebra, tuple t is in the subtraction of relation s from relation r if it is an element of r but not an element of s. Thus, the probabilistic subtraction finds the probability that t is in r but not in s.

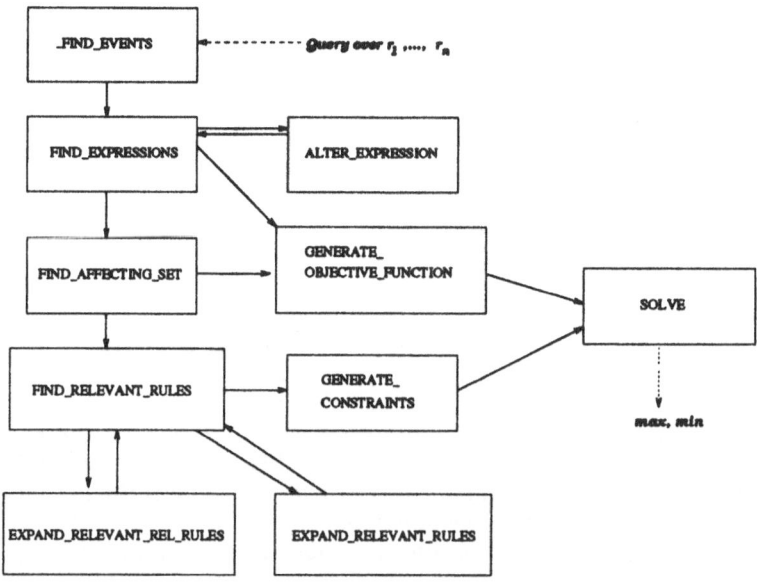

Figure 3: Functional Architecture of Query Processor

So $prob(r(t) \wedge \neg s(t))$ given the relevant facts of the factbase becomes the objective function of the mathematical program generated by the events $r(t)$ and $s(t)$.

6 Query processing

In the previous section we showed how the probabilistic relations for a KB are generated. In [11] relational operators are defined that work over those relations. In practice, the complete set of probabilistic relations would not be physically generated. Instead, the user would pose a query over those virtual relations, and the result probabilistic relation would be output. In this section we present a functional architecture for processing queries.

Figure 3 illustrates the functional architecture of the query processor. A query Q over relations $r_1, \ldots, r_n$ is input to the query processor. The first module, FIND_EVENTS, generates all the possible events for each r_i in Q. Recall that the set of events for a relation is simply the Cartesian Product of the scopes of the attributes for that relation. These classical relations are passed to the FIND_EXPRESSIONS module whose purpose is two-fold : to derive the classical result relation for query Q and to assign to each tuple in the result relation an expression which has to be true in order for the tuple to be an element of this relation. This expression is a conjunction and/or disjunction of events which is derived from the definitions of the operators presented in the previous section.

For each tuple in the result relation generated by FIND_EXPRESSIONS, the expression for that tuple is passed to the FIND_AFFECTING_SET module. For each event in the expression the affecting set is found. The union of these affecting sets is then taken. This union of affecting sets is then passed to the FIND_RELEVANT_RULES module whose task it is to find and expand the relevant rules from the RB and relevancy base. It consults the modules EX-PAND_RELEVANT_REL_RULES and EXPAND_RELEVANT_RULES so that only the relevant rules are expanded.

At this stage, the constraints can be generated. This is realized by the FIND_CONSTRAINTS module which takes as input the relevant rules.

Recall that to find the probability of an event, both the constraints and the objective function must be specified. We have so far described how the constraints are generated and we now turn our attention to the objective function. FIND_OBJECTIVE_FUNCTION module proceeds much the same way as was described in the previous but in this case the event is not atomic but is a conjunction and disjunction of atomic events. The affecting set (really a union of affecting sets) is input from the FIND_AFFECTING_SET module and the (composite) event is provided by the FIND_EXPRESSIONS module.

The output from the FIND_OBJECTIVE_FUNCTION and FIND_CONSTRAINTS module, along with the event whose probability is of interest (from the FIND_EXPRESSIONS module) is sent to the solver which finds the minimum and maximum value for the objective function.

We now present an example to illustrate how the query processing algorithm works.

Example 5.1. Consider the query: what is the probability that the company will have to pay Fred more than \$2000 in the next year. This can be expressed in RA_p as:

$$\Pi_{NAME,AMT}(\sigma_{Claim_p.TYPE=Payment_p.TYPE}(\sigma_{NAME='fred'}(Claim_p) \times \sigma_{AMT='\$2001-\$3000'}(Payment_p)))$$

The above expression is interpreted the following way. For each claim type, we find the probability that Fred will make a claim of that type **and** that the claim type will cost the company more than \$2000. Then, since the type of the claim does not matter, INS_NAME and AMT are projected on to yield the desired answer (i.e. we get the probability that Fred will be paid more than \$2000 from an accident **or** a theft claim.

The first step in processing the query is to identify the events for the relations in the query:

$$Event(Claim_p) = \{\ e_1 : Claim(fred, accident),$$
$$e_2 : \ Claim(wilma, accident),$$
$$e_3 : \ Claim(fred, theft),$$
$$e_4 : \ Claim(wilma, theft)\ \}.$$
$$Event(Payment_p) = \{\ e_5 : \ Payment(accident, \$1000\text{-}\$2000),$$
$$e_6 : \ Payment(accident, \$2001\text{-}\$3000),$$
$$e_7 : \ Payment(theft, \$1000\text{-}\$2000),$$
$$e_8 : \ Payment(theft, \$2001\text{-}\$3000)\ \}$$

Notice that $Event(Claim_p)$ and $Event(Payment_p)$ can be regarded as classical relations. The query is processed over these relations in the classical way with the result of each subquery being a classical relation. For each tuple in the intermediate result relations, we associate an expression which is a (normally composite) event which must be true in order for the tuple to be an element of that relation. The event associated with a tuple is derived from the events in the sets $Event(Claim_p)$ and $Event(Payment_p)$.

We now show how the example query would be processed, going step by step through each subquery.

$$SUB\_QUERY_1 = \sigma_{AMT='\$2001-\$3000'} (Payment_p)$$

TYPE	AMT	EXPRESSION
accident	\$2001 − \$3000	e_6
theft	\$2001 − \$3000	e_8

In the above result relation of the subquery shown, the tuple $< accident, \$2001-\$3000 >$ is an element of the relation SUB_QUERY_1 if the event e_6 is true.

$$SUB\_QUERY_2 = \sigma_{NAME='fred'} (Claim_p)$$

NAME	TYPE	EXPRESSION
fred	accident	e_1
fred	theft	e_3

$$SUB\_QUERY_3 = SUB\_QUERY_2 \times SUB\_QUERY_1 4$$

NAME	TYPE	TYPE	AMT	EXPRESSION
fred	accident	accident	\$2001 − 3000	$(e_1 \wedge e_6)$
fred	accident	theft	\$2001 − \$3000	$(e_1 \wedge e_8)$
fred	theft	accident	\$2001 − \$3000	$(e_3 \wedge e_6)$
fred	theft	theft	\$2001 − \$3000	$(e_3 \wedge e_8)$

In SUB_QUERY_3, the tuple $<fred, accident, accident, \$2000-\$3001>$ is an element of SUB_QUERY_3, if the composite event $(e_1 \wedge e_6)$ is true.

$$SUB\_QUERY_4 = \sigma_{Claim_p.TYPE=Payment_p.TYPE} (SUB\_QUERY_3)$$

NAME	TYPE	TYPE	AMT	EXPRESSION
fred	accident	accident	\$2001 − 3000	$(e_1 \wedge e_6)$
fred	theft	theft	\$2001 − \$3000	$(e_3 \wedge e_8)$

$$ANSWER = \prod_{NAME,AMT}(SUB\_QUERY_4)$$

NAME	AMT	EXPRESSION
fred	\$2001 − 3000	$((e_1 \wedge e_6) \vee (e_3 \wedge e_8))$

The answer relation has one tuple $< fred, \$2001-\$3000 >$, with the associated expression $((e_1 \wedge e_6) \vee (e_3 \wedge e_8))$. Since $< fred, \$2001 - \$3000 >$ is true if the expression $((e_1 \wedge e_6) \vee (e_3 \wedge e_8))$ is true, the probability of $< fred, \$2001-\$3000 >$ being an element of the answer is equal to the probability that $((e_1 \wedge e_6) \vee (e_3 \wedge e_8))$ is true.

To calculate the probability of the event $((e_1 \wedge e_6) \vee (e_3 \wedge e_8))$, the affecting set for each of e_1, e_6, e_3 and e_8 is found and the union of these sets is taken. The union is $\{e_1, e_3, e_5, e_6, e_7, e_8, e_9, e_{11}, e_{12}\}$.

Using the events above, the relevant rules of the rule base and relevancy base are expanded and from these rules and all the possible worlds which can be generated from the events, the mathematical constraints are set up.

In order to set up the expression which will be converted into the objective function, the events which refer to definite predicates of the affecting set must be identified. These are $\{e_9, e_{11}, e_{12}\}$. The events e_9 and e_{12} are true in the factbase and e_{11} is false. Thus, the expression to derive the objective function from is $prob(((e_1 \wedge e_6) \vee (e_3 \wedge e_8))|e_9 \wedge \neg e_{11} \wedge e_{12})$.

7 Summary and future research

Reasoning with probabilistic knowledge arises in many areas in computer science including knowledge-base systems and expert systems. While many logical systems of reasoning have been developed for this purpose, relatively little work has been done on the related topic of representation and manipulation of probabilistic information in the form of a probabilistic database. Probabilistic databases are important not only because they can provide an effective methodology for dealing with uncertain information arising in many database applications, but also because they can form the algebraic backbone for probabilistic logic programming, for which one scheme was recently introduced by Ng and Subrahmanian [13].

In this paper we introduced a probabilistic model which has certain advantages over models so far proposed: a language with which to assign probabilities to tuples, the option of specifying an incomplete probabilistic model and the ability to represent a conditional probabilities between data items.

Inherent in the management of probabilistic data is the complexity of the algorithms to compute the probabilities. The price of the strong modelling power of our probabilistic database is the important requirement of dealing with this complexity. Further research should concentrate on methods of lessening the complexity either by heuristics or by some approximation algorithms that would give less precise bounds to the probabilistic intervals assigned to tuples.

Another direction of research is to investigate how the language could be strengthened to allow it to incorporate a wider variety of probabilistic information.

In that the type of probabilistic data that an application needs to manage might be complex, the requirement for a model to be able to handle this data is very important. Our work takes a first step in this direction and gives a framework for future research in this topic.

References

[1] Ben-Bassat M, Carlson EW, Puri VK, Lipnick E, Portigal LD, Weil MH. Pattern-based interactive diagnosis of multiple disorders: the medas system. IEEE Trans on Pattern Analysis in Machine Intelligence 1980; PAMI-2:148–160

[2] Barbara C, Garcia-Molina H, Porter D. A probabilistic relational data model. In: Proc Advancing Database Technology EDBT'90, 1990; pp 60–64

[3] Carnap R. Logical foundations of probability. University of Chicago Press, 1950

[4] Cooper GF. Nestor, a computer-based medical diagnostic aid that integrates knowledge. Technical Report STAN-CS-84-1031, Stanford University, 1984

[5] Cavallo R, Pittarelli M. The theory of probabilistic databases. In: Proc of the Thirteenth Conference on Very Large Databases, Brighton, 1987, pp 71–81

[6] Duda RO, Hart PE, Barnett P, et al. Development of the prospector consultant system for mineral exploration, final report for sri projects 5821 and 6915. Technical Report, Artificial Intelligence Center, SRI International, 1978

[7] Fagin R, Halpern J, Megiddo J. A logic for reasoning about probabilities. Information and Computation 1990; 87(1/2):78–128

[8] Gelenbe E, Hebrail G. A probability model of uncertainty in databases. In: IEEE Conference on Data Engineering, 1986

[9] Halpern J. An analysis of first-order logics of probability. Artificial Intelligence 1990; 46:311–350

[10] Kim J. CONVINCE, A CONVersational Inference Consolodation Engine. PhD thesis, University of California, Los Angeles, 1983

[11] Lakshmanan VS, Johnstone HL. A relational data model for manipulating probabilistic knowledge. Technical Report, Concordia University, 1993

[12] Nilsson NJ. Probabilistic logic. Artificial Intelligence 1986; 28:71–86

[13] Ng R, Subrahmanian VS. Probabilistic logic programming. Information and Computation 1992; 101(2):150–201

[14] Pearl J. Bayesian and belief-functions formalisms for evidential reasoning: a conceptual analysis. In: Shafer G, Pearl J (eds) Readings in uncertain reasoning. Morgan Kaufmann, San Mateo, California, 1990

[15] Raju KVSVN, Majumdar A. Fuzzy functional dependencies and lossless join decomposition of fuzzy relational database systems. ACM TODS 1988; 13:660–669

[16] Sadri F. Reliability of answers to queries in relational databases. IEEE Transactions on Knowledge and Data Engineering 1991; 3(2):245–251

[17] Spiegelhalter DJ, Knill-Jones RP. Statistical and knowledge-based approaches to clinical decision support systems, with an application to gastroenterology. JR Stat Soc 1984; A(147):35–77

[18] Steger N, Schmidt H, Guntzer U, Kiessling W. Semantics and efficient compilation of quantitative deductive databases. IEEE Conference on Data Engineering 1989; 660–669

[19] van Emden MH. Quantitative deduction and its fixpoint theory. Journal of Logic Programming 1986; 4(1):37–53

[20] Zadeh LA. Fuzzy sets. Information and Control 1965; 8:338–353

A Full Rulebase for Insurance Example

1. $(\forall X)(0.2 \leq prob(Claim(X, accident)) \leq 0.2)$

2. $(\forall X)(0.33 \leq prob(Claim(X, theft)|Residence(X, downtown)) \leq 0.33)$

3. $(\forall X)(0.5 \leq prob(Residence(X, downtown)) \leq 0.5)$

4. $(\forall X)(0.2 \leq prob(Claim(X, theft)|Owns(X, honda)\wedge) \leq 0.2)$

5. $(\forall X)(0.33 \leq prob(Owns(X, honda)|Claim(X, theft)) \leq 0.33)$

6. $(\forall X)(0.5 \leq prob(Residence(X, downtown)|Claim(X, theft)) \leq 0.5)$

7. $0.8 \leq prob(Payment(accident, \$1000 - \$2000)) \leq 0.8$

8. $0.2 \leq prob(Payment(accident, \$2001 - \$3000)) \leq 0.2$

9. $(\forall XYZ)(0 \leq prob(Payment(X, Y)|Payment(X, Z) \wedge Y \neq Z) \leq 0)$

10. $(\forall X)(0 \leq prob(Claim(X, theft)|Residence(X, downtown)\wedge Owns(X, honda))$
    $- prob(Claim(X, theft)|Residence(X, downtown)) \leq 1)$

11. $(\forall X)(0 \leq prob(Claim(X, theft)|Residence(X, downtown)\wedge Owns(X, honda))$
    $- prob(Claim(X, theft)|Owns(X, honda)) \leq 1)$

12. $(\forall XY)(0 \leq prob(Residence(X, Y)|Residence(X, Z) \wedge Y \neq Z) \leq 0)$

Uncertainty as a Function of Expertise*

Nematolaah Shiri   Hasan M. Jamil[†]

Department of Computer Science

Concordia University

Montreal, Canada

{shiri,jamil}@cs.concordia.ca

Abstract

Information Source Tracking (IST) method is an elegant framework proposed for the representation and manipulation of inaccurate data. In IST, sources contribute data in the database and the reliability of data depends on the reliability of the contributing sources. While IST is capable of managing inaccurate data, it is incapable of accommodating reliability revision of sources and apparently can not assign reliability to sources as a function of their expertise. In this paper we introduce the concept of *context* in the IST to accommodate the notion of context dependent reliability of sources. We show that the introduction of the concept of contexts greatly enhances the naturality and the conceptual modeling capability of the basic IST model. We also show that under the assumption of *reliability independence* among sources in different contexts, an extended IST database is IST reducible. Finally, we extend the definitions of the relational operators proposed for basic IST to accommodate contexts, and show that the extended operators are *information preserving*.

Key Words: information source, contextual data, uncertainty, data reliability.

1   Introduction

Uncertainty in artificial intelligence and databases mathematics is a well studied subject and still is an active field of research. While uncertainty takes several forms, *incompleteness* and *imprecision* are the most prevalent kinds that are being investigated in database community. Another type of uncertainty, called *inaccuracy* [5], results when data in the database are contributed by different *sources* and the reliability of data depends on the reliability of the sources. That is, the reliability of data is abstracted into the reliability of the contributing sources.

Sadri [3, 4, 5] proposed an extended relational model, called *Information Source Tracking* (IST) method for the modeling and manipulation of uncertain and inaccurate data in relational databases. IST is capable of modeling

---

*This research was supported in part by grants from the Natural Sciences and Engineering Research Council of Canada and the Fonds Pour Formation De Chercheurs Et L'Aide À La Recherche of Quebec.

†This author's research was additionally supported in part by grants from the Canadian Commonwealth Scholarship and Fellowship Plan, and the University of Dhaka, Bangladesh. The author is on leave from the University of Dhaka, Bangladesh.

(probabilistic) dependent and independent data, an issue which causes substantial difficulties in other frameworks. A sound and complete set of extended relational operators have also been proposed.

The approach in the IST differs from the other works in that IST does not associate certainties directly with information. It assumes that the information is contributed, or confirmed, by information sources, and the reliability of the contributing sources determines the reliability of information. For each "piece" of data, i.e., tuples in a relation, the contributing sources are also recorded. An answer to a query identifies the sources contributing to the answer, as well as their nature of contribution. Reliability calculations are left as a final step of query processing. This separation of data and its reliability in IST makes it a clean and effective framework to deal with the issue of dependent and independent data, an issue which creates substantial difficulties in other techniques.

More recently, there has been interest in investigating extensions and applications of IST in several directions. Lakshmanan and Sadri [2] extended IST to deductive databases. They studied query processing in the model and showed that the top-down and bottom-up evaluation techniques of logic programming and deductive databases can be extended to their model. In some other applications, such as stock exchange or learning, it is essential to capture the time dependent behavior of the sources. That is, the source reliability must be revised and maintained in real time. In IST, however, sources are assigned a fixed reliability which does not change over time. Recently Jamil and Sadri [1] proposed a method to maintain reliability of sources based on observation and evidence. In their proposal, all inaccurate data are viewed as predictions and all data are observed until they become true or false (fail to be true). The reliability of the sources are then statistically estimated based on the observed data at the time of query processing.

In applications like medicine and expert systems, reliability depends on the expertise of the sources in various fields, or *contexts*. That means a source may have several reliability depending on the context in which the source has supplied information. In this paper, we study the issue of assigning reliabilities to sources based on contexts. That is, we relax the restriction that a source should have a fixed reliability all over the database. Although, we can statically assign different reliability to the same source, the real issue is to assign reliability to sources on derived relations or views[1], so that reliability of tuples in the views may be calculated. In this paper, we do not consider the issue of source reliability maintenance as proposed in [1], which can be accommodated, however, as an orthogonal extension to our current proposal.

In the next section we review the basic IST model. In Section 3 we formulate the problem and give an outline of our proposed extension to the IST model. We also discuss pertinent issues and identify problems that arise when we attempt to extend relational algebra operators to our model. We then propose extensions to basic IST algebra operators in section 4 to accommodate contexts. Then, we present a reduction technique of EIST database to an equivalent IST database and claim that they are *information preserving*. Finally, we give our conclusion.

---

[1]Notice that the answer to a query is a relation and may be regarded as a view.

2 The basic IST method

In this section we review the basic concepts of IST proposed by Sadri [3, 4, 2]. An IST database scheme $\mathbf{R}$ is a set of *extended relation schemes* $\{R_1, \ldots, R_n\}$. An *extended relation scheme* (*relation scheme*, for short) R_i is a set of attributes $A_{i_1}, \ldots, A_{i_m}, A_I$, where A_{i_j}s are *normal attributes* as in a relational database, and A_I is a special attribute called the *information source attribute* (*source attribute*, for short). The domain D_I of the attribute A_I is the set of all vectors[2] of length k with entries in $\{+1, -1, 0\}$, where k is the number of sources $S = \{s_1, \ldots, s_k\}$ which supply (or confirm) the information in the database. That is,

$$D_I = \{(a_1 \ldots a_k) \mid a_i \in \{+1, -1, 0\},\ i = 1, \ldots, k\}.$$

Let R_i be a relation scheme. An *extended relation (instance)* r_i of R_i is a finite subset of $D_{i_1} \times \ldots \times D_{i_m} \times D_I$, where D_{i_j} (for $j = 1, \ldots, m$) is the domain corresponding to the normal attribute A_{i_j} in R_i, and D_I is the domain of A_I. An IST database (instance) $\mathbf{D}$ over $\mathbf{R}$ is a set of relation instances $r_1, \ldots, r_n$, where r_i is defined over the relation scheme $R_i \in \mathbf{R}$, for $i = 1, \ldots, n$. As usual, each relation $r_i \in \mathbf{D}$ is called a *base relation*.

Each tuple in a base relation r_i is of the form $t@u$, where t is the component of the tuple corresponding to the normal attributes and $u \in D_I$ is the component corresponding to the source attribute A_I. If $t@u$ is a tuple in r_i, then we refer to t as the *visible component* of the tuple, since this is the component visible to a user of the database. We refer to u as the source vector associated with t. The users are transparent of the source vectors associated with each tuple. To the users, the database is a pure relational database. The IST model allows a tuple t in an extended relation r to be associated with a set of source vectors. If r contains a tuple of the form $t@\{u_1, \ldots, u_l\}$, where $l \geq 1$, this is a short form denoting that r contains the tuples $t@u_1, \ldots, t@u_l$. We will use x, y, or z, with or without subscripts, to denote a set of source vectors, and use u or v, subscripted or otherwise, to denote a single source vector.

2.1 Source vectors

Let r be a relation in an IST database. Suppose r contains a tuple $t@x$. This is denoted as $r(t)$. To simplify the description, further suppose that x contains a single source vector v. The source vector v indicates the nature of contribution of each source in t. If the i-th element of v is 1, it means that the source s_i has confirmed the fact $r(t)$. In this case, we say s_i has contributed positively to t. If the i-th element of v is -1, it means s_i denies $r(t)$. The source s_i in this case is said to have contributed negatively. If the i-th element of v is 0, it denotes that s_i has no contribution to t, positively or negatively.

That is, the source s_i in this case is non-committal about $r(t)$. A source vector associated with a tuple represents a logical *expression*. This is illustrated in the following example from [5].

Example 1 Let $S = \{s_1, s_2, s_3, s_4\}$ be the set of sources in an IST database $\mathbf{D}$. Let r be a relation in $\mathbf{D}$ with the following tuples.

---

[2]The meaning of the (source) vectors will be described shortly.

$$t_1@(1 \quad 0 \quad -1 \quad 0)$$
$$t_2@(1 \quad -1 \quad 0 \quad 1)$$
$$t_2@(0 \quad 0 \quad -1 \quad 1)$$

The first tuple indicates that $r(t_1)$ is true if source s_1 is correct and s_3 is wrong. This fact can be represented by the logical expression $s_1 \wedge (\neg s_3)$, obtained from the source vector associated with t_1. Similarly, $r(t_2)$ is true if either s_1 and s_4 are correct and s_2 is wrong, or s_4 is correct and s_3 is wrong. The logical expression corresponding to t_2 is

$$(s_1 \wedge (\neg s_2) \wedge s_4) \vee ((\neg s_3) \wedge s_4).$$

As in the example above, s_i is a logical variable representing the i-th source vector, for all $1 \leq i \leq k$. A source vector u represents a conjunction of variables (in case of 1) and negation of variables (in case of -1). Formally, let $u = (a_1 \ldots a_k)$ be a source vector associated with a tuple t, and S^+, S^- be two sets of sources contributed to t positively and negatively, respectively. Then the expression $e(u)$ corresponding to t is defined as

$$e(u) = \bigwedge_{s_i \in S^+} s_i \bigwedge_{s_j \in S^-} s_j.$$

The expression $e(x)$ corresponding to a tuple which is associated with a set x of source vectors is

$$e(x) = \bigvee_{u \in x} e(v).$$

The special source vector $\top$ denotes a contradiction. We say that a source s has supplied contradictory information w.r.t. a tuple t in a relation r if s has both confirmed and denied t in r. In this case, we say that the tuple t is contradictory, denoted $t@\top$, and the expression corresponding to t is $e(\top) = false$.

Sadri [3, 5] extended the relational algebra operations to IST for manipulating visible components of the tuples as well as their associated source vectors. We will describe the extended operations later. As a result of applying the extended operations, each tuple in a derived relation r will be associated with a set of source vectors. As illustrated earlier, source vector(s) associated with each tuple t defines a logical expression. The expression corresponding to t, in turn, will be used for calculating the reliability of t being in r, i.e., the probability that $r(t)$ is correct. The algorithms for calculating reliabilities of tuples are presented in [5], and their correctness are proved in [3]. Basically, reliability of a tuple t is defined as a function of reliability of the sources encoded in the expression corresponding to t.

IST makes a fundamental assumption that each source $s_i \in S$ has a single reliability in all the relations in the database. Stated formally, reliability of the sources in S in an IST database $\mathbf{D}$ is defined as a function $\rho : S \rightarrow [0, 1]$. We will relax on this assumption, and argue that this is natural and that it increases the conceptual view of a database.

2.2 Relational algebra operations for IST

To make this report self-contained, we present the basic (selection, projection, union, difference, and Cartesian product) extended relational algebra operations of IST from [3, 5]. The elements in the information source attribute

$A_I = \{+1, -1, 0, \top\}$ constitute a lattice, where $\top$ is the top element and 0 is the bottom element. The partial order $\prec$ is defined among the elements of A_I as $0 \prec 1 \prec \top$ and $0 \prec -1 \prec \top$. This order is useful in defining $\overset{s}{\wedge}$, which is an operator defined on source vectors as follows. Let $v_1(a_1 \ldots a_k)$ and $v_2 = (b_1 \ldots b_k)$ be source vectors different from $\top$, and let $v = v_1 \overset{s}{\wedge} v_2$, defined as the following. If for some i, $a_i \times b_i = -1$, then $v = \top$. Otherwise, $v = (c_1 \ldots c_k)$, where $c_i = lub(a_i, b_i)$, for all $i = 1, \ldots, k$, where lub is the least upper bound operator. The conjunction of two sets of source vectors x and y is defined as follows.

$$x \overset{s}{\wedge} y = \{v \overset{s}{\wedge} w \mid v \in x \text{ and } w \in y\}.$$

The negation operator $\overset{s}{\neg}$ applies to a (set of) source vector(s) and is defined as follows. Let $v = (a_1 \ldots a_k) \neq \top$ be a source vector. Then $\overset{s}{\neg} v = \{u_1, \ldots, u_k\}$, where each u_i is a source vector obtained from a_i as the following. If $a_i = 1(-1)$, then the i-th entry in u_i is $-1(1)$, and the rest 0. If $a_i = 0$, then u_i need not be included. The negation of a set $x = \{u_1, \ldots, u_m\}$ of source vectors is defined as $\overset{s}{\neg} x = (\overset{s}{\neg} u_1) \overset{s}{\wedge} \ldots \overset{s}{\wedge} (\overset{s}{\neg} u_m)$. The disjunction of two sets of source vectors x and y, denoted by $x \overset{s}{\vee} y$, is their union, i.e., $x \overset{s}{\vee} y = x \cup y$.

Following are the definitions of the extended relational algebra operations for IST as presented in Sadri [3, 5]. It is easy to see that as far as the visible components of the tuples are concerned, the extended operations are the same as the "classical" relational algebra operations. In the following definitions, p and q are extended relation instances in an IST database, C in $\sigma_C(p)$ is a selection condition on only the normal attributes of p. X in $\Pi_X(p)$ denotes a list of normal attributes of p.

$$\sigma_C(p) = \{t@z \in p \mid t \text{ satisfies condition } C\}$$
$$\Pi_X(p) = \{t[X]@z \in p \mid t@z \in p\}$$
$$p \cup q = \{t@z \in r \mid t@z \in p, \text{ or } t@z \in q\}$$
$$p - q = \{t@z \mid t@z \in p \text{ and } q \text{ does not contain any tuple whose visible}$$
$$\text{component is } t, \text{ or } t@x \in p, \; t@y \in q, \text{ and } z = x \overset{s}{\wedge} (\overset{s}{\neg} y)\}$$
$$p \times q = \{t_1.t_2@(v_1 \overset{s}{\wedge} v_2) \mid t_1@v_1 \in p \text{ and } t_2@v_2 \in q\}$$

where $t_1.t_2$ denotes the concatenation of t_1 and t_2.

3   Introducing context in IST

Our objective is to extend the IST model so that a source may be assigned different reliabilities in different "contexts" or "topics". In practice, every relation in a database models a real world entity, and thus captures a single concept. We view each such concept as a context. In this paper, we will use the terms context and relation interchangeably. We will refer to an extended IST model as EIST. We define an EIST database as a 4-tuple $\langle \mathbf{R}, \mathbf{D}, S, \psi \rangle$, where $\mathbf{R}$ is an extended database scheme, $\mathbf{D}$ is a set of extended relation instances r_j on scheme $R_j \in \mathbf{R}$, S is a set of sources, and ψ is a reliability assignment function that assigns reliability to every source $s_i \in S$ in every context, i.e., $\psi : S \times \mathbf{R} \to [0, 1]$. We will, however with abuse of notation, use $\mathbf{D}$ to represent both the database and an instance of the database scheme **R** when there is no ambiguity.

3.1 The issues

It should be easy to see that in IST, deducing the source vectors during relational operations is relatively simple using the $\overset{\bullet}{\wedge}$ and $\overset{\bullet}{\neg}$ operators, since each source has a single reliability in every relation in the database. Recall that, these vectors carry the source information with the data, which can then be used to calculate the reliability of the data. However, if the reliability of a source varies with the base relations in a database, as is the case we have in mind, then the picture becomes very different. In order to obtain the reliability of the tuples in a derived relation, or view, R_i, we should either (1) be able to use the reliability of the sources in the base relations from which the instance of R_i is derived, or (2) know the reliability of each source in the context of R_i. The former case can be restated as follows. Given an EIST database **R** with the sources in S, and a reliability assignment function $\psi : S \times \mathbf{R} \rightarrow [0, 1]$, we want to obtain the reliability of each tuple in a derived relation R_i. Note that, since $R_i \notin \mathbf{R}$, the reliability of the sources $s \in S$ in the context of R_i is not known, i.e., ψ only assigns reliability to sources in base relations. The latter case is an interesting problem, which we call Reliability Assignment Problem (RAP). Since ψ does not assign reliability to sources in derived relations or views, the idea here is to extend ψ such that reliability for each source in the virtual context can be assigned, to calculate the reliability of tuples in the answer relation, or if we decide to materialize the view. Notice the difference in the two cases. In the first case, the reliability of a source may change from tuple to tuple in the same view, whereas in the second, the reliability will be the same for a source for all the tuples. In this paper, however, we will address the first issue, and the second will be addressed in a companion paper.

3.1.1 Reliability calculation in extended IST

In this section we will try to convince the reader through a series of examples that except for unary operators, a straightforward extension of relational operators for IST is not enough to accommodate the concept of contexts. Then in the next section we will present a basis for the tuple reliability in derived relations based on which extensions to IST operators will be proposed.

In the case of unary operations σ and Π, it is straightforward to determine the reliability of the sources in the derived relations or contexts, and hence the reliability of the tuples. For example, let $r = \sigma_C(R_i)$, where C is the selection condition, and $R_i \in \mathbf{R}$. Clearly the scheme of the relation r is the same as R_i, and whatever tuple qualifies to be in r, their reliability should be the same as in r_i, since nothing has changed for those tuples. Also logically, r is nothing but a horizontal partition of r_i, and thus its scheme models the same context as does the scheme of r_i. Hence the reliability of each source in the scheme of r should be the same as R_i. Following a similar reasoning, we conclude that for $r = \Pi_X(R_i)$, where $R_i \in \mathbf{R}$ and X is a list of normal attributes of R_i, the reliability of the sources in the scheme of R should be the same as in the scheme of R_i. We will see next, that in case of binary operators like $\cup$ (union), $-$ (difference), etc., the analysis are not that simple.

Let P and Q be the schemes of union compatible base relations in an EIST database. Let the set of sources in the database be $S = \{s_1, s_2\}$, and ψ be a reliability assignment function. For simplicity, let us also assume that the tuples in the instances of P and Q, p and q respectively, have only one one source vector associated with them. Now, consider the following example.

Example 2 Let $\mathbf{D} = \{p, q\}$, where $p = \{t@1\ 0\}$, and $q\{t@0\ 1\}$, and that $r = p \cup q$. Let ψ assigns a reliability to each source as $\psi(s_1, P) = 0.7$, $\psi(s_2, P) = 0.8$, $\psi(s_1, Q) = 0.7$, and $\psi(s_2, Q) = 0.9$. In this case, r would contain[3] the tuples $t@1\ 0$ and $t@0\ 1$. The reliability of t in r, denoted $re(r(t))$, may be computed as follows, with a slight twist in the algorithm[4] proposed by Sadri [3].

$$re(r(t)) = 1 - (1 - 0.7)(1 - 0.9) = 0.97 = 97\%.$$

It can be easily seen that if we switch the tuples , i.e., $t@0\ 1 \in p$ and $t@1\ 0 \in q$, then the contents of r would be as before, but with a different reliability as calculated below. This is because we are now considering the contexts of the tuples.

$$re(r(t)) = 1 - (1 - 0.8)(1 - 0.7) = 0.94 = 94\%.$$

The above example suggests that we should know exactly the origin of the tuples, i.e., the base relations from which the tuples in r are supplied. This can be achieved, for instance, by labelling the source vectors in the (base) relations. We will use the relation names as the labels for the vectors. Thus, the relation p in Example 2 would contain $t@(1\ 0)_p$, q would contain $t@(0\ 1)_q$. Therefore, r would contain $t@\{(1\ 0)_p \overset{s}{\vee} (0\ 1)_q\}$. Next examples illustrate the problems with labeled source vectors.

Example 3 Let $p = \{t@(1\ 0)_p\}$, $q = \{t@(1\ 1)_q\}$, and $r = \{t@\{(1\ 0)_p \overset{s}{\vee} (1\ 1)_q\}\}$ $= p \cup q$, with source vectors labelled. Let ψ be the same as in Example 2. Now, let us determine the value $re(r(t))$. If we expand the source [3] vector $(1\ 0)_p$, we would get $t@\{(1\ 1)_p \overset{s}{\vee} (1\ -1)_p \overset{s}{\vee} (1\ 1)_q\}$. IST requires that one of the repeated source vectors $(1\ 1)_p$ or $(1\ 1)_q$ should be removed. However, we can not do so in this case, since contexts of the vectors are not the same although the vectors themselves are the same, and removing one or the other will result in different reliabilities. For instance, if $(1\ 1)_p$ is removed, we get

$$
\begin{aligned}
re(r(t)) &= re(r(t@(1\ -1)_p)) + re(r(t@(1\ 1)_q)) \\
&= 0.7 \times 0.2 + 0.7 \times 0.9 = 0.77 = 77\%.
\end{aligned}
$$

However, if $(1\ 1)_q$ is removed, we obtain

$$
\begin{aligned}
re(r(t)) &= re(r(t@(1\ 1)_p)) + re(r(t@(1\ -1)_p)) = 0.7 = 70\%
\end{aligned}
$$

Example 4 Now, let $r = p - q$, where $p = \{t_1@(0\ 1)_p, t_2@(1\ 0)_p\}$, and $q = \{t_1@(0\ 1)_q\}$, and ψ is as before. In this case, r would contain the tuples $t_1@\{(0\ 1)_p \overset{s}{\wedge} (0\ -1)_q\}$, and $t_2@(1\ 0)_p$. Note that in an IST database we would

---

[3] The tuples in r could also be represented shortly as the single tuple $t@\{1\ 0 \overset{s}{\vee} 0\ 1\}$.

[4] Recall that in IST, a source has a single reliability in all relations.

have had $r = \{t_2@(1\ 0)\}$, since the source vector associated with t_1 in r would be $(0\ 1)\dot{\wedge}(0\ -1) = \top$, and hence $re(t_1(r)) = 0$. We, however, in our EIST database can simplify the source vector associated with t_1 in r and get $t_1@(0\ \ 1_p \wedge -1_q)$. Note that 0 is the first entry in the source vector and $1_p \wedge -1_q$ is its second entry. The reliability $re(r(t_1))$ can then be calculated as

$$re(r(t_1)) = \psi(s_2, P) \times (1 - \psi(s_2, Q)) = 0.8 \times (1 - 0.9) = 0.08 = 8\%$$

The series of examples above show that a straightforward labelling of source vectors is not enough, and new algorithm should be developed for reliability calculation which will be capable in taking into consideration the contexts of the tuples in a derived relation.

3.1.2 Basis of reliability calculation in EIST

In this section, we discuss the basis for calculating reliability of the tuples in the answer to a query in an EIST database. This will serve as a correctness criterion for the algorithm we propose later. We will describe a key observation that leads to a natural and simple algorithm for reliability calculation. To illustrate the point, consider the following example.

Example 5 Let $\mathbf{D} = \{p, q\}$ be an EIST database and $S = \{s\}$. Suppose $p = \{t@1\}$ and $q = \{t@1\}$. If $r = p \cup q$, then clearly r would contain $t@1$.

The question now is, what is $re(r(t))$? In the IST model, the reliability of a source over a database is a fixed global value in $[0, 1]$. It is also assumed in an IST database that a source is either wrong every where in the database or it is correct. That is, IST does not allow situations where a source could be wrong about part of the information and be correct about the rest. In Example 5, as long as the source s was correct about confirming that t belongs to p and/or q, we can safely conclude that t is in r. If we assume the events of different pieces of information supplied by the same source but in different relations are "independent", then $re(r(t))$ could be calculated as

$$re(r(t)) = re(p(t)) + re(q(t)) - re(p(t)) \times re(q(t)).$$

If we have more than one source, the above simple formula does not apply. To see this, suppose $t@1\ 0 \in p$ and $t@1\ 1 \in q$. Let s_1 and s_2 be the sources in this case. Then, the question is when can we safely deduce that $t \in r$? Clearly, as long as s_1 was correct about t's membership in p, or it was correct about t's membership in q and so was s_2. If we calculate $re(r(t))$ from the values of $re(p(t))$ and $re(q(t))$, then in some sense some information is lost when we derived the values $re(p(t))$ and $re(q(t))$; the fact that s_1 confirms t's membership in both p and q is somehow lost. If we assume the information supplied by the same source in different relations is independent and formalize the above intuition about when we can safely conclude that $t \in r$, we get the following.

$$
\begin{aligned}
re(r(t)) &= Prob[c(s_1, p(t)) \vee (c(s_1, q(t)) \wedge c(s_2, q(t)))] \\
&= Prob[c(s_1, p(t))] + Prob[c(s_1, q(t))] \times Prob[c(s_2, q(t))] - \\
&\quad Prob[c(s_1, p(t))] \times Prob[c(s_1, q(t))] \times Prob[(s_2, q(t))] \\
&= \psi(s_1, P) + \psi(s_1, Q).\psi(s_2, Q) - \psi(s_1, P).\psi(s_1, Q).\psi(s_2, Q).
\end{aligned}
$$

In the above, $Prob[c(s, p(t))]$ denotes the probability that the source s is correct in confirming that t is a tuple in relation p. Therefore, the first identity says that the reliability of t being in r is equal to the probability that either s_1 is correct in confirming $t \in p$, or that both s_1 and s_2 are correct in confirming t's membership in q. Note that the resulting reliability $re(r(t))$ is essentially an expression with the building blocks of the form $\psi(s_i, R_j)$. It is assumed in the EIST model that *all the tuples in a context (relation) contributed by a source are correct or all are wrong*. In particular, it allows for a source to be correct in some contexts and wrong in others. We can express the notion of "independence of sources" in the form of conditional probability statements. This form also represents the distinction between IST and EIST, as follows. For each source $s \in S$ and for all contexts R_1 and R_2 in an IST database, we have that

$$Prob(Correct(s, R_1) \mid Correct(s, R_2)) = 1, \text{ and}$$
$$Prob(Wrong(s, R_1) \mid Wrong(s, R_2)) = 1,$$

whereas, in an EIST database we have

$$Prob(Correct(s, R_1) \mid Correct(s, R_2)) = Prob[Correct(s, R_1)]$$
$$= \psi(s, R_1), \text{ and}$$
$$Prob(Wrong(s, R_1) \mid Wrong(s, R_2)) = Prob[Wrong(s, R_1)]$$
$$= 1 - \psi(s, R_1)$$

where the predicate $Correct(s, P)$ means that source s is correct in all the information it contributed to the base relation P. The meaning of $Wrong(s, P)$ should now be obvious. This notion of independence provides a basis for tuple reliability calculation using labelled source vectors in EIST. Now, if we revisit Example 3, we would calculate a reliability for t as follows, under the assumptions just described.

$$re(r(t)) = \psi(s_1, P) + \psi(s_1, Q) \times \psi(s_2, Q) - \psi(s_1, P) \times \psi(s_1, Q) \times \psi(s_2, Q) = 0.889.$$

4 Accommodating contexts in relational algebra of IST

In this section, we present the relational algebra operations for EIST. These operations are identical to the ones defined for IST in Section 2, with the exception for the source vector operators $\overset{s}{\wedge}$ and $\overset{s}{\neg}$. Basically, we introduce the source vector operators $\overset{s}{\wedge}$ and $\overset{s}{\neg}$ to replace, respectively, $\wedge$ and $\neg$ in IST. The resulting relational algebra operations naturally extend the ones proposed for IST [3]. We now define $\overset{s}{\wedge}$ and $\overset{s}{\neg}$.

In order to obtain reliabilities of the tuples in an EIST database **D** over a scheme **R**, it was shown in the previous section that we can label the source vectors associated with the tuples. As a result, the i-th entry of a source vector may be 0 or it may be a conjunction of the form:

$$\bigwedge_{p \in A} 1_p \bigwedge_{q \in B} -1_q$$

$conj_i$	$conj'_i$	$conj''_i$
1_p	1_q	$1_p \wedge 1_q$
1_p	-1_q	$1_p \wedge -1_q$
1_p	0_q	1_p
-1_p	1_q	$-1_p \wedge 1_q$
-1_p	-1_q	$-1_p \wedge -1_q$
-1_p	0_q	-1_p
0_p	1_q	1_q
0_p	-1_q	-1_q
0_p	0_q	0

Table 1: Definition of $\overset{s,}{\wedge}$ for the i-th entry, where $conj''_i = conj_i \overset{s,}{\wedge} conj'_i$.

where A and B are subsets of $\mathbf{R}$. If $t@v$ is a tuple in a derived relation in $\mathbf{D}$, then v is a labelled source vector of the form $v = (conj_1 \ldots conj_k)$, where $conj_i$ is a conjunction denoting the contributions that the source s_i has with respect to t. Note that if $A \cap B \neq \emptyset$, then $v = \top$. As an example, let $t@(0 \ 1_p \wedge 1_q \wedge -1_r)$ be a tuple in a context $R \in \mathbf{R}$. Then, t is in r if the source s_2 is correct in confirming t in p and q, and s_2 is wrong in confirming t's membership in r. We will refer to each of the atomic formulas 1_p, 1_q, and -1_r as a conjunct. Note that each entry $conj_i$ in v may consists of at most $n = |\mathbf{R}|$ conjuncts, which happens only if s_i has a positive or negative contribution with respect to any tuple t in all the contexts in $\mathbf{R}$. In the case where s_i has contributed both positively and negatively in the same context with respect to $t@v$, then there is an inconsistency which will be denoted by $t@\top$ with evaluation $e(\top) = false$.

The binary operator $\overset{s,}{\wedge}$ takes two (sets of) labelled source vectors and produces a (set of) labelled source vector(s), described as follows. Let $v_1 = (conj_1 \ \ldots \ conj_k) \neq \top$ and $v_2 = (conj'_1 \ \ldots \ conj'_k) \neq \top$ be labelled source vectors associated with a tuple t in two contexts, where the conjunction $conj_i$ (and $conj'_i$) is the i-th entry denoting the contribution of source s_i in $\mathbf{D}$. Then $v = v_1 \overset{s,}{\wedge} v_2 = (conj''_1 \ \ldots \ conj''_k)$ is a labelled source vector where $conj''_i = conj_i \wedge conj'_i$. This definition is given in Table 1, where p and q are base relations. Note that if $\mathbf{D}$ is an IST database, the above definition of $\overset{s,}{\wedge}$ reduces to the definition of $\wedge$. The negation operator $\overset{s,}{\neg}$ is a unary operator that takes a (set of) labelled source vector(s) and produces a set of labelled source vectors. Let $v = (conj_1 \ \ldots \ conj_k) \neq \top$ be a labelled source vector associated with a tuple t in a context in an EIST database $\mathbf{D}$. Then $\overset{s,}{\neg}v = \{x_1, \ldots, x_k\}$, where each x_i is a set of labelled source vectors obtained from $conj_i$, as the following. If $conj_i = 0$, we need not include x_i.[5] For each conjunct 1_{r_j} (-1_{r_j}) in $conj_i$, include in x_i a source vector whose i-th entry is -1_{r_j} (1_{r_j}) and the rest are 0. For instance, if $v = (0 \ 1_p \wedge 1_q \wedge -1_r \ 1_p)$, then $\overset{s,}{\neg}v = \{(0 \ 1_p \ 0), (0 \ 1_q \ 0), (0 \ -1_r \ 0), (0 \ 0 \ 1_p)\}$.

---

[5] We can ignore the label of a conjunct in $conj_i$ if source s_i is non-committal, i.e., $0_{r_j} = 0$, for all $r_j \in \mathbf{D}$.

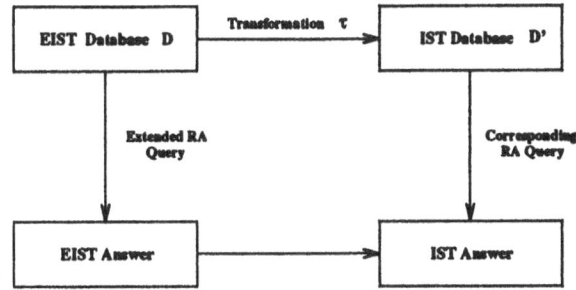

Figure 1: Commutative diagram showing the relationship between IST and EIST

4.1 Reduction of EIST to IST

In this section, we describe a transformation τ that takes an EIST database instance $\mathbf{D}$ as input and produces an IST database $\mathbf{D}'$ such that, if the sources are assumed independent, the reliability of each tuple in the result of a query posed to $\mathbf{D}$ and $\mathbf{D}'$ will be the same. Our goal is illustrated in the commutative diagram in Fig. 1.

The idea of the transformation is as follows. Let $\mathbf{D}$ be an EIST database over $\mathbf{R}$, and S be the set of sources, where $|\mathbf{R}| = n$, $\mathbf{R} = \mathbf{R}'$, and $|S| = k$. Let also $\psi : S \times \mathbf{R} \rightarrow [0, 1]$ be a reliability assignment function. Now, we can define an IST database $\mathbf{D}'$ over $\mathbf{R}'$ with sources S', where $|\mathbf{R}'| = n$ and $|S'| = k \times n$, such that for each $s_i \in S$ and for each relation $R_j \in \mathbf{R}$, we have a source $s_{ij} \in S'$, and a relation scheme $R_j' \in \mathbf{R}'$. If $t@(a_1, \ldots, a_k)$ is a tuple in $r_j \in \mathbf{D}$, then there would be a tuple $t@v$ in the relation r_j' in $\mathbf{D}'$, where v is a source vector of length $k \times n$. The entries $k \times (i - 1) + 1, \ldots, k \times (i - 1) + k$ in v are $a_1, \ldots, a_n$, respectively, and the others are 0. The reliability assignment function ρ for the sources in S' is defined as $\rho(s_{ij}) = \psi(s_i, R_j)$. It is easy to see that the transformation process above can be automated. The following example further clarifies the transformation process.

Example 6 Let $\mathbf{R} = \{R_1, R_2, R_3\}$ be an EIST database with the sources $S = \{s_1, s_2\}$. Let r_1, r_2, and r_3 be relation instances over R_1, R_2, and R_3, respectively, where $r_1 = \{t_1@1\ 0\}$, $r_2 = \{t_2@0\ 1\}$, and $r_3 = \{t_2@1\ 0\}$. Suppose the reliability of the sources in S are given as $\psi(s_1, R_1) = 0.7$, $\psi(s_2, R_1) = 0.8$, $\psi(s_1, R_2) = 0.7$, $\psi(s_2, R_2) = 0.9$, $\psi(s_1, R_3) = 0.9$, and $\psi(s_2, R_3) = 0.85$. Assume $r = r_1 \cup r_2$. As the result of the transformation τ of $\mathbf{D}$, we get an IST database $\mathbf{R}' = \{R_1', R_2', R_3'\}$, with the sources $S' = \{s_{11}, s_{12}, s_{13}, s_{21}, s_{22}, s_{23}\}$. The reliability of the sources in S' can then be defined as $\rho(s_{11}) = \psi(s_1, R_1) = 0.7$, $\rho(s_{12}) = \psi(s_1, R_2) = 0.7$, $\rho(s_{13}) = \psi(s_1, R_3) = 0.9$, $\rho(s_{21}) = \psi(s_2, R_1) = 0.8$, $\rho(s_{22}) = \psi(s_2, R_2) = 0.9$, and $\rho(s_{23}) = \psi(s_2, R_3) = 0.85$. The transformation τ of the relations r_1, r_2, and r_3 in $\mathbf{D}$ will produce respectively the relations $r_1' = \{t_1@1\ 0\ 0\ 0\ 0\ 0\}$, $r_2' = \{t_2@0\ 0\ 0\ 1\ 0\ 0\}$, and $r_3' = \{t_2@0\ 0\ 0\ 0\ 1\ 0\}$. The relation $r' = r_1' \cup r_2'$ in the IST database $\mathbf{D}'$ with the scheme $\mathbf{R}'$ would then contain the tuples $t_1@1\ 0\ 0\ 0\ 0\ 0$ and $t_2@0\ 0\ 0\ 1\ 0\ 0$.

We have the following result, which states that, under the assumption of source independence, the commutative diagram in Section 3 is correct and for any EIST database, there exist an IST database that is information preserving.

Definition 1 Let ϕ be a relational operator defined using $\overset{s}{\wedge}$ and $\overset{s}{\dashv}$, and ϕ' be the same operator defined using $\overset{s}{\wedge}$ and $\overset{s}{\dashv}$ respectively. Let r be an EIST relation, S be a set of sources, and ψ be any reliability assignment function. We say that ϕ' is *information preserving* if the reliability of each tuple $t \in \phi(r)$ is identical to the corresponding tuple $t \in \phi'(r)$. □

Theorem 1 *Let D be an EIST database, S be the sources in D, and τ be a transformation of D into an IST database D'. If the sources in S are independent, and the reliability of the same source in different contexts are independent, then D is IST reducible via τ and $\tau(D)$ is information preserving.*

Proof: Omitted for want of space. □

4.2 Reliability calculation algorithm for EIST databases

Now, we describe how to compute the reliability of answer tuples defined by an EIST expression (using our extended operations). Let $\mathbf{R} = \{R_1, \ldots, R_n\}$ be an EIST database scheme, $S = \{s_1, \ldots, s_k\}$ be the set of sources, and $\psi : S \times \mathbf{R} \to [0, 1]$ be the reliability assignment function. Let $r = Exp(\mathbf{R})$, where $Exp(\mathbf{R})$ is a relational algebra expression involving the relations in $\mathbf{R}$. Suppose that $t@x$ is a tuple in r where x is a set of labelled source vectors $x_1, \ldots, x_l$. Note that since $|S| = k$, each x_i is a k-tuple $(c_1 \ldots c_k)$, where each c_j is either 0, or is a conjunction of labelled confirmations (1s) of sources in different contexts, as described in Section 4.

Case 1: If $x_i \in x$ and that $x_i = \top$, then $re(r(t))$ the reliability of t being a member of r is 0, and hence we can delete such source vectors from x in calculating $re(r(t))$ (see Section 2.1).

Case 2: Let $x = \{x_i\}$ and $x_i \neq \top$. Also let that $c_{j_1}, \ldots, c_{j_k}$ $(j_k \leq k)$ are all be non-zero entries in x_i. Let A_{j_1} be the set of relation schemes such that source s_{j_1} has contributed positively w.r.t. the tuple t. Recall that this provides a 1 in the conjunction c_{j_1} with the corresponding relation's name as its label. Similarly, let B_{j_1} be the set of relation schemes such that s_{j_1} has contributed negatively w.r.t. the tuple t. Define $A = \bigcup A_{j_i}$ and $B = \bigcup B_{j_i}$, for $j_1 \leq j_i \leq j_k$. Then, we have

$$re(r(t)) = \prod_{p \in A} \psi(s, p) \times \prod_{q \in B} (1 - \psi(s, q)).$$

Case 3: Let $x = \{x_1, \ldots, x_l\}$ such that no $x_i = \top$. Then,

$$re(r(t)) = 1 - (1 - re_1) \times \ldots \times (1 - re_l),$$

where re_i is the reliability of $t@x_i$ being in r, obtained in Case 2 above.

The following example illustrates the algorithm above.

Example 7 Let $\mathbf{D} = \{p, q\}$ be an EIST database over the scheme $\mathbf{R} = \{P, Q\}$, and $S = \{s_1, s_2, s_3\}$ be the set of sources, where $\psi(s_1, P) = 0.7$, $\psi(s_2, P) = 0.7$, $\psi(s_3, P) = 0.8$, $\psi(s_1, Q) = 0.9$, $\psi(s_2, Q) = 0.8$, and $\psi(s_3, Q) = 0.6$. Let also $r = Exp(\mathbf{R})$ be an extended relational algebra expression. Suppose that r contains the tuple $t@x$, where $x = \{(1_p 1_q \quad 0 \quad 1_p 1_q), (0 \quad -1_p \quad 1_q)\}$. We have Case 3 of the above algorithm. Thus, we first determine re_1 and re_2, where $re_1 = re(r(t@(1_p 1_q \quad 0 \quad 1_p 1_q)))$, and $re_2 = re(r(t@(0 \quad -1_p \quad 1_q)))$, each of which is an instance of Case 2 of the algorithm.

$$re_1 = \psi(s_1, P) \times \psi(s_3, P) \times \psi(s_3, Q) \times (1 - \psi(s_1, Q)) = 0.0336.$$
$$re_2 = \psi(s_3, Q) \times (1 - \psi(s_2, P)) = 0.18.$$

Thus,

$$
\begin{aligned}
re(r(t)) &= 1 - (1 - re_1) \times (1 - re_2) \\
&= 1 - (1 - 0.0336) \times (1 - 0.18) \\
&= 0.027.
\end{aligned}
$$

5 Conclusions

We have introduced the idea of contexts in the basic IST model, and allowed sources to have different reliabilities in different contexts. In this paper we have assumed that every relation in a database models a real world entity and thus captures a single concept. We viewed each such concept as a context. We have extended the relational algebra operations of Sadri [3, 5] to capture the concept of context and to enable the system to manipulate the source information to finally calculate the tuple reliability. We have also shown that an EIST database is IST reducible and the reduction is information preserving. These results are based on the assumption that all the sources are independent and the reliability of a source in different contexts are also independent.

An issue that remains yet to be investigated and deserves due attention is that how to assign reliabilities to sources in materialized views. Clearly, the reliability should depend on the reliability of the sources in the contributing relations from which the tuples in the view are derived. Another interesting issue is that of accommodating different modes of reliability dependency of a source in different contexts. For example, the reliability of a source may be partially dependent in two contexts, while they may be independent in other contexts. Thus, it might be possible to let the user define a mix of combination modes of reliability dependency of the sources in a database, and hence better reflect real life situations. In this case the functionality, and consequently the relational operators, should be extended in such a way that it takes into account the dependency mode of the source reliability and compute the expected reliability of the tuples. A related issue is to define the concept of context at a finer level of granularity, say, at the attribute level. These are some of the issues we plan to investigate in our future research.

Acknowledgement

We thank Professor Laks V.S. Lakshmanan and Professor Fereidoon Sadri for many helpful suggestions and useful discussions during the development of this paper.

References

[1] Jamil H, Sadri F. Trusting an information agent. Proc of the International Workshop on Rough Sets and Knowledge Discovery, Banff, Canada, 1993, pp 348–359

[2] Lakshmanan VS, Sadri F. Modeling uncertainty in deductive databases, Technical Report, Concordia University, 1993

[3] Sadri F. Information source tracking. Technical Report, Concordia University, 1991

[4] Sadri F. Integrity constraints in the information source tracking method. Technical Report, Concordia University, 1991

[5] Sadri F. Reliability of answers to queries in relational databases. IEEE Trans on Knowledge and Data Engineering 1991; 3(2)

Unnesting Fuzzy SQL Queries in Fuzzy Databases*

Qi Yang, Weining Zhang, Chenjie Luo, Clement Yu, H. Nakajima

Department of EECS, University of Illinois at Chicago
Omron Corporation, Kyoto 617, Japan
{yang,yu}@dbis.eecs.uic.edu

Abstract

The efficiency of processing fuzzy queries in fuzzy databases is a major concern. We provide techniques to unnest fuzzy queries (of two blocks) of type N, type J, type JA, and nested queries with quantifiers. We show that by unnesting the queries, efficiency can be improved significantly. The results obtained in the paper form the basis for unnesting fuzzy queries of arbitrary blocks in fuzzy databases.

1 Introduction

A fuzzy database system has been built by Omron Corporation, and relational SQL has been extended for fuzzy relations [7,8]. As in ordinary SQL, nested queries are allowed in fuzzy SQL so that users can express their queries in a convenient way. However, the evaluation of nested queries will be very inefficient if they are implemented as nested loops.

We extend and modify unnesting techniques [3,4,5,6] for ordinary relational nested SQL queries to nested fuzzy SQL queries. We also provide some new techniques for unnesting fuzzy SQL queries. All nested fuzzy queries involving outer fuzzy relation R and inner fuzzy relation S can be evaluated by performing some type of merge-join between R and S, and the I/O cost is reduced dramatically. Specifically, the following results are obtained.

1. For type N and type J nesting, the technique for ordinary relational queries is applicable to fuzzy relational queries.

2. For type JA queries, the techniques for ordinary relational queries in [4] and [6] are modified, and pipelining technique [3, 6] is adapted to further reduce I/O cost.

3. For queries with quantifier ALL, new techniques are provided. In addition, a necessary and sufficient condition is obtained as to when such queries can be transformed to type A or type JA queries.

*Research supported in part by NSF under IRI–9111988, Omron Corporation, and Omron Management Center of America.

For queries with quantifier *ALL* and without a join predicate in the inner block, no sorting is needed, and the I/O cost for unnested queries is $P(R) + 2P(S)$, where $P(X)$ is the size in pages of relation X. In all other cases, the I/O cost for unnested queries is $SORT(R) + SORT(S) + P(R) + P(S)$, where $SORT(X)$ is the I/O cost of sorting relation X. For most practical situations, $SORT(X)$ takes $4P(X)$ [10]. In contrast, when relations are very large, the I/O cost for processing a nested fuzzy query in a naive manner is $P(R) + P(S) + \alpha|R| \times P(T)$ when there is no join predicate in the inner block, and $P(R) + \alpha|R| \times P(S)$ otherwise, where $|R|$ is the number of tuples of R, α the fraction of R-tuples that satisfy other predicates in the outer block, and T the temporary relation generated from the inner block. In this case, the I/O cost for a nested query is dominated by the product $\alpha|R| \times P(T)$ or $\alpha|R| \times P(S)$, and may be much larger than that for the corresponding unnested query.

2 Fuzzy databases

2.1 Fuzzy databases

A fuzzy database system has been established in Omron Corp. based on fuzzy set theory [8]. For a fuzzy set F, each crisp value v belongs to F with a membership degree $\mu_F(v)$ between 0 and 1. In a fuzzy relation, the value of an attribute of a tuple may be either a crisp value or a fuzzy term representing a fuzzy set. For example, a relation about people may have an attribute AGE and the values for AGE may be 28 or "about 35" or "young". Both "about 35" and "young" are fuzzy terms, and their membership functions are shown in *Figure 1*. A person of age 32 will be "about 35" with degree 0.4 and be "young" with degree 0.6; a person of age 35 will be "about 35" with degree 1.0 and be "young" with degree 0.0. The graph of $\mu_{about\ 35}(v)$ is a triangle and such a fuzzy term is called a fuzzy number; the graph of $\mu_{young}(v)$ is a trapezoid and such a fuzzy term is called a fuzzy label. Notice that a fuzzy term corresponds to an interval, e.g., "about 35" to [30, 40] and "young" to [20, 35].

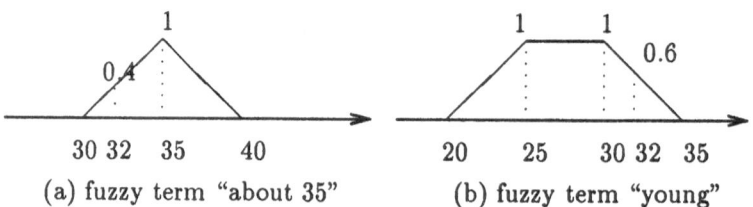

(a) fuzzy term "about 35"   (b) fuzzy term "young"

Figure 1 Membership functions for two fuzzy terms

An attribute is called a *fuzzy attribute* if its domain contains crisp values as well as fuzzy numbers or/and fuzzy labels; a relation is called a *fuzzy relation* if at least one attribute is a fuzzy attribute. A fuzzy relation R itself is also a fuzzy set with a membership degree $\mu_R(r)$ for each tuple r, and we indicate the membership degree explicitly only when necessary. The answer to a query Q on a fuzzy database is also a fuzzy set, i.e., each tuple t in the answer has a satisfaction degree $\mu_Q(t)$ which is the membership degree of t in the answer to Q.

2.2 Fuzzy SQL

The standard SQL has been extended to a fuzzy database language called *Fuzzy SQL*, and rules are given to compute the satisfaction degree for a tuple in the answer [7, 8]. There are three basic rules for computing the degrees. The first one is for computing the truth value of the *WHERE* clause of a given query. We assume that the *WHERE* clause of a query is a conjunction of predicates. But the membership degrees of tuples involved should also be taken into account. Thus, as a default, the truth value of the clause is taken as the minimal one among all truth values for the individual predicates in the clause and the membership degrees of the tuples involved.

$$
\begin{aligned}
&\text{SELECT} && R.X \\
&\text{FROM} && R,\, S \\
&\text{WHERE} && p_1 \text{ AND } R.Y = S.Z \text{ AND } p_2
\end{aligned}
$$

In the query above, predicate p_1 involves only R and p_2 involves only S. For any pair of tuples r and s, the truth value of the *WHERE* clause is defined as

$$ d'_{r,s} = min(\mu_R(r), \mu_S(s), d(p_1(r)), d(p_2(s)), d(r.Y = s.Z)), $$

where $d(p_i())$ is the truth value of p_i on the corresponding tuple, and $d(r.Y = s.Z)$ is the truth value of predicate $r.Y = s.Z$.

The second rule is concerned with the *SELECT* clause. As a default, only when the truth value of the *WHERE* clause is positive, the required attribute value is selected. In the example above, $r.X$ is retrieved only when $d'_{r,s} > 0$. However, other conditions are sometimes needed. In *Fuzzy SQL*, a new clause *WITH* is introduced to enforce any conditions as to when a tuple should be generated. For example, if there is a clause *WITH* $D > 0.5$ following the *WHERE* clause in the above query, then $r.X$ is added to the answer only when $d'_{r,s} > 0.5$.

The last rule deals with elimination of duplicates. The same tuple may be generated more than once; the answer is a set and should not contain duplicate occurrences of the same value (especially when *DISTINCT* is issued in the *SELECT* clause). In this case, the maximal degree is maintained. This can be considered as a disjunction of several predicates. In the above example, an x value in $R.X$ is in the answer with the final degree $max_{r.X=x}(d'_{r,s})$.

In this paper, we will introduce some new operators and structures into *Fuzzy SQL* in order to optimize query processing in fuzzy databases. However, when no special operators are present, we always assume the three default rules.

2.3 Fuzzy joins

Consider the join $R \bowtie_{R.X=S.X} S$, where R and S are two fuzzy relations and X is a common fuzzy attribute. As an example, when X is the attribute AGE, the above join requests all pairs of persons, one from R and another from S, who have the same age. Two persons can not have the same age if one is 28 and the other is "about 35", since "about 35" means between 30 and 40. However two persons may have the same age if one is "young" and the other is "about 35", since "young" means between 20 and 35. But we do not know for sure

170

that they have the same age. So, unlike joins of ordinary relations, the join predicate $R.X = S.X$ may be true for two tuples of fuzzy relations even they have different values for the joining attribute, and can only be checked with some uncertainty.

In general, the truth value of a predicate in fuzzy logic is a value between 0 and 1. In Omron's system, the truth value for "about 35" = "young" is computed by taking the highest intersection point of the two corresponding membership functions as illustrated in Figure 2. There are other ways to compute the truth value of such a fuzzy predicate, e.g., to use the area under membership functions. In any case, the truth value can be computed in constant time.

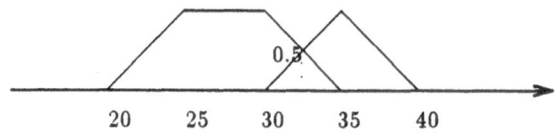

Figure 2   The truth value of "about 35" = "young" is 0.5.

The semantics of the join $R \bowtie_{R.X = S.X} S$ is defined as follows. For any pair of tuples r of R and s of S, the truth value of $R.X = S.X$, $d(r.X = s.X)$, is computed first, a satisfaction degree for the pair, $d_{r,s}$, is then computed as $MIN(\mu_R(r), \mu_S(s), d(r.X = s.X))$, and finally a tuple is generated with degree $d_{r,s}$ when $d_{r,s} > 0$. Notice that tuple r is in R with $\mu_R(r) > 0$, and s is in S with $\mu_S(s) > 0$. Thus, $d_{r,s} > 0$ if and only if $d(r.X = s.X) > 0$.

There is analytical and experimental evidence that hashed join is the most effective method for joins of ordinary relations, but the method may not be as efficient for computing joins of fuzzy relations, since two tuples may still join even they have different values on the joining attribute.

One way to process a fuzzy join efficiently is sort-merge. In [11], we define a partial order on the set of R-tuples (or S-tuples) and describe how sort-merge join can be conducted for fuzzy relations efficiently. The range of a tuple r of R, $Rng(r)$, is a subset of S such that a tuple s of S can not join with a tuple r of R, i.e., $d(r.X = s.X) = 0$, if s is not in $Rng(r)$. After both R and S are sorted, the fuzzy join $R \bowtie_{R.X = S.X} S$ can be completed by reading both R and S only once.

3   Type N and type J nested queries

A nested query of type N or type J [5] does not have an aggregate function in the $SELECT$ clause of the inner block. The difference between them is that a type J query contains a join predicate in the inner block that references the outer relation. The following Query N is of type N while Query J is of type J, where predicate p_1 involves only R and p_2 involves only S.

Query N
SELECT $R.X$
FROM R
WHERE p_1 AND $R.Y$ is in

Query J
SELECT $R.X$
FROM R
WHERE p_1 AND $R.Y$ is in

```
(SELECT S.Z              (SELECT S.Z
 FROM  S                  FROM  S
 WHERE p₂ )               WHERE p₂ AND S.V = R.U )
```

We first discuss the semantics of Query N in fuzzy databases. The inner block should be processed first, independent of the outer block, since it contains no join predicate referencing the outer relation. Let T be the temporary relation produced from the inner block. To produce T, relation S is scanned, and a satisfaction degree, d_s, is computed for each tuple s in S to be

$$d_s = min(\mu_S(s), d(p_2(s))).$$

When $d_s > 0$, the value $s.Z$ is stored; after removing duplicates, a value z is in T with degree

$$\mu_T(z) = \max_{s.Z=z}(d_s).$$

After T is computed, the outer block is processed. For any tuple r of R, its satisfaction degree is

$$d_r = min(\mu_R(r), d(p_1(r)), d(r.Y \text{ is in } T)).$$

To compute d_r, we need to compute the degree of $r.Y$ is in T, $d(r.Y \text{ is in } T)$. Given a fuzzy or crisp value v and a fuzzy set F, the degree of the predicate (v is in F) is defined as follows [8]:

$$d(v \text{ is in } F) = \begin{cases} \max_{e\in F}(min(\mu_F(e), d(e=v))), & \text{when } F \neq \emptyset; \\ 0, & \text{otherwise.} \end{cases}$$

Then, $\quad d_r = min(\mu_R(r), d(p_1(r)), \max_{z\in T}(min(\mu_T(z), d(r.Y=z)))).$

When $T = \emptyset$, $d_r = 0$. When $d_r > 0$, the value $r.X$ is retrieved. After removing duplicates, a value x is in the answer with degree

$$\mu_N(x) = \max_{r.X=x}(d_r).$$

It is possible that T can reside in the main memory. In this case, the inner block reads relation S once to produce T, which resides in the main memory; the outer block reads relation R only once. Thus, the I/O cost for processing Query N is $P(R)+P(S)$. However, when T can not reside in the main memory, for each R-tuple that yields a positive degree on p_1, the entire T may have to be read in, and the I/O cost would be increased to $P(R)+P(S)+\alpha|R| \times P(T)$.

For ordinary databases, Query N is equivalent to the following unnested Query N' and can be processed by some efficient join algorithm to reduce the I/O cost.

Query N'
```
SELECT   R.X
FROM     R, S
WHERE    p₁ AND R.Y = S.Z AND p₂
```

According to the default rules, the semantics of Query N' in fuzzy databases is as follows. For a pair of tuples r and s, the satisfaction degree is

$$d'_{r,s} = min(\mu_R(r), \mu_S(s), d(p_1(r)), d(p_2(s)), d(r.Y = s.Z));$$

$r.X$ is retrieved when $d'_{r,s} > 0$; after eliminating duplicates, a value x is in the answer with degree

$$\mu_{N'}(x) = max_{r.X=x} max_{s \in S}(d'_{r,s}).$$

In fuzzy database systems, Query N' can be processed by the merge-join method [11]. We sort R on $R.Y$ and sort S on $S.Z$. Then a tuple r joins with all S-tuples in $Rng(r)$, the value of $d'_{r,s}$ is computed for each s in $Rng(r)$, and $r.X$ is inserted into the answer with degree $max_{s \in Rgn(r)}(d'_{r,s})$, which is the same as $max_{s \in S}(d'_{r,s})$, since $d(r.Y = s.Z)$ and hence $d'_{r,s}$ are zero for any s not in $Rng(r)$. The degree $\mu_{N'}(x)$ is obtained by maintaining the maximal value when eliminating duplicates.

Since the fuzzy join incurs linear I/O cost, the total I/O cost for Query N' is $SORT(R) + SORT(S) + P(R) + P(S)$. Before sorting either R or S, predicate p_1 or p_2 should be evaluated to reduce the size of the relation. This will reduce the sorting cost and the later joining cost. For the sake of simplicity of presentation, we assume that R and S are to be sorted. For the original nested query, if the temporary relation, T, can not reside in the main memory, the I/O cost is dominated by the product $\alpha|R| \times P(T)$ and may be much larger than that for the unnested query. If Query N' is equivalent to Query N in fuzzy databases, then we can unnest the original query and let the system optimizer choose the better method to improve the I/O performance.

Lemma 3.1 For any $n \geq 1$ and any $m \geq 1$,

(a) $\quad min(\min_{1 \leq i \leq n}(a_i), b_1, \ldots, b_m) = min(a_1, \ldots, a_n, b_1, \ldots, b_m);$

(b) $\quad min(\max_{1 \leq i \leq n}(a_i), b_1, \ldots, b_m) = \max_{1 \leq i \leq n}(min(a_i, b_1, \ldots, b_m)).$

Theorem 3.1 Query N' is equivalent to Query N in fuzzy databases.

Proof: We prove $\mu_N(x) = \mu_{N'}(x)$ for each x in the domain of $R.X$, where $\mu_N(x)$ and $\mu_{N'}(x)$ are the membership degrees of x in the answers to Query N and Query N', respectively. This implies that Query N' generates the same answer set as Query N does, since x is in the answer to Query N (Query N') if and only if $\mu_N(x) > 0$ $(\mu_{N'}(x) > 0)$.

For Query N', x is in the answer with degree

$$\mu_{N'}(x) = \max_{r.X=x} \max_{s \in S}(d'_{r,s})$$

$$= \max_{r.X=x} \max_{s \in S}(min(\mu_R(r), \mu_S(s), d(p_1(r)), d(p_2(s)), d(r.Y = s.Z))).$$

For Query N, we have

$$\mu_N(x) = \max_{r.X=x}(d_r)$$

$$= \max_{r.X=x}(min(\mu_R(r), d(p_1(r)), \max_{z \in T}(min(\mu_T(z), d(r.Y = z)))))$$

$$= \max_{r.X=x} (\max_{z \in T}(min(\mu_R(r), d(p_1(r)), min(\mu_T(z), d(r.Y = z)))))$$

by Lemma 3.1 (b)

$$= \max_{r.X=x} (\max_{z \in T}(min(\mu_R(r), d(p_1(r)), \mu_T(z), d(r.Y = z))))$$

by Lemma 3.1 (a)

$$= \max_{r.X=x} (\max_{z \in T}(min(\mu_R(r), d(p_1(r)), \max_{s.Z=z}(d_s), d(r.Y = z))))$$

$$= \max_{r.X=x} (\max_{z \in T}(\max_{s.Z=z}(min(\mu_R(r), d(p_1(r)), d_s, d(r.Y = z)))))$$

by Lemma 3.1 (b)

$$= \max_{r.X=x} (\max_{z \in T}(\max_{s.Z=z}$$

$$(min(\mu_R(r), d(p_1(r)), min(\mu_S(s), d(p_2(s))), d(r.Y = z)))))$$

$$= \max_{r.X=x} (\max_{z \in T}(\max_{s.Z=z}(min(\mu_R(r), d(p_1(r)), \mu_S(s), d(p_2(s)), d(r.Y = z)))))$$

by Lemma 3.1 (a)

$$= \max_{r.X=x} \max_{s \in S}(min(\mu_R(r), d(p_1(r)), \mu_S(s), d(p_2(s)), d(r.Y = s.Z)))$$

In the last step,

$\max_{r.X=x} \max_{z \in T} \max_{s.Z=z} (min(*))$

is replaced by

$\max_{r.X=x} \max_{s \in S}(min(*))$.

The latter expression may cover more pairs of tuples than the former. A pair of tuples r and s will not be covered by the former but will be by the latter if $r.X = x$ and $s.Z$ is not in T. As discussed earlier in this section,

$d_s = min(\mu_S(s), d(p_2(s)))$, and $\mu_T(z) = \max_{s.Z=z}(d_s)$.

Then, $s.Z$ is not in T implies $d(p_2(s)) = 0$, which in turn implies $min(*) = 0$ since $d(p_2(s))$ is inside the expression $(*)$. That is, each pair covered by the latter but not covered by the former yields a value of zero. We can replace the former by the latter, because $(min(*))$ always gives non-negative values and the maximum value is chosen from all values produced by $(min(*))$. For instance, if $T = \emptyset$, which implies $d(p_2(s)) = 0$ for all tuples s, then $\mu_N(x) = \mu_{N'}(x) = 0$ for any x although the former covers no pairs of tuples. Thus, $\mu_N(x)\mu_{N'}(x)$ for any value x and the proof is completed. ∎

For ordinary relations, Query J can be unnested to the following Query J' [5]. This is also true for fuzzy databases.

Query J'

SELECT	$R.X$
FROM	R, S
WHERE	p_1 AND $R.Y = S.Z$ AND p_2 AND $R.U = S.V$

Theorem 3.2 Query J' is equivalent to Query J in fuzzy databases.

The evaluation algorithm for Query J' is very similar to that for Query N'. For Query J', either join predicate can be used for the merge, although $R.Y = S.Z$ is obtained from the *is in* predicate of the original query. Suppose R is sorted on $R.Y$ and S on $S.Z$. For each tuple r of R, all tuples that may join with r are in $Rng(r)$ and can be loaded into the main memory. Then, for each s in $Rng(r)$, a satisfaction degree is computed w.r.t. r:

$$d'_{r,s} = min(\mu_R(r), \mu_S(s), d(p_1(r)), d(p_2(s)), d(r.Y = s.Z), d(r.U = s.V)),$$

and $r.X$ is retrieved $d'_{r,s} > 0$. Finally, after removing duplicates, a value x is in the answer with degree

$$\mu_{J'}(x) = \max_{r.X=x}(d'_{r,s}).$$

4 Type JA nested queries

The following Query JA is of type JA nesting [5], where the inner block contains a join predicate that references the outer relation and has an aggregate function in the *SELECT* clause. Both op_1 and op_2 are comparison operators in $\{<, >, \le , \ge, =\}$, and AGG is one of the aggregate functions MAX, MIN, AVG, SUM and $COUNT$. (When no join predicate exists in the inner block, the inner block produces the same single value for any tuple of R, and no unnesting is needed.)

Query JA
```
         SELECT   R.X
         FROM     R
         WHERE    p₁ AND R.Y op₁
                  ( SELECT AGG(S.Z)
                    FROM   S
                    WHERE p₂ AND S.V op₂ R.U )
```

We propose to unnest fuzzy Query JA by using two temporary relations, T_1 and T_2. T_1 is obtained from R by restricting R with p_1 and projecting on $R.U$. Duplicates are removed from T_1.

```
T₁(U) = ( SELECT R.U      T₂(U,A) = ( SELECT   T₁.U, AGG(S.Z)
          FROM    R                   FROM     T₁, S
          WHERE  p₁ )                 WHERE    p₂ AND S.V op₂ T₁.U
                                      GROUPBY T₁.U )
```

T_2 is obtained by joining T_1 with S. The join operation is on $S.V\ op_2\ T_1.U$ (p_2 can be applied to S before the join). There is a $GROUPBY$ clause in T_2. Such a clause in fuzzy databases is carried out by the identity predicate $\equiv$ and not by the fuzzy equality predicate. That is, for each value u in T_1, all tuples s such that $d(s.V\ op_2\ u) > 0$ (and $d(p_2(s)) > 0$) are grouped together, and their $S.Z$ values form a set, $T'(u)$. Then, a result, $A'(u)$, is computed from $T'(u)$ by AGG, and a tuple $(u, A'(u))$ is inserted into T_2.

When AGG is not $COUNT$, Query JA' gives the final answer by joining R with T_2 on $R.U \equiv T_2.U$. A tuple r joins with at most one tuple of T_2. If r joins with $t = (u, A'(u))$ of T_2, then the satisfaction degree of r, d'_r, is computed; the value $r.X$ is retrieved when $d'_r > 0$. If r does not join with any tuple of T_2, then $d'_r = 0$ and $r.X$ is not inserted into the answer.

Query JA'

  SELECT $R.X$
  FROM R, T_2
  WHERE p_1 AND $R.U \equiv T_2.U$ AND $R.Y$ op_1 $T_2.A$

When AGG is $COUNT$, the *left outer join* operator, denoted by $+$, is used together with the identity predicate and the final answer is given by Query COUNT'. A tuple r of R joins with at most one tuple of T_2 because of the identity predicate.

Query COUNT'

  SELECT $R.X$
  FROM R, T_2
  WHERE p_1 AND
        $R.U+ \equiv T_2.U$
    $[R.Y$ op_1 $T_2.A: R.Y$ op_1 $0]$

We use the left outer join operator (e.g., [2]) to preserve each tuple of the left relation R, since only $R.X$ is projected. As in [6], a square bracket following the outer join predicate is used to specify an *IF-THEN-ELSE* structure. The square bracket has two parts separated by a colon, and the *WHERE* clause is evaluated as follows:

If tuple r of R joins with tuple $t = (u, A'(u))$ of T_2, i.e., $r.U \equiv u$, then the degree of the outer join is determined by the first part in the square bracket;

else (r does not join with any tuple of T_2, i.e., $T'(r.U) = \emptyset$) the degree of the outer join is determined by the second part of the bracket.

Theorem 4.1 Query JA' (Query COUNT') is equivalent to Query JA in fuzzy databases when $AGG \neq COUNT$ ($AGG = COUNT$).

 Although we use three queries to unnest Query JA, by pipelining the result of one query to another, the three queries can be carried out together in the main memory as in merge-join of R and S. We sort R on $R.U$ and S on $S.V$ (after applying predicate p_1 to R and predicate p_2 to S, respectively). We assume that the join predicate op_2 is the equality predicate. Let r_1 be the smallest R-tuple (according to $\prec$). Then, $u_1 = r_1.U$ is the smallest U value (according to $\prec$) and projected first (Query T_1). The value u_1 is pipelined to Query T_2, and u_1 joins with all tuples s in $Rng(r_1)$ to generate $T'(u_1)$. If $T'(u_1) \neq \emptyset$, $A'(u_1)$ is computed (Query T_2). The value $A'(u_1)$ is then pipelined to Query JA' or Query COUNT', and for all R-tuples r with $r.U \equiv u_1$ including r_1, the satisfaction degree d'_r is computed, and the value $r.X$ is projected accordingly. If $T'(u_1) = \emptyset$ and $AGG = COUNT$, the left outer join in Query COUNT' is evaluated, and $r.X$ may still be retrieved for a tuple r with $r.U \equiv u_1$. If $T'(u_1) = \emptyset$ and $AGG \neq COUNT$, the processing for u_1 ends. After that, the second smallest U value is to be computed, and the process continues until all R-tuples are processed. The total I/O cost for the unnested query is $SORT(R) + SORT(S) + P(R) + P(S)$, while that for the nested one is $P(R) + \alpha|R| \times P(S)$.

5 Queries with quantifier ALL

A nested query may have a quantifier such as *EXISTS*, *SOME* and *ALL* in the *WHERE* clause. Ganski and Wong [4] replaced each quantifier with an appropriate aggregate function and unnested such queries in ordinary SQL easily. Nested fuzzy queries with quantifiers can also be unnested, but not as easily as in ordinary databases. In addition to computing degrees in evaluating fuzzy queries, a major complication is that the ordering of fuzzy terms is not necessarily consistent with the predicate *less than* (or *greater than*). We discuss nested fuzzy queries with quantifier *ALL*. The discussion for other quantifiers is similar.

Consider the following Query JALL, which has quantifier *ALL* in the outer block and a join predicate in the inner block referencing the outer relation. For the sake of simplicity of presentation, we omit both p_1 and p_2 and use $<$ instead of *op* in the query. The discussion will be similar for any other comparison operator in $\{<, \leq, >, \geq\}$, and for the situation where p_1 and/or p_2 are present.

> Query JALL
> > SELECT $R.X$
> > FROM R
> > WHERE $R.Y < $ ALL
> > (SELECT $S.Z$
> >   FROM S
> >   WHERE $S.V = R.U$)

A method is given in Fuzzy SQL [8] to compute the degree of $v_1 < v_2$ for two fuzzy or crisp elements, but it does not guarantee that $d(v < ALL\ F)$ is the same as $d(v < MIN(F))$. Consequently, $< ALL\ F$ can not be replaced by $< MIN(F)$ in fuzzy databases. We will discuss later when this transformation is valid.

We propose to unnest fuzzy Query JALL by using two temporary relations T_1 and T_2. We assume that $R.K$ is a key of relation R. We indicate the computed degree, D, when necessary. In the query for T_1, the *WITH* clause contains an expression $d(R.U = S.V) > 0$ AND $D \geq 0$. As a consequence, no tuple will be generated when joining r and s if $d(r.U = s.V) = 0$; only when $d(r.U = s.V) > 0$, the satisfaction degree, $d'_{r,s}$, is computed, and a tuple is generated even when $d'_{r,s} = 0$ because of $D \geq 0$. The *GROUPBY* clause groups all generated tuples by the combination of $R.K$ and $S.Z$.

> $T_1(K, Z, D) = ($ SELECT $R.K, S.Z, MAX(D)$
> > FROM R, S
> > WHERE $R.U = S.V$ AND $R.Y < S.Z$
> > WITH $d(R.U = S.V) > 0$ AND $D \geq 0$
> > GROUPBY $R.K$ AND $S.Z$)

T_2 groups T_1 by $T_1.K$. The *HAVING* clause in standard SQL is used to indicate when a tuple should be generated when the *GROUPBY* clause is present. As a result, one tuple is always generated for each group, even though the degree may be zero. It is important to keep tuples with degree zero, since such a tuple indicates that the temporary relation, $T(r)$, produced w.r.t. tuple r

from the inner block of Query ALL is not empty, but the degree of $r.Y <$ ALL $T(r)$ is zero. Otherwise, there is no way to distinguish this case from that of $T(r) = \emptyset$.

$$
\begin{array}{ll}
T_2(K,D) = (\ \text{SELECT} & T_1.K, MIN(D) \\
\text{FROM} & T_1 \\
\text{GROUPBY} & T_1.K \\
\text{HAVING} & MIN(D) \geq 0\ )
\end{array}
$$

In Query JALL', the left outer join combined with the identity operator is applied to R and T_2. A tuple r can join with at most one tuple of T_2 because of the identity operator. If r joins with a tuple t of T_2, the degree of the left outer join is $t.D$, and the satisfaction degree of r is $d'_r = min(\mu_R(r), t.D)$. This corresponds to the case where $T(r) \neq \emptyset$ in the original query, and $d'_r = 0$ is equivalent to $t.D = 0$ which implies that $d(r.Y < z) = 0$ for some z in $T(r)$. Otherwise, the degree of the outer join is 1, and $d'_r = min(\mu_R(r), 1) = \mu_R(r)$. This corresponds to the case where $T(r) = \emptyset$ in the original query.

Query JALL'
$$
\begin{array}{ll}
\text{SELECT} & R.X \\
\text{FROM} & R, T_2 \\
\text{WHERE} & R.K+ \equiv T_2.K \\
& [T_2.D : 1]
\end{array}
$$

Theorem 5.1 Query JALL' is equivalent to Query JALL in fuzzy databases.

By sorting R on $R.U$ and S on $S.V$ and employing pipelining, Query JALL' with the two temporary relations can be processed with I/O cost $SORT(R) + SORT(S) + P(R) + P(S)$, while Query JALL requires I/O cost of $P(R) + \alpha |R| \times P(S)$.

For ordinary relations, $v <$ ALL F is equivalent to $v < MIN(F)$ (be cautious when $F = \emptyset$), and Query JALL may be transformed to a type JA query and unnested easily [4]. An interesting question is: Under what conditions can $<$ ALL F be replaced by $< MIN(F)$ in fuzzy databases? We have found that the inconsistency between the ordering of fuzzy terms and predicate *less than* occurs when two fuzzy terms have different angles on the left side of their membership functions as illustrated in *Figure 3*.

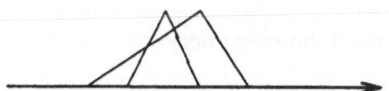

Figure 3 Two fuzzy terms having different angles on the left side.

If this does not occur, then $v <$ ALL F and $v < MIN(F)$ are equivalent, provided that the degree of $MIN(F)$ is defined to be the minimum degree over all values in F. From the $COUNT$ *Bug*, we need to be careful when $F = \emptyset$. In this case, $MIN(F) = null$ and $v < MIN(F)$ is false. But $v <$ ALL F is true with degree 1 when $F = \emptyset$. To handle this case, we introduce a new comparison operator $<\sim$. The predicate $x <\sim y$ gives degree 1 when $x \neq null$ (it is assumed that all entries in a tuple are non-null) and $y = null$, otherwise gives the same degree as $x < y$. Then, Query JALL can be transformed to the following Query MIN', which is of type JA and can be unnested.

Query MIN'

SELECT	$R.X$
FROM	R
WHERE	$R.Y <\sim$
	(SELECT $MIN(S.Z)$
	FROM S
	WHERE p_2 AND $S.V = R.U$)

Theorem 5.2 Query MIN' is equivalent to Query JALL if and only if fuzzy terms in the domain of $S.Z$ have the same angle on the left side and the degree of $MIN(F)$ is the minimum degree over all values in F.

We now discuss the following Query ALL, which has quantifier ALL but does not contain a join predicate in the inner block.

Query ALL

SELECT	$R.X$
FROM	R
WHERE	$R.Y <$ ALL
	(SELECT $S.Z$
	FROM S
	WHERE p_2)

The result of *Theorem 7.2* also applies to Query ALL, and Query ALL can be transformed to a type A nested query when the condition holds. Although for many fuzzy relations of practical interest the condition in *Theorem 7.2* is true, some relations may violate the condition. Let T be the temporary relation generated from the inner block of Query ALL. When the condition in *Theorem 7.2* is not true and T is too large to reside in the main memory, the I/O cost for Query ALL will be $P(R) + P(S) + \alpha|R| \times P(T)$. However, we do not need the entire T even when *Theorem 7.2* does not apply. Assume that MZ and MD are the minimum value in T and the minimum degree over all values in T, respectively. It can be shown that it is equivalent to consider those values in T joining with MZ. Let
$$T' = \{z : z \in T \text{ and } d(z = MZ) > 0 \}.$$
That is, T' contains all values in T that join with the minimum value in T including MZ. We also let the degree of each z in T' be MD. Then Query ALL can be unnested to the following query.

Query ALL'

SELECT	$R.X$
FROM	R
WHERE	$R.Y <$ ALL T'

Theorem 5.3 Query ALL' with T' defined above is equivalent to Query ALL in fuzzy databases.

The values of MZ and MD can be produced by scanning S once; then T' can be produced by scanning S again[1]. T' can be considered as $Rng(MZ)$ in

---

[1] Under some additional conditions, T' can be produced together with MZ and MD. But this is not true in general.

the notations for fuzzy joins (Section 2), and should be much smaller than T. The I/O cost of Query ALL' is $P(R) + 2P(S)$, while the I/O cost of Query ALL is $P(R) + P(S) + \alpha|R| \times P(T)$.

References

[1] Bosc P, Galibourg M, Hamon G. Fuzzy querying with SQL: extensions and implementation aspects. Fuzzy Sets and Systems 1988; 28:333–349

[2] Codd EF. Extending the database relational model to capture more meaning. ACM TODS 1979

[3] Dayal U. Of nests and trees: a unified approach to processing queries that contain nested queries, aggregates, and quantifiers. VLDB 1987

[4] Ganski RA, Wong HKT. Optimization of nested SQL queries revisited. ACM SIGMOD 1987; 23–33

[5] Kim W. On Optimizing an SQL-like Nested Query. ACM Trans on Database Systems 1982; 7(3):443–469

[6] Muralikrishna M. Improved unnesting algorithms for join aggregate SQL queries. VLDB 1992, Vancouver, Canada, pp 91–102

[7] Nakajima H. Development of an efficient fuzzy SQL for large scale fuzzy relational database. Proc. of 5th International Fuzzy Systems Association World Congress, 1993, pp 517–520

[8] Fuzzy LUNA - Fuzzy database system library user's manual. Fuzzy LUNA - Fuzzy database system library reference manual. OMRON Corporation, 1992

[9] Shenoi S, Melton A. An extended version of the fuzzy relational database model. Information Sciences 1990; 52:35–52

[10] Salzberg B, Tsukerman A, Gray J, Stewart M, Uren S, Vaughan B. Fast-Sort: a distributed single-input single-output external sort. SIGMOD 1990; 94–101

[11] Yang Q, Yu C, Nakajima H. A parallel scheme using the divide-and-conquer method. Submitted

[12] Zadeh LA. Fuzzy logic. IEEE Computer 1988; 83–93

[13] Zhang W, Yu C, Wang G, Pham T, Nakajima H. A relational model for imprecise queries. Int'l Symposium on Methodologies in Intelligent Systems, Trondheim, Norway, 1993

A Logical Explication of the Concepts of Incomplete and Uncertain Information

Urszula Wybraniec-Skardowska

Department of Computer Science and Applied Logic

University of Opole

wspopole@mvax.ci-pwr.wroc.edu.pl

1 Introduction

Discovery of elementary knowledge and its constituents, i.e. information contained in objects of reality is realized through asking questions including certain aspects called attributes in this paper. We describe a fragment of a discovered reality as an *information system* (cf. Pawlak [1,3,4]), which consists of the *universum* U of all the objects of this reality we are concerned with, and of a set A of *attributes* understood as functions each of which assigns to every object of U 1) a value of given attribute belonging to A or 2) an interval of approximate values of this attribute, i.e. an established set of possible values of this attribute. From the point of view of the cognitive agent and his knowledge of the attributes of this information system, such system is a *complete system* when the values of all its attributes for any objects are known, contrary to *incomplete system*, in which value or, respectively, set of values for an attribute are unknown or are not available, though at the same time the only possible. A complete system in the case of 1) is called by us *exact* and in the case of 2) is called by us *approximate*. An incomplete system is called by us *inexact, or uncertain, or vague,* in the case of 1) or *strongly uncertain, or strongly vague* in the case of 2).

The information systems discussed above allow to determine information about particular objects as either *complete* and *exact* (resp. *complete* and *approximate*) or *incomplete* and *uncertain* (resp. *incomplete* and *strongly vague*). They also allow to determine suitable *elementary knowledge* about the whole universum of a system (see Pawlak [5]). Complete information of an object of universum, with respect to a given attribute, corresponds here to the class of *indiscernible* objects assigned by this object with respect to values of this attribute, i.e. the class of objects of the same property (possessing the same value of this attribute), identified with this property, that is to say with *basic notion* the extension of which is such a class. Incomplete information of an object of U, with respect to a given attribute, corresponds to some of such classes creating an extension of indefinite notion assigned to this information of this object. Information of an object of universum, with respect to a set A of attributes of a system, corresponds to intersection of all such classes for particular attributes from A, identified with intersection of suitable basic notions, i.e. definite *elementary notion*. *Elementary knowledge on* U is a sum of information of elements of U and it may be identified with a union of elementary notions. It is divided into *complete* and *incomplete* depending on a kind of a given information system. *Elementary knowledge of U* is the family of information of elements of U and can be identified with the set of elementary notions.

Referring to Pawlak's theory of rough sets [2,5] below we provide strict formal definitions of the mentioned notions and derivative notions. In our considerations we will confine ourselves to information systems with one-argument attributes (cf. Pawlak [1,3]). Some generalizations of the notions are specified in a work of the author [6].

2 One-valued information systems

Let us consider a fragment of reality grasped as an information system S. *One-valued information system* or *deterministic information system* is called here an ordered pair

$$S = \langle U, A \rangle,$$

where U is a nonempty, finite set called the universe of S, and A is a nonempty, finite *set of attributes*, each of which is a function:

(i) $$\forall a \in A \quad a : U \to V_a,$$

where V_a is the *set of values of a*.

The following set represents the knowledge K_a of the cognitive agent of the attribute $a \in A$ of the system S:

$$K_a = \{(u, V_a^u) : u \in U\},$$

where $V_a^u \subseteq V_a$ and V_a is the set of possible values of the attribute a for the object u from the point of view of the agent discovering reality S. Further we assume that such knowledge is *not empty*, i.e. $V_a^u \neq \varnothing$ for any $a \in A$ and $u \in U$.

If the knowledge K_a of any attribute a of the system S is *complete*, i.e. the following condition holds:

(1°) $$\forall a \in A \forall u \in U \quad |V_a^u| = 1,$$

which, assuming that $V_a^u = \{v_a^u\}$, we will write down in the following form:

(1) $$\forall a \in A \forall u \in U \quad a(u) = v_a^u,$$

then the system S with respect to the knowledge K_a, for any a, is called *exact information system* here.

If the condition (1°) does not hold and the knowledge K_a of an attribute $a \in A$ is *incomplete*, i.e. the following condition holds:

(2°) $$\exists a \in A \exists u \in U \quad |V_a^u| \geq 2,$$

then the system S with respect to the knowledge K_a of its some attribute $a \in A$ is called *inexact*, or *uncertain*, or *vague information system*.

Assuming that $V_a^u = \{v_{a,l}^u\}_{l\in I}$ the condition (2°) will be written down in the following form:

$$(2) \qquad\qquad \exists a \in A \exists u \in U \, a(u) = x_a^u,$$

where $a(u) = x_a^u$ is an equation with one unknown quality x_a^u the range of which is the set V_a^u.

The incomplete knowledge K_{a_1} of $a_1 \in A$ for $u_1 \in U$ such that $V_{a_1}^{u_1} = \{v_{a_1,l}^{u_1}\}_{l\in I}$ and $|V_{a_1}^{u_1}| \geq 2$ determines the whole family of the information systems $F = \{S_l\}_{l\in I}$ corresponding to the system S. This family is defined in the following way:

$$S_l = (U, A_l) \in F \Leftrightarrow A_l = (A - \{a_1\}) \cup \{a_l\} \wedge a_l : U \to V_{a_1} \wedge$$

$$\wedge \forall u \in U[(u \neq u_1 \Rightarrow a_l(u) = a_1(u)) \wedge a_l(u_1) = v_{a_1,l}^{u_1}].$$

An example of an exact information system is a system S_1 defined by the Table 1. An example of an uncertain system is the system S_2 defined by Table 2. Universum of those systems is compounded of seven persons — candidates for a managing post in a given firm, who volunteered to a competition on the basis of given criteria: required AGE — 40–45 years, desired QUALIFICATIONS — economist or lawyer, required TRAINING PERIOD — at least 10 years of active work on an independent post. The attributes are: AGE with a set of values (years of life) $V_{AGE} = \{0, 1, ..., 125\}$, QUALIFICATIONS with a set of values $V_{QUAL.}$ compounded of all the jobs and TRAINING PERIOD with a set values (years of work) $V_{TR.P} = \{0, 1, ..., 70\}$. Here we have to deal with an uncertain system S_2 defined by Table 2 e.g., when the candidates put forward incomplete data but compatible with the criteria, or when only such data are presently useful or known. Occurring in the system indefinite values of the attributes AGE and QUALIFICATIONS, namely the unknown quantities REQUIRED and respectively DESIRED, have of course the range compatible with the criteria: $V_{AGE}^{p_3} = V_{AGE}^{p_6} = \{40, 41, ..., 45\}$ and $V_{QUAL}^{p_3} = V_{QUAL}^{p_6} = \{\text{economist, lawyer}\}$. Table 2 shows that the candidate p_7 is not without chances, despite the fact that he hardly matches the criterion of age.

U	AGE	QUALIFICATIONS	TRAINING PERIOD
p_1	41	economist	12
p_2	45	economist	14
p_3	45	lawyer	12
p_4	45	economist	11
p_5	45	economist	14
p_6	44	lawyer	13
p_7	39	lawyer	13

Table 1

U	AGE	QUALIFICATIONS	TRAINING PERIOD
p_1	41	economist	12
p_2	45	economist	14
p_3	REQUIRED	DESIRED	12
p_4	45	economist	11
p_5	45	economist	14
p_6	REQUIRED	DESIRED	13
p_7	39	lawyer	13

Table 2

Table 2 can be regarded as the scheme of all the tables obtained by substitution for the variables "REQUIRED" and "DESIRED" of the possible data corresponding to the values of sets $V_{AGE}^{p_3}$, $V_{AGE}^{p_6}$ and $V_{QUAL}^{p_3}$, $V_{QUAL}^{p_6}$. One of such tables represented by such scheme-Table 2 is Table 1.

3   Many valued information systems

Let $S = \langle U, A \rangle$ be an information system satisfying condition (i). A many valued information system or non-deterministic information system is called an ordered pair here

$$S^* = \langle U, A \rangle,$$

where U is the universum of S^* and A is the set of attributes, each of which satisfies the following condition:

(ii) $\forall a \in Aa : U \to P(V_a) - \{\oslash\},$

where $P(V_a)$ is a family of all the subsets of the set V_a of values for the attribute a of the system S.

The knowledge K_a of the cognitive agent of the attribute $a \in A$ of the system S^* is the following set

$$K_a = \{(u, V_a^u) : u \in U\},$$

where $V_a^u \subseteq P(V_a) - \{\oslash\}$ and V_a^u is the set of possible values of the attribute a for the object u from the point of view of the agent discovering reality given by the system S^*.

If the knowledge K_a of any attribute a of the system S^* is complete, i.e. the following condition holds:

(3°) $\forall a \in A \forall u \in U \quad |V_a^u| = 1 ,$

which, assuming that $V_a^u = \{\underline{V_a^u}\}$ we will write down in the following form

(3) $\forall a \in A \forall u \in U \quad a(u) = \underline{V_a^u} ,$

then the system S^* with respect to the knowledge K_a, for any a, is called approximate information system here.

If the condition (3°) does not hold and the knowledge K_a of an attribute $a \in A$ is incomplete, i.e. the following condition holds:

(4°) $\exists a \in A \exists u \in U \quad |V_a^u| \geq 2 ,$

then the system S^* with respect to the knowledge K_a of its some attribute $a \in A$ is called *strongly uncertain*, or *strongly vague information system*.

Assuming that $V_a^u = \{V_{a,l}^u\}_{l \in I}$ the condition ($4°$) will be written down in the following form:

(4)
$$\exists a \in A \exists u \in U \quad a(u) = X_a^u,$$

where $a(u) = X_a^u$ is an equation with one unknown quality X_a^u the range of which is the set V_a^u.

The incomplete knowledge K_{a_1} of $a_1 \in A$ determines the whole family of the information systems F^* corresponding to the system S^* defined in the similar way as in the part 2.

The exact or approximate systems are called *complete*. The uncertain or strongly vague system are called *incomplete*.

An example of an approximate system is a many valued information system S_3 corresponding to the system S_1 and defined by Table 3. An example of a strongly vague system is a many valued system S_4 corresponding to the system S_2 and defined by Table 4. Let us notice that assignation of the set {lawyer, economist} to objects p_3 and p_7 of the S_3 and S_4 systems, with respect to QUALIFICATIONS does not exclude a possibility that the candidates p_3 and p_7 are lawyers and economists at the same time. In the S_4 system there are three unknown quantities: ABOUT 40, EXCELLENT and MORE THAN 10 YEARS. We can assume in our examples that the range of these unknown quantities are respectively the following subfamilies of the families $P(V_{AGE})$, $P(V_{QUAL.})$ and $P(V_{TR.P.})$: $V_{AGE}^{p_1} = V_{AGE}^{p_7} = \{\{38\}, \{38,39\}, \{38,39,40\}, \{38,39,40,41\}, \{38,39,40,41,42\}, \{38,39,40,41,42,43\}\}$; $V_{QAL}^{p_7} = \{$ {lawyer} $\cap$ {economist}, {lawyer}, {economist}, {lawyer,economist} $\}$; $V_{TR.P}^{p_1} = V_{TR.P}^{p_7}$ $= \{\{11\}, \{11,12\}, \{11,12,13\}, \{11,12,13,14\}, \{11,12,13,14,15\}, \{11,12,13,14,15,16\}\}$.

The given families are respectively the extensions of indefinite *vague attribute notions:* AGE ABOUT 40 YEARS, EXCELLENT QUALIFICATIONS, TRAINING PERIOD OF WORK MORE THAN 10 YEARS. These families possess the greatest lower bound (the lower approximation) and the least upper bound (the upper approximation) and can be understood as *rough sets* (cf. Pawlak [2,5], Wybraniec-Skardowska [6]).

U	AGE	QUALIFICATIONS	TRAINING PERIOD
p_1	$\{38,39,40,41\}$	{economist}	$\{12\}$
p_2	$\{45\}$	{economist}	$\{14\}$
p_3	$\{40, \cdots, 45\}$	{lawyer,economist}	$\{11,12,13\}$
p_4	$\{45\}$	{economist}	$\{11\}$
p_5	$\{45\}$	{economist}	$\{14\}$
p_6	$\{40, \cdots, 45\}$	{lawyer}	$\{13,14\}$
p_7	$\{38,39\}$	{lawyer,economist}	$\{13\}$

Table 3

U	AGE	QUALIFICATIONS	TRAINING PERIOD
p_1	ABOUT 40	{economist}	MORE THAN 10 YEARS
p_2	{45}	{economist}	{14}
p_3	{40, $\cdots$, 45}	{lawyer,economist}	{11, 12, 13}
p_4	{45}	{economist}	{11}
p_5	{45}	{economist}	{14}
p_6	{40, $\cdots$, 45}	{lawyer}	{13, 14}
p_7	ABOUT 40	EXCELLENT	MORE THAN 10 YEARS

Table 4

Table 4, similarly to Table 2, is the scheme represented in particular Table 3, and also all other tables obtained by substitutions of variables "ABOUT 40", "EXCELLENT", "MORE THAN 10 YEARS" with possible data corresponding to the values of ranges of the unknown quantities: ABOUT 40, EXCELLENT, MORE THAN 10.

4 Complete and incomplete information

The starting point for characterization of notions of complete and incomplete information and their variant are suitable definitions of indiscernibility relations. If S (resp. S^*) is a complete information system satisfying the conditions (i) and (1) (resp. (ii) and (3)), then a binary relation IND_a^1 (resp. IND_a^3) defined as follows:

$$IND_a^1 = \{(u,t) \in U^2 : v_a^u = v_a^t\}$$

(and respectively

$$IND_a^3 = \{(u,t) \in U^2 : V_a = V_a\})$$

is called an *indiscernibility relation with respect to an attribute a* in the complete information system S (resp. S^*). If S (resp. S^*) is an incomplete information system satisfying the conditions (i) and (2) (resp. (ii) and (4)), then a binary relation IND_a^2 (resp. IND_a^4) satisfies the following condition:

$$IND_a^2 \in \{IND_a^1 \cup IND_{a,l}^2\}_{l \in I} \, ,$$

i.e.

$$IND_a^2 = \{(u,t) \in U^2 : v_a^u = v_a^t \vee \exists^1 l \in I \ (u,t) \in IND_{a,l}^2\}$$

(and respectively

$$IND_a^4 \in \{IND_a^3 \cup IND_{a,l}^4\}_{l \in T} \, ,$$

i.e.

$$IND_a^4 = \{(u,t) \in U^2 : \underline{V_a^u} = \underline{V_a^t} \vee \exists^1 l \in I \ (u,t) \in IND_{a,l}^4\}) \, ,$$

where for any $l \in I$ (resp. $l \in T$)

$$IND_{a,l}^2 = \{(u,t) \in U^2 : v_a^u = v_{a,l}^t \vee v_{a,l}^u = v_a^t \vee v_{a,l}^u = v_{a,l}^t\}$$

(and respectively

$$IND_{a,l}^4 = \{(u,t) \in U^2 : \underline{V_a^u} = V_{a,l}^t \vee V_{a,l}^u = \underline{V_a^t} \vee V_{a,l}^u = V_{a,l}^t\}),$$

is called an *indiscernibility relation with respect to an attribute a in the incomplete information system S* (resp. S^*).

Notice that all the indiscernibility relations introduced here are equivalence relations. Likewise every following l-th relation called *an indiscernibility relation with respect to A* is an equivalence relation:

$$IND_A^l = \bigcap \{IND_a^l\}_{a \in A}, \quad l = 1, 2, 3, 4.$$

Any l-th ($l = 1, 2, 3, 4$) indiscernibility relation with respect to $a \in A$ (resp. with respect to A) determines a suitable *information* $\overrightarrow{IND_a^l}$ (resp. $\overrightarrow{IND_A^l}$) with respect to a given information system and the attribute $a \in A$ (resp. the set attributes A). The relation $\overrightarrow{IND_a^l}$ (resp. $\overrightarrow{IND_A^l}$) is the IND_a^l-image (resp. IND_A^l-image) function determined by the relation IND_a^l (resp. IND_A^l). So that, $\overrightarrow{IND_a^l}$ and $\overrightarrow{IND_A^l}$ are the functions satisfying the following conditions:

$$\overrightarrow{IND_a^l} : U \to P(U), \qquad \overrightarrow{IND_A^l} : U \to P(U)$$

and for every $u \in U$

$$\overrightarrow{IND_a^l}(u) = [u]_{IND_a^l}, \qquad \overrightarrow{IND_A^l}(u) = [u]_{IND_A^l} = \bigcap \{[u]_{IND_a^l}\}_{a \in A},$$

where $[u]_{IND_a^l}$ and $[u]_{IND_A^l}$ are the abstraction classes determined by IND_a^l and IND_A^l, respectively, with representative u. These classes create a *unit information of u* with respect to the attribute $a \in A$ and a *unit information of u* with respect to the set A of all the attributes, respectively. The unit information of u is *complete*, if $l = 1, 3$. For $l = 1$ it is called *exact*, and for $l = 3$ it is called *approximate*. They can be understood as extensions of suitable basic or elementary notions assigned to these information, respectively. The unit information of u is *incomplete*, if $l = 2, 4$ and

$$\overrightarrow{IND_a^2}(u) \in \{[u]_{IND_a^1 \cup IND_{a,l}^2}\}_{l \in I} \qquad \overrightarrow{IND_a^4}(u) \in \{[u]_{IND_a^3 \cup IND_{a,l}^4}\}_{l \in T}$$

and

$$\overrightarrow{IND_A^2}(u) = \bigcap \{[u]_{IND_a^2}\}_{a \in A} \qquad \overrightarrow{IND_A^4}(u) = \bigcap \{[u]_{IND_A^4}\}_{a \in A}.$$

Then for $l = 2$ it is called *uncertain*, or *inexact*, or *vague* and for $l = 4$ it is called *strongly uncertain* or *strongly vague*. Notice that the family of all the equivalence classes compounded from u and all such objects t of universum of S (resp. S^*) that u and t are indiscernible in the sense $IND_{a,l}^2$ (resp. $IND_{a,l}^4$), where $l \in I$ (resp. $l \in T$), corresponds to the unit incomplete information of u in system S (resp. S^*) with respect to the attribute $a \in A$. This family is understood as an extension of a *vague basic notion* assigned to the information of u and as a rough set. It is easy to see that also some family of sets corresponds to the unit information of u with respect to the set A of attributes. This family is compounded of intersections of particular equivalence classes which can create unit information of u with respect to any attribute $a \in A$. This family can be understood as an extension of a vague elementary notion assigned to this information.

For example, the class $[p_3]_{IND^2_{AGE}}$ being a class belonging to the following family (see Table 2): $\{\{p_3\}, \{p_1, p_3\}, \{p_3, p_6\}, \{p_1, p_3, p_6\}, \{p_2, p_3, p_4, p_5\},$ $\{p_2, p_3, p_4, p_5, p_6\}\}$ is the incomplete and uncertain vague information of p_3 in S_2 with respect to AGE determining vague notion of the CANDIDATE WITH REQUIRED AGE. If the variable REQUIRED in Table 2 will be replaced as in Table 1 then we obtain the complete and exact information of p_3 in S_1, i.e. the set $[p_3]_{IND^1_{AGE}} = \{p_2, p_3, p_4, p_5\}$ determining the basic sharp notion FORTY FIVE YEAR OLD CANDIDATE.

The class $[p_3]_{IND^2_{QUAL.}}$ being a class of the family: $\{\{p_3\}, \{p_3, p_7\}, \{p_3, p_6,$ $p_7\}, \{p_1, p_2, p_3, p_4, p_5\}, \{p_1, p_2, p_3, p_4, p_5, p_6\}\}$ is the incomplete and vague information of p_3 in S_2 with respect to QUALIFICATIONS determining the vague notion of the CANDIDATE WITH DESIRED QUALIFICATIONS. If we replace the variable DESIRED with the data as in Table 1, then we obtain the complete information of p_3 in S_1, i.e. the set $[p_3]_{IND^1_{QUAL.}} = \{p_3, p_6, p_7\}$. It is the extension of basic sharp concept LAWYER CANDIDATE. Notice that in S_1 and S_2 $[p_3]_{IND^2_{T.R.P.}} = [p_3]_{IND^1_{T.R.P.}} = \{p_1, p_3\}$. This set is the extension of the basic notion CANDIDATE WITH TWELVE YEARS' TRAINING PERIOD OF WORK. Elementary knowledge of p_3 in S_2, i.e. set $[p_3]_{IND^2_A}$, where A is the set of all the attributes of S_2, is the class $\{p_3\}$ or the class $\{p_1, p_3\}$. It is obvious that the singleton $\{p_3\}$ is elementary knowledge of p_3 in S_1. $\{p_3\}$ is the extension of the elementary notion - the intersection of the mentioned basic notions.

In the system S_4 (see Table 4) a strongly uncertain strongly vague information of a potential candidate p_7 with respect to AGE is the class $[p_7]_{IND^4_{AGE}}$ belonging to the following family which is the extension of strongly vague basic notion ABOUT 40 YEAR OLD CANDIDATE: $\{\{p_7\}, \{p_1, p_7\}\}$, with respect to QUALIFICATIONS the class $[p_7]_{IND^4_{QUAL.}}$ belonging to the following family of which is the extension of strongly vague basic notion of the EXCELLENT CANDIDATE: $\{\{p_7\}, \{p_6, p_7\}, \{p_1, p_2, p_4, p_5, p_7\}, \{p_3, p_7\}\}$ and with respect to TRAINING PERIOD the class $[p_7]_{IND^4_{T.R.P.}}$ being a class of the following family — the extension of strongly vague notion of the CANDIDATE WITH MORE THAN 10 YEARS OF TRAINING PERIOD OF WORK: $\{\{p_7\},$ $\{p_1, p_7\}, \{p_4, p_7\}, \{p_3, p_7\}, \{p_1, p_3, p_7\}, \{p_1, p_4, p_7\}\}$. The vague elementary knowledge $[p_7]_{IND^4_A}$ with respect to all the attributes in S_4 is determined by the family $\{\{p_7\}, \{p_1, p_7\}\}$. It is the extension of the vague elementary notion: EXCELLENT ABOUT 40 YEAR OLD CANDIDATE WITH MORE THAN 10 YEARS OF TRAINING PERIOD OF WORK. The approximate elementary knowledge $[p_7]_{IND^3_A}$ with respect to all the attributes in S_3 is the set $\{p_7\}$. It is extension of the approximate notion: 38 OR 39 YEAR OLD LAWYER OR ECONOMIST WITH 13 YEARS OF TRAINING PERIOD OF WORK.

It is easy to notice that the sum of the unit information of $u \in U$ in S or

S^* of definite kind yields the definite kind information (knowledge) on U in S or S^*:

$$\overrightarrow{IND}_a^l(U) = \bigcup_{u \in U} \overrightarrow{IND}_a^l(u) = \bigcup_{u \in U} [u]_{\overrightarrow{IND}_a^l},$$

$$\overrightarrow{IND}_A^l(U) = \bigcup_{u \in U} \overrightarrow{IND}_A^l(u) = \bigcup_{u \in U} [u]_{\overrightarrow{IND}_A^l}, \quad \text{for } l = 1,2,3,4.$$

The family $U/IND_a^l = \{[u]_{IND_a^l}\}_{u \in U}$ $(l = 1,2,3,4)$ can be treated as the *basic knowledge of* U with respect to $a \in A$ in S or S^*, respectively, and the family $U/IND_A^l = \{[u]_{IND_A^l}\}_{u \in U}$ as the *elementary knowledge* of U in S or S^*, respectively.

5 Acknowledgement

The author appreciates the discussion, remarks and suggestions of Professors Andrzej Skowron and Zdzisław Pawlak. The author used their suggestions in above paper and is much grateful to them.

References

[1] Pawlak Z. Information systems–theoretical foundations. Information Systems 1981; 6(3):205–218

[2] Pawlak Z. Rough sets. International Journal of Computer Sciences 1982; 11:341–356

[3] Pawlak Z. Information systems–theoretical foundations. PWN Warsaw, 1983 (in Polish)

[4] Pawlak Z. Rough sets–theoretical aspects of reasoning about data. Kluwer Academic Publishers, 1991

[5] Pawlak Z. Knowledge from rough sets perspective. Research Reports of the Institute of Computer Science. W.U.T., 23/92, 1992 (in Polish)

[6] Wybraniec-Skardowska U. Status of rough information and the problem of vagueness. Biblioteka Myśli Semiotycznej, vol 36, 1993 (in Polish) to appear

Evolution of Intelligent Database Systems: A Personal Perspective

Laks V.S. Lakshmanan

Department of Computer Science

Concordia University

Montreal, Canada

laks@cs.concordia.ca

1 Introduction

With the need driven by next-generation applications such as computer aided design, VLSI, satellite image data analysis, genomic databases, there has been considerable research into extending databases into knowledge-bases. One approach to knowledge-bases that has evolved from database research is based on deductive databases. (See Ceri, et. al. [8] and Ullman [40, 41] for excellent introductions to the subject. See Ceri, et. al. [7] for a quick informal introduction and a discussion of the fundamental concepts needed.) Deductive databases represent a significant extension to the more traditional relational databases in bringing in important concepts of rule based programming, modular development, and recursion from the field of logic programming. In terms of expressive power alone, deductive databases constitute a non-trivial extension to relational databases. The following example illustrates the basic concepts in deductive databases.

Example 1.1 r_0: $route(X, Y) \leftarrow link(X, Y), \neg broken(X), \neg broken(Y)$.
r_1: $route(X, Y) \leftarrow route(X, Z), route(Z, Y)$.

The formalism of deductive databases is based on first-order predicate calculus. Formulas such as r_0, r_1 above are known as generalized Horn clauses. In the context of databases, function symbols are usually not used. The fragment of first-order logic used is thus the function-free generalized Horn clauses. Such formulas are often termed rules. Rules r_0, r_1 define the predicate $route(X, Y)$ in terms of other predicates. Presumably, the definitions of predicates such as $link(X, Y)$ and $broken(X)$ are explicitly stored as facts, much like the relations in a traditional relational database. The latter predicates are called *extensional database* (EDB) predicates since their definition is explicitly stored in the database. The predicate $route(X, Y)$, whose definition is implicit, is known as an *intensional database* (IDB) predicate. Intuitively, rule r_0 says that there is a (reliable) route between nodes X and Y in a network, provided there is a direct link between them and neither node is broken. Rule r_1 says there is a route between X and Y as long as there are routes between X and Z and Z and Y. Clearly, this is a recursive definition. Notice in addition that the subgoals $broken(X)$ and $broken(Y)$ occur negatively in the body of r_1, while all other subgoal occurrences are positive. Queries in this formalism are easily expressed as goal clauses in the style of logic programming. For instance, the goal clause $\leftarrow route(montreal, X)$ expresses the query "Find all nodes to which there is a reliable route from Montreal".

It is well known that the price of enhanced expressive power in deductive databases is the increased complexity of (recursive) query processing. This has sparked an extensive research into efficient (recursive) query processing for nearly a decade (see Bancilhon and Ramakrishnan [5], Naughton and Ramakrishnan [29], and Ceri et. al. [7] for surveys). While most of the above works concentrate on efficient processing of specific queries, there is another body of literature concentrating on query independent properties of programs that make them amenable for efficient evaluation for the class of all queries against those programs. Examples of such properties include *boundedness*, and *linearizability*. A program is bounded w.r.t. a given predicate (viewed as a query predicate) provided it is equivalent to a non-recursive program, also defining that predicate. A program is linearizable if it is equivalent to a linear recursive program. When a program is bounded or linearizable, queries against such a program can be evaluated much more efficiently than for arbitrary programs. Extensive work has been done in this area, and we refer the reader to [18, 38, 25] for recent surveys.

The upshot of the "mainstream" research done on deductive databases is that it is possible to extend relational databases with the useful expressive power, logic programmability, and modularity offered by the framework of deductive databases. Well understood paradigms now exist for efficient query processing in deductive databases, making it possible to support a declarative interface to the users of the database while relegating efficiency issues to the system in the form of query optimization. Indeed, several prototype deductive database systems have been developed (*e.g.* , LDL [9], NAIL! [28], glue-NAIL! [30], Aditi [43], CORAL [37], to name a few). A steady stream of published applications for this technology is emerging (*e.g.* , see [39, 21, 27, 36, 31]). However, it has been noted that deductive databases still are inadequate for supporting anticipated next generation applications for the database technology. In our view, some of the most serious such shortcomings include (i) the lack of modeling power to support complex structuring and behavioral aspects, (ii) lack of support for handling incomplete information, (iii) lack of support for uncertainty, (iv) lack of support for temporal aspects, and (v) the highly restrictive forms of query answering.

In this paper, we are mainly concerned with the last aspect above. This has to do not only with the manner in which queries can be posed against (deductive) databases but also the forms of answers extracted from the database. We first remark that the criticism that the form of query answering is restrictive is applicable not just to deductive databases, but essentially every known database system.

Conventionally, queries to databases are expressed in some query language, and amount to asking for all "objects"[1] which satisfy the properties stated in the query. Notice that the differences due to the nature of the query interface (*e.g.* whether it is declarative, functional, or procedural)[2] are irrelevant to the

---

[1] Clearly, we are not referring to objects in the sense of object-oriented databases. We are using the term in a neutral sense. For instance, for the relational model, "objects" would correspond to tuples.

[2] We will not define these terms here. Instead, we appeal to the reader's intuition about these terms. For concreteness, we can take languages based on logic, relational algebra, and

issue we are after. The point is regardless of the actual level of the query language interface, we can still abstract the essential characteristics of queries allowed in conventional interfaces in the above manner. To better appreciate the restrictions associated with this (customary) notion of queries, we must ask ourselves what kind of "properties" are allowed to be imposed as part of a query statement[3]. It is easy to see that we can characterize the class of queries allowed in conventional interfaces as statements which ask "which objects in the database satisfy properties expressed as query bindings?".

The next natural question that arises is "what kind of answers can be expected?". Using the same abstract terms, we can categorize answers as sets of objects from the database which satisfy given query bindings. It is our contention that for database systems to evolve as knowledge-base systems, it is essential that the users and application programmers be liberated from this highly restrictive mode of interaction with the database system. For instance, for applications such as planning, CAD, etc., it will be necessary to deal with incomplete knowledge, and find out what the outcomes would be if one of several design alternatives were chosen. This is an example of a "what if ..." query which is radically different from the queries allowed in conventional interfaces. Furthermore, it is desirable to be able to query about situations, and generate explanations or plans pertaining to the situation queried about. Both these functionalities are unavailable in current database systems, and worse, it is not very clear how implemented systems can be extended to support these functionalities. Notice that this issue is important since in developing the technology needed for next generation applications, we wish to retain the advantages of traditional database systems, in particular, their 3-level architecture, query optimization, transaction processing, concurrency control, recovery and resiliency. Any advances proposed should thus be capable of being integrated into the robust existing technology. In this paper, we shall discuss a framework for extending (deductive) database technology with the ability to incorporate both types of queries mentioned above. We shall show that this framework naturally extends the traditional framework of deductive databases.

Section 2 begins with a review of work on relational databases with incomplete information in the form of null values. In Section 3, we shall consider deductive databases with null values and briefly discuss a sample application to fault diagnosis. Section 4 contains a brief introduction to hypothetical reasoning. We introduce the notion of hypothetical answers to queries. Finally, we discuss an approach to extend deductive databases to support hypothetical query answering. The framework of Section 4 involves hiLog, the syntactic higher-order logic recently introduced by Kifer et. al. [10], augmented with two types of null values – atomic nulls (these are the conventional nulls), and rel-nulls (which can take on whole relations as values). We also outline an approach to query processing on databases involving atomic and re-nulls. Section 5 summarizes the paper, and concludes with directions for future research.

---

say CODASYL DML as examples of these categories.

[3]Again, depending on the data model, the queries can be simply an SQL statement, a query program expressed in a high level language, or some code in a low level language. We gloss over these differences by adopting the neutral term *query statement*.

2 Relational databases with null values

Codd [11] originally proposed an extension to the relational model with the ability to handle incomplete information. This was in keeping with the fact that available information about real-life applications (enterprises) is typically incomplete. Different types of null values have been proposed in the literature (*e.g.* see Zaniolo [44]), and one of the most popular forms of nulls correspond to saying "a value exists but not known at present". To quote a nearly "invariant" example, consider the situation where *Smith* is an employee (so he must be earning something), with an unknown salary. Suppose our relation scheme is *employee(NAME, SALARY)*. Then this situation can be modeled, in logic, by the sentence $(\exists\ S)employee(smith, S)$, and more concisely as *employee(smith,* $\perp$), where $\perp$ is a new symbol appearing nowhere else in the database. In the context of relational databases with null values, both logical and algebraic approaches have been studied. However, we should point out a subtle departure from the viewpoint associated with databases, once we move from complete information databases to those with null values. Classical databases are traditionally viewed as (finite) first-order structures. Thus query answering can be conceptually understood in simple terms as that of generating all variable assignments ν over the structure $\mathcal{D}$ such that the given query $\phi(X_1, \ldots, X_n)$, a first-order formula with free variables $X_1, \ldots, X_n$, is true in $\mathcal{D}$ under ν, or in symbols, $\mathcal{D} \models \phi(X_1, \ldots, X_n)$ $[\nu]$. It is well known (*e.g.* see Reiter [33]) that this simple viewpoint breaks down when we move from complete information databases to databases with null values. The culprit, of course, is the null values. The problem is that in a database with complete information, all individuals occurring in the database are known to be distinct. When nulls are introduced, this is no longer the case. The cure, as pointed out by Reiter [33], is to view databases as logical theories. As shown in the beginning of this section, every tuple with null values has a natural 1-1 correspondence with a logical sentence. Exploiting this viewpoint, Reiter formalized the notion of answers as follows. Let $\mathcal{D}$ be a database with nulls and $\phi(X_1, \ldots, X_n)$ as before. Then a tuple of individuals (which could be normal constants or nulls) $\bar{d}$ is an answer to this query against $\mathcal{D}$ iff $\mathcal{D}_e \models \phi(\bar{d})$. Here, $\mathcal{D}_e$ is an extension of $\mathcal{D}$ obtained by axioms that make the intention of such a database explicit, using the so-called *closed world assumption* (CWA). Reiter introduced 3 such axioms: unique name axioms (UNA), domain closure axioms (DCA), and completion axioms (COMP). For details, the reader is referred to Reiter [32, 34], but we shall merely give the intuition behind each axiom here. UNA makes the distinct identity of the normal constants in the database explicit, by means of inequalities. DCA essentially says that the only individuals that exist are those that occur in the database. COMP says that for each predicate (relation) r in the database the only tuples that are true of r are exactly those tuples t such that $r(t) \in \mathcal{D}$.

In the context of databases with nulls, answers to queries are not categorically determined, unlike in the classical case. For instance, revisiting the earlier example, assume that employees earning more than $50,000$ are not eligible for bonus. Then for a query asking whether Smith is eligible for bonus, we cannot give a categorical answer. To resolve this situation, we can follow Codd's proposal [11], and return the answer "maybe". Indeed, Codd introduced both *sure* and *maybe* answers, and these were later formalized by Biskup [2]. One of the early pioneering studies is that of Lipski [23] and Imielinski and Lipski [19]. They formalized the notions of *internal* and *external* representation of information (in a database with nulls) and used modal logic to characterize these notions as well as the notions of *certain* answers and *possible* answers. Possible answers are closely related to the notion of "maybe tuples" introduced by Codd. Vardi [42] has shown several intractability results for databases with nulls. Indeed, two of the major concerns in query processing with null values are completeness of query answering and the computational complexity of generating these answers. Lakshmanan [20] showed there is a tradeoff between completeness and complexity and proposed the notion of *feasible completeness*. The framework of databases is traditionally based on classical logic. More precisely, the classical entailment relation $\models$ is used for traditional query processing. Clearly, any notion of completeness has an underlying notion of semantic entailment. By changing it, one gets different notions of completeness. Lakshmanan showed that completeness in the sense of intuitionistic logic is indeed feasible: he showed that intuitionistically complete answers to queries can be generated in polynomial time in the database size. He also proposed an intuitionistic version of relational algebra and showed its equivalence to the intuitionistic version of relational calculus.

One of the lessons learned from the research into databases with incomplete information is that incompleteness can be used as a modeling device, which can be used to advantage when answering queries. To appreciate this, note that under incomplete information, we can now answers queries by providing the traditional component of answers (*i.e.* tuples satisfying query bindings) and then qualify each answer with an explanation which says either that the answer is *certain* or that it is *possible*. More precisely, $p(t)$ is a certain answer just in case it is provable from the theory associated with the database. It is a possible answer if it is consistent with the theory of the database.

The following example illustrates this.

Example 2.1 *Consider a database with the relations employee(NAME, DEPT, SALARY), department(DEPT, PROJECT). The following tables show the contents of the database.*

employee

NAME	DEPT	SALARY
smith	marketing	$\perp_1$
$\perp_2$	sales	70K
mary	promotion	75K
mike	engineering	72K
jane	$\perp_4$	$\perp_5$

project

DEPT	PROJECT
markerting	survey
engineering	machinery
$\perp_3$	pollution

Suppose the given constraints dictate the inequalities $\perp_i \neq \perp_j, \forall i, j, 1 \leq i \neq j \leq 5 : \neg(i = 4 \wedge j = 3 \vee i = 3 \wedge j = 4)$. Then consider the query which asks "Find the name and salary of employees working on the pollution project". This can be answered by joining employee and project and projecting the result on NAME and SALARY. In the framework proposed in Lakshmanan [20], the relational algebraic expression $\pi_{NAME,SALARY}(employee \bowtie project)$ where the operators are interpreted as their intuitionistic versions as discussed in that paper, would generate the (only) answer $< jane, \perp_5 >$, possibly. (In that paper, the terminology of definite *and* indefinite *answers adopted.)*

The point to be noted is that, if a rigid notion of query answers (*e.g.* by provability from the database theory) is adopted, then this would cover only the certain answers. In many situations, it is necessary to be "open-minded" about possible scenarios, particularly when not all information is available about a (*e.g.* design) application and various alternatives have to be tried out. In that respect, possible (and certain) answers provide us with a way to generate informative answers to queries on databases with null values. In Section 3, where we will introduce the notion of *conditional answers* we will revisit this example and show that it is possible to generate more informative forms of answers.

3 Deductive databases with null values

In this section, we shall review the framework of deductive databases with incomplete information. Representative works on this topic include Abiteboul et. al. [1], Liu [24], Demolombe and Cerro [12], and Dong and Lakshmanan [14, 13].

Abiteboul et. al. [1] consider different algebraic models of databases with nulls, using various types of tables with variables representing null values with different types of conditions acting on them. They establish several complexity results on query processing with null values for various query classes, including recursive ones. Among other things, they show that *certain* query answers can be generated in polynomial time in the database size for Datalog, while for *possible* query answers the problem is NP-complete.

Demolombe and Cerro [12] extend the conventional relational algebra by incorporating semantic equality (as opposed to syntactic identity). They use the notion of extended models (capturing semantic equality) and establish a link between provability w.r.t. a Horn clause theory (featuring null values) and satisfiability in the extended model of the theory. They argue that their extended relational algebra can be used for bottom-up query processing with nulls. However, important issues in bottom-up processing include (i) rewriting query programs into query-equivalent but more efficient ones, and (ii) extending the idea of sideways information passing. The rewriting has to minimize the useless tuples generated during a bottom-up evaluation of the program. Item (ii) can be essentially regarded as one of the main ingredients of the rewriting strategy itself. In [12], the authors do not address these issues, and without these a bottom-up evaluation can be prohibitively expensive.

Liu [24] considers incomplete information in the form of "S-constants". S-constants are similar to marked nulls with additional information which specifies the exact set of possible values the null may take. He also establishes a model-theoretic and fixpoint-theoretic semantics and proposed a sound and "weakly" complete proof procedure for query answering. Besides this, Liu does not consider any explicit constraints on the null values. To appreciate the significance of constraints on nulls, notice that in real life, partial knowledge on the possible exact values for nulls may often be available. It is essential to capture this information. Although the set of possible values assumed for S-constants does fill this need in some sense, it may be inconvenient (when the set is large) or even impossible (when the set is infinite) to assume such an enumeration of possible values. This shows the fundamental importance of allowing constraints on null values. A final remark is that Liu's framework forces a null (or S-constant) to take on one of the *known* values. In many applications, this assumption may be restrictive. As a simple example, if a null corresponds to evolving information (*e.g.* affected by technological developments) then its exact value could either correspond to a previously known item or to a recent invention/development which may not appear in the database as yet.

Dong and Lakshmanan [14, 13] followed a logical approach along the lines of Reiter [34] and formalized deductive databases with null values in the form of Datalog$^\perp$ theories. In simple terms, consider any datalog program with null values, together with any constraints on nulls. The constraints considered in those works involve the usual arithmetic comparison predicates. The datalog$^\perp$ theory associated with the given program is the theory consisting of the following axioms: unique name axioms, domain closure axioms, and predicate completion axioms, and given constraints on nulls. They motivated the problem of generating maximally informative responses to queries, and formalized it in the form of *conditional answers*. For a query $\phi(X_1, \ldots, X_n)$ against a datalog$^\perp$ theory P, *conditional answer set* is defined as

$$\|Q\|_P^c = \{(\bar{d}, E) \mid P \cup E \text{ is consistent and } P \models E \rightarrow \phi(\bar{d})\}.$$

Here, $\bar{d}$ is an n-tuple of constants (either normal or null) appearing in the theory P. E is a set of equality conditions involving nulls (and possibly nonnulls). We blur the distinction between a set of such equality atoms and their conjunction, both for convenience and conceptual clarity. Intuitively, the conditional answers to a query $\phi(X_1, \ldots, X_n)$ are those tuples of constants which would be answers if certain conditions – in this case represented by E – were to hold. For avoiding redundant answers, we insist that the answers be *minimal* in the following sense. Define a preorder on the set of all answers to Q, as follows: $(\bar{d}, E) \preceq (\bar{d}, E')$ provided, $P \models E \rightarrow E'$. Then an answer $(\bar{d}, E)$ is *minimal* provided for every answer $(\bar{d}, E')$, whenever $(\bar{d}, E) \preceq (\bar{d}, E')$, we also have $(\bar{d}, E') \preceq (\bar{d}, E)$.

Some preprocessing is required before queries can be processed against a datalog$^\perp$ theory P. The reason is that null values are embedded in the P and each null may have several constraints associated with it. Basically, we need to ensure these constraints are brought up to a level where they will bear on query processing directly. Following Vardi's idea, we can exploit the fact that each null value indeed represents a mapping to possible values. Let us introduce predicate $map(\Omega, X)$ to assert that a null Ω is mapped to a value (represented by X). The constraints on the null can then be modeled as constraints on the possible extension of the predicate $map(\Omega, X)$. Using this observation, Dong and Lakshmanan proposed a transformation of a datalog$^\perp$ theory into an equivalent theory (referred to as a program in the sequel, for convenience) which helps bring the program into a syntactic form closer to that of conventional datalog query programs. The only difference is that (i) a special predicate $map(\Omega, X)$ may occur in rule bodies, and (ii) this predicate is constrained by a set of axioms.

The following example, adapted from [14], illustrates the transformation.

Example 3.1 *Consider the usual ancestor example[4], but this time with incomplete information: the parent-child relationships for certain individuals are not known exactly.*

---

[4] The point of this example is simplicity and illustration of ideas. The purpose of deductive databases with nulls goes far beyond such "toy" examples, as we shall later see.

	parent
CHILD	*PARENT*
cathy	jim
paul	$\perp_1$
$\perp_2$	george
john	$\perp_2$
mary	$\perp_2$

The ancestor rules are the usual ones:

r_0: $anc(X, Y) \leftarrow par(X, Y)$.

r_1: $anc(X, Y) \leftarrow par(X, Z), anc(Z, Y)$.

Then the facts in the edb are transformed into the rules:

r_2: $par(cathy, jim) \leftarrow$.

r_3; $par(paul, \perp_1) \leftarrow map(\perp_1, X_1)$.

r_4; $par(X_2, george) \leftarrow map(\perp_2, X_2)$.

r_5; $par(john, X_2) \leftarrow map(\perp_2, X_2)$.

r_6; $par(mary, X_2) \leftarrow map(\perp_2, X_2)$.

Suppose the given constraints on the nulls are:

C: $\{\perp_1 \neq \perp_2, \perp_1 \neq jim, \perp_1 \neq paul, \perp_2 \neq george\}$.

The following axioms constrain the extension of the map predicate.

1. $map(c, c)$, *for every normal constant c occurring in the database.*
2. $(\forall X)(\exists! Y) map(X, Y)$.
3. $(\forall X_1, X_2)[map(\perp_1, X_1) \land map(\perp_2, X_2) \rightarrow (X_1 \neq X_2 \land X_1 \neq jim \land X_1 \neq paul \land X_2 \neq george)$.

For brevity, we do now show the UNA, DCA, and COMP axioms explicitly in the example above. The first axiom says *map* is an identity on each normal constant. The second one says *map* acts as a function. The last axiom above says, we can let X_1, X_2 play the roles of $\perp_1, \perp_2$ just in case they respect the given constraints on these nulls.

The SLD$^{\perp}$-resolution proof procedure proposed by Dong and Lakshmanan is an extension of the standard SLD-resolution procedure. The main idea is to distinguish between three kinds of predicates: database predicates (which are the edb and idb predicates defined by the program), built-in predicates involving constraints, and *map* predicates. The following issues arise. (1) Not every mgu (in the usual sense) is applicable; (2) even when unification is possible in the conventional sense, a goal can fail because of the interaction of constraints; and (3) the answer substitution involves more than a mere composition of the mgu's used in a derivation. The following example illustrates these issues. The original proof procedure presented in [14] requires the constraints on nulls to be explicitly made part of the derivation. Here we shall simplify matters by carrying the constraints in the background. In either case, the key requirement is to ensure that the constraints are never violated.

Example 3.2 *Let us return to Example 3.1. Consider the query $\leftarrow anc(mary, U)$. The following is one possible derivation. We assume that the left-most database literal is selected at each step.*

1. $(\leftarrow anc(mary, U)$, *variant of* r_1, *mgu:* $\theta_0 = \{X/mary, Y/U\})$.
2. $(\leftarrow par(mary, Z_0), anc(Z_0, U)$, *variant of* r_6, *mgu:* $\theta_1 = \{X_2/Z_0\})$.
3. $(\leftarrow map(\perp_2, Z_0), anc(Z_0, U)$, *variant of* r_1, *mgu:* $\theta_2 = \{X/Z_0, Y/U\})$.
4. $(\leftarrow map(\perp_2, Z_0), par(Z_0, Z_1), anc(Z_1, U)$, *variant of* r_5,
   mgu: $\theta_3 = \{Z_0/john, X_2'/Z_1\})$.

5. $(\leftarrow map(\perp_2, john),\ map(\perp_2, Z_1),\ anc(Z_1, U),\ variant\ of\ r_0,$
   mgu: $\theta_4 = \{X'/Z_1, U/Y'\}).$
6. $(\leftarrow map(\perp_2, john),\ map(\perp_2, Z_1),\ par(Z_1, U),\ r_2,$
   mgu: $\theta_5 = \{Z_1/cathy, U/jim\}).$

At this point, the mgu θ_5 would normally qualify as an acceptable mgu to resolve the subgoal $par(Z_1, U)$ against the edb fact r_2 (see Example 3.1). However, because null values are involved, we must ensure that (i) no null value is committed to more than one distinct value (null or non-null) and (ii) a null is not assigned to a value that would violate the constraints on any null. This necessitates the notion of a constrained mgu. *Intuitively, constrained mgu's keep track of constraints on nulls and make sure they are respected during unification. In our example, the constrained mgu at step 6 can be obtained by noting that there is more than one map literal involving the same null and different values. Specifically, we have the subgoals $map(\perp_2, john)$ and $map(\perp_2, Z_1)$. We then introduce the* constraint substitution $\{Z_1/john\}$. *Then the constrained substitution is obtained as $\theta'_5 = \{Z_1/john\} \circ \theta_5 = \{Z_1/john, U/jim\}$. The important thing to note here is that θ'_5 does not unify the current goal with r_2, which is as it should be, since unifying it would commit $\perp_2$ to two distinct values – john and cathy.*

Now, consider a successful derivation starting with the same query, which is identical to the above derivation up to step 2. Replace step 3 by unifying the ancestor subgoal with the head of r_0 and the resulting parent subgoal with the head of r_5. We say a goal is the bottom goal *provided it does not contain any database literals. The reader can check that the bottom goal that would be obtained is $\leftarrow map(\perp_2, john)$. The answer substitution associated with this derivation (as defined in the standard manner) is $\{U/john\}$. At this point, two steps are necessary: (i) ensuring the constraints C are not violated: this is done by adding the constraints with each occurrence of $\perp_2$ in C replaced by the constant john and testing the resulting conjunction for consistency; (ii) generating the conditions E of the conditional answer: in the present example, the only condition is suggested by the map literal $map(\perp_2, john)$ in the bottom goal. The reader can check that the constraints are not violated and that $(john, \{\perp_2 = john\})$ is a valid conditional answer.*

In Dong and Lakshmanan [14] SLD$^\perp$-resolution proof procedure is shown to be sound and complete. In general, the architecture proposed for top-down query evaluation involves a resolution proof procedure which at each step of the derivation involves an invocation of a consistency (of constraints) checker. Efficient consistency checkers based on graph theory can be easily implemented, keeping the resulting overhead to a minimum.

Dong and Lakshmanan [14] also develop a bottom-up query processing strategy by extending the well-known magic sets rewriting method and the semi-naive evaluation method. They also show that their extended bottom-up query evaluation procedure is sound and complete. For further details, the reader is referred to that paper. We conclude this section with a brief note on an application of deductive databases with null values to fault diagnosis.

One of the earliest formal approaches to fault diagnosis was proposed by Reiter [35]. Let C be a set of interacting system components. Suppose the I/O specifications of the system are supplied, in the form of sentences in first-order logic. Some observations (in the form of input, output pairs), which possibly conflict with the specifications, are also given. The problem is to identify the (alternate) minimal sets of components, called *diagnoses*, whose possible faulty behavior would explain the discrepancy between the specifications and the observations. Clearly, a unique solution rarely exists and typically several solutions might be of interest. Reiter's idea was to formalize the diagnoses in terms of an intermediate concept called *conflict sets*. In expecting the behavior as prescribed by the specifications, we tacitly assume all components are behaving *normally*. This can be made explicit using the well-known abnormality predicate in AI. A conflict set is any minimal subset $\Delta \subseteq C$ of components such that the assumption that all components in Δ are normal (together with the specifications and observations) gives rise to an inconsistent theory. Once conflict sets are determined, it is straightforward to compute diagnoses using the principle of hitting sets [35]. It was shown in Dong and Lakshmanan [14] that datalog$^\perp$ offers a viable medium for system I/O specifications. Indeed, null values serve two purposes in this application: (i) they can be used to capture the (unknown!) components which can be supposed to be abnormal to produce a diagnosis; (ii) they can also be used to capture values of inputs (to components) which are irrelevant to the present diagnosis. (*E.g.* , if the output of an AND gate is a 0 and one of its inputs is 0, then the other input is irrelevant.) A central result of Dong and Lakshmanan [14] is that conflict sets can be computed as conditional answers to queries.

4 Hypothetical query answering

The following example, expanded from Bonner [4], illustrates hypothetical reasoning in the form of embedded implications.

Example 4.1 *Consider the following rules.*
r_0: *near-grad*$(X) \leftarrow (grad(X) \Leftarrow takes(X,C))$.
r_1: *grad*$(X) \leftarrow total\text{-}credits(X,Y)$, $Y \geq 64$.
r_2: *total-credits*$(X,T) \leftarrow transcript(X,Creditset)$,
    aggregate$(sum, Creditset, T)$.
r_3: *transcript*$(X, < Credits >) \leftarrow takes(X,C)$, *course*$(C, Credits)$.

Rule r_3 groups courses by student names and r_2 calculates the total number of credits from this. According to r_1, anyone with 64 or more credits can graduate (assuming no failures!). Finally, r_0 says X is a near-graduate provided (s)he is short of graduating by just one course, *i.e. if (s)he took one more course, then (s)he would graduate*. The difference with other rules is the use of an embedded Horn rule as a subgoal which involves proving subgoals in a context obtained by extending the present context by the clauses (in this case just literals) appearing in its own "body". Extensive work has been done on embedded implications, in the context of hypothetical reasoning as well as in other contexts such as modules in logic programming (*e.g.* , see [4, 3, 26, 17]). In Dong and Lakshmanan [15, 16], the problem of extending deductive databases with the ability to generate plans and explanations as answers to appropriate queries was motivated. The authors showed that it is possible to incorporate this functionality by extending deductive databases to capture hypothetical reasoning. To motivate some of these issues, we reproduce below the proof system for embedded implications, proposed by Bonner [4]. Here, R denotes a set of embedded implications, ψ_i any embedded implications and A, B_j any atoms.

1. $R \vdash_i A$ if $A \in R$.
2. $R \vdash_i A$ if $A \leftarrow \psi_1, \ldots, \psi_n \in R$, and $R \vdash_i \psi_j, \forall j$.
3. $R \vdash_i A \Leftarrow B_1, \ldots, B_m$ if $R \cup \{B_1, \ldots, B_m\} \vdash_i A$.

The last rule captures the essence of the locality of context introduced by the use of embedded Horn rules. In the context of databases for planning or CAD, where "what if ..." queries and queries expecting explanations of situations as answers are very important, we would like to know not only whether a certain conclusion is hypothetically derivable, but also under what hypotheses (if any) it would be derivable. Indeed, the hypotheses associated with a derivation are just as important as the yes/no answer. Unfortunately, no known system for hypothetical reasoning addresses this issue. It turns out that even a precise definition of *hypothetical answer* is non-trivial. This notion was first formalized in Dong and Lakshmanan [15]. A second problem is that in practice we typically have constraints on which hypotheses are "acceptable". This notion is typically driven by the application semantics. Integrity constraints offer an elegant means with which to capture such constraints [15]. We shall first develop the necessary intuitions.

Example 4.2 *Consider the following rules.* $R = \{r_0: E \leftarrow (D \Leftarrow F); r_1: A \leftarrow (B \Leftarrow C); r_2: F \leftarrow B; r_3: D \leftarrow F, A; r_4: B \leftarrow C; r_5: C \leftarrow (F \Leftarrow B)\}$. *Suppose the integrity constraints are* $IC = \{\leftarrow C, F\}$. *Consider the query* $\leftarrow E$. *One derivation of E from R is as follows.*

$$\frac{R \vdash_i E}{R \vdash_i D \Leftarrow F.} \text{ (by } r_0\text{)}.$$

$$\frac{R \cup \{F\} \vdash_i D.}{R \cup \{F\} \vdash_i F \quad R \cup \{F\} \vdash_i A} \text{ (by } r_3\text{)}.$$

$$\frac{R \cup \{F\} \vdash_i B \Leftarrow C.}{R \cup \{F, C\} \vdash_i B.} \text{ (by } r_1\text{)}.$$

$$\frac{}{R \cup \{F, C\} \vdash_i C.} \text{ (by } r_4\text{)}.$$

From the proof, it appears that the (embedded hypotheses used for proving E are C, F. If the integrity constraints are not given, then this would be a satisfactory explanation. If not, we should look for other hypotheses (if any). Even if the integrity constraints are not given, the above is by no means a unique explanation. E.g. , notice that from $R \cup \{C\}$ *we can deductively derive F, suggesting that F is a redundant hypothesis. Thus, we can say that when no ICs are given,* $\{C\}$ *is a non-redundant set of embedded hypotheses associated with (deriving) E (from R). When* $IC = \{\leftarrow C, F\}$ *is given, then this is indeed the only set of embedded hypotheses associated with E. The term deductively derived is important here. If we do not make this distinction and simply allowed hypothetical derivations, we would be in trouble. For notice that the hypothesis C is hypothetically derivable from R, i.e.* $R \vdash_i C$ *using rules* r_5 *and* r_2. *This would suggest the embedded hypotheses associated with the derivation of E from R should be regarded empty, which is clearly unintuitive.*

The above example shows that ensuring non-redundancy of hypothesis sets is non-trivial. It obviously cannot be done by minimality w.r.t. set inclusion. Nor can it be done by minimizing the set w.r.t. the provability relation $\vdash_i$. The answer to this question must lie in a proper use of the term deductive derivability. How can we formalize deductive derivability in the context of embedded implications? The example above is illuminating. The key observation can be explained as follows. Suppose $\{A_1, \ldots, A_m\}$ is a set of embedded hypotheses associated with some atom B. When can we say a hypothesis A_i is redundant in this set? The main idea is that A_i can be regarded as redundant provided it is derivable from R together with the rest of the hypotheses $\{A_1, \ldots, A_{i-1}, A_{i+1}, \ldots, A_m\}$, but in *this* latter derivation no embedded hypotheses shall be introduced. In simple terms, the entire proof of A_i from $R \cup \{A_1, \ldots, A_{i-1}, A_{i+1}, \ldots, A_m\}$ must take place in exactly this context. This can be formalized using an alternate notion of provability, $\vdash_d$ denoting deductive derivability. The rules below are reproduced from [16].

1. $R \vdash_d A$ if $A \in R$.
2. $R \vdash_d A$ if $A \leftarrow \psi_1, \ldots, \psi_n \in R$, and $R \vdash_d \psi_j, \forall j$.
3. $R \vdash_d A \Leftarrow B_1, \ldots, B_m$ if $R \vdash_d B_j, \forall j$, and $R \vdash_d A$.

Notice that deductive derivability, unlike hypothetical derivability, does not permit the context of a proof to be ever altered. In particular, in rule 3, proving an embedded Horn rule in the deductive sense involves (deductively) proving both the body and the head (from the current context). This can be understood by interpreting this rule as saying that the provability of the head does not depend on the body subgoals being added s hypotheses, since they can be also be proved (deductively).

In Dong and Lakshmanan [16], the model-theoretic and fixpoint-theoretic semantics are given for embedded implications together with integrity constraints. The notion of hypothetical answers to queries is formalized in this context. The said fixpoint procedure is extended for directly extracting hypothetical query answers. In addition, the paper also establishes a firm relationship between deductive databases with null values and embedded implications. Specifically, it is shown that every deductive database with nulls can be transformed into a set of embedded implications, in such a manner that the conditional answers of the deductive database with nulls exactly correspond to the hypothetical query answers of the transformed embedded implications. In the other direction, it is shown that embedded implications involving only existentially quantified variables in rule bodies can be transformed into query equivalent deductive databases with null values. Since the semantics of embedded implications is rich, a syntactically higher-order logic is used for expressing the transformed deductive databases with null values. It is this direction we focus on in this paper. A full description of the transformation algorithms for both directions as well as proofs of correctness (*i.e.* equivalence preservation) can be found in [16, 22]. Here, we first illustrate the transformation from embedded implications into deductive databases with null values, with an example. We shall use the higher-order logic called HiLog, recently introduced by Kifer, et. al. [10] for illustrating this transformation. The reader is assumed to be familiar with (at least the basic ideas behind) hiLog. A formal introduction is given in [10]. We just highlight here that in hiLog, there is no distinction between function symbols and predicate symbols, and between terms and atomic formulas. Terms can appear in places corresponding (normally) to predicate symbols. However, hiLog has a first-order semantics, making it attractive for advanced logic programming.

An Extended Example

Consider again the near-grad example.

r_0: $near\text{-}grad(X) \leftarrow (grad(X) \Leftarrow takes(X, C))$.

r_1: $grad(X) \leftarrow total\text{-}credits(X, Y), Y \geq 64$.

For simplicity, let us suppress the details of how $total\text{-}credits(X, Y)$ is computed.

Firstly, the following axioms are a standard part of every transformed program.

A_1: $holds(A, add(\phi, A), \phi) \leftarrow hypo(A)$.

A_2: $hypo(A) \leftarrow holds(A, D, \phi)$.

A_3: $holds(A, D, diff(H, D)) \leftarrow holds(A, D', H), subset(D', D)$.

The atom $hypo(A)$ says A is an embedded hypothesis. The atom $holds(A, D, H)$ asserts that A is hypothetically derivable from the rulebase $R \cup D$ where H is a set of embedded hypotheses used in the derivation. Here, the rule base R is kept in the background. A_1 says whenever A is a hypothesis, it is trivially hypothetically derivable from $R \cup \{A\}$ without introducing further hypotheses. A_2 says if A can be hypothetically derived, then it can be used as a hypothesis whenever necessary. A_3 says whenever A is hypothetically derivable from $R \cup D'$ where $D' \subseteq D$, under hypotheses H, then we can assert that A is hypothetically derivable from $R \cup D$ where the associated hypotheses are H minus any that are common to H and D. Terms (or atoms!) such as $add(H,A)$ and $diff(H,D)$ correspond to the set of atoms $\{A\} \cup H$ or to the set $D - H$ respectively. It is readily possible to write hiLog rules defining these atoms. E.g. , $add(H,A)$ can be defined as follows.

$add(H, A)(A) \leftarrow$.

$add(H, A)(B) \leftarrow H(B)$.

In like manner, we can define other predicates convenient for manipulating sets and formalize them as hiLog rules. In the following, we shall freely make use of several such predicates without always giving their rule definition.

Next, deductive derivability is captured using the predicate $derived(H, D)$ which asserts that a set of atoms H is deductively derived from the rulebase $R \cup D$. (Recall that this means no embedded hypotheses are introduced during this derivation. We have the following rules.

DD_1: $derived(\phi, D)$.

DD_2: $derived(add(A, H), D) \leftarrow holds(A, D, \phi), derived(H, D)$.

The main transformed rules corresponding to the given embedded implications follow.

$holds(near\text{-}grad(X), D, H) \leftarrow holds(p_1(X), D, H)$.

$holds(grad(X), D, H) \leftarrow holds(total\text{-}credits(X, Y), D, H), Y \geq 64$.

$holds(p_1(X), del(D, takes(X, C)), add(H, takes(X, C))) \leftarrow$

$holds(grad(X), D, H), hypo(takes(X, C))$.

We need rules for generating embedded hypotheses. The following rule is used to accomplish this.

$hypo(takes(X, C)) \leftarrow \omega(X, C)$.

Here, ω is a *rel-null* which means it is a null value (and therefore its exact extension is unknown) but is of higher order. Indeed, it can take on a whole relation (in this case, a binary one) as its value.

A Proposal for Top-down Query Evaluation

Here, we shall sketch an approach for processing queries top-down, in the framework of the DDB with nulls obtained by transformation from embedded implications. Remember that the DDB is expressed in the language of hiLog which allows arbitrary terms to appear as names of relations. Additional complications are introduced by the fact that we have to deal with rel-nulls which are higher-order in nature. Our methodology combines traditional SLD-resolution with semantic query optimization and constraint programming. Figure 1 illustrates the architecture of the query processor.

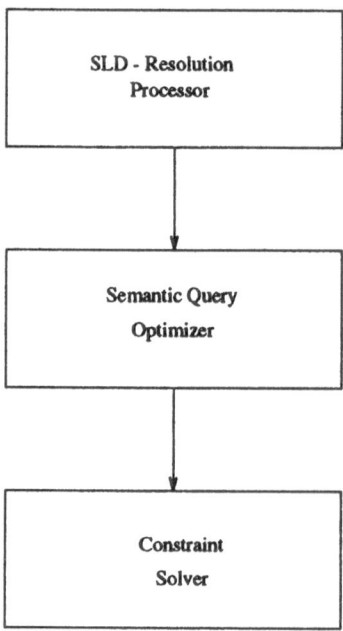

Fig. 1. An Architecture for Query Processing

To appreciate the importance of the roles played by all modules, we shall use an example featuring constraints. The following set of embedded implications correspond to a circuit consisting of gates and adders. The example is from [16]. Since we emphasize the query evaluation strategy here, we suppress other details of the circuit.

1. $e(X) \leftarrow a(Y), b(Z), X = Y + Z$.
2. $d(X) \leftarrow a(Y), c(Z), X = Y + Z$.
3. $f(X) \leftarrow (\exists Y, Z)[d(X) \Leftarrow a(Y), b(Z)], [e() \Leftarrow b(Z)]$.

4. $e() \leftarrow b(X), X \leq 3.$

Integrity Constraints:

5. $X = Y \leftarrow a(X), a(Y).$
6. $X = Y \leftarrow b(X), b(Y).$

Consider the query $\leftarrow f(14)$. The intention is to find the conditions on the inputs X, Y which would enable the output of the module f to be 14. In the present framework, this corresponds to generating the embedded hypotheses associated with the atom $f(14)$ against the given set of embedded implications. The transformed (hiLog) program is as follows, where we have suppressed some of the axioms which are an invariant part of every such transformed program (see the detailed example above).

1. $holds(c(X), D, union(H_1, H_2)) \leftarrow holds(a(Y), D, H_1), holds(b(Z), D, H_2),$
   $X = Y + Z.$
2. $holds(d(X), D, union(H_1, H_2)) \leftarrow holds(a(Y), D, H_1), holds(c(Z), D, H_2),$
   $X = Y + Z.$
3. $holds(f(X), D, union(H_1, H_2)) \leftarrow holds(p_1(X), D, H_1), holds(p_2(), D, H_2).$
4. $holds(p_1(X), del*(D, a(Y), b(Z)), add*(H, a(Y), b(Z))) \leftarrow holds(d(X), D, H),$
   $hypo(a(Y)), hypo(b(Z)).$
5. $holds(p_2(), del(D, b(X)), add(H, b(X))) \leftarrow holds(e(), D, H), hypo(b(X)).$
6. $holds(e(), D, H) \leftarrow holds(b(X), D, H), X \leq 3.$
7. $hypo(a(X)) \leftarrow \omega_1(X).$
8. $hypo(b(X)) \leftarrow \omega_2(X).$

Transformed ICs:

9. $X = Y \leftarrow holds(a(X), D, \phi), holds(a(Y), D, \phi).$
10. $X = Y \leftarrow holds(b(X), D, \phi), holds(b(Y), D, \phi).$

In the transformed program, $add * (H, a(Y), b(Z))$ abbreviates $add(add(H, a(Y)), b(Z))$, and similarly for $del*$.

Rules 7 and 8 are used to generate instances of embedded hypotheses.

Since we are dealing with constraints, the domains of the appropriate variables come into play here. We assume that constants used to generate instances of embedded hypotheses must be bound by the constraints appearing in the program.

The given query $(\leftarrow f(14))$ corresponds to the query $\leftarrow holds(f(14), \phi, H)$ against the transformed program above. A sequence of resolutions against the program above followed by an application of the ICs and constraint (in this case, just equality) simplification would eventually produce the following goal. (Notice that to apply ICs, we need to perform subsumption tests as usual – e.g. , see Chakravarthy et. al. [6].)

$\leftarrow holds(a(Y), D', H'_{11}), holds(a(Y_2), D', H'_{121}), holds(b(Z_2), D', H'_{122}),$
$holds(b(Z), D'', H'_2), Z' = Y_2 + Z_2, 14 = Y + Z', Y = Y_2, Z = Z_2, Z_2 = Z_3,$
$Z = Z_3, H'_{12} = union(H'_{121}, H'_{122}), H'_1 = union(H'_{11}, H'_2), H_1 = add *$
$(H'_1, a(Y), b(Z)), D = del * (D', a(Y), b(Z)), Z_3 \leq 3, D = del(D'', b(Z_3)),$
$H_2 = add(H'_2, b(Z_3)), \omega_1(Y), \omega_2(Z).$

We can now use the axioms to infer, e.g. ,
$holds(a(Y), add(\phi, a(Y)), \phi) \leftarrow hypo(a(Y))$ and hence
$holds(a(Y), add(\phi, a(Y)), \phi) \leftarrow \omega_1(a(Y)).$

This implies the bindings $D' = add(\phi, a(Y))$ and $H'_{11} = \phi$. Notice that the axioms also imply $holds(a(Y), add(\phi, a(Y)), \phi) \rightarrow holds(a(Y), S, \phi)$, where S is any superset of $add(\phi, a(Y))$. Thus, we also get the bindings (from the subgoals $holds(a(Y_2), D', H'_{121})$ above) the bindings $D' = add(add(\phi, a(Y)), a(Y_2))$ and $H'_{121} = \phi$. Notice that this situation is unlike any other arising with conventional bindings, as we have to (as far as the axioms permit) "update" the bindings as we process the subgoals from left to right. Likewise, we update our bindings to $D' = add(add(add(\phi, a(Y)), a(Y_2)), b(Z_2))$, $H'_{121} = \phi$. The constraints at this point are $14 = Y + Z'$, $Z' = Y_2 + Z_2$, $Z_3 \leq 3$, $Y = Y_2$, $Z = Z_2$, $Z_2 = Z_3$, $Z = Z_3$. A constraint solver would give $Z = Z_2 = Z_3 = 2$ and $Y = Y_2 = 6$ as the unique solution to these constraints. This would in turn lead to the following bindings. $H'_{12} = union(\phi, \phi)$, $H_1 = add * (\phi, a(6), b(2))$, $D = del * (D', a(6), b(2))$, $D = del(D'', b(2))$, $D'' = add(\phi, b(2))$, $H'_2 = \phi$.

Further simplification leads to the embedded hypotheses $a(6)$ and $b(2)$ for the given query above. Note that in this process, we need to recognize that the terms $del * (add(add(add(\phi, a(6)), a(6)), b(2)), a(6), b(2))$, and $del(add(\phi, b(2)), b(2))$ are equivalent.

From this example, we see that (top-down) query evaluation for the transformed program involves resolution (as usual) together with constraint simplification (or solving) on the fly combined with sideways information passing. Finally, we need equality theory for recognizing *equivalent* bindings (as opposed to just identical bindings). In general, it can be non-trivial to infer term equivalence, because we are dealing with terms which (in their role as atoms) are defined by rules. However, we need to recognize that the undecidability of arbitrary program equivalence is not attendant upon this problem. The reason is that we are dealing with a fixed number of terms which have a fixed (rule-based) definition. On the other side of the coin, to appreciate the difficulty associated with this task, notice that (*e.g.*) we have a fixed definition given for $add(H, A)$ where H is any set of atoms and A is any atom. Based on this definition, we would like to decide whether two *add*-terms are equivalent. When we are only dealing with total (*i.e.* completely ground) bindings, all we need to do is test whether the *set* of subterms occurring in the two given *add*-terms are identical. This is straightforward to implement. More research is needed for dealing with partial bindings. The theory of term rewriting might play a useful role here.

5   Conclusions

There are several aspects to making database systems "intelligent" enough to play a major role in supporting the next generation applications. We have argued that one prudent way is to base the underlying technology of such systems on the deductive database technology and extend it in directions where it is found lacking. This is primarily because of the unique advantages that go with this technology. A common goal to all directions of extensions to the DDB technology is that of boosting the application potential. Here, we have primarily focused on enhancing the query answering interface by enhancing the quality of answers generated from the database. In this respect, we have reviewed work done in the literature on extending DDBs to handle null values. We also briefly sketched an application of this extension to fault diagnosis. We then discussed an extension of the DDB technology with the ability to support hypothetical query answering. Hypothetical query answering is useful in the context of generating plans and explanations pertaining to "real-life" problem situations. It turns out that the hypothetical query answering functionality can be implemented by transforming embedded implications into a query equivalent DDB with null values, expressed in a higher-order language (hiLog). We finally outlined an approach for top-down query evaluation for generating the embedded hypotheses from the transformed DDB.

More research is needed on the following fronts. (1) Efficient top-down and bottom-up query evaluation for DDBs with nulls (both atomic and rel-nulls) together with ICs is a topic of high priority. (2) A topic of equal importance is real-life application development using the extended technology. One application that we have already developed is fault diagnosis. More applications involving planning, design, etc. are necessary to demonstrate the usefulness of the extended technology.

References

[1] S. Abiteboul, P. Kanellakis, and G. Grahne. On the representation and querying of sets of possible worlds. *Theoretical Computer Science*, 78:159–187, 1991.

[2] J. Biskup. A foundation of codd's relational maybe operations. *ACM Transactions on Database Systems*, 8, 4:608–636., Dec. 1983.

[3] A.J. Bonner, L.T. McCarty, and K. Vadaparty. Expressing database queries with intuitionistic logic. In *Proc. North American Conf. on Logic Programming*, October 1989.

[4] A.J. Bonner. A logic for hypothetical reasoning. Technical Report DCS-TR-230, Rutgers University, March 1991. (Preliminary version appeared in Proc. AAAI 1987.).

[5] F. Bancilhon and R. Ramakrishnan. An amateur's introduction to recursive query-processing strategies. In *Proc. ACM SIGMOD International Conference on Management of Data*, pages 16–52, 1986.

[6] U.S. Chakravarthy, J. Grant, and J. Minker. Logic based approach to semantic query optimization. *ACM Trans. on Database Systems*, pages 162–207, June 1990.

[7] S. Ceri, G. Gottlob, and L. Tanca. What you always wanted to know about datalog (and never dared to ask. *IEEE Transactions on Knowledge and Data Engineering*, 1(1), March 1989.

[8] S. Ceri, G. Gottlob, and L. Tanca. *Logic programming and Databases*. Berlin, New York: Springer-Verlag, c1990, 1990.

[9] D. *et al.* Chimenti. The ldl system prototype. *IEEE Trans. on Knowledge and Data Eng.*, 2(1):76–90, 1989.

[10] W. Chen, M. Kifer, and D. S. Warren. A foundation for higher-order logic programming. Technical report, SUNY at Stony Brook, 1990.

[11] E.F. Codd. Further normalization of the database relational model. In R. Rustin, editor, *Database Systems*, pages 33–64, Englewood Cliffs, NJ, 1972. Prentice Hall.

[12] R. Demolombe and L.F.D. Cerro. An algebraic evaluation method for deduction in incomplete data bases. *Journal of Logic Programming*, 5:183–205, 1988.

[13] Fangqing Dong and Laks V. S. Lakshmanan. Modeling deductive databases with incomplete information. In *Proc. Workshop on Formal Methods in Databases and Software Engineering*, Montreal, Quebec, May 1992. Springer Verlag, London.

[14] Fangqing Dong and Laks V. S. Lakshmanan. Deductive databases with incomplete information. In *Joint Int. Conf. and Symp. on Logic Programming*, Washington, D.C., Nov 1992. (extended version available as Technical Report, Concordia University, Montreal, 1993).

[15] Fangqing Dong and Laks V. S. Lakshmanan. A deductive approach to hypothetical query answering. In *Int. Symp. on Logic Programming*, Van Couver, BC, Oct. 1993.

[16] Fangqing Dong and Laks V.S. Lakshmanan. Intuitionistic interpretation of deductive databases with incomplete information. *Theoretical Computer Science*, October 1994. to appear.

[17] L. Giordano and A. Martelli. Structuring logic programs: A modal approach, 1994.

[18] G. G. Hillebrand, H. G. Mairson, and M. Y. Vardi. Tools for datalog boundedness. In *Proc. ACM Symp. PODS*, pages 1–12, 1991.

[19] T. Imielinski and W. Lipski. Incomplete information in relational databases. *Journal of the ACM*, 31(4), October 1984.

[20] V.S. Lakshmanan. Query evaluation with null values: How complex is completeness? In *Proc. 9th Int. Conf. Foundations of Software Technology and Theoretical Computer Science*, Bangalore, India, Dec. 1989. Lecture Notes in Computer Science, vol. 405, pp. 204-222.

[21] V.S. Laks Lakshmanan, editor. *ILPS Workshop on Deductive Databases*, San Diego, CA, October 1991. in conjunction with Int. Logic Programming Symposium.

[22] Laks V. S. Lakshmanan and Fangqing Dong. On the power of deductive databases with null values. Technical report, Concordia University, Montreal, Canada, July 1993.

[23] W. Lipski. On semantic issues connected with incomplete information databases. *ACM Transactions on Database Systems*, 4(3), Sept 1979.

[24] Y. Liu. Null values in definite programs. In *Proc. North American Conf. on Logic Programming*, pages 273–288, Austin, TX, Nov. 1990.

[25] L.V.S. Lakshmanan, Ashraf Karima, and Han Jiawei. Homomorphic tree embeddings and their applications to recursive program optimization. In *Eight Annual IEEE Symposium on Logic in Computer Science*, pages 344–353, 1993.

[26] D. Miller. A logical analysis of modules in logic programming. *Journal of Logic Programming*, pages 79–108., 1989.

[27] Inderpal Singh Mumick, editor. *ACM SIGMOD Workshop on Combining Declarative and Object-Oriented Databases*, Washington, DC, May 1993. in cooperation with ACM SIGMOD.

[28] K. Morris, J.D. Ullman, and A. Van Gelder. Design overview of the nail! system. In *Proc. 3rd Int. Conf. on Logic Programming*, pages 554–568, 1986.

[29] J. Naughton and R. Ramakrishnan. Bottom-up evaluation of logic programs. *Journal of Logic Programming*, 1992.

[30] G. Phipps, M. Derr, and K.A. Ross. Glue-nail: A deductive database system. In *Proc. ACM-SIGMOD Int. Conf. on Management of Data*, 1991.

[31] R. Ramakrishnan, editor. *ILPS Workshop on Programming with Logic Databases*, Vancouver, BC, October 1993. in conjunction with Int. Logic Programming Symposium.

[32] R. Reiter. On closed world databases. In H. Gallaire and J. Minker, editors, *Logic and Databases*, pages 55–76. Plenum Press, 1978.

[33] R. Reiter. Towards a logical reconstruction of relational database theory. In M. L. Brodie, J. Myoploulos, and J. W. Schmidt, editors, *On Conceptual Modelling*. Springer-Verlag, New York, 1984.

[34] R. Reiter. A sound and sometimes complete query evaluation algorithm for relational databases with null values. *Journal of the ACM*, 33:349–370, April 1986.

[35] R. Reiter. A theory of diagnosis from first principles. *Artificial Intelligence*, 32:57–95, 1987.

[36] K. Ramamohanarao, J. Harland, and G. Dong, editors. *JICSLP Workshop on Deductive Databases*, Washington, DC, November 1992. in conjunction with Joint Int. Conf. and Symp. on Logic Programming.

[37] R. Ramakrishnan, D. Srivastava, and S. Sudarshan. Coral: Control, relations, and logic. In *Proc. Int. Conf. on Very Large Databases*, 1992.

[38] R. Ramakrishnan, Y. Sagiv, J. D. Ullman, and M. Vardi. Proof-tree transformation theorems and their applications. In *Proc. 8TH ACM Symp. PODS*, pages 172–181, 1989.

[39] Tsur S. Deductive databases in action. In *ACM Principles of Databases Systems*, pages 142–153, 1991.

[40] J. D. Ullman. *Principles of Database and Knowledge-Base Systems*, volume I. Computer Science Press, Maryland, 1989.

[41] J. D. Ullman. *Principles of Database and Knowledge-Base Systems*, volume II. Computer Science Press, Maryland, 1989.

[42] M. Y. Vardi. Querying logical databases. In *Proceedings of the Fourth ACM SIGACT-SIGMOD Symposium on Principles of Database Systems*, pages 57–65, 1985.

[43] J. Vaghani, K. Ramamohanarao, D.B. Kemp, Z. Somogyi, and P.J. Stuckey. Design overview of the Aditi deductive database system. In *Proc. IEEE Int. Conf. on Data Engineering*, Kobe, Japan, April 1991.

[44] C. Zaniolo. Database relations with null values. *Journal of Computer and System Sciences*, 28:142–166, 1984.

Extracting Exact and Approximate Rules from Databases

Rokia Missaoui
Robert Godin

Département de Mathématiques et d'Informatique
Université du Québec à Montréal
C.P. 8888, succursale "Centre-Ville", Montréal, Canada, H3C 3P8

Ameur Boujenoui

Ecole des Hautes Etudes Commerciales
5255, avenue Decelles, Montréal, Canada, H3T 1V6

Abstract

In addition to being a technique for classifying objects and defining concepts from data, the concept lattice may be exploited to discover functional dependencies as well as exact and approximate (probabilistic) implication rules between properties (descriptors). This paper presents algorithms for rule generation and shows that the lattice is an interesting framework for that purpose.

1 Introduction

The ability to extract knowledge from large databases is becoming an important feature of data/knowledge based systems [1, 3, 10, 22], offering a better understanding of the semantics of the data, an effective decision making, and an efficient knowledge and data management (e.g., semantic query optimization).

Knowledge discovery techniques as they currently stand cannot be applied to many database applications. There are at least two reasons for this. One is the fact that databases (DB)s are generally complex, voluminous, noisy and continually changing. Two is the fact that the overhead due to the application of discovery techniques may be high. That is why researchers in this area [22] recommend that discovery algorithms for database applications be *incremental*, sufficiently *efficient* to have at most a quadratic growth with respect to the size of input, and *robust* enough to cope with noisy data.

Cai *et al* [2] presents an induction algorithm which extracts classification and characterization rules from relational databases by performing a step by step generalization on individual attributes. Classification rules discriminate the concepts of one class from that of the others and help predict the class of newly introduced objects. They take the form: *if ⟨description⟩ then ⟨class⟩*, where the description stands for the properties common to the objects of a given class. Characteristic rules characterize a class independently from the other classes and are expressed by *if ⟨class⟩ then ⟨description⟩*. Ioannidis *et al* [11] uses two machine learning algorithms to generate concept hierarchies from queries addressed to a database. The extracted knowledge is used for physical and logical database reorganization. Kaufman *et al* [12] describes the INLEN system which integrates a relational database, a knowledge base as well as machine learning tools for manipulating data and knowledge, and for discovering rules, concepts and equations. In [20], a survey of methods, theories and implementations of *Inductive Logic Programming* (ILP) is given. ILP is a new discipline defined as the convergence of inductive learning and logic programming. Learning in that discipline starts from examples and background knowledge to inductively build first-order clausal theories. In [9], a set of efficient algorithms for generating concepts and rules are presented. Theoretical and empirical studies of the algorithms are also provided. The algorithms described in [9] offer most of the functionalities presented in [1], and are implemented in Smalltalk within the environment of ObjectWorks (release 4.0).

The procedure for choosing which attributes in a binary relation $\mathcal{R}$ should be the left-hand side (LHS) of a functional dependency is in the worst case exponential in the total number of attributes (say n) since there are 2^n possible sets. There are many works in the rough set community [21, 24] and the database area that have dealt with the issue of generating functional dependencies from a binary relation [13]. In [19] we show that the concept lattice is an appropriate framework for FD generation and checking, and propose two procedures: one which scans the concept lattice to compute the degree of accuracy of a given FD: $Y \rightarrow Z$ [21, 24], and another one which starts from a set of implication rules to generate a set of FDs.

This paper extends our previous work on knowledge discovery from databases [9, 18, 19]. In the next section we give a background on the concept lattice theory, and some basic definitions. Section 3 provides algorithms for generating exact and probabilistic implication rules. Finally, a brief discussion on further refinements is proposed.

2 Background

2.1 The concept lattice

From the context $(\mathcal{O}, \mathcal{D}, \mathcal{R})$ describing a set $\mathcal{O}$ of objects, a set $\mathcal{D}$ of descriptors (properties) and a binary relation $\mathcal{R}$ (Table 2.1) between $\mathcal{O}$ and $\mathcal{D}$, there is a unique ordered set which describes the inherent lattice structure defining natural groupings and relationships among the objects and their descriptors (Figure 2.2). This structure is known as a concept lattice [4, 26] or Galois lattice [9]. The notation $x\mathcal{R}x'$ is used to express the fact that an element x from $\mathcal{O}$ is related to an element x' from $\mathcal{D}$. Each element of the lattice $\mathcal{L}$ derived from the context $(\mathcal{O}, \mathcal{D}, \mathcal{R})$ [26] is a couple, noted (X, X'), composed of an object set X of the power set $\mathcal{P}(\mathcal{O})$ and a property set $X' \in \mathcal{P}(\mathcal{D})$. Each couple must be complete with respect to $\mathcal{R}$, which means that the following two properties hold:
(i) $X' = f(X)$ where $f(X) = \{x' \in \mathcal{D} \mid \forall x \in X, x\mathcal{R}x'\}$.
(ii) $X = f'(X')$ where $f'(X') = \{x \in \mathcal{O} \mid \forall x' \in X', x\mathcal{R}x'\}$.
The following partial order holds.

Given $C_1 = (X_1, X_1')$ and $C_2 = (X_2, X_2')$, $C_1 \leq C_2 \Leftrightarrow X_1' \subset X_2'$ [1]. The partial order is used to generate the graph in the following way: there is an edge from C_1 to C_2 if $C_1 < C_2$ and there is no other element C_3 in the lattice such that $C_1 < C_3 < C_2$. The graph is usually called a Hasse diagram and the precedent order means that C_1 is parent of C_2. Given, $\mathcal{C}$, a set of elements from the lattice $\mathcal{L}$, $inf(\mathcal{C})$ and $sup(\mathcal{C})$ will denote respectively the infimum and the supremum of the elements in $\mathcal{C}$.

The fundamental theorem on concept lattices [26]. Let $(\mathcal{O}, \mathcal{D}, \mathcal{R})$ be a context. Then $\langle \mathcal{L}; \leq \rangle$ is a complete lattice for which infimum and supremum of any subset of $\mathcal{L}$ are given by

$$\bigwedge_{i \in I}(X_i, X_i') = (f'f(\bigcup_{i \in I} X_i), \bigcap_{i \in I} X_i'),$$

$$\bigvee_{i \in I}(X_i, X_i') = (\bigcap_{i \in I} X_i, ff'(\bigcup_{i \in I} X_i')).$$

The task of inducing a concept hierarchy in an incremental manner is called *incremental concept formation* [5]. This inductive approach falls into the category of *unsupervised learning* since the concepts to learn are not predetermined by a teacher, and the instances are not pre-classified with respect to these concepts. This approach falls also into the class of *empirical inductive learning* [14] since no background knowledge is needed. As pointed out by [10], there are two main differences between machine learning and data mining. The first difference is that the ultimate goal of databases is quite distinct from data mining and therefore, attributes that may be relevant to the data dredging process do not necessarily exist in the schema of the database. The second difference is that in machine learning applications (e.g., scientific and medical files), observations have a limited size and are carefully collected and checked, while in database applications, information may be very voluminous and incomplete.

For illustration, the following example will be used.

Table 2.1 The input relation.

Objects	Attributes				
	F	R	E	M	S
Tiger	f_1	r_1	e_1	m_1	s_1
Horse	f_2	r_1	e_3	m_1	s_1
Sheep	f_2	r_1	e_3	m_1	s_0
Penguin	f_3	r_2	e_1	m_0	s_1
Frog	f_3	r_2	e_1	m_0	s_2
Rat	f_1	r_1	e_2	m_1	s_1

The attributes and their values have the following meaning:
$F=$ Feet; f_1=claw, f_2=hoof, f_3=web.

---

[1] Since we shall focus on generating rules for descriptors rather than for objects, the partial order as well as infimum and supremum definitions are given with respect to descriptors instead of objects as in Wille.

212

R=Ears; r_1= external, r_2= middle.
E=Eats; e_1= meat, e_2= grain, e_3=grass.
M=Gives milk; m_0= no milk, m_1=milk.
S=Swims; s_0=unable, s_1=able, s_2=well.

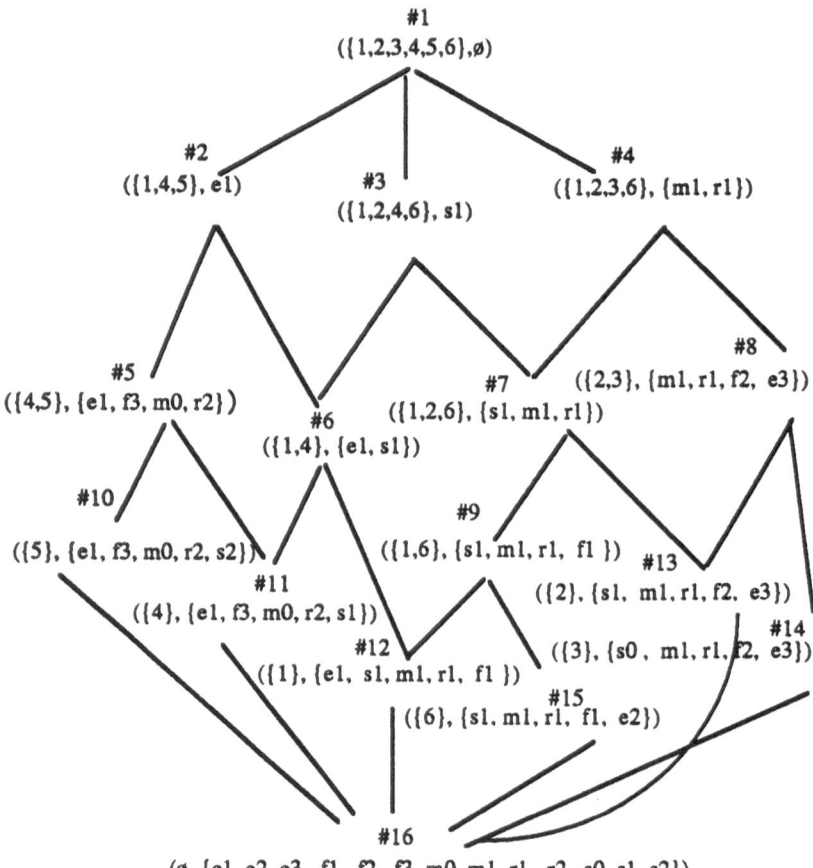

Figure 2.2 The Concept lattice.

2.2 Implication rules

In the following we use P and Q to denote sets of properties (called complex descriptors), while we use X and Y to name sets of attributes. An elementary property q_i is a pair $\langle A, V_i \rangle$ stating that V_i is the value of the attribute A for a given object x. The notation $Attrib(P)$ gives the set of attributes involved in the complex descriptor P. Since a node N of the lattice is a couple of sets, $Extent(N)$ and $Intent(N)$ will express the extent (set of objects) and intent (set of descriptors) of N, respectively.

Definition 1. A *conjunctive* implication rule for *descriptors* (IRD) is an implication rule of the form $P \Rightarrow Q$ where P and Q are subsets of $\mathcal{D}$ [9]. A context

$(\mathcal{O}, \mathcal{D}, \mathcal{R})$ satisfies the IRD $P \Rightarrow Q$ if for every object x in $\mathcal{O}$, whenever x is described by P it has also properties Q, i.e.,

$$f(x) \supseteq P \Longrightarrow f(x) \supseteq Q$$

Proposition 1. $P \Rightarrow Q$ is a *conjunctive* IRD $\Leftrightarrow [[(Z, Z') = inf\{(X, X') \in \mathcal{L} \mid P \subset X' \text{ and } X \neq \emptyset\}] \Rightarrow Q \subset Z']$. $\qquad\square$

The following definitions are borrowed from the implication theory on functional dependencies [15] and apply to implication rules as well.

Given a set Σ of IRDs, the *closure* Σ^+ is the set of rules implied by Σ by application of the inference axioms. $P \Rightarrow Q$ is *redundant* in the set Σ of IRs if $\Sigma - \{P \Rightarrow Q\} \models P \Rightarrow Q$

$P \Rightarrow Q$ is *full* (or left-reduced) if $\nexists P' \subset P$ such that $(\Sigma - \{P \Rightarrow Q\}) \cup \{P' \Rightarrow Q\} \equiv \Sigma$

$P \Rightarrow Q$ is *right-reduced* if $\nexists Q' \subset Q$ such that $(\Sigma - \{P \Rightarrow Q\}) \cup \{P \Rightarrow Q'\} \equiv \Sigma$

$P \Rightarrow Q$ is *reduced* if it is left-reduced and right-reduced, and $Q \neq \emptyset$.

The *closure* P^+ of a set P according to Σ is defined by: $P^+ = P \cup \{Q \mid Z \subseteq P^+ \text{ and } Z \Rightarrow Q \in \Sigma\}$.

Definition 2. $P \Rightarrow Q$ is an *existence* implication rule if
$\nexists Z \subset P$ such that $Z^+ \subset P^+$.

A *composite* rule is one for which the precedent condition does not hold.

For example, $m_1 \Rightarrow r_1$ is an existence rule (see Table 3.1) while $e_1 m_1 \Rightarrow r_1 s_1 f_1$ is a full composite rule since there exists $Z = \{m_1\}$ in the premise $P = \{e_1 m_1\}$ of the second rule such that $Z^+ \subset P^+$, i.e., $\{m_1 r_1\} \subset \{e_1 m_1 r_1 s_1 f_1\}$.

3   Exact and probabilistic rule generation

From a finite set of objects (observations, individuals), there are many models and different types of knowledge that can be extracted using different inductive learning techniques. In this section we propose a set of algorithms that make use of an already built lattice to generate *exact* as well as *probabilistic* rules. Under the assumption of an upper bound K on the number of descriptors per object, it can be shown that the time complexity of the following algorithms is $O(\|\mathcal{O}\|)$.

In addition to being a technique for concept hierarchy formation, the concept lattice may be exploited to discover implication rules as well as functional dependencies [19]. The process of implication rule learning can be undertaken in many ways, depending on the peculiarities of the DB under consideration and the needs of the users. Databases can have different levels of size, complexity, and may be subject to different degrees of updates. Users' needs can be of different kinds, such as:

(i) derive a set of exact implications rules from the lattice,

(ii) check if a given rule $P \Rightarrow Q$ holds,

(iii) find a rule with P as a left-hand side and estimate its accuracy (certainty degree), and

(iv) build rules when $Attrib(P)$ and $Attrib(Q)$ are given.

The first kind of queries can be answered using Algorithm 3.1 which scans the whole lattice to generate a set of rules. Such a processing is useful in a knowledge-based environment to enrich the knowledge base with the new generated rules, and for relatively stable databases. Since databases are usually evolutive, an efficient algorithm for incrementally updating both the lattice and the set of generated rules is proposed in [9].

To handle the second type of queries, we have either to show that the hypothesis $P \Rightarrow Q$ can be derived from the set Σ of rules produced by Algorithm 3.1, or to look for the smallest node (w.r.t. descriptors) containing the premise components of that hypothesis, and check if the conclusion components also occur in the intent of that node. The motivation behind this kind of queries is that it often happens that one wants to confirm a hypothesis or invalidate a claim based on the analysis of input data. We have experimented a DB application about divestment of units in a firm, and in many cases, the analyst wanted to confirm individual hypotheses such as the following one: *"If both the divested unit and the firm to which it belongs had a performance rate higher than the average in the industry, and the divested unit was created by internal development, then the motif of the divestment is a strategic reorientation."*

Algorithm 3.2 deals with the third type of queries and is particularly helpful under the following situations: (i) there is no (non trivial) conjunctive IRD with P as a premise, and/or (ii) a probabilistic (non deterministic) rule is tolerated, and even desirable.

The last type of queries is particularly interesting in scientific and medical applications to establish relationships between attributes (e.g., diagnosis rules for diseases), and can be handled by Algorithm 3.3.

In the following, we present algorithms for generating exact rules as well as approximate rules. As in many studies in knowledge discovery [1, 10, 22], data analysis and rough sets [21], we attach two measures to each rule: a support ratio s which indicates the percentage of objects supporting the rule, and either a certainty ratio c which expresses the ratio of objects that satisfy the conclusion Q when the premise P is true (see Algorithm 3.2), or a more elaborated entropy measure as indicated in Algorithm 3.3.

3.1 Generation of exact implication rules

Based on Proposition 1 defined before, Algorithm 3.1 computes a complete set of IRDs from an already built lattice. In [9], additional algorithms for exact implication rule generation are proposed, including one algorithm that incrementally builds the lattice and computes the set of rules in one shot.

Algorithm 3.1 *SetOfExactRules*

Input: A lattice $\mathcal{L}$.

Output: A set Σ of conjunctive IRDs: $P \Rightarrow Q$ (possibly redundant or non-reduced), and the array $Rules[1 \cdots \|\mathcal{L}\|]$, where an element $Rules[N]$ represents the set of IRDs associated with the node N.

> **Function** *GenerateRulesForNode(N)*
> /* Returns the complete set of rules generated from the node N */
> **begin**
> $\Delta := \emptyset;$

If $Extent(N) \neq \emptyset$ and $\|Intent(N)\| > 1$ **then** /* discard some trivial rules */

  For each non empty set $P \in \{\mathcal{P}(Intent(N)) - Intent(N)\}$ in ascending $\|P\|$ **do**

    If $\not\exists \, M = (Y, Y')$ parent of N such that $P \subseteq Y'$ **then**

      If $\not\exists \, P' \Rightarrow Q \in \Delta$ such that $P' \subset P$ **then**

        $\Delta := \Delta \cup \{P \Rightarrow Intent(N) - P\}$

      endIf

    endIf

  endFor

endIf

return(Δ)

end $\{GenerateRulesForNode\}$

begin

$\Sigma := \emptyset$; /* the cumulative set of IRDs */

For each node $N \in \mathcal{L}$ in ascending $\|Intent(N)\|$ **do**

  begin

  $Rules[N] := GenerateRulesForNode(N)$

  $\Sigma := \Sigma \cup Rules[N]$

  end

endFor

return(Σ)

end $\{SetOfExactRules\}$

The first test inside the *For* loop in the *GenerateRulesForNode* function ensures that $P \Rightarrow Q$ is valid by checking if the current node is the smallest concept containing P in its intent. Algorithm 3.1 generates a set of (possibly composite) exact rules. To get only existence rules, the second *If* test of the *GenerateRulesFromNode* function should be reworded as follows:

If $\not\exists \, M = (Y, Y')$, a parent node of N such that $P \cap Y'$ is non empty **then**. The *If* tests inside the *GenerateRulesFromNode* function help eliminate redundant rules produced by a same node. However, redundancy occurring between rules generated from two different nodes of the lattice is not detected by the algorithm, and can later be removed using the polynomial time algorithm for nonredundant cover generation [15].

Example. The IRD: $s_2 \Rightarrow f_3 r_2 e_1 m_0$ is generated from node #10 (see Figure 2.2), and can later be reduced to $s_2 \Rightarrow f_3$ based on the fact that $f_3 \Rightarrow r_2 e_1 m_0$ holds from node #5 and the inference axioms for IRDs. The reader may notice in Table 3.1 that the rule $e_1 m_1 \Rightarrow f_1 r_1 s_1$ is a full composite rule generated from node #12, and that no existence rule can be generated from that node.

Table 3.1 Generating IRDs from the lattice.

Nodes	Exact Rules	
	Composite IRDs	Existence IRDs
4	$m_1 \Rightarrow r_1$ $r_1 \Rightarrow m_1$	$m_1 \Rightarrow r_1$ $r_1 \Rightarrow m_1$
5	$f_3 \Rightarrow r_2 e_1 m_0$ $m_0 \Rightarrow f_3 r_2 e_1$ $r_2 \Rightarrow f_3 e_1 m_0$	$f_3 \Rightarrow r_2 e_1 m_0$ $m_0 \Rightarrow f_3 r_2 e_1$ $r_2 \Rightarrow f_3 e_1 m_0$
7	$r_1 s_1 \Rightarrow m_1$ $m_1 s_1 \Rightarrow r_1$	
8	$f_2 \Rightarrow r_1 e_3 m_1$ $e_3 \Rightarrow f_2 r_1 m_1$	$f_2 \Rightarrow r_1 e_3 m_1$ $e_3 \Rightarrow f_2 r_1 m_1$
9	$f_1 \Rightarrow r_1 m_1 s_1$	$f_1 \Rightarrow r_1 m_1 s_1$
10	$s_2 \Rightarrow e_1 m_0 f_3 r_2$	$s_2 \Rightarrow e_1 m_0 f_3 r_2$
11	$f_3 s_1 \Rightarrow r_2 e_1 m_0$ $r_2 s_1 \Rightarrow f_3 e_1 m_0$ $m_0 s_1 \Rightarrow f_3 r_2 e_1$	
12	$r_1 e_1 \Rightarrow f_1 m_1 s_1$ $e_1 m_1 \Rightarrow f_1 r_1 s_1$ $f_1 e_1 \Rightarrow r_1 m_1 s_1$	
13	$f_2 s_1 \Rightarrow r_1 e_3 m_1$ $e_3 s_1 \Rightarrow f_2 r_1 m_1$	
14	$s_0 \Rightarrow f_2 r_1 e_3 m_1$	$s_0 \Rightarrow f_2 r_1 e_3 m_1$
15	$e_2 \Rightarrow f_1 r_1 m_1 s_1$	$e_2 \Rightarrow f_1 r_1 m_1 s_1$

3.2 Generation of probabilistic implication rules

Patterns, concepts and relationships extracted from large databases are frequently probabilistic rather than fully exact. This is due to the fact that databases have noisy data, missing information, and do not form a representative sample of data of real-world applications. Moreover, databases are usually designed and managed for purposes other than learning tasks [10]. In particular, attributes describing objects (individuals) are chosen for retrieval rather than for learning and data analysis. Since databases are usually large, discovery techniques and tools need to be applied on a sample of the data. The sampling operation brings additional uncertainty to the knowledge discovered from data. Uncertainty in data mining applications and systems takes the form of weights that express belief measures, accuracy ratios, frequencies of success (e.g., probability that a classification rule correctly classifies a new object in the DB), and so on. Techniques used for estimating the uncertainty attached to patterns and relationships are mainly based on statistics, probability theory and information theory. They rely either on simple frequency ratios or more sophisticated estimations such as bayesian methods and maximum entropy. As opposed to exact rules, probabilistic (approximate) rules $P \Rightarrow Q$ reflect the probability that Q is true when P holds.

Algorithm 3.2 determines the (exclusive) *disjunctive* form of the right-hand side (RHS) part of a rule when a left-hand side (LHS) and a threshold are given. This algorithm is a variant of one of the algorithms described in [9].

Algorithm 3.2 *OneApproximateRule*

Input: A (possibly complex) descriptor P in $\mathcal{D}$, a lattice $\mathcal{L}$, and a threshold α.

Output: The RHS of a rule $P \Rightarrow Q$ such that $Q = Q_1 \vee \cdots \vee Q_k$ holds with a certainty ratio c when P is true.

begin

$L := Nil$, $n := \|Extent(Inf(\mathcal{L}))\|$, $m := 0$, $i := 0$, $RHS := True$;

Step (1) Collect in the list L the pairs $\langle Q_i, n_i \rangle$, where n_i is the number of objects supporting $P \Rightarrow Q_i$.

For each parent node N_i of $sup(\mathcal{L})$ such that $Extent(sup(\mathcal{L})) = \emptyset$ **do**

   If $P \subseteq Intent(N_i)$ **then**

   $L := Cons(\langle (Intent(N_i) - P), Extent(N_i) \rangle, L)$ /* Append $\langle Q_i, n_i \rangle$ to L */

   endIf

endFor

Step (2) Form the smallest disjunction of Q_i such that $\sum_{i=1}^{k} n_i/n \geq \alpha$

Sort L in a decreasing order of the second component of pairs $\langle Q_i, n_i \rangle$

While $\alpha > m/n$ **do**

begin

   $i := i + 1$;

   $Element := Nth(L, i)$;   /* Return the i-th element of the list L */

   $m := m + Second(Element)$ /* take the second component of the pair $\langle Q_i, n_i \rangle$ */

   $RHS := RHS \vee (First(Element) - P)$

end

endWhile

return(RHS, m/n)

end {*OneApproximateRule*}

   To collect the alternate descriptors Q_i that P implies in a disjunctive (and exclusive) way, Algorithm 3.2 selects all the parent nodes N_i of $sup(\mathcal{L})$ such that these nodes include P in their intent, and then takes the descriptors other than P. Step 1 collects all the Q_i that P may imply as well as their corresponding strength. Step 2 progressively forms the disjunction of Q_i by taking the strongest Q_i first (i.e. those that are more likely true when P holds). The process ends when the threshold α is reached. For example, a non-deterministic characteristic rule for s_1 allowing a certainty ratio of .75 is $s_1 \Rightarrow m_1(e_1 f_1 \vee e_2 \vee e_3) \vee f_3$. This assertion may be approximated by $m_1 \vee f_3$ which states that animals that can roughly swim give milk in .75 of cases.

Algorithm 3.3 explores the concept lattice to compute a set of probabilistic implication rules that hold between a set Y of attributes and a given decision attribute A. To estimate the goodness of the probabilistic rules, this algorithm borrows some ideas found in [23, 25]. Smyth and Goodman [25] propose an entropy measure, called J-measure, which estimates *the information content* (the goodness) of a rule based on the product of $Prob(P)$ (i.e., the probability that P holds) and the predictive value of the rule expressed by the distance between *a posteriori* belief and *a priori* belief about A. The second factor of the product in the J-measure uses a log scale involving $Prob(q_i \mid P)$ (i.e., the probability that q_i holds when P is true) and $Prob(q_i)$. In [23], the second factor is expressed as the difference between $Prob(q_i \mid P)$ and $Prob(q_i)$. We make use of the simplified formula in the following algorithm.

Algorithm 3.3 *ConjunctiveApproximateRules*

Input: A set Y of attributes, a decision attribute A, a lattice $\mathcal{L}$.

Output: A list of pairs $\langle P_i \Rightarrow q_i, rk_i \rangle$ where $P_i \Rightarrow q_i$ is such that $Attrib(P_i) = Y$, and $Attrib(q_i) = A$, and rk_i is a goodness measure for the approximate rule.

begin

Step (1) Collect in the list L_1 the pairs $\langle r_i, n_i \rangle$, where r_i is a conjunctive IRD involving the attributes of Y in its LHS and a descriptor q_i for A in its RHS, and n_i is the number of objects supporting $P_i \Rightarrow q_i$. In list L_2, collect the pairs $\langle q_j, n_j \rangle$ where n_j is the number of occurrences of the descriptor q_j for the attribute A. In list L_3, put the pairs $\langle P_k, n_k \rangle$ where n_k is the number of occurrences of P_k (related to Y) in the data.

$L_1 := Nil$, $L_2 := Nil$, $L_3 := Nil$, $n := \|Extent(Inf(\mathcal{L}))\|$, $\Delta := \emptyset$;

$Mark_Y[i] := 0$, $Mark_A[i] := 0$, and $Mark_{YA}[i] := 0$, for $i = 1, \ldots, \|\mathcal{L}\|$;

While $\Delta \subset Extent(Inf(\mathcal{L}))$ **do**

For each node $H \in \mathcal{L}$ in ascending $Intent(H)$ such that $Extent(H)$ is not empty **do**

begin

    If $(Y \cup A) \subseteq Attrib(Intent(H))$ and $Mark_{YA}(H) \neq 1$ **then**

    $m := \|Extent(H)\|$

    $L_1 := Cons(\langle P_i \Rightarrow q_i, m \rangle, L_1)$ such that $Attrib(P_i) = Y$ and $Attrib(q_i) = A$.

    $Mark_{YA}(N) := 1$ for each descendant N of H

        /* Mark all the descendants of H as visited */

    $\Delta := \Delta \cup Extent(H)$

endIf

If $A \in Attrib(Intent(H))$ and $Mark_A(H) \neq 1$ **then**

$\quad m := \|Extent(H)\|$

$\quad L_2 := Cons(\langle q_i, m \rangle, L_2)$ such that $Attrib(q_i) = A$.

$\quad Mark_A(N) := 1$ for each descendant N of H

endIf

If $Y \subseteq Attrib(Intent(H))$ and $Mark_Y(H) \neq 1$ **then**

$\quad m := \|Extent(H)\|$

$\quad L_3 := Cons(\langle P_i, m \rangle, L_3)$ such that $Attrib(P_i) = Y$.

$\quad Mark_Y(N) := 1$ for each descendant N of H

endIf

end

endFor

endWhile

Step (2) Compute the goodness of the approximate rules.

For each pair $\langle P_i \Rightarrow q_i, n_i \rangle$ in L_1 **do**

begin

$\qquad f_1 := Nth(L_3, 2)/n;\ f_2 := Nth(L_2, 2)/n;\ f_3 := Nth(L_1, 2)/n;$

$\qquad Nth(L_1, 2) := f_1 \times (f_3/f_1 - f_2);$

end

endFor

return(L_1)

end $\{ConjunctiveApproximateRules\}$

The three similar *If* tests aim at determining all the smallest nodes containing descriptors related to $Y \cup A$, A, and Y respectively. For example, L_3 serves to collect all the possible descriptors related to Y that are found in the data.

Example. Table 3.2 below shows the set of probabilistic rules relating the attribute E (see Table 2.1) to the attribute S. For a given rule, $p(s\&e)$ and $p(s \mid e)$ denote the probability that S takes the value s and E the modality e, and the conditional probability of the modality s of S when the value e of E holds, respectively. Even though the third and fourth rules have the same (and the highest) predictive value expressed by $p(s \mid e) - p(s)$, the rule $e_3 \Rightarrow s_0$ is more relevant than $e_2 \Rightarrow s_1$ since its LHS occurs more frequently in the data.

Table 3.2 Approximate rules and their goodness.

Rules	Probabilities					Goodness
	$p(s\&e)$	$p(s\mid e)$	$p(s)$	$p(s\mid e)-p(s)$	$p(e)$	
$e_1 \Rightarrow s_1$	2/6	2/3	4/6	0	3/6	0
$e_1 \Rightarrow s_2$	1/6	1/3	1/6	1/6	3/6	0.08
$e_2 \Rightarrow s_1$	1/6	1	4/6	2/6	1/6	0.055
$e_3 \Rightarrow s_0$	1/6	1/2	1/6	2/6	2/6	0.11
$e_3 \Rightarrow s_1$	1/6	1/2	4/6	-1/6	2/6	-0.055

4 Conclusion and further research

This paper is an extension to our previous work on knowledge discovery from databases [9, 18, 19]. It deals with the generation of probabilistic implication rules using a concept lattice framework.

Our current research concerns the development of pruning techniques that help overcome the complexity in the size and the structure of data. We believe that some kinds of pruning can be undertaken before or during the process of knowledge mining: (i) input pruning, (ii) lattice pruning, and (iii) rule pruning.

Input pruning can be handled either by selecting the appropriate portion of the binary relation that is potentially useful for generating the relevant concepts and rules, or by choosing a sample of the relation, or by preprocessing the data using exploratory data analysis techniques to get hints about attributes and objects that play a significant role in discriminating objects [6]. In that way, only the objects and attributes that are most likely relevant and representative are selected. The second type of pruning consists of discarding some possibly irrelevant concepts. In [7, 16], a variant of the concept lattice, called the knowledge space, contains nodes such that their intent includes at least a descriptor not found in the parent nodes. The rule pruning can be handled by discarding some relationships with a weak support and/or a low certainty ratio. Moreover, the application of the well-known minimal cover algorithm [15] guarantees the elimination of redundant and non-reduced rules and FDs. The rule pruning process includes also the ability to confirm a rule $P \Rightarrow Q$ by selecting the smallest node (in the lattice) with a description P without necessarily generating the whole set of rules. This task can be done in a constant time.

Acknowledgments

This research has been supported by NSERC (the Natural Sciences and Engineering Research Council of Canada) under grants No OGP0041899 and OGP0009184.

References

[1] Agrawal R, Imielinski T and Swami A. Mining association rules between sets of items in large databases. Proc. ACM SIGMOD'93 Conf., 1993 pp 207-216

[2] Cai Y, Cercone N and Han J. Attribute-oriented induction in relational databases. In: Piatetsky-Shapiro G and Frawley WJ (eds) Knowledge Discovery from Databases. Menlo Park, CA, AAAI Press/The MIT Press, 1991 pp 213-228

[3] Cercone N. and Tsuchiya M (eds). Special issue on learning and discovery in knowledge-based databases. In: Knowledge and Data Engineering, 5(6), 1993

[4] Davey BA and Priestley HA. Introduction to Lattices and Order. Cambridge University Press, Cambridge, 1990, p 248

[5] Gennari JH, Langley P and Fisher D. Models of incremental concept formation. In: Carbonell J (ed) Machine learning: paradigms and methods. MIT Press, Amsterdam, The Netherlands, 1990, pp 11-62

[6] Gale WA (ed). Artificial Intelligence and Statistics. Addison-Wesley, Reading, Menlo Park, Don Mills, 1986

[7] Godin R, Mineau G and Missaoui R. Rapport de la phase 2 du projet Macroscope pour le volet Réutilisation, 1993

[8] Godin R, Missaoui R and Alaoui H. Incremental concept formation algorithms based on Galois (concept) lattices. Technical Report, Département de Mathématiques et d'Informatique, Université du Québec à Montréal, 1994. Also submitted for publication.

[9] Godin R and Missaoui R. An incremental concept formation approach for learning from databases. Technical Report, Département de Mathématiques et d'Informatique, Université du Québec à Montréal, 1994. Also submitted for publication.

[10] Holsheimer M and Siebes A. Data mining: the search for knowledge in databases. Technical Report CS-R9406, 1993

[11] Ioannidis YE, Saulys T and Whitsitt AJ. Conceptual learning in database design. ACM Trans. on Information Systems, 10(3), 1992, pp 265-293

[12] Kaufman KA, Michalski RS and Kerschberg L. Mining for knowledge in databases: goals and general description of the INLEN system. In: Piatetsky-Shapiro G and Frawley WJ (ed) Knowledge Discovery from Databases, AAAI Press/The MIT Press, Menlo Park, CA, 1991, pp 449-462

[13] Kivinen J and Mannila H. Approximate dependency inference from relations. In: Biskup J and Hull R (ed) 4th Int. Conf. on Database Theory, Springer-Verlag, London, 1992, pp 86-98

[14] Michalski RS and Kodratoff Y. Research in machine learning: recent progress, classification of methods, and future directions. In: Kodratoff Y and Michalski RS (ed) Machine Learning: An Artificial Intelligence Approach, Morgan Kaufmann, San Mateo, CA, 1990, pp 1-30

[15] Maier D. The theory of Relational Databases, Computer Science Press, Rockville, Md, 1983

[16] Mineau G and Godin R. Automatic structuring of knowledge bases by conceptual clustering. IEEE Trans. on Knowledge and Data Engineering, accepted for publication

[17] Minker J (ed). Foundations of Deductive Databases and Logic Programming. Morgan Kaufmann, Los Altos, CA, 1988

[18] Missaoui R and Godin R. An incremental concept formation approach for learning from databases. In: Alagar VS, Lakshmanan VS and Sadri F (ed) Workshop on Formal Methods in Databases and Software Engineering. Montreal, May 15-16, 1992. Springer-Verlag, London, 1993, pp 39-53

[19] Missaoui R and Godin R. Search for concepts and dependencies in databases. In: Ziarko W (ed) International Workshop on Rough Sets and Knowledge Discovery. Banff, October 1993. Springer-Verlag, London, 1994, to appear

[20] Muggleton S, De Raedt L. Inductive logic programming: theory and methods. Submitted to The Journal of Logic Programming, 1993

[21] Pawlak Z. Rough sets: theoretical aspects of reasoning about data. Kluwer Academic, Dordrecht, Boston, London, 1992

[22] Piatetsky-Shapiro G and Frawley WJ (ed). Knowledge discovery in databases AAAI Press/The MIT Press, Menlo Park, CA, 1991, p 525

[23] Piatetsky-Shapiro G. Discovery, analysis, and presentation of strong rules. In: Piatetsky-Shapiro G and Frawley WJ (eds) Knowledge Discovery in Databases. AAAI Press/The MIT Press, Menlo Park, CA, 1991, pp 229-248

[24] Slowinski R (ed). Intelligent decision support. In: Handbook of Applications and Advances of the Rough Sets Theory, Kluwer Academic, Dordrecht, Boston, London, 1992

[25] Smyth P and Goodman RM. Rule induction using information theory. In: Piatetsky-Shapiro G and Frawley WJ (eds) Knowledge Discovery in Databases. AAAI Press/The MIT Press, Menlo Park, CA, 1991, pp 159-167

[26] Wille R. Knowledge acquisition by methods of formal concept analysis. In: Diday E (ed) Data Analysis, Learning Symbolic and Numeric Knowledge. Nova Science, New York, 1989, pp 365-380

Logic of Rough Sets

Mohua Banerjee*   M.K. Chakraborty

Department of Pure Mathematics
University of Calcutta
35, Ballygunge Circular Road
Calcutta 700 019, India

Abstract

It is shown that the modal system S_5 captures the basic propositional aspects of rough set theory. The system S_5 is enhanced to define a consequence relation called 'rough consequence' to ensure derivability of 'roughly equal' formulae. A predicate logic that includes in its ambit all the existing notions of rough set theory, is presented. Its semantics is studied in some detail.

Key Words: Rough sets, Modal system S_5, Kripke semantics.

1   Introduction

Since the theory of rough sets was proposed [11], there have been quite a few attempts [4,8,9,10,13,14] to accommodate its basic features in formal theories. During these attempts, its modal nature was felt by many [8,10,13]. It is seen, in this paper, that the modal system S_5, in terms of its syntax and semantics (Kripke), is capable of capturing some fundamental notions like lower and upper approximations of sets, rough equality of sets and rough truth [11,12]. Further, a 'rough consequence' relation is introduced into the system which allows us, unlike the standard consequence relation, to derive 'roughly equal' formulae. All of the above are dealt with in the next section.

A predicate logic without equality is represented in section 3. The syntax of the logic proposed by Rasiowa and Skowron [13] is similar to that of this logic, but one of the additional features in the latter is the incorporation of the notion of rough quantifiers, introduced by Szczerba in [14]. A number of theorems involving these quantifiers are syntactically derivable here. Moreover, a distinctive feature of our predicational system is its semantics, defined keeping parity with the Kripke semantics of the propositional system S_5–this in order that it can also serve as rough set semantics. A special binary predicate '$\approx$' in the language is interpreted as an equivalence relation, and the final interpretation is carried out over an induced approximation space. Notions of rough truth, rough falsity, rough validity are brought in again and quite a few properties are cited, in proving some of which the soundness of the system is exploited. It is still our opinion that our system is not fully satisfactory and that there is scope for improvement.

---

*Research supported by the Council of Scientific and Industrial Research, New Delhi, India.

2 Propositional logic

2.1 Modal system S₅ redefined

The language of the modal system S_5 consists of the following:

propositional variables   : $p, q, r, \ldots$;

logical symbols   : $\sim, \rightarrow$, L (the necessity operator) ;

parentheses   :   (,) .

The formation rules are as usual. The connectives $\wedge, \vee, \leftrightarrow$ are also defined in the usual way. M (the possibility operator) stands for $\sim L \sim$.

Axiom schemata:

1. $\phi \rightarrow (\psi \rightarrow \phi)$.

2. $(\phi \rightarrow (\psi \rightarrow t)) \rightarrow ((\phi \rightarrow \psi) \rightarrow (\phi \rightarrow t))$.

3. $(\sim \psi \rightarrow \sim \phi) \rightarrow (\phi \rightarrow \psi)$.

4. $L (\phi \rightarrow \psi) \rightarrow (L \phi \rightarrow L \psi)$.

5. $L \phi \rightarrow \phi$.

6. $L \phi \rightarrow L L \phi$.

7. $M \phi \rightarrow L M \phi$.

Rules of inference:

1. Modus ponens : $\dfrac{\phi , \phi \rightarrow \psi}{\psi}$.

2. Necessitation: $\dfrac{\phi}{L \phi}$.

2.2 Rough set semantics

We recall that a Kripke model [6] of S_5 is a triple $M \equiv \langle A, R, \pi \rangle$, where A is a non-empty set, R is an equivalence relation on A and π is a map from the set of propositional variables to subsets of A.

We see then that $\langle A, R \rangle$ is an approximation space in which the lower and upper approximations $\underline{S}$ and $\overline{S}$ respectively of any subset S of A is defined as in [11].

π is now extended over the set of all well-formed formulae (wffs) thus:

$\pi(\sim \phi) \equiv A \setminus \pi(\phi)$,

$\pi(\phi \rightarrow \psi) \equiv (A \setminus \pi(\phi)) \cup \pi(\psi)$ and

$\pi(L \phi) \equiv \underline{\pi(\phi)}$.

Thus any wff ϕ is interpreted as a subset $\pi(\phi)$ in the approximation space $\langle A, R \rangle$ and hence $\langle A, R, \pi(\phi) \rangle$ is a rough set [1].

Defining, for any wff ϕ, the notions of truth in a model and validity in the usual manner, it can be proved [7] that ϕ is a theorem of S_5 ($\vdash \phi$) if and only if ϕ is valid (soundness and completeness theorems).

2.3   Rough consequence

We define next a binary connective ' $\approx$ ' (read 'roughly equal') [2] in the language of S_5. The intention is to bring the notion of rough equality [11] into the syntax. $\phi \approx \psi$ is the abbreviation of $(L \phi \leftrightarrow L \psi) \wedge (M \phi \leftrightarrow M \psi)$, which is true in a model $M \equiv \langle A, R, \pi \rangle$ if and only if the interpretations of ϕ and ψ are roughly equal in the approximation space $\langle A, R \rangle$. Now we would like to be able to derive a wff ψ if ϕ has been derived and if $\vdash \phi \approx \psi$, i.e. $\pi(\phi)$ roughly equals $\pi(\psi)$ in every model $M \equiv \langle A, R, \pi \rangle$. But the ordinary consequence relation available in S_5, does not allow us to do so. A notion of 'rough consequence' is introduced [3], which permits this kind of derivation. This consequence relation is defined with two new rules $(RMP)_1$ and $(RMP)_2$. More explicitly, we have the following for any set of wffs Γ and wff ϕ.

Definition 1 ϕ is said to be a rough consequence of Γ (written $\Gamma \hspace{0.5mm}\vert\!\sim\phi$), if and only if there is a sequence $\phi_1, \ldots, \phi_n (= \phi)$ such that each ϕ_i, $i = 1, \ldots, n$, is either

(i) a theorem of S_5, or

(ii) a member of Γ, or

(iii) derived from some of the wffs $\phi_1, \ldots, \phi_{i-1}$ by one of the following rules:

$(RMP)_1$: $\dfrac{\phi \qquad \vdash \phi' \to \psi}{\psi}$,   where $\vdash M \phi \to M \phi'$;

$(RMP)_2$: $\dfrac{\vdash \phi \qquad \phi' \to \psi}{\psi}$,   where $\vdash L \phi \to L \phi'$.

If Γ is empty, we write $\vert\!\sim \phi$ and say that ϕ is a rough theorem.

'Rough truth' was defined in [12]. We extend it to 'rough validity' ($\approx\!\!\vDash$) and obtain the soundness theorem for any theory with respect to the rough consequence relation $\vert\!\sim$ [3]. Moreover, any roughly valid formula is a rough theorem, so that $\vert\!\sim \phi$ if and only if $\approx\!\!\vDash \phi$. 'Rough truth' and 'rough validity' will come in again during our discussion of rough set semantics for the predicate logic, to be presented in the following section.

3 Predicate logic

3.1 The language

The language consists of

variables : $x_1, x_2, \ldots$;

predicate symbols : $p_1, p_2, \ldots$ of different arities ;

one special binary predicate symbol : $\approx$;

logical symbols : $\sim, \rightarrow$, L (the necessity operator) ;

quantifier : $\forall$ and

parentheses : (,) .

We take usual formation rules and shall use the predicate symbol $\approx$ between two terms. $\phi(y/x)$ means replacement of all free occurrences of x in ϕ by y.

Standard defined symbols: $\wedge, \vee, \leftrightarrow$, M (the possibility operator),
$\dashv$ (strict implication), $\Leftrightarrow$, $\exists$.

Also, $\phi \approx \psi$, $\forall x_i \, \phi$ and $\exists x_i \, \phi$ are respectively abbreviations of $(L \, \phi \leftrightarrow L \, \psi) \wedge (M \, \phi \leftrightarrow M \, \psi)$, $\forall \, x_i \exists \, y(x_i \approx y \wedge \phi(y/x_i))$, where y is the first variable not occurring in ϕ, and $\exists \, x_i \forall \, y(x_i \approx y \rightarrow \phi(y/x_i))$, where y is as before. The symbols $\forall$ and $\exists$ may be called 'rough quantifiers', read as 'roughly all' and 'roughly some' respectively.

3.2 Rough set semantics

Let $\langle A, R \rangle$ be an approximation space. For each positive integer n, an equivalence relation R_n is induced in A^n as follows.

$\langle a_1, \ldots, a_n \rangle \, R_n \, \langle b_1, \ldots, b_n \rangle$ if and only if $a_i \, R \, b_i, i = 1, \ldots, n$.

Also in A^∞ (the set of all infinite sequences over A) an equivalence relation R_∞ is induced thus:

$\overline{a} \, R_\infty \, \overline{b}$ if and only if $a_i \, R \, b_i$, $i = 1, 2, \ldots, \overline{a}, \overline{b} \in A^\infty$.

Definition 2 By an interpretation of the language defined before, we shall mean a relation structure $\mathcal{U} \equiv \langle A, R, P_1, P_2, \ldots \rangle$, where A is a non-empty set, R an equivalence relation on A and P_i, $i = 1, 2, \ldots$, is a relation on A corresponding to the predicate symbol p_i with the arity of p_i.

Definition 3 A model $M_{\mathcal{U}}$ relative to the structure $\mathcal{U}$ is the triple $\langle A^{\infty}, R_{\infty}, \pi \rangle$, where π is a map from the set of atomic formulae to subsets of A^{∞} defined as follows.

$$\pi(x_i \approx x_j) \equiv \{\bar{a} : a_i \ R \ a_j \text{ holds}\}.$$

$$\pi(p_j x_{i_1} \cdots x_{i_k}) \equiv \{\bar{a} : \langle a_{i_1}, \ldots, a_{i_k} \rangle \in P_j\}.$$

If for an atomic formula ϕ, $\bar{a} \in \pi(\phi)$, $\bar{a}$ is said to satisfy ϕ. The notion of satisfaction can be extended to the set of all wffs as follows.

$\bar{a}$ satisfies $\sim \phi$ if and only if $\bar{a}$ does not satisfy ϕ.

$\bar{a}$ satisfies $\phi \rightarrow \psi$ if and only if either $\bar{a}$ does not satisfy ϕ or $\bar{a}$ satisfies ψ.

$\bar{a}$ satisfies $L \ \phi$ if and only if for every $\bar{b}$ with $\bar{a} \ R_{\infty} \ \bar{b}$, $\bar{b}$ satisfies ϕ.

$\bar{a}$ satisfies $\forall \ x_i \ \phi$ if and only if for all $d \in A$, $\bar{a}(d/i)$ satisfies ϕ.

As a consequence to the above definition of satisfaction, we get the following.

$\bar{a}$ satisfies $\phi \wedge \psi$ if and only if $\bar{a}$ satisfies ϕ and $\bar{a}$ satisfies ψ.

$\bar{a}$ satisfies $\phi \vee \psi$ if and only if either $\bar{a}$ satisfies ϕ or $\bar{a}$ satisfies ψ.

$\bar{a}$ satisfies $M \ \phi$ if and only if there exists $\bar{b}$ such that $\bar{a} \ R_{\infty} \ \bar{b}$ and $\bar{b}$ satisfies ϕ.

$\bar{a}$ satisfies $\exists \ x_i \ \phi$ if and only if for some $d \in A$, $\bar{a}(d/i)$ satisfies ϕ.

$\bar{a}$ satisfies $\overline{\forall} x_i \ \phi$ if and only if for all $d \in A$, there exists $d' \in A$ such that $d \ R \ d'$ and $\bar{a}(d'/j)$ satisfies $\phi(x_j/x_i)$, where x_j is the first variable not occurring in ϕ.

$\bar{a}$ satisfies $\overline{\exists} x_i \ \phi$ if and only if there exists $d \in A$ such that for all $d' \in A$, if $d \ R \ d'$ holds then $\bar{a}(d'/j)$ satisfies $\phi(x_j/x_i)$, where x_j is as before.

The function π is now extended over the set of all wffs by:

$$\pi(\phi) \equiv \{\bar{a} : \bar{a} \text{ satisfies } \phi\}.$$

Proposition. For any wffs ϕ and ψ,

$$\pi(\sim \phi) = A^{\infty} \setminus \pi(\phi),$$

$$\pi(L \ \phi) = \underline{\pi(\phi)},$$

$$\pi(M \ \phi) = \overline{\pi(\phi)},$$

$$\pi(\phi \wedge \psi) = \pi(\phi) \cap \pi(\psi) \quad \text{and}$$

$$\pi(\phi \vee \psi) = \pi(\phi) \cup \pi(\psi).$$

Let $\mathcal{U} \equiv \langle A, R, P_1, P_2, \ldots \rangle$ be an interpretation of the language and $M_{\mathcal{U}} \equiv \langle A^\infty, R_\infty, \pi \rangle$ the corresponding model. Let ϕ be a wff.

Definition 4

ϕ is true in $M_{\mathcal{U}}$ if and only if $\pi(\phi) = A^\infty$.

ϕ is false in $M_{\mathcal{U}}$ if and only if $\pi(\phi) = \emptyset$.

ϕ is valid if and only if ϕ is true in every model.

The notion of falsity is a departure from Pawlak's [12], but is in conformity with the standard lower predicate calculus.

Definition 5 For any set Γ of wffs of the language, $\Gamma \models \phi$ (ϕ is a semantic consequence of Γ) if and only if for any model $M_{\mathcal{U}} \equiv \langle A^\infty, R_\infty, \pi \rangle$, $\pi(\gamma) = A^\infty$ for all $\gamma \in \Gamma$ implies $\pi(\phi) = A^\infty$.

3.3   The syntax

Axiom schemata:
   Axiom schemata 1–7 of the propositional logic (cf. section 2).

8. $\forall x_i(\phi \rightarrow \psi) \rightarrow (\forall x_i \phi \rightarrow \forall x_i \psi)$.

9. $\forall x_i \phi \rightarrow \phi(x_j/x_i)$, x_j is free for x_i in ϕ .

10. $\phi \rightarrow \forall x_i \phi$, x_i is not free in ϕ .

11. $x_i \approx x_i$.

12. $x_i \approx x_j \rightarrow x_j \approx x_i$.

13. $x_i \approx x_j \wedge x_j \approx x_k \rightarrow x_i \approx x_k$.

14. $x_i \approx x_j \wedge L\,\phi(x_i) \rightarrow L\,\phi(x_j/x_i)$.

15. $\forall x_{i_1} \ldots \forall x_{i_k}((x_{j_1} \approx x_{i_1} \wedge \ldots \wedge x_{j_k} \approx x_{i_k}) \rightarrow \phi(x_{i_1}/x_{j_1}, \ldots, x_{i_k}/x_{j_k}))$
$\rightarrow L\,\phi(x_{j_1}, \ldots, x_{j_k})$, where $\{x_{j_1}, \ldots, x_{j_k}\}$ is the set of free variables in ϕ.

16. $\phi \rightarrow L\,\phi$, for any closed wff ϕ .

17. If ϕ is an axiom and x_i is free in ϕ then $\forall x_i \phi$ is an axiom.

Rules of inference:

1. Modus ponens: $\dfrac{\phi\,,\ \phi \rightarrow \psi}{\psi}$.

2. Necessitation: $\dfrac{\phi}{L\,\phi}$.

Metatheorem (Soundness)   If $\Gamma \vdash \phi$ then $\Gamma \models \phi$.
   The proof is standard, showing the validity of the axioms and that the rules preserve truth, but requiring augmentation to meet the needs of the new system.

3.4 Theorems

We shall state now some theorems of the system. A few of these have proofs using the identity axioms 11, 12, 13 and/or axiom 16; some involve the new quantifiers $\forall$, $\exists$. In [14], some of the wffs of the latter kind have been mentioned, but claimed valid from the semantic standpoint. We recall that Deduction Theorem can be used if the derivation does not involve the necessitation rule. For proofs we refer [4].

1. $\vdash x \approx y \wedge M\ \phi(x) \rightarrow M\ \phi(y/x)$.

2. $\vdash M\ \phi(x) \rightarrow \exists\ y(x \approx y \wedge \phi(y/x))$, if x is the only free variable in ϕ .

3. $\vdash L\ \phi(x) \rightarrow \forall\ y(x \approx y \rightarrow \phi(y/x))$, provided y is not free in $\phi(x)$.

4. $\vdash \exists\ y(x \approx y \wedge \phi(y/x)) \rightarrow M\ \phi(x)$, provided y is not free in $\phi(x)$.

5. $\vdash x \approx y \wedge \phi(x) \rightarrow M\ \phi(y/x)$.

6. $\vdash M\ \phi \rightarrow \phi$, where ϕ is any closed wff .

7. $\vdash \forall\ x(L\ \phi(x) \rightarrow \psi(x) \wedge L\ \psi(x) \rightarrow \phi(x)) \leftrightarrow \forall\ x(L\ \phi(x) \leftrightarrow L\ \psi(x))$, if x is the only free variable in ϕ and ψ .

8. $\vdash \forall\ x(\phi(x) \rightarrow M\ \psi(x) \wedge \psi(x) \rightarrow M\ \phi(x)) \leftrightarrow \forall\ x(M\ \phi(x) \leftrightarrow M\ \psi(x))$, if x is the only free variable in ϕ and ψ.

9. $\vdash \forall\ x\ \phi(x) \rightarrow \ \forall x\ \phi(x)$.

10. $\vdash \ \forall x\ \phi(x) \rightarrow \exists\ x\ \phi(x)$.

11. $\vdash \ \forall x\ L\ \phi(x) \rightarrow \forall\ x\ \phi(x)$.

12. $\vdash \forall\ x(\phi(x) \rightarrow \psi(x)) \rightarrow (\ \forall x\ \phi(x) \rightarrow \ \forall x\ \psi(x))$.

13. $\vdash \ \forall x(\phi(x) \ni \psi(x)) \rightarrow (\ \forall x\ \phi(x) \rightarrow \ \forall x\ \psi(x))$.

14. $\vdash \ \forall x(\phi(x) \wedge \psi(x)) \rightarrow (\ \forall x \phi(x) \wedge \ \forall x\ \psi(x))$.

15. $\vdash \ \forall x(\phi(x) \Longleftrightarrow \psi(x)) \rightarrow (\ \forall x\ \phi(x) \leftrightarrow \ \forall x\ \psi(x))$.

16. $\vdash \exists\ x\ \phi(x) \leftrightarrow \sim \ \forall x \sim \phi(x)$.

17. $\vdash \ \forall x\ \phi(x) \leftrightarrow \sim \exists\ x \sim \phi(x)$.

18. $\vdash \exists\ x\ \phi(x) \rightarrow \exists\ x\ \phi(x)$.

19. $\vdash \forall\ x\ \phi(x) \rightarrow \exists\ x\ \phi(x)$.

20. $\vdash \ \forall x\ L\ \phi(x) \rightarrow \exists\ x\ \phi(x)$.

21. $\vdash \exists\ x\ \phi(x) \rightarrow \exists\ x\ M\ \phi(x)$.

22. $\vdash (\exists\ x\ \phi(x) \vee \exists\ x\ \psi(x)) \rightarrow \exists\ x\ (\phi(x) \vee \psi(x))$.

23. $\vdash \forall\ x(\phi(x) \rightarrow \psi(x)) \rightarrow (\exists\ x\ \phi(x) \rightarrow \exists\ x\ \psi(x))$.

24. $\vdash \forall x(\phi(x) \supset \psi(x)) \rightarrow (\exists x \, \phi(x) \rightarrow \exists x \, \psi(x))$.

25. $\vdash \forall x \exists y(x \approx y \wedge \phi(y/x)) \leftrightarrow \forall y \exists x(x \approx y \wedge \phi(x))$.

Note. The last theorem establishes the equivalence between our definition of $\forall$ and that of Szczerba [14].

All the preceding theorems of the system are, in fact, theorem schemata. We mention a few types of wffs which are not theorem schemata. This is established by choosing a proper formula under the types, constructing models in which they are not true and then using the soundness theorem.

1. $\forall x \, \phi(x) \rightarrow \phi(x)$.

2. $\forall x(\phi \rightarrow \psi) \rightarrow (\phi \rightarrow \psi)$.

3. $\forall x(\phi(x) \rightarrow \psi(x)) \rightarrow (\forall x \, \phi(x) \rightarrow \forall x \, \psi(x))$.

4. $\forall x \, \phi(x) \rightarrow \exists x \, \phi(x)$.

Remark. The above brings forth differences between the classical and rough quantifiers.

Metatheorem (Equivalence theorem)
$\vdash \forall x_{i_1} \ldots \forall x_{i_k}(U \leftrightarrow V) \rightarrow (\phi_U \leftrightarrow \phi_V)$, where ϕ_U contains U as a subformula, ϕ_V is obtained from ϕ_U by replacing some occurrences of U in ϕ_U by V and

(i) Free ϕ_U = Free ϕ_V ,

(ii) Free $\phi_U \cup (((\text{Free } U) \cup (\text{Free } U)) \cap (Bd \, \phi_U)) \subseteq \{x_{i_1}, \ldots, x_{i_k}\}$.

3.5 More on the semantics

Definition 6 Let $\mathcal{U} \equiv \langle A, R, P_1, P_2, \ldots \rangle$ be an interpretation of the language and $M_{\mathcal{U}} \equiv \langle A^\infty, R_\infty, \pi \rangle$ the corresponding model. Let ϕ be a wff.

ϕ is roughly true in $M_{\mathcal{U}}$ if and only if $\overline{\pi(\phi)} = A^\infty$.

ϕ is roughly false in $M_{\mathcal{U}}$ if and only if $\underline{\pi(\phi)} = \emptyset$.

ϕ is roughly valid if and only if ϕ is roughly true in every model.

Many interesting consequences of these definitions immediately follow.

(i) ϕ is true implies ϕ is roughly true.

(ii) ϕ is false implies ϕ is roughly false.

(iii) ϕ is valid implies ϕ is roughly valid.

(iv) ϕ is roughly true implies ϕ is not false.

(v) ϕ is roughly false implies ϕ is not true.

(vi) ϕ is roughly true if and only if M ϕ is true.

(vii) ϕ is roughly false if and only if L ϕ is false.

(viii) L ϕ is roughly true if and only if ϕ is true.

(ix) M ϕ is roughly false if and only if ϕ is false.

(x) $L\phi \leftrightarrow L\psi$ is false implies $\phi \leftrightarrow \psi$ is roughly false.

Proof. Let $L\phi \leftrightarrow L\psi$ be false in $M_\mathcal{U} \equiv \langle A^\infty, R_\infty, \pi \rangle$.

As $\vdash L(\phi \leftrightarrow \psi) \to (L\phi \leftrightarrow L\psi)$, using soundness theorem,

$$\pi(\phi \leftrightarrow \psi) = \pi(L(\phi \leftrightarrow \psi)) \subseteq \pi(L\phi \leftrightarrow L\psi) = \emptyset .$$

(xi) $\phi \approx\approx \psi$ is roughly true if and only if $\phi \approx\approx \psi$ is true.
Proof. Let $\phi \approx\approx \psi$ be roughly true in $M_n \equiv \langle A^\infty, R_\infty, \pi \rangle$. Then

$$\pi(M((L\phi \leftrightarrow L\psi) \wedge (M\phi \leftrightarrow M\psi))) = A^\infty. \text{ Now for any wffs } \mu, v,$$

$$\vdash M(\mu \wedge v) \to (M\mu \wedge Mv). \text{ Using soundness theorem,}$$

$$\pi(M(L\phi \leftrightarrow L\psi) \wedge M(M\phi \leftrightarrow M\psi)) = A^\infty, \text{ i.e.}$$

$$\pi(M(L\phi \leftrightarrow L\psi)) \cap \pi(M(M\phi \leftrightarrow M\psi)) = A^\infty, \text{ which means}$$

$$\pi(M(L\phi \leftrightarrow L\psi)) = A^\infty = \pi(M(M\phi \leftrightarrow M\psi)).$$

By the same reasoning,

$$A^\infty = \pi(M(L\phi \to L\psi)) = \pi(M(L\psi \to L\phi)) = \pi(M(M\phi \to M\psi)) = \pi(M(M\psi \to M\phi)).$$

Also, for any wffs μ, v,

$\vdash M(\mu \vee v) \leftrightarrow (M\mu \vee Mv), \vdash M(\sim L\mu) \leftrightarrow \ \sim LL\mu, \vdash LL\mu \leftrightarrow L\mu, \vdash LM\mu \leftrightarrow M\mu,$
$\vdash M(\sim M\mu) \leftrightarrow \ \sim LM\mu, \vdash ML\mu \leftrightarrow L\mu, \vdash MM\mu \leftrightarrow M\mu.$
So, taking into account soundness once more, we get

$$
\begin{aligned}
A^\infty &= (A^\infty \setminus \pi(L(\phi)) \cup \pi(L(\psi)) = (A^\infty \setminus \pi(L\psi)) \cup \pi(L(\phi)) \\
&= (A^\infty \setminus \pi(M(\phi)) \cup \pi(M\psi) \\
&= (A^\infty \setminus \pi(M\psi)) \cup \pi(M\phi).
\end{aligned}
$$

Then $\pi(L\phi) = \pi(L\psi)$ and $\pi(M(\phi)) = \pi(M\psi)$.

So
$\pi(L\phi \leftrightarrow L\psi) = A^\infty = \pi(M\phi \leftrightarrow M\psi)$, i.e. $\pi((L\phi \leftrightarrow L\psi) \wedge (M\phi \leftrightarrow M\psi)) = A^\infty$
and thus $\pi(\phi \approx\approx \psi) = A^\infty$, i.e. $\phi \approx\approx \psi$ is true in $M_\mathcal{U}$.

The converse follows from consequence (i).

(xii) There may be ϕ which is both roughly true and roughly false.
In fact, in any language with at least one predicate symbol other than $\approx$, there
is a wff ϕ and a model in which ϕ is both roughly true and roughly false.

Example 1 Let us take a k-ary predicate p_j which is different from $\approx$ and the wff $\phi \equiv p_j\, x_1 \ldots x_k$. We consider $A = \{a, b, c, d\}$ and an equivalence relation R on A that partitions A into the classes $\{a, c\}$, $\{b, d\}$. It can be shown that in the approximation space $\langle A^k, R_k \rangle$, each equivalence class has at least two distinct elements. Choosing an element from each class, a subset P_j of A^k may be formed, so that there is at least one element of A^k outside P_j in each class. Let P_j correspond to the predicate p_j. For any n-ary predicate p_i, $i \neq j$, let $P_i = A^n$. We take the interpretation $\mathcal{U} \equiv \langle A, R, P_1, P_2, \ldots \rangle$. Then $M_{\mathcal{U}} \equiv \langle A^\infty, R_\infty, \pi \rangle$ serves as a model in which ϕ is both roughly true and roughly false.

Observation. There is no model in which $x_i \approx x_j$ is both roughly true and roughly false.

(xiii) There may be ϕ which is neither roughly true nor roughly false.
In fact, there is a wff ϕ in every language and a model in which ϕ is neither roughly true nor roughly false.

Example 2 We consider the wff $x_i \approx x_j$ and a model $M_{\mathcal{U}}$ corresponding to any interpretation $\mathcal{U} \equiv \langle A, R, P_1, P_2, \ldots \rangle$ such that $R \neq A \times A$.

(xiv) There may be ϕ which is roughly true, but not true.

(xv) There may be ϕ which is roughly false, but not false.

(xvi) There may be ϕ which is roughly valid, but not valid.

In case of each of (xiv), (xv) and (xvi), there is a wff ϕ in any language having a predicate different from $\approx$ and a model $M_{\mathcal{U}}$ such that ϕ possesses the stated property. To serve as examples for (xiv) and (xv), one may take the same ϕ and $M_{\mathcal{U}}$ considered to establish (xiii). For (xvi), we have the following.

Example 3 Let p_j be any k-ary predicate different from $\approx$ and ϕ the wff $p_j\, x_1 \ldots x_k \rightarrow L\, p_j\, x_1 \ldots x_k$. $M(p_j\, x_1 \ldots x_k \rightarrow L\, p_j\, x_1 \ldots x_k)$ is valid and hence $p_j\, x_1 \ldots x_k \rightarrow L\, p_j\, x_1 \ldots x_k$ is roughly valid (using consequence (vi)). Then considering an interpretation $\mathcal{U} \equiv \langle A, A \times A, P_1, P_2, \ldots \rangle$ where $A = \{a, a'\}$ and P_i, with arity n, consists of the n-tuple $\langle a, a, \ldots, a \rangle$ only, it can be shown that the element $\langle a, a, \ldots \rangle$ of A^∞ does not satisfy the wff. Thus the wff cannot be valid.

4 Concluding remarks

The predicate logic presented here cannot include constants, i.e. names of individuals, in its language. This is because, with constants included, axiom 14 and the necessitation rule cannot be taken together. For a detailed discussion on this issue and a comparison of various systems proposed for rough logic, we refer to [5]. Non-acceptability of constants stands in the way of adopting a Gödel-Henkin-like method in proving the completeness of the system. It is our hope that a better system will emerge.

References

[1] Banerjee M, Chakraborty MK. A category for rough sets. Foundations of Computing and Decision Sciences 1993; 18(3-4):167–180

[2] Banerjee M, Chakraborty MK. Rough algebra. Bull Pol Acad Sc (Math) to appear

[3] Chakraborty MK, Banerjee M. Rough consequence. Bull Pol Acad Sc (Math) to appear

[4] Chakraborty MK, Banerjee M. Rough logic with rough quantifiers. Bull Pol Acad Sc (Math) to appear

[5] Chakraborty MK, Banerjee M. Rough logics. preprint, 1994

[6] Chellas BF. Modal logic - an introduction. Cambridge University Press, 1980

[7] Hughes GE, Cresswell MJ. A companion to modal logic. Methuen, 1984

[8] Krynicki M. A note on rough concepts logic. Fundamenta Informaticae XIII 1990; 227–235

[9] Krynicki M, Tuschik HP. An axiomatization of the logic with the rough quantifier. Journal of Symb Logic 1991; 56(2):608–617

[10] Orłowska E. Kripke semantics for knowledge representation logics. Studia Logica XLIX 1990; 255–272

[11] Pawlak Z. Rough sets. Int Journal of Comp and Inf Sci 1982; 11(5):341–356

[12] Pawlak Z. Rough logic. Bull Pol Acad Sc (Technical Sc) 1987; 35(5-6):253–258

[13] Rasiowa H, Skowron A. Rough concepts logic. In: Skowron A (ed) Computation Theory, 1985, pp. 288–297 (Lecture notes in computer science no. 208)

[14] Szczerba LW. Rough quantifiers. Bull Pol Acad Sc (Math) 1987; 35(3-4):251–254

Author Index

Published in 1990–92

AI and Cognitive Science '89, Dublin City
University, Eire, 14–15 September 1989
Alan F. Smeaton and Gabriel McDermott (Eds.)

**Specification and Verification of Concurrent
Systems,** University of Stirling, Scotland,
6–8 July 1988
C. Rattray (Ed.)

Semantics for Concurrency, Proceedings of the
International BCS-FACS Workshop, Sponsored
by Logic for IT (S.E.R.C.), University of
Leicester, UK, 23–25 July 1990
M. Z. Kwiatkowska, M. W. Shields and
R. M. Thomas (Eds.)

Functional Programming, Glasgow 1989
Proceedings of the 1989 Glasgow Workshop,
Fraserburgh, Scotland, 21–23 August 1989
Kei Davis and John Hughes (Eds.)

Persistent Object Systems, Proceedings of the
Third International Workshop, Newcastle,
Australia, 10–13 January 1989
John Rosenberg and David Koch (Eds.)

Z User Workshop, Oxford 1989, Proceedings of
the Fourth Annual Z User Meeting, Oxford,
15 December 1989
J. E. Nicholls (Ed.)

**Formal Methods for Trustworthy Computer
Systems (FM89),** Halifax, Canada,
23–27 July 1989
Dan Craigen (Editor) and Karen Summerskill
(Assistant Editor)

Security and Persistence, Proceedings of the
International Workshop on Computer
Architectures to Support Security and Persistence
of Information, Bremen, West Germany,
8–11 May 1990
John Rosenberg and J. Leslie Keedy (Eds.)

**Women into Computing: Selected Papers
1988–1990**
Gillian Lovegrove and Barbara Segal (Eds.)

3rd Refinement Workshop (organised by
BCS-FACS, and sponsored by IBM UK
Laboratories, Hursley Park and the Programming
Research Group, University of Oxford),
Hursley Park, 9–11 January 1990
Carroll Morgan and J. C. P. Woodcock (Eds.)

Designing Correct Circuits, Workshop jointly
organised by the Universities of Oxford and
Glasgow, Oxford, 26–28 September 1990
Geraint Jones and Mary Sheeran (Eds.)

Functional Programming, Glasgow 1990
Proceedings of the 1990 Glasgow Workshop on
Functional Programming, Ullapool, Scotland,
13–15 August 1990
Simon L. Peyton Jones, Graham Hutton and
Carsten Kehler Holst (Eds.)

4th Refinement Workshop, Proceedings of the
4th Refinement Workshop, organised by BCS-
FACS, Cambridge, 9–11 January 1991
Joseph M. Morris and Roger C. Shaw (Eds.)

AI and Cognitive Science '90, University of
Ulster at Jordanstown, 20–21 September 1990
Michael F. McTear and Norman Creaney (Eds.)

Software Re-use, Utrecht 1989, Proceedings of
the Software Re-use Workshop, Utrecht,
The Netherlands, 23–24 November 1989
Liesbeth Dusink and Patrick Hall (Eds.)

Z User Workshop, 1990, Proceedings of the Fifth
Annual Z User Meeting, Oxford,
17–18 December 1990
J.E. Nicholls (Ed.)

IV Higher Order Workshop, Banff 1990
Proceedings of the IV Higher Order Workshop,
Banff, Alberta, Canada, 10–14 September 1990
Graham Birtwistle (Ed.)

ALPUK91, Proceedings of the 3rd UK
Annual Conference on Logic Programming,
Edinburgh, 10–12 April 1991
Geraint A.Wiggins, Chris Mellish and
Tim Duncan (Eds.)

Specifications of Database Systems
International Workshop on Specifications of
Database Systems, Glasgow, 3–5 July 1991
David J. Harper and Moira C. Norrie (Eds.)

**7th UK Computer and Telecommunications
Performance Engineering Workshop**
Edinburgh, 22–23 July 1991
J. Hillston, P.J.B. King and R.J. Pooley (Eds.)

Logic Program Synthesis and Transformation
Proceedings of LOPSTR 91, International
Workshop on Logic Program Synthesis and
Transformation, University of Manchester,
4–5 July 1991
T.P. Clement and K.-K. Lau (Eds.)

Declarative Programming, Sasbachwalden 1991
PHOENIX Seminar and Workshop on Declarative
Programming, Sasbachwalden, Black Forest,
Germany, 18–22 November 1991
John Darlington and Roland Dietrich (Eds.)